*The United Nations
in the 21st Century*

Dilemmas in World Politics

Series Editor: Jennifer Sterling-Folker, University of Connecticut

Why is it difficult to achieve the universal protection of human rights? How can democratization be achieved so that it is equitable and lasting? Why does agreement on global environmental protection seem so elusive? How does the concept of gender play a role in the shocking inequalities of women throughout the globe? Why do horrific events such as genocide or ethnic conflicts recur or persist? These are the sorts of questions that confront policymakers and students of contemporary international politics alike. They are dilemmas because they are enduring problems in world affairs that are difficult to resolve.

These are the types of dilemmas at the heart of the Dilemmas in World Politics series. Each book in the Dilemmas in World Politics series addresses a challenge or problem in world politics that is topical, recurrent, and not easily solved. Each is structured to cover the historical and theoretical aspects of the dilemma, as well as the policy alternatives for and future direction of the problem. The books are designed as supplements to introductory and intermediate courses in international relations. The books in the Dilemmas in World Politics series encourage students to engage in informed discussion of current policy issues.

BOOKS IN THIS SERIES

FOURTH EDITION

The United Nations in the 21st Century

KAREN A. MINGST

AND

MARGARET P. KARNS

WESTVIEW
PRESS

A Member of the Perseus Books Group

Westview Press was founded in 1975 in Boulder, Colorado, by notable publisher and intellectual Fred Praeger. Westview Press continues to publish scholarly titles and high-quality undergraduate- and graduate-level textbooks in core social science disciplines. With books developed, written, and edited with the needs of serious nonfiction readers, professors, and students in mind, Westview Press honors its long history of publishing books that matter.

Copyright © 2012 by Westview Press
Published by Westview Press,
A Member of the Perseus Books Group

Find us on the World Wide Web at www.westviewpress.com.

Every effort has been made to secure required permissions for all text, images, maps, and other art reprinted in this volume.

Westview Press books are available at special discounts for bulk purchases in the United States by corporations, institutions, and other organizations. For more information, please contact the Special Markets Department at the Perseus Books Group, 2300 Chestnut Street, Suite 200, Philadelphia, PA 19103, or call (800) 810-4145, ext. 5000, or e-mail special.markets @perseusbooks.com.

Library of Congress Cataloging-in-Publication Data

Mingst, Karen A., 1947–
    The United Nations in the 21st century / Karen A. Mingst and Margaret P. Karns.—
4th ed.
        p.   cm.
    Includes bibliographical references and index.
ISBN 978-0-8133-4538-3 (pbk. : alk. paper)—ISBN 978-0-8133-4539-0 (e-book)
1. United Nations. 2. International cooperation. 3. Security, International. I. Karns,
Margaret P. II. Title. III. Title: United Nations in the twenty-first century.
JZ5005.M56 2011
341.23—dc23   2011037198

10 9 8 7 6 5 4 3

Contents

List of Illustrations

Cartoons

Preface

In revising and updating this book, we have been reminded that we do, indeed, live in a world of rapid change. When we did the third edition, we were dealing with a new millennium marked by the effects of globalization, the September 11, 2001, attacks on the World Trade Center and the Pentagon, divisions provoked by the US war in Iraq and other unilateralist actions by the world's sole superpower, the threats to human security from global climate change and the HIV/AIDS pandemic, and the failure, once again, to respond to genocide in Africa. The United Nations had been shaken by the scandal over the Oil-for-Food Programme, sexual misconduct by peacekeepers, and doubts about its capacity for reforms that would enable it to better serve today's rather than yesterday's governance needs. Now, with this fourth edition, the twenty-first century is more than a decade old; the dynamics of world politics are being shaped by rising powers and the sole superpower's diminished influence, huge budget deficits, and far-flung military commitments. The UN has more peacekeepers in the field than at any time in its sixty-five years. Its role in international economic relations, however, is still further diminished as the IMF, World Bank, World Trade Organization, G-20, and other bodies play more important roles in dealing with financial crises, trade, and development. The effects of climate change are ever more apparent, yet the political will to take concrete steps to address it remains elusive. And despite the seeming consensus on the responsibility to protect civilians at risk in armed conflicts and humanitarian and natural disasters, the reality continues to be a very selective will to act.

In updating the book, we reduced material on the earlier history of the UN and sought to deal more with the challenges the UN faces today. We have added new case studies of peacekeeping in the Democratic Republic of the Congo, human trafficking, and the challenges of statebuilding for human security in Haiti. UN reform-related issues are discussed throughout the book. In the process, we have benefited from comments provided by several anonymous reviewers. We wish also to thank Alexander Kreidenweis for his assistance in updating figures and tables and Lynne Rienner for allowing us to use material on the United Nations from the second edition of our book *International Organizations: The Politics and Processes of Global Governance* (2009).

We dedicate this fourth edition to our children and grandchild, Ginger, Brett, Paul, and Anna, whose generations must sustain the United Nations in the twenty-first century. And we wish to thank our husbands, Robert Stauffer and Ralph Johnston, whose continuing patience, support, and encouragement have enabled us to bring this work to fruition.

Karen A. Mingst
Margaret P. Karns

Acronyms

AI	Amnesty International
ANC	African National Congress
ASEAN	Association of Southeast Asian Nations
AU	African Union
BRICS	Brazil, Russia, India, China, and South Africa (emerging powers)
CACM	Central American Common Market
CEDAW	Convention on the Elimination of All Forms of Discrimination Against Women
CFCs	chlorofluorocarbons
CGIAR	Consultative Group on International Agricultural Research
CONGO	Conference of Non-Governmental Organisations in Consultative Status with United Nations Economic and Social Council
CSD	Commission on Sustainable Development
CSO	civil society organization
CSW	Commission on the Status of Women
CTC	Counter-Terrorism Committee
CTED	Counter-Terrorism Executive Directorate
DPKO	Department of Peacekeeping Operations
DRC	Democratic Republic of the Congo
ECA	Economic Commission for Africa
ECE	Economic Commission for Europe
ECLA	Economic Commission for Latin America
ECOSOC	United Nations Economic and Social Council
ECOWAS	Economic Community of West African States
EPTA	Expanded Programme of Technical Assistance
ESCAP	Economic and Social Commission for Asia and the Pacific
EU	European Union (previously referred to as the European Community [EC] or the European Economic Community [EEC])
FAO	Food and Agriculture Organization

GATT   General Agreement on Tariffs and Trade
GAVI   Global Alliance for Vaccines and Immunization
GEF   Global Environmental Facility
GNP   gross national product
GONGOs government-organized nongovernmental organizations
G-7   Group of 7
G-77   Group of 77
GSP   Generalized System of Preferences
G-20   Group of 20
HDI   Human Development Index
HIPC   Heavily Indebted Poor Countries Initiative
HIV/AIDS human immunodeficiency syndrome
HRC   Human Rights Council
HRW   Human Rights Watch
IAEA   International Atomic Energy Agency
IATA   International Association of Transport Airlines
IBRD   International Bank for Reconstruction and Development
        (also known as the World Bank)
ICAO   International Civil Aviation Organization
ICC   International Criminal Court
ICJ   International Court of Justice
ICRC   International Committee of the Red Cross
ICSID   International Centre for Settlement of Investment Disputes
ICTR   International Criminal Tribunal for Rwanda
ICTY   International Criminal Tribunal for the Former Yugoslavia
IDA   International Development Association
IDB   Inter-American Development Bank
IFAD   International Fund for Agricultural Development
IFC   International Finance Corporation
IFOR   Implementation Force (NATO force in the
        former Yugoslavia)
IGO   international intergovernmental organization
IHR   International Health Regulations
ILO   International Labour Organization
IMF   International Monetary Fund
IMO   International Maritime Organization
INGO   international nongovernmental organization
INSTRAW International Research and Training Institute for the
        Advancement of Women
IO   international organization
IPCC   Intergovernmental Panel on Climate Change

ISAF International Security Assistance Force
ITU International Telecommunications Union
KFOR NATO force in Kosovo
LDCs less developed countries (also referred to as "the South")
LRA Lord's Resistance Army
MDGs Millennium Development Goals
MIGA Multilateral Investment Guarantee Agency
MINUSTAH UN Stabilization Mission in Haiti
MNC multinational corporation
MONUC UN Organization Mission in the Democratic Republic of the Congo
MONUSCO UN Organization Stabilization Mission in the Democratic Republic of the Congo
NAM Nonaligned Movement
NATO North Atlantic Treaty Organization
NEPAD New Partnership for Africa's Development
NGO nongovernmental organization
NIEO New International Economic Order
NNWS non–nuclear weapon states
NPT Treaty on the Non-Proliferation of Nuclear Weapons
NWS nuclear weapon states
OAS Organization of American States
OAU Organization of African Unity
OFFP Oil-for-Food Programme
OHCHR Office of the High Commissioner for Human Rights
OIHP Office International d'Hygiène Publique
OPEC Organization of Petroleum Exporting Countries
OSCE Organization for Security and Cooperation in Europe
PBC Peacebuilding Commission
P-5 permanent members of the UN Security Council
PLO Palestine Liberation Organization
PRC People's Republic of China
REDD reducing emissions from deforestation and degradation process
RFP Rwandan Patriotic Front
ROC Republic of China (Taiwan)
R2P responsibility to protect (also RtoP)
SADC Southern African Development Community
SARS severe acute respiratory syndrome
SFOR NATO Stabilization Force (in the former Yugoslavia)
SWAPO South West Africa People's Organization

UN	United Nations
UNAIDS	United Nations Joint Programme on HIV/AIDS
UNAMID	African Union/United Nations Hybrid Mission in Darfur
UNAMIR	United Nations Assistance Mission in Rwanda
UNCED	United Nations Conference on the Environment and Development
UNCHE	United Nations Conference on the Human Environment
UNCLOS	United Nations Conference on the Law of the Sea
UNCTAD	United Nations Conference on Trade and Development
UNDOF	United Nations Disengagement Observer Force
UNDP	United Nations Development Programme
UNEF I, II	United Nations Emergency Force (in Egypt)
UNEP	United Nations Environment Programme
UNESCO	United Nations Educational, Scientific, and Cultural Organization
UNFICYP	United Nations Force in Cyprus
UNFPA	United Nations Fund for Population Activities
UNHCR	United Nations High Commissioner for Refugees
UNICEF	United Nations Children's Fund
UNIDO	United Nations Industrial Development Organization
UNIFEM	United Nations Development Fund for Women
UNIFIL	United Nations Interim Force in Lebanon
UNIHP	United Nations Intellectual History Project
UNIKOM	United Nations Iraq-Kuwait Observer Mission
UNITA	National Union for the Total Independence of Angola
UNITAF	Unified Task Force (in Somalia, also known as Operation Restore Hope)
UNMIK	United Nations Mission in Kosovo
UNMIT	UN Integrated Mission in Timor
UNMOVIC	United Nations Monitoring, Verification, and Inspection Commission (in Iraq)
UN-NGLS	UN Non-Governmental Liaison Service
UNODC	UN Office of Drugs and Crime
UNOSOM	United Nations Operation in Somalia
UNPROFOR	United Nations Protection Force (in the former Yugoslavia)
UNSCOM	United Nations Special Commission for the Disarmament of Iraq
UNTAC	United Nations Transitional Authority in Cambodia
UNTAET	United Nations Transitional Administration in East Timor
UNTAG	United Nations Transition Assistance Group (in Namibia)
UPR	Universal Periodic Review

WCED World Commission on Environment and Development
WFP World Food Programme
WHA World Health Assembly
WHO World Health Organization
WID women-in-development
WIPO World Intellectual Property Organization
WMD weapons of mass destruction
WTO World Trade Organization

1

◄○►

The United Nations in World Politics

It is hard to imagine a world without the United Nations. Despite many ups and downs over more than sixty-five years, the UN has not only endured but also played a key role in reshaping the world as we know it. It has embodied humankind's hopes for a better world through the prevention of conflict. It has promoted a culture of legality and rule of law. It has raised an awareness of the plight of the world's poor, and it has boosted development by providing **technical assistance**. It has promoted concern for human rights, including the status of women, the rights of the child, and the unique needs of indigenous peoples. It has formulated the concept of environmentally sustainable development. It has contributed immensely to making multilateral diplomacy the primary way in which international norms, public policies, and law are established. It has served as a catalyst for global policy networks and partnerships with other actors. It plays a central role in **global governance**. Along the way, the UN has earned several Nobel Peace Prizes, including the 2005 award to the International Atomic Energy Agency (IAEA) and its chief, Mohamed ElBaradei; the 2001 prize to the UN and Secretary-General Kofi Annan; the 1988 award to UN peacekeepers; and the 1969 honor to the International Labour Organization (ILO).

In the many areas of UN activity, we can point to the UN's accomplishments and also to its shortcomings and failures. More than sixty-five years after its creation, the UN continues to be the only **international organization (IO)** or, more correctly, **international intergovernmental organization (IGO)** of global scope and nearly universal membership that has an agenda encompassing the broadest range of governance issues. It is a complex system that serves as the central site for multilateral diplomacy, with the UN's General Assembly as center stage. Three weeks of general debate at the opening of each fall assembly session draw foreign ministers and heads of state from small and large states to take advantage of the opportunity to address the nations of the world and to engage in intensive diplomacy.

1

As an intergovernmental organization, however, the UN is the creation of its member states; it is they who decide what it is that they will allow this organization to do and what resources—financial and otherwise—they will provide. In this regard, the UN is very much a political organization, subject to the winds of world politics and the whims of member governments. To understand the UN today, it is useful to look back at some of the major changes in world politics and how they affected the UN.

THE UNITED NATIONS IN WORLD POLITICS: VISION AND REALITY

The establishment of the United Nations in the closing days of World War II was an affirmation of the desire of war-weary nations for an organization that could help them avoid future conflicts and promote international economic and social cooperation. As we discuss further in Chapter 2, the UN's Charter built on lessons learned from the failed League of Nations created at the end of World War I and earlier experiments with international unions, conference diplomacy, and dispute-settlement mechanisms. It represented an expression of hope for the possibilities of a new global security arrangement and for fostering the social and economic conditions necessary for peace to prevail.

The United Nations and Politics in the Cold War World

The World War II coalition of great powers (the United States, the Soviet Union, Great Britain, France, and China), whose unity had been key to the UN's founding, was nevertheless a victim of rising tensions almost before the first General Assembly session in 1946. Developments in Europe and Asia between 1946 and 1950 soon made it clear that the emerging Cold War would have fundamental effects on the UN. How could a **collective security** system operate when there was no unity among the great powers on whose cooperation it depended? Even the admission of new members was affected between 1950 and 1955 because each side vetoed applications from states that were allied with the other.

The Cold War made Security Council actions on threats to peace and security extremely problematic, with repeated sharp exchanges and frequent deadlock. Some conflicts, such as the French and American wars in Vietnam and the Soviet interventions in Czechoslovakia and Hungary, were never brought to the UN at all. The UN was able to respond to the North Korean invasion of South Korea in 1950 only because the Soviet Union was boycotting the Security Council at the time.

In order to deal with a number of regional conflicts, the UN developed something never mentioned in its charter, namely, **peacekeeping**; this has involved the prevention, containment, and moderation of hostilities between or within states through the use of lightly armed multinational forces of soldiers, police, and civilians.

Peacekeeping was a creative response to the breakdown of great-power unity and the spread of East-West tensions to regional conflicts. UN peacekeeping forces were used extensively in the Middle East and in conflicts arising out of the decolonization process during the Cold War period. Thirteen operations were deployed from 1948 to 1988. The innovation of peacekeeping illustrates what the Cold War did to the UN: "It had repealed the proposition that the organization should undertake to promote order by bringing the great powers into troubled situations. . . . Henceforward, the task of the United Nations was to be defined as that of keeping the great powers out of such situations."[1]

The Effects of the Nuclear Revolution. The UN Charter had just been signed when the use of two atomic bombs on Japan on August 6 and 10, 1945, began a scientific and technological revolution in warfare that would have a far-reaching impact on the post–World War II world. At the United Nations, the earliest and most obvious effect of nuclear weapons was to restore the issue of disarmament (and its relative, arms control) to the agenda. Disarmament as an approach to peace had been discredited during the interwar era. The UN almost from its inception in early 1946 became a forum for discussions and negotiations on **arms control and disarmament**. Hence, the nuclear threat not only transformed world politics but also made the UN the key place where statespersons sought to persuade each other that war had become excessively dangerous, that disarmament and arms control were imperative, and that they were devoted to peace and restraint.

The Role of the United Nations in Decolonization and the Emergence of New States. At the close of World War II, few would have predicted the end of colonial rule in Africa and Asia. Yet twenty-five years after the UN Charter was signed, most of the former colonies had achieved independence with relatively little threat to international peace and security. Membership in the UN more than doubled from 51 states in 1945 to 118 in 1965 and had tripled by 1980 (see Figure 1.1), the vast majority of these new members being newly independent states. The UN played a significant role in this remarkably peaceful transformation, much of which took place during the height of the Cold War. Twenty-six new states were later seated in the UN after the Cold War's end, mostly as a result of the dissolution of the Soviet Union and Yugoslavia.

The UN Charter endorsed the principle of **self-determination**. Already independent former colonies, such as India, Egypt, Indonesia, and the Latin American states, used the UN as a forum to advocate an end to colonialism and independence for territories ruled by Great Britain, France, the Netherlands,

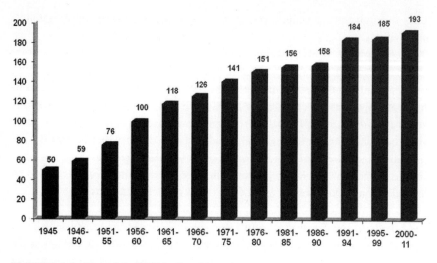

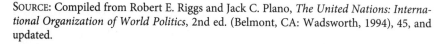

FIGURE 1.1. Growth in UN Membership, 1945–2011

SOURCE: Compiled from Robert E. Riggs and Jack C. Plano, *The United Nations: International Organization of World Politics*, 2nd ed. (Belmont, CA: Wadsworth, 1994), 45, and updated.

Belgium, Spain, and Portugal. Success added new votes to the growing anti-colonial coalition.

By 1960 a majority of the UN's members favored decolonization. General Assembly Resolution 1514 that year condemned the continuation of colonial rule and preconditions for granting independence (such as a lack of preparation for self-rule) and called for annual reports on the progress toward independence for all remaining colonial territories. The UN provided an important forum for the **collective legitimation** of a change in international norms (that is, colonialism and imperialism were no longer acceptable patterns of state behavior, and colonial peoples had a right to self-determination). The international system was fully internationalized to include all sovereign, independent states that sought membership.

The consequences of decolonization and the expanded number of independent states were manifold. The less developed, often newly independent states of Africa, Asia, and Latin America formed a strong coalition within the UN known as the **Group of 77 (G-77)**; after 1960 this coalition commanded a majority of votes on a broad range of issues. Whereas the Cold War had shaped politics in the UN until 1960, the G-77, and what became known as "North-South issues," shaped much of the politics thereafter. The two sets of issues became entwined in complex ways, and political divisions changed. The Soviet Union and many Western European states often sided with the G-77, and the United States frequently found itself in a small minority.

Beginning in the 1960s, new issues proliferated on the UN's agenda, many at the urging of the G-77. For example, in 1967, Arvid Pardo, the representative from Malta, argued on behalf of newly independent states that the resources found on the deep seabed were the "common heritage of mankind," not the property of any specific nation. This would subsequently have an impact on emerging environmental issues as well as on the law of the sea. Of all the issues pushed by the G-77, however, none received more attention than the drive for economic and social development.

The North-South Conflict. By the late 1960s, UN agendas were dominated by issues of economic and social development and the relations between the developed countries of the industrial North and the less developed countries (LDCs) of the South. The ideological leaning of the G-77 in the 1960s and 1970s toward a heavy government role in economic development and redistribution of wealth shaped many UN programs and activities. In the 1970s the G-77 pushed for a **New International Economic Order (NIEO)**, marshaling support in the UN General Assembly for "A Declaration on the Establishment of a New International Economic Order" and "A Charter of Economic Rights and Duties of States." For most of the decade, the NIEO debates dominated and polarized the UN system, with the deep divide between North and South at times making agreement on both economic and security issues impossible to achieve.

The North-South conflict continues to be a central feature of world politics, and hence of the UN, although the rhetoric and issues of the NIEO sharply diminished in the late 1980s and 1990s. For example, the UN's treatment of environmental issues, which first began with the Stockholm Conference on the Human Environment in 1972, has been permeated by North-South differences. The 1997 Kyoto Conference on Climate Change heard echoes of the North-South conflict when developing countries insisted that industrial countries make the first reductions in carbon dioxide emissions. Those echoes still persisted at the 2009 Copenhagen conference on climate change. The G-77, however, is no longer as cohesive a group; its members' interests increasingly diverged in the 1980s when some states, especially in Southeast Asia, achieved rapid economic growth and as many developing countries shifted from statist-oriented economic policies to neoliberal ones, calling for open markets and privatization. Chapter 5 discusses these shifts further as well as the increased emphasis on poverty alleviation that accompanied the **Millennium Development Goals (MDGs)** approved in 2000.

World Politics Since the Cold War's End

The Cold War's end in 1990 meant not only new cooperation among the five permanent members of the Security Council but also a resurgence of nationalism, civil wars, and ethnic conflicts; the new phenomenon of failed states; and a related series of humanitarian crises. The consequence was greater demands than ever before on the United Nations to deal with threats to peace and security as well as environmental and developmental issues, democratization, population growth, humanitarian crises, and other problems. UN peacekeepers were called on to rebuild Cambodia; create peace in Bosnia; organize and monitor postconflict elections in Nicaragua, Namibia, and many other places; monitor human rights violations in El Salvador; and oversee humanitarian relief in Bosnia, Somalia, Rwanda, Kosovo, the Democratic Republic of the Congo (DRC), East Timor, and Afghanistan. Beginning with Iraq's invasion of Kuwait in 1990, the UN's enforcement powers were used more in the post–Cold War era than at any previous time.

With the spread of **democratization** to all regions of the globe from Latin America, Eastern Europe, and states created from the former Soviet Union to Africa and Asia, many authoritarian governments in the late 1980s and 1990s were forced to open their political processes to competing political parties, adopt more stringent human rights standards, and hold free elections. Since 1990 the UN has been in heavy demand to provide observers for elections in countries around the world. UN-sanctioned intervention in Haiti in 1993 marked the first time the UN took action to restore a democratically elected government. In Namibia, Kosovo, Bosnia, and East Timor, the UN was called upon to assist with organizing the elements of newly independent states, including the provision of transitional administrations, writing of constitutions, training of police and judges, and organization of elections.

By 1995, however, the early post–Cold War optimism about the United Nations had faded. The peacekeepers in Somalia, Bosnia, and Rwanda found little peace to be kept, although their presence did alleviate much human suffering. Despite almost continuous meetings of the UN Security Council and numerous resolutions, the UN's members lacked the political will to provide the military, logistical, and financial resources needed to deal adequately with these and other complex situations. In addition, the UN faced a deep financial crisis in the late 1990s caused by the increased cost of peacekeeping and other activities and the failure of many members, including the United States, to pay their assessed contributions. The organization clearly needed significant reforms to meet the increased demands and address weaknesses in its structures and operations, but member states failed to use either the occasion of the UN's fiftieth anniversary in 1995 or the UN's sixtieth anniversary in 2005 to approve many of the necessary changes. The UN did not stand still, however. Some changes could be made without member states' approval; other reforms were approved at the 2005 World Summit. And, in its responses to many complex conflicts, humanitarian crises, new threats to peace posed by nuclear weapons proliferation and terrorism, as well as persistent global poverty, the UN demonstrated that it was still central to many aspects of global governance, as discussed in subsequent chapters.

Well before the Cold War's end, the UN played an important role on a nexus of **interdependence** issues by convening global conferences and summits on topics ranging from the environment, food, housing, the law of the sea, disarmament, women, and water to human rights, population and development, and social development. These conferences have articulated new international norms; expanded international law; set agendas for governments, as well as for the UN itself, through programs of action; and promoted linkages among the growing communities of **nongovernmental organizations (NGOs)** active on different issues, the UN, and member states' governments.

Still, the UN has never played a central role in international economic relations. Although economic topics have appeared on the agendas of the General Assembly and the United Nations Economic and Social Council (ECOSOC), the major decisionmaking has always taken place in institutions that have never really been part of the UN system: the World Bank, the International Monetary Fund (IMF), the World Trade Organization (WTO), and the **Group of 7 (G-7)**, as well as in Washington, Tokyo, London, and the headquarters of major corporations and banks. The UN has, however, been active from its earliest years in efforts to promote economic and social development, introducing the ideas of development aid in the 1950s, sustainable development in the 1980s, and human development in the 1990s. Many of the global conferences contributed other ideas and reinforced understanding of the way development overlaps with the status of women, population, food, and other problems. UN Secretary-General Kofi Annan used the occasion of the new millennium to convene a Millennium Summit in 2000. In suggesting the special gathering, the secretary-general hoped "to harness the symbolic power of the millennium to the real and urgent needs of people everywhere."[2] His special report, *We the Peoples*, provided his views of the state of the world, the major global challenges, and the need for structural reform of the UN itself. The three days of meetings drew the largest gathering of world leaders ever: There were 147 heads of state or government and representatives from forty-four other countries.

The Millennium Declaration adopted at the close of the extraordinary summit reflected the high degree of consensus on two priorities: peace and development. Different leaders had stressed different aspects of the issues, ranging from globalization and nuclear weapons to fairer economic systems, ethnic tolerance, and human immunodeficiency syndrome (HIV/AIDS). They had disagreed about how to restructure the UN, but not about the importance of the world organization; they concurred with lofty language about values and principles and also committed themselves to the series of specific objectives known as the MDGs that include halving the number of people living on less than one dollar a day by the year 2015 and reversing the spread of HIV/AIDS, malaria, and other major diseases. The declaration outlined special measures to meet the needs of Africa, and it intensified efforts to reform the Security Council, to strengthen ECOSOC and the International Court of Justice (ICJ), to make the General Assembly a more effective deliberative and policymaking body, and to ensure that the UN has the resources to carry out its mandates. The MDGs and their implementation are discussed further in Chapters 5 and 7.

Rising globalization has been a major feature of world politics since the Cold War's end. **Globalization** is the process of increasing worldwide integration of politics, economics, social relations, and culture that often appears to undermine state sovereignty. In the 1990s this process of increased connectivity greatly accelerated, especially in the area of economic activities across state borders with the rapid growth in flows of finance, goods and services (trade), and investment, as well as diffusion of technology. Many regard globalization as desirable because it has fueled greater prosperity and higher standards of living in many parts of the world. Others, however, point to the growing inequality among and within nations and the ways in which globalization creates both winners and losers, such as those whose jobs in developed countries are lost to workers in developing countries who are paid lower wages. There is also the dark side of globalization that has facilitated the growth of trafficking in drugs, persons, and other criminal enterprises.

The UN itself and various **specialized agencies** within the UN system have struggled to address globalization issues. Although the International Labour Organization, World Health Organization (WHO), and World Intellectual Property Organization (WIPO) are very much involved in globalization-related issues of labor, health, and intellectual property rights, the fact that the targets of antiglobalization protesters have been the World Bank, IMF, G-7, and WTO underscores the UN's marginal role in international economic relations. Yet globalization has fueled the growth of NGOs. Subsequent chapters illustrate how the UN and NGOs, which represent what some have called global civil society, are working out new partnerships that will make each more responsive to globalization issues.

The emergence of the United States as the world's sole superpower has been a related aspect of post–Cold War world politics, the era of globalization, and the early twenty-first century. The economic and military capabilities of the United States have far exceeded those of any other state, and, with the collapse of the Soviet Union, the United States had no serious rival. Many worried that this development would result in the UN's marginalization, particularly if, or when, the United States chose to act unilaterally. This view was borne out when the United States invaded Iraq in 2003 in defiance of international opposition. An alternative view was that the UN could become a puppet of the sole superpower, dependent upon its goodwill for funding and subservient in authorizing US actions. Yet in the late 1990s and first decade of the twenty-first century, we have seen groups of states and of NGOs willing to push ahead with policy initiatives even when the United States has opposed them, examples being the International Criminal Court, the Convention on Landmines, the Kyoto Protocol on Climate Change, and its successor. Although its support has fluctuated, in fact, the United States has always been important to the United Nations, as discussed further in Chapter 3.

Now, with the rapid rise of China, India, South Africa, Brazil and other emerging powers as well as the reassertiveness of Russia (a group collectively known as the **BRICS**), world politics is again shifting, and the years ahead will likely see significant changes in how these shifts play out within the UN. Already in international economic relations, the G-7 has been effectively replaced by the **Group of 20 (G-20)**, and the emerging powers have pushed for changes in their voting shares within the World Bank and IMF. The reform of UN Security Council membership will gain new attention and urgency with these power shifts.

To understand the links between world politics and the United Nations, it is also important to examine the major international relations theories to see how they explain global changes and the roles of IGOs such as the UN.

CONTENDING INTERNATIONAL RELATIONS THEORIES

For much of the post–World War II era, **realist theory**, or **realism**, provided the dominant explanation for international politics. Realists see states as the most important actors in the international system. They view states as unitary actors that define their national interests in terms of maximizing power and security. States' **sovereignty** means that they coexist in an anarchic international system and, therefore, must rely primarily on themselves to manage their own insecurity through balance of power, alliances, and deterrence. International rules (law) and norms, as well as international organizations, do not carry much weight with realists because they lack enforcement power. In realists' view, IGOs and NGOs are marginal actors. IGOs, in particular, do not enjoy autonomy or capability for independent action on the world stage. Rather, they reflect the interests of their members, especially the most powerful ones. In this

view, the UN is constrained by its members' willingness to work through it in
dealing with specific problems, to comply with and support its actions, to provide peacekeeping contingents (military or civilian), and to pay for its regular
operations and special programs. In realist theory, cooperation among states is
not impossible, but states have little incentive to enter into international
arrangements, and they are always free to exit from them.[3]

For many international relations scholars, however, realist theory is an inadequate theoretical framework for analyzing world politics, and especially the
rapid changes since the Cold War's end as well as the expanded practice of
multilateralism and the activities of the UN and other IGOs. One major alternative is **liberalism**.[4]

Liberals regard states as important actors, but they place importance on a variety of other actors in the international system, including IGOs, NGOs, **multinational corporations (MNCs)**, and even individuals. States, in their view, are
pluralistic, not unitary, actors. Moral and ethical principles, power relations,
and bargaining among different domestic and transnational groups and changing international conditions shape states' interests and actions. There is no single definition of national interest; rather, states vary in their goals, and their
interests change. Liberal theorists characterize the international system as an
interdependent one in which there is both cooperation and conflict and where
actors' mutual interests tend to increase over time. States' power matters, but it
is exercised within a framework of international rules and institutions that help
to make cooperation possible.

Neoliberal institutionalists have provided a somewhat different explanation for
why cooperation occurs. For classical liberals, cooperation emerges from establishing and reforming institutions that permit cooperative interactions and prohibit coercive actions. For neoliberal institutionalists, cooperation emerges when
actors have continuous interactions with each other. Institutions help prevent
cheating; they reduce transaction and opportunity costs for those who seek gains
from cooperation within them. Institutions are essential; they build upon common interests. They help to shape state's interests and state preferences. IGOs such
as the United Nations make a difference in world politics by altering state preferences and establishing rules that constrain states. They are not merely pawns of
the dominant powers but actually modify state behavior by creating habits of cooperation and serving as arenas for negotiation and policy coordination.

For some liberal theorists, the growth of multilateralism, IGOs, and international law is indicative of a nascent international society in which actors consent to common rules and institutions and recognize common interests as well
as a common identity or sense of "we-ness." Within this emerging society, international institutions are changing the way states and other actors interact

with each other. Many scholars argue that the growing role of nongovernmental actors represents an emerging global civil society.[5]

A third and relatively recent approach to international relations is **constructivism**, which has become important for studying various aspects of global governance, particularly the role of norms and institutions. Constructivism has several variants, and questions have arisen about whether it is a theory of politics. Yet it offers a valuable way of studying how shared beliefs, rules, organizations, and cultural practices shape the behavior of states and other actors as well as their identities and interests. Among the key norms affecting state behavior in constructivists' view is multilateralism. Several studies have examined the impact of norms and principled beliefs on international outcomes such as the evolution of the international human rights **regime**, bans on certain types of weapons, and humanitarian intervention in which the UN and other IGOs have played a role. They have found that international organizations can be not only "teachers" but also "creators" of norms; as such, they can socialize states into accepting certain political goals and values.[6]

Constructivists tend to see IGOs as actors that can have independent effects on international relations and as arenas in which discussions, persuasion, education, and argument take place that influence government leaders', businesspeople's, and NGO activists' understandings of their interests and of the world in which they live. The consequences are not always positive, however, because IGOs can also stimulate conflicts, their actions may not necessarily be in the interests of their member states, and IGO bureaucracies such as the UN Secretariat may develop agendas of their own, be dysfunctional, lack accountability, tolerate inefficient practices, and compete for turf, budgets, and staff.[7]

Realism, liberalism, and constructivism, then, are different "lenses" through which scholars view world politics and the United Nations.

DILEMMAS THE UN FACES IN THE 21ST CENTURY

No matter which theory one finds most valuable, understanding the role of the UN in the twenty-first century requires the exploration of three dilemmas.

Dilemma 1: Needs for Governance Versus the UN's Weaknesses

The United Nations has faced increasing demands that it provide peacekeeping and peacebuilding operations, initiate international regulation to halt environmental degradation and alleviate poverty and inequality in the world, promote greater human economic and social well-being, provide humanitarian relief to victims of natural disasters and violence, and protect human rights for various groups. These are demands for global governance—not world government—demands for rules, norms, and organizational structures to manage transboundary and interdependence problems that states acting alone cannot solve, such as terrorism, crime, drugs, environmental degradation, pandemics, and human rights violations.[8]

These governance demands test the capacity and the willingness of states to commit themselves to international cooperation and the capacity of the UN and other international organizations to function effectively. Can they meet these new demands without simply adding more programs? How can the initiatives be funded? Can the UN be more effective in coordinating the related activities of various institutions, states, and NGOs? Can it improve its own management and personnel practices? Can it adapt to deal with the changing nature of conflicts and persistent poverty and inequality? The most important issues concerning the global economy are discussed and decided outside the UN system. The UN Charter's provisions are designed for interstate conflicts, yet most post–Cold War conflicts have been intrastate civil wars. The UN's membership has grown from 50 to 193 states. The Security Council was structured to reflect power realities in 1945, not the twenty-first century.

Clearly, the UN needs to reform to increase its capacity to meet new demands, to mobilize resources, to reflect the changing distribution of power and authority in the twenty-first century, and to strengthen its links with nonstate actors. One of the UN's strengths to date has been its flexibility in response to new issues and a membership more than three times the size of the original membership. Its weaknesses are the rigidity of its central structures, its slowness to accommodate nonstate actors and the changing realities of geopolitics, and the continuing inability of member states to agree about major reforms. It has also been weakened by states' failure to meet their commitments for funding and their reluctance to empower the UN Secretariat too much. Yet the current demands for global governance require the commitment of states and enhanced institutional capacity in the UN; they therefore also require that states give up more of their sovereignty. This leads to the second dilemma.

Dilemma 2: Sovereignty Versus Challenges to Sovereignty

The longstanding principles of state sovereignty and nonintervention in states' domestic affairs are affirmed in the UN Charter, yet sovereignty has eroded on many fronts and is continually challenged in this era of globalization by issues and problems that cross states' borders and that states cannot solve alone. Historically, sovereignty empowered each state to govern all matters within its territorial jurisdiction. **Nonintervention** is the related principle that obliges other states and international organizations not to intervene in matters within the internal or domestic jurisdiction of a sovereign state. Global telecommunications, including the Internet, and economic interdependencies such as global financial markets, international human rights norms, international election monitoring, and environmental regulation are among the many developments that infringe on states' sovereignty and traditional areas of domestic jurisdiction. The growing activities of IGOs and NGOs have eroded the centrality of states as the primary actors in world politics. For example, Amnesty International (AI) and the International Commission of Jurists have been key actors in promoting human rights, sometimes exerting more influence than states themselves. Multinational corporations with operations in several countries and industry groups such as oil, steel, textiles, automobiles, and shipping are important players in trade and climate change negotiations, some having more resources than some states. Partnerships between the UN and private sector, including multinational corporations, have become increasingly important for a variety of governance challenges. The Global Compact initiated by UN Secretary-General Kofi Annan in 1999 was a step in this direction.

How is sovereignty challenged by these developments? Global telecommunications and particularly the Internet as well as heightened economic interdependence have diminished the control that governments can exercise over the information their citizens receive, the value of their money, financial transactions, and the health of their countries' economies. NGOs can influence legislators and government officials both from within countries and from outside through transnational networks and access to the media.

International norms and rules, such as those on trade, the seas, intellectual property rights, ozone-depleting chlorofluorocarbons (CFCs), and women's rights, have been established through UN-sponsored negotiations. They set standards for states and relevant industries as well as for consumers and citizens. When states themselves accept commitments to uphold these standards (by signing and ratifying international treaties and conventions), they are simultaneously exercising their sovereignty (the commitment they make) and accepting a diminution of that sovereignty (the agreement to international standards that will then be open to international monitoring). Climate change poses particularly daunting challenges for both global governance and state sovereignty.

Although multilateral institutions in theory take actions that constitute intervention in states' domestic affairs only with their consent, there is now a growing body of precedent for **humanitarian intervention**, which has emerged as a new norm of **responsibility to protect (R2P)** to justify international actions to alleviate human suffering during violent conflicts without the consent of the "host" country. It was first invoked to provide food relief and reestablish civil order in Somalia in 1993–1994, then to justify the bombing of Yugoslavia and Kosovo by the North Atlantic Treaty Organization (NATO) in 1999, and to call for international action against genocide in the Darfur region of Sudan in 2005–2006. The

2005 World Summit endorsed the R2P norm, but many states, particularly developing countries, feared its consequences for the norms of nonintervention and sovereignty. The case of Libya in 2011 is discussed in Chapter 4.

Despite these apparent limitations on states' sovereignty, the reality remains that "the capacity to mobilize the resources necessary to tackle global problems also remains vested in states, therefore effectively incapacitating many international institutions."[9] That includes the United Nations. Thus, the dilemma associated with state sovereignty links also to the third dilemma: the need for leadership.

Dilemma 3: The Need for Leadership

World politics in the twenty-first century was marked initially by the dominance of the United States as the sole superpower and a diffusion of power among many other states, the European Union (EU), and a wide variety of nonstate actors that exercise influence in different ways. As noted above, however, even before the end of the first decade, it was apparent that the rise of emerging nations such as Brazil, India, and China as well as constraints on the United States were leading to shifting patterns of power and leadership. Yet traditional measures of power in international politics do not necessarily dictate who will provide leadership or be influential within the UN.

Multilateral institutions such as the UN create opportunities for small and middle powers as well as for NGOs, groups of states, and IGOs' executive heads to exercise initiative and leadership. UN secretaries-general, in fact, have often been important figures in the international arena depending on their personality and willingness to take initiatives such as mediating conflicts or proposing responses to international problems that may or may not prove acceptable to member states. Both Boutros Boutros-Ghali and Kofi Annan are noted, for example, for their leadership both within and outside the UN. Prominent individuals, such as former Australian prime minister Gareth Evans and Mohamed Sahnoun of Algeria, who chaired the independent International Commission on Intervention and State Sovereignty that in 2001 proposed the new norm of responsibility to protect as an obligation of states, can exercise leadership through technical expertise and diplomatic skill. Middle powers such as Australia, Canada, Brazil, and India have been influential in international trade negotiations on agricultural issues, as they have long been in peacekeeping and development. Canada provided leadership for the effort in the late 1990s to ban antipersonnel land mines, while Norway led a similar effort on cluster munitions that culminated in a treaty in 2008. Brazil, Japan, and India led the effort in 2005 to secure Security Council reform.

NGOs can also provide leadership along with states, UN secretaries-general, and other prominent individuals. The success of both the land-mine and cluster-munitions efforts owed much to the leadership of coalitions of NGOs. The Inter-governmental Panel on Climate Change (IPCC) has been a lead actor in interna-tional efforts since the late 1980s to analyze data on climate and to promote efforts to address the problem.

Still, states matter, and leadership from major powers with resources and in-fluence matters. Hence, the dilemma. With the demise of the Soviet Union in 1991, the United States became the sole remaining superpower—the only state with intervention capabilities and interests in many parts of the globe. US eco-nomic, military, technological, and other resources still vastly exceed those of all other countries, notwithstanding China's rapid economic growth and emer-gence as a major economic power. The US gross domestic product is more than two and a half times that of China, whose GDP surpassed Japan's in 2010, and the American military expenditure is almost half that of the entire world. Power disparity such as this may still make the United States "bound to lead," but the style of leadership required in a world marked by multilateralism is not one of unilateral action but one geared to building coalitions and consensus and achieving active consultation and cooperation.

Furthermore, dominance tends to inspire resistance. A dominant power can rely on its sheer weight to play hardball and get its way—up to a point. The pro-longed insurgency and failures in Iraq following US military intervention in 2003 demonstrated the limits of hard power. Leadership (and inspiring follower-ship) depends on soft power's inspiration and cultivation. In the late 1990s, US opposi-tion to the creation of the International Criminal Court, the convention banning antipersonnel land mines, the Comprehensive Test Ban Treaty, and the Kyoto Protocol on Climate Change signaled a "go-it-alone" pattern that continued in the early years of the twenty-first century with the Bush administration's opposi-tion to international treaties and invasion of Iraq.[10] This made many countries less willing to accept US dominance.[11] It also fueled anti-Americanism in many parts of the world.[12] Consequently, the United States lost a good deal of its soft power and ability to lead. President Obama has rectified some of that and been more inclined to forge international consensus, limiting US interventions, mind-ful also of the constraints of the US budget deficit and military commitments. In any case, the history of US engagement with the UN is one of "mixed messages" and considerable variation. As discussed further in Chapter 3, Congress blocked full payment of US dues to the UN from the mid-1980s until 2000, and with the huge budget deficit, as well as Republican majority in the House of Representa-tives following the 2010 midterm elections, US payments to the UN are targeted for cuts again.

In a world of emerging powers, the likelihood that the United States can lead, even when it chooses to, is inevitably diminished. Yet those rising powers may not be willing or able to assume leadership either.

CONCLUSION

Subsequent chapters explore these dilemmas in the context of different areas of UN activity. Chapter 2 outlines the historical foundations of the United Nations and describes the various structures, politics, and processes within it as well as efforts at reform. Chapter 3 considers the major actors in the UN system, including NGOs, coalitions and blocs, small states and middle powers, and the United States and other major powers, as well as the UN secretary-general and the Secretariat. Chapter 4 deals with the UN's role in peace and security issues, including peacekeeping, enforcement, peacebuilding, humanitarian intervention, counterterrorism, and nuclear proliferation, with case studies of Somalia, Bosnia, the Democratic Republic of the Congo, and Darfur. In Chapter 5, which covers the role of the UN system in promoting development, we explore case studies of women and development and the MDGs and poverty alleviation. Chapter 6 analyzes the role of the UN in the evolution of international human rights norms with case studies of the anti-apartheid movement, the women's rights agenda, human trafficking, and the issues of genocide, crimes against humanity, and war crimes. Chapter 7 on **human security** deals with environmental degradation and health issues, with case studies of ozone and climate change and HIV/AIDS. It also includes a case study of statebuilding for human security in Haiti. Chapter 8 explores the questions of what the UN has done best, where it has fallen short, and whether and how it can make a difference in the world of the twenty-first century.

To aid readers in pursuing further research on the subject matter in the book, we have provided lists by topic area of sources for additional research at the end of the book along with Internet sites. The notes with each chapter are also an excellent place to start for learning more.

Notes

1. Inis L. Claude Jr., *The Changing United Nations* (New York: Random House, 1965), 32.

2. Christopher S. Wren, "Annan Says All Nations Must Cooperate," *New York Times,* September 6, 2000.

3. See, for example, Hans Morgenthau, *Politics Among Nations,* 4th ed. (New York: Alfred A. Knopf, 1967); and John J. Mearsheimer, "The False Promise of International Institutions," *International Security* 13, no. 3 (1994–1995): 5–49.

4. See, for example, Michael W. Doyle, "Liberalism and World Politics," *American Political Science Review* 80, no. 4 (December 1986): 1151–1169; Hedley Bull, *The Anarchical Society: A Study of Order in World Politics* (New York: Columbia University Press, 1977); Robert O. Keohane and Joseph S. Nye, *Power and Interdependence,* 3rd ed. (New York: Longman, 2001); and Robert O. Keohane and Lisa L. Martin, "The Promise of Institutionalist Theory," *International Security* 20, no. 1 (1995): 39–51.

5. See, for example, Ronnie Lipschutz, "Reconstructing World Politics: The Emergence of Global Civil Society," *Millennium: Journal of International Studies* 21, no. 3 (1992): 398–399; and Craig Warkentin, *Reshaping World Politics: NGOs, the Internet, and Global Civil Society* (Lanham, MD: Rowman and Littlefield, 2001).

6. See, for example, John Gerard Ruggie, "Multilateralism: The Anatomy of an Institution," in *Multilateralism Matters: The Theory and Praxis of an Institutional Form,* ed. John Gerard Ruggie (New York: Columbia University Press, 1993), 3–47; Martha Finnemore, *National Interests in International Society* (Ithaca: Cornell University Press, 1996); and Martha Finnemore and Kathryn Sikkink, "Taking Stock: The Constructivist Research Program in International Relations and Comparative Politics," *Annual Review of Political Science* 4 (2001): 391–416.

7. Michael Barnett and Martha Finnemore, *Rules for the World: International Organizations in Global Politics* (Ithaca: Cornell University Press, 2004).

8. Margaret P. Karns and Karen A. Mingst, *International Organizations: The Politics and Processes of Global Governance,* 2nd ed. (Boulder: Lynne Rienner, 2009).

9. Thomas G. Weiss and Ramesh Thakur, *Global Governance and the UN: An Unfinished Journey* (Bloomington: Indiana University Press, 2010).

10. Stewart Patrick and Shepard Forman, eds., *Multilateralism and U.S. Foreign Policy: Ambivalent Engagement* (Boulder: Lynne Rienner, 2002).

11. David M. Malone and Yuen Foong Khong, eds., *Unilateralism and U.S. Foreign Policy: International Perspectives* (Boulder: Lynne Rienner, 2003).

12. Joseph S. Nye Jr., *Bound to Lead: The Changing Nature of American Power* (New York: Basic Books, 1990); Joseph S. Nye, *The Paradox of American Power: Why the World's Only Superpower Can't Go It Alone* (Oxford: Oxford University Press, 2002).

2

⊰◦⊱

The Evolution of the
United Nations System

The United Nations was established at the end of World War II, but its roots can be traced to sixteenth-century European ideas about international law and organization, a series of developments in the nineteenth century, and the League of Nations established after World War I. For example, beginning in 1815, the European states participated in the **Concert of Europe**. Under the Concert system, the leaders of the major European powers came together in multilateral meetings to settle problems and coordinate actions. Meeting more than thirty times between 1815 and 1878, the major powers legitimized the independence of new European states such as Belgium and Greece. At the last meeting in Berlin in 1878, they extended the reach of European imperialism by dividing up the previously uncolonized parts of Africa. These Concert meetings solidified some important practices that persist today in the UN, including multilateral consultation, collective diplomacy, and special status for great "powers" in the Security Council.

Also in the nineteenth century, a number of public international unions were established among European states to deal with problems stemming from the expanding commerce, communications, and technological innovation of the Industrial Revolution: for example, health standards for travelers, shipping rules on the Rhine River, increased mail volume, and the cross-boundary usage of the newly invented telegraph. These practical problems of expanding international relations led to the creation of the International Telegraph Union in 1865 and the Universal Postal Union in 1874. Thus, the public international unions gave rise to **functionalism**—the theory that IGOs can help states deal with practical problems in their international relations—and many are now specialized agencies within the UN system.

The public international unions spawned several procedural innovations; among them were international secretariats, that is, permanent bureaucrats hired from a variety of countries to perform specific tasks. They also developed the practice of involving specialists from outside ministries of foreign affairs as well as private interest groups in their work. Multilateral diplomacy was no longer the exclusive domain of traditional diplomats. In addition, the public unions began to develop techniques for multilateral conventions—law- or rule-making treaties. Many additional such organizations were established in the twentieth century, including the International Maritime Organization and the International Civil Aviation Organization.

In addition, a pair of conferences of European and non-European states convened in The Hague (Netherlands) in 1899 and 1907 by Czar Nicholas II of Russia set a number of precedents that also shaped the UN as we know it today. The conferences were intended to consider techniques that would prevent war and the conditions under which arbitration, negotiation, and legal recourse would be appropriate. Exploring such issues in the absence of a crisis was a novelty. They led to the Convention for the Pacific Settlement of International Disputes, ad hoc international commissions of inquiry, and the Permanent Court of Arbitration, which still exists and has been used, for example, to handle claims arising from the 1979–1980 Iran hostage crisis.

The Hague conferences also produced several major procedural innovations. This was the first time that participants included both small and non-European states. The Latin American states, China, and Japan were given an equal voice, an advance that not only established the principle of universality but also bolstered legal equality. Thus, what had been largely a European state system until the end of the nineteenth century became a truly international system at the beginning of the twentieth. For the first time, multilateral diplomacy employed such techniques as the election of chairs, the organization of committees, and roll call votes, all of which became permanent features of twentieth-century organizations, including the UN. The Hague conferences also advanced the codification of international law and promoted the novel idea that humankind has common interests.

The institutional developments of the nineteenth century, however, did not prevent war among the major European powers. The Concert system broke into two competing military alliances at the turn of the twentieth century. Cooperation in other areas of interest proved insufficient to prevent war when national security was at stake. Hence, the outbreak of World War I pointed vividly to the weaknesses of the nineteenth-century arrangements. The war had hardly begun when private groups and prominent individuals in Europe and the United States began to plan for the postwar era. Nongovernmental groups such as the League to Enforce Peace in the United States and the League of Nations in Great Britain were eager to develop more permanent frameworks for preventing future wars. President Woodrow Wilson's proposal to create a permanent international organization in the Versailles Peace Treaty was based on these plans. Because the League of Nations had a significant influence on its successor, the United Nations, we examine it in more detail.

THE LEAGUE OF NATIONS

The League of Nations reflected the environment in which it was conceived.[1] Almost half of the League Covenant's twenty-six provisions focused on preventing war. Two basic principles were paramount: Member states agreed to respect and preserve the territorial integrity and political independence of states and to try different methods of dispute settlement. If they failed, the League had the power under Article 16 to enforce settlements through sanctions. The second principle was firmly embedded in the proposition of collective security, namely, that aggression by one state should be countered by all members acting together as a "league of nations" with economic sanctions and force if necessary.

The League Covenant established an assembly and a council, the latter recognizing the special prerogative of great powers, a lasting remnant of the European Concert system, and the former giving pride of place to universality of membership (about sixty states at that time). Authority rested with the council, composed of four permanent and four elected members. The council was to be the settler of disputes, the enforcer of sanctions, and the implementer of peaceful settlements. The requirement of unanimity, however, made action difficult.

The League did enjoy a number of successes, many of them on territorial issues. It conducted plebiscites in Silesia and the Saar and then demarcated the German-Polish border. It settled territorial disputes between Lithuania and Poland, Finland and Russia, and Bulgaria and Greece, and it guaranteed Albanian territorial integrity against encroachments by Italy, Greece, and Yugoslavia.

Despite these successes, the League's council failed to act decisively against the aggression of Italy and Japan in the 1930s. Collective security failed as Britain and France pursued their national interests. Voluntary sanctions approved after Italy's invasion of Ethiopia in 1935 carried little effect. The absence of great-power support for the League was particularly evident in the failure of the United States, as a result of congressional opposition and a resurgence of isolationism, to join the organization.

The League could not prevent the outbreak of World War II, yet it represented an important step forward in the process of international organization. Planning for the post–World War II peace began even before the United States entered the war and involved several high-level meetings of the Allied leaders—Roosevelt, Churchill, and Stalin—as well as other officials in Allied governments. Most important, this planning built on the lessons of the League in laying the ground-work for its successor, the United Nations. Despite the League's shortcomings, there was consensus on the importance of such an international organization, albeit one whose scope would be far greater than the League's. President Roosevelt, a firm believer in the importance of such an organization, early on sought to ensure domestic support for US participation.

THE ORIGINS OF THE UNITED NATIONS

The Atlantic Charter of August 14, 1941—a joint declaration by US president Franklin Roosevelt and British prime minister Winston Churchill calling for collaboration on economic issues and a permanent system of security—was the foundation for the Declaration by the United Nations in January 1942. Twenty-six nations affirmed the principles of the Atlantic Charter and agreed to create a new universal organization to replace the League of Nations. The UN Charter was then drafted in two sets of meetings, between August and October 1944, at Dumbarton Oaks in Washington, DC. The participants agreed that the organization would be based on the principle of the sovereign equality of members and that all "peace-loving" states would be eligible for membership, thereby excluding the Axis powers—Germany, Italy, Japan, and Spain. It was also agreed that decisions on security issues would require unanimity of the permanent members of the Security Council, the great powers.

When the United Nations Conference on International Organization convened in San Francisco on April 25, 1945, delegates from the fifty participating states modified and finalized what had already been negotiated among the great powers. On July 28, 1945, with Senate approval, the United States became the first country to ratify the Charter, and it would take only three more months to obtain a sufficient number of ratifications (legal consents) from other countries. (An abridged and amended version of the UN Charter can be found in the Appendix.)

One conference participant made the following comments after the Charter was signed:

> One of the most significant features was the demonstration of the large area of agreement which existed from the start among the 50 nations. . . . Everyone exhibited a serious minded determination to reach agreement on an organization which would be more effective than the League of Nations. . . . Not a single reservation was made to the Charter when it was adopted. . . . The conference will long stand as one of the landmarks in international diplomacy. . . . [Nonetheless] one wonders—will the conversations of men prove powerful enough to curb the might of military power or to harness it to more orderly uses?[2]

THE ORGANIZATION OF THE UNITED NATIONS

Basic Principles

Several principles undergird the structure and operation of the UN and represent fundamental legal obligations of all members. These are contained in Article 2 of the Charter as well as in other Charter provisions.

The most fundamental principle is the sovereign equality of member states. Since the Peace of Westphalia of 1648, states as political units do not recognize any higher governing authority. "Equality" refers to the legal status of states, not to their size, military power, or wealth; Russia, Lithuania, China, and Singapore, for instance, are thus equals. Sovereign equality is the basis for each state having one vote in the General Assembly. Yet inequality is also part of the UN framework, embodied in the permanent membership and veto power of five states in the Security Council: the United States, Russia, China, Great Britain, and France.

Closely related to the UN's primary goal of maintaining peace and security are the twin principles that all member states shall refrain from threatening or using force against the territorial integrity or political independence of any state, and from acting in any manner inconsistent with UN purposes, and that they shall settle their international disputes by peaceful means. Many times over the years, states have failed to honor these principles, often failing even to submit their disputes to the UN for settlement. Yet the UN's members continue to demonstrate strong support for these core principles, as evidenced by their firm response to Iraq's occupation of Kuwait in 1990.

Members also accept the obligation to support **enforcement actions**, such as economic sanctions, and to refrain from giving assistance to states that are the objects of UN preventive or enforcement action. They have the collective responsibility to ensure that nonmember states act in accordance with these principles as necessary for the maintenance of international peace and security.

A further key principle is the requirement that member states fulfill in good faith all the obligations assumed by them under the Charter; this affirms a fundamental norm of all international law and treaties, *pacta sunt servanda*—treaties must be carried out. Those obligations include payment of assessed annual contributions (dues) to the organization, compliance with sanctions, and provision of troops for peacekeeping operations.

Finally, Article 2(7) asserts that "nothing in the present Charter shall authorize the United Nations to intervene in matters which are essentially within the domestic jurisdiction of any state or shall require the Members to submit such matters to settlement under the present Charter . . . [although] this principle shall not prejudice the application of enforcement measures under Chapter

VII." This provision underscores the longstanding norm of nonintervention in the domestic affairs of states. But who decides what is an international problem and what is a domestic one? Since the UN's founding in 1945, the scope of what is considered international has broadened, with UN involvement in human rights, development, and humanitarian intervention. Since the Cold War's end, most UN peacekeeping operations have involved intrastate rather than interstate conflicts, that is, conflicts within rather than between states, as well as intrusive peacebuilding efforts. The UN's founders recognized the tension between the commitment to act collectively against a member state and the affirmation of state sovereignty represented in the nonintervention principle. They could not foresee the dilemmas that changing definitions of security, new issues, and ethnic conflicts would pose, let alone shifting interpretations of sovereignty itself.

The Preamble and Article 1 of the UN Charter both contain references to human rights and obligate states to show "respect for the principle of equal rights and self-determination of peoples." Hence, discussions about human rights have always been regarded as a legitimate international activity rather than solely a domestic concern. Actions to promote or enforce human rights have been more controversial. Since the late 1990s, there have been extensive debates over "sovereignty as responsibility" and the responsibility to protect peoples at risk in situations of humanitarian crisis.

In Article 51, the Charter affirms states' "right of individual or collective self-defence" against armed attack. Thus, states are not required to wait for the UN to act before undertaking measures in their own (and others') defense. They are obligated to report their responses, and they may create regional defense and other arrangements. This "self-defence" principle, not surprisingly, has led to many debates over who initiated hostilities and who was the victim of aggression.

Structure of the United Nations

The structure of the United Nations as outlined in the Charter includes six major bodies: the General Assembly, the Security Council, the Economic and Social Council, the Trusteeship Council, the International Court of Justice, and the Secretariat. Each has changed during the life of the organization in response to external realities, internal pressures, and interactions with other organs.[3]

In reality, it is more accurate to speak of the **United Nations system**, because the UN has evolved into far more than these six organs.[4] Articles 57 and 63 of the Charter called for the affiliation with the UN of various specialized agencies established by separate international agreements to deal with particular issues, as discussed later in this chapter. The General Assembly, the Security Council, and ECOSOC have also used their powers to create separate and subsidiary bodies; in doing so, they have illustrated the phenomenon of "IGOs creating other IGOs."[5] For example, in 1964, developing countries, with their large majority in the General Assembly, created the United Nations Conference on Trade and Development (UNCTAD) to focus more attention on the trade and development problems of newly independent and developing states. The entry into force of the UN Convention on Chemical Weapons in 1997 led to the creation of the Organization for the Prohibition of Chemical Weapons. Figure 2.1 shows the complexity of the UN system.

In the sections that follow, we discuss how the six major UN organs have evolved in practice and some of their political dynamics. We also provide brief discussions of one specialized agency and of UN-sponsored global conferences. Subsequent chapters will illustrate the relationships among different parts of the UN system.

The General Assembly. The General Assembly, like the League of Nations assembly, was designed as the general debate arena where all members would be equally represented according to a one-state/one-vote formula. It is the organization's hub, with a diverse agenda and the responsibility for coordinating and supervising subsidiary bodies but with power only to make recommendations to members, except on internal matters such as elections and the budget. It has exclusive competence over the latter, giving it a measure of surveillance and control over all UN programs and subsidiary bodies. The assembly has important elective functions: electing the nonpermanent members of the Security Council, ECOSOC, and the Trusteeship Council; appointing judges to the International Court of Justice; and, upon the recommendation of the Security Council, admitting states to UN membership and appointing the secretary-general. In many ways, the General Assembly comes closer than any other international body to embodying what is often called the "international community." It is a "forum where 'the masses' can rally to counterbalance the 'the aristocracy' of the permanent five."[6] To paraphrase Shakespeare, if "all the world's a stage," the UN General Assembly is center stage—particularly for small states such as Fiji, Malta, and Burundi.

The General Assembly can consider any matter within the purview of the UN Charter (Article 10) and make nonbinding recommendations. Over time, the number of items on the assembly's agenda has continually grown, from 46 in 1946 to more than 150 in recent years. Many items, however, are repeated year after year, because they either constitute routine UN business or represent efforts by member states to reiterate support for some cause. The issues range from conflict situations such as the Israeli-Palestinian conflict to arms control, development, global resource management, human rights, legal issues, and the

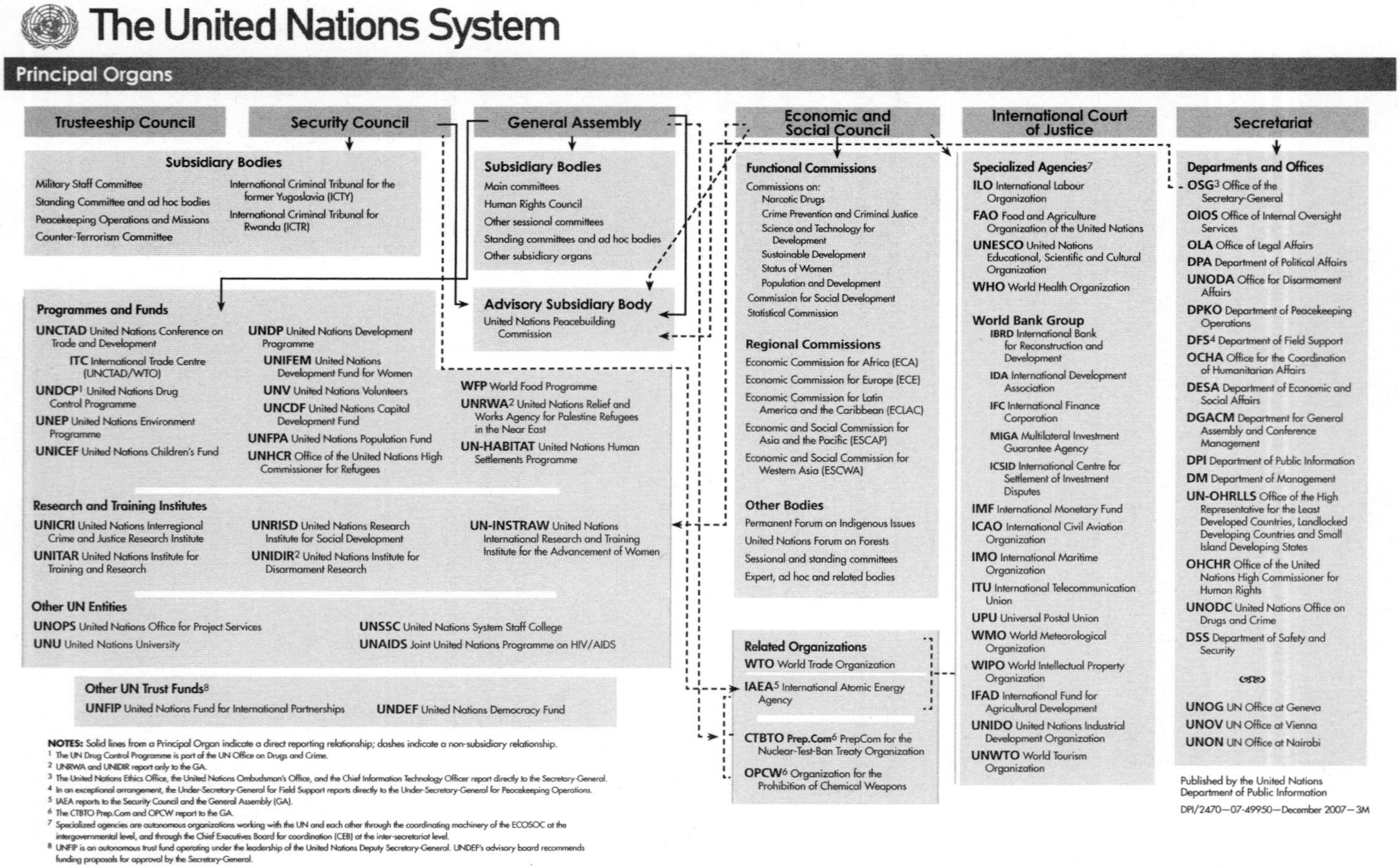

The United Nations System

Principal Organs

Trusteeship Council

Security Council

General Assembly

Economic and Social Council

International Court of Justice

Secretariat

Subsidiary Bodies

Military Staff Committee
Standing Committee and ad hoc bodies
Peacekeeping Operations and Missions
Counter-Terrorism Committee

Subsidiary Bodies

Main committees
Human Rights Council
Other sessional committees
Standing committees and ad hoc bodies
Other subsidiary organs

Advisory Subsidiary Body

United Nations Peacebuilding Commission

Programmes and Funds

UNCTAD United Nations Conference on Trade and Development
 ITC International Trade Centre (UNCTAD/WTO)
UNDCP¹ United Nations Drug Control Programme
UNEP United Nations Environment Programme
UNICEF United Nations Children's Fund

UNDP United Nations Development Programme
 UNIFEM United Nations Development Fund for Women
 UNV United Nations Volunteers
 UNCDF United Nations Capital Development Fund
UNFPA United Nations Population Fund
UNHCR Office of the United Nations High Commissioner for Refugees

WFP World Food Programme
UNRWA² United Nations Relief and Works Agency for Palestine Refugees in the Near East
UN-HABITAT United Nations Human Settlements Programme

Research and Training Institutes

UNICRI United Nations Interregional Crime and Justice Research Institute
UNITAR United Nations Institute for Training and Research

UNRISD United Nations Research Institute for Social Development
UNIDIR² United Nations Institute for Disarmament Research

UN-INSTRAW United Nations International Research and Training Institute for the Advancement of Women

Other UN Entities

UNOPS United Nations Office for Project Services
UNU United Nations University

UNSSC United Nations System Staff College
UNAIDS Joint United Nations Programme on HIV/AIDS

Other UN Trust Funds⁸

UNFIP⁷ United Nations Fund for International Partnerships

UNDEF United Nations Democracy Fund

Subsidiary Bodies

International Criminal Tribunal for the former Yugoslavia (ICTY)
International Criminal Tribunal for Rwanda (ICTR)

Functional Commissions

Commissions on:
 Narcotic Drugs
 Crime Prevention and Criminal Justice
 Science and Technology for Development
 Sustainable Development
 Status of Women
 Population and Development
 Commission for Social Development
Statistical Commission

Regional Commissions

Economic Commission for Africa (ECA)
Economic Commission for Europe (ECE)
Economic Commission for Latin America and the Caribbean (ECLAC)
Economic and Social Commission for Asia and the Pacific (ESCAP)
Economic and Social Commission for Western Asia (ESCWA)

Other Bodies

Permanent Forum on Indigenous Issues
United Nations Forum on Forests
Sessional and standing committees
Expert, ad hoc and related bodies

Related Organizations

WTO World Trade Organization
IAEA³ International Atomic Energy Agency
CTBTO Prep.Com⁴ PrepCom for the Nuclear-Test-Ban Treaty Organization
OPCW⁴ Organization for the Prohibition of Chemical Weapons

Specialized Agencies⁷

ILO International Labour Organization
FAO Food and Agriculture Organization of the United Nations
UNESCO United Nations Educational, Scientific and Cultural Organization
WHO World Health Organization

World Bank Group
 IBRD International Bank for Reconstruction and Development
 IDA International Development Association
 IFC International Finance Corporation
 MIGA Multilateral Investment Guarantee Agency
 ICSID International Centre for Settlement of Investment Disputes

IMF International Monetary Fund
ICAO International Civil Aviation Organization
IMO International Maritime Organization
ITU International Telecommunication Union
UPU Universal Postal Union
WMO World Meteorological Organization
WIPO World Intellectual Property Organization
IFAD International Fund for Agricultural Development
UNIDO United Nations Industrial Development Organization
UNWTO World Tourism Organization

Departments and Offices

OSG⁵ Office of the Secretary-General
OIOS Office of Internal Oversight Services
OLA Office of Legal Affairs
DPA Department of Political Affairs
UNODA Office for Disarmament Affairs
DPKO Department of Peacekeeping Operations
DFS⁶ Department of Field Support
OCHA Office for the Coordination of Humanitarian Affairs
DESA Department of Economic and Social Affairs
DGACM Department for General Assembly and Conference Management
DPI Department of Public Information
DM Department of Management
UN-OHRLLS Office of the High Representative for the Least Developed Countries, Landlocked Developing Countries and Small Island Developing States
OHCHR Office of the United Nations High Commissioner for Human Rights
UNODC United Nations Office on Drugs and Crime
DSS Department of Safety and Security

UNOG UN Office at Geneva
UNOV UN Office at Vienna
UNON UN Office at Nairobi

Published by the United Nations Department of Public Information
DPI/2470—07-49950—December 2007—3M

NOTES: Solid lines from a Principal Organ indicate a direct reporting relationship; dashes indicate a non-subsidiary relationship.

1 The UN Drug Control Programme is part of the UN Office on Drugs and Crime.
2 UNRWA and UNIDIR report only to the GA.
3 The United Nations Ethics Office, the United Nations Ombudsman's Office, and the Chief Information Technology Officer report directly to the Secretary-General.
4 In an exceptional arrangement, the Under-Secretary-General for Field Support reports directly to the Under-Secretary-General for Peacekeeping Operations.
5 IAEA reports to the Security Council and the General Assembly (GA).
6 The CTBTO Prep.Com and OPCW report to the GA.
7 Specialized agencies are autonomous organizations working with the UN and each other through the coordinating machinery of the ECOSOC at the intergovernmental level, and through the Chief Executives Board for coordination (CEB) at the inter-secretariat level.
8 UNFIP is an autonomous trust fund operating under the leadership of the United Nations Deputy Secretary-General. UNDEF's advisory board recommends funding proposals for approval by the Secretary-General.

FIGURE 2.1. UN System Chart

SOURCE: Published by the United Nations Department of Public Information, DPI/2470—07-49950—December 2007

UN's finances. Resolutions may be aimed at individual member states, non-members, the Security Council or other organs, the secretary-general, or even the assembly itself.

Although the Security Council is the primary organ for dealing with threats to international peace and security, the assembly can make inquiries and studies with respect to conflicts (Articles 13, 14), it may discuss a situation and make recommendations if the council is not exercising its functions (Articles 11, 12), and it has the right to be kept informed by the Security Council and the secretary-general (Articles 10, 11, 12). The **Uniting for Peace Resolution** passed during the Korean War in 1950, however, ignited controversy over the respective roles of the two bodies. Under the resolution, the General Assembly claimed authority to recommend collective measures when the Security Council was deadlocked by a veto. It was subsequently used to deal with crises in Suez and Hungary (1956), the Middle East (1958, 1967, 1980, 1982), the Congo (1960), and Palestine-Israel (1997). In all, ten emergency special sessions of the General Assembly have dealt with threats to international peace when the Security Council was deadlocked. Since the early 1990s, however, the permanent members of the Security Council have tacitly agreed that only the Security Council should authorize the use of armed force, and this is widely accepted. In any case, the General Assembly is a cumbersome body for dealing with delicate situations concerning peace and security. It is a far better organ for the symbolic politics of agenda setting and for mustering large majorities in support of resolutions.

The UN Charter also gave the General Assembly an important role in the development of international law (Article 13). Although it is not a world legislature, its resolutions may lay the basis for new international law by articulating new principles, such as one that called the seas the "common heritage of mankind," and new concepts such as sustainable development. When reiterated in resolutions over several years, these can become the basis for "soft law"—norms that represent a widespread international consensus. This norm-creating role is now recognized as one of the UN's major contributions. In some instances, new norms may be subsequently incorporated in "hard law"—creating treaties and conventions drafted under General Assembly authorization. For example, the "common heritage" principle was incorporated into the 1967 Treaty on Outer Space and 1982 Convention on Law of the Sea.

Over time, the General Assembly has produced a large number of multilateral lawmaking treaties, including the 1961 Vienna Convention on Diplomatic Relations, the 1969 Vienna Convention on the Law of Treaties, the 1968 Treaty on the Nonproliferation of Nuclear Weapons, and the 1994 Convention on the Safety of United Nations and Associated Personnel. Assembly resolutions have also approved all the major conventions on international human rights, although most were drafted in the former Commission on Human Rights that functioned under ECOSOC, as discussed in Chapter 6.

The Security Council and General Assembly share responsibilities for Charter revision. The assembly can propose amendments with a two-thirds majority; two-thirds of the member states, including all the permanent members of the Security Council, must then ratify the changes. The General Assembly and Security Council together may also call a general conference for the purpose of Charter review. There have been only two instances to date, however, of Charter amendment, both enlarging the membership of the Security Council (1965) and ECOSOC (1965 and 1973).

How the General Assembly Functions. Regular annual meetings of the General Assembly are held for three months (or longer) each fall; they begin with a "general debate" period when heads of state, prime ministers, and foreign ministers speak before the assembly. Each year, the General Assembly elects a president and seventeen vice presidents who serve for that year's session. By tradition, presidents come from small and middle-power states. Only once (in 1969) has a woman been elected. The president's powers come largely from personal influence and political skills in guiding the assembly's work, averting crises, bringing parties to agreement, ensuring that procedures are respected, and accelerating the large agenda. In addition to regular sessions, there have been twenty-eight special sessions called to deal with specific problems (for example, with HIV/ AIDS in 2001 and with children in 2002). These special sessions should not be confused with the assembly's emergency special sessions convened under a Uniting for Peace Resolution or with the global conferences the UN has sponsored since the 1970s.

The bulk of the General Assembly's work is done in six functional committees on which all members sit: the First, or Disarmament and International Security Committee; the Second, or Economic and Financial Committee; the Third, or Social, Humanitarian, and Cultural Committee; the Fourth, or Special Political and Decolonization Committee; the Fifth, or Administrative and Budgetary Committee; and the Sixth, or Legal Committee. The assembly also has created other, smaller committees to carry out specific tasks, such as studying a question (the ad hoc Committee on International Terrorism) or framing proposals and monitoring (the Committee on Peaceful Uses of Outer Space and the Disarmament Commission).

Member states' delegations are key to the assembly's functioning. The Charter provides that each member can have no more than five representatives in the assembly, but alternates and advisers are permitted. Delegates are organized in permanent missions, a practice begun with the League of Nations. Missions vary in size from about 120 (the United States) to one or two persons of diplomatic rank. Small and poor states often combine their UN mission with their embassy in

Washington, DC, to save money; most states' missions grow significantly during the fall assembly sessions, sometimes including a few parliamentarians or legislators. (The US House and Senate alternate in having representatives on the US delegation each year.) Ties between UN missions and home governments vary from loose to tight. Some delegations have considerable autonomy in dealing with the various issues on assembly agendas and determining how best to represent their countries' interests. Others operate on a "tighter leash" and must seek instructions from their capitals on what strategies to use and how to vote on given resolutions.

Delegates attend assembly and committee sessions, participate in efforts to shape agendas and debate, and represent national interests. Expertise matters and enables some delegates to be more influential than others. Because almost all states of the world are represented at the annual assembly sessions, there are many opportunities for informal bilateral and multilateral contacts, which countries may use to deal with issues outside the assembly's agenda. Multilateral diplomacy requires different skills, more akin to those of a parliamentary body than to traditional bilateral diplomacy.

Politics and Decisionmaking in the General Assembly. Politics within the General Assembly has mirrored world politics; it is the place to set the agendas of world politics, to get ideas endorsed or condemned, to have actions taken or rejected. Any state can propose an agenda item, and the assembly has been an especially valued tool of small and developing states. Under the one-state/one-vote system, it takes a simple majority of member states present and voting (50 percent plus one) to approve most resolutions. For those items determined to be "important questions," such as resolutions dealing with the maintenance of peace and security, admission of new members, suspension or expulsion of a member, and budgetary questions, a two-thirds majority is required.

Since the General Assembly often mirrors world politics, it is not surprising that member states have formed **voting blocs** to coordinate positions on particular issues and build support for them. As discussed further in Chapter 3, there emerged during the Cold War two competing coalitions aligned with either the US or the Soviet Union; later, the North-South coalitions tended to dominant assembly discussions and voting patterns, although those coalitions were never completely unified and changed over time. Thus, while the assembly's agenda was dominated by Cold War and decolonization issues in the 1950s, from the 1960s to the 1980s, developing countries used their voting power to push a number of Third World goals, as discussed in Chapter 5. The lopsided voting and frequent condemnations of US policies led the United States, in particular, to regard the General Assembly as a "hostile place" by the mid-1970s. Assembly agendas still largely reflect developing countries' interests in self-determination, economic development, global inequalities, and neocolonialism, but since the late 1980s, differences in social and economic conditions among Asian, African, and Latin American countries have made common policy positions difficult to forge. The South is splintered between a number of more developed countries such as Brazil, China, India, South Africa, Mexico, and Malaysia; a large number of very poor countries; and others in between. The developed countries have never been as cohesive as the South. Many European states have been more supportive of developing countries' concerns than the United States, weakening the North's ability to operate as a coalition in responding to the South. Chapter 3 explores further the phenomenon of blocs and coalitions.

Although coalitions and blocs emerged in response to the Charter's provisions for "equitable geographical distribution" in elections and voting, more General Assembly decisionmaking in recent years has been done by consensus, that is, by acclamation or acquiescence without any formal vote. In this case, the assembly president consults with delegations and then announces that a resolution is adopted. Consensus, therefore, refers to a decision "supported by, or at least not objectionable to, all parties involved."[7] When the assembly does vote, Article 18, paragraph 2, specifies that it use a simple majority of those states "present and voting" to decide all questions other than "important questions" dealing with peace and security, elections, budget, and admission or suspension of members. Coalitions and blocs are as active in trying to forge consensus as in marshaling votes, but the outcome is less divisive because states' individual positions are not revealed as in a roll call vote.

Many criticisms directed at the UN are really criticisms of the General Assembly. Many resolutions are "ritual resolutions"—their texts repeated almost verbatim year after year. The number of resolutions passed in the General Assembly steadily increased over time, from about 117 annually during the first five years to a peak of 360 in 2001–2002. During the 1970s, for example, resolutions dealing with the proposed New International Economic Order were repeatedly passed over the opposition of most developed countries; in recent years, resolutions on such issues as self-determination and disarmament have been approved with little concern for enforcement. This situation has led to arguments that there are too many resolutions with redundant or watered-down content, calling for too many reports, with delegates showing too little concern about commitments made.[8]

Since the Cold War's end, the General Assembly's importance within the UN system has declined as the epicenter of UN activity shifted to the Security Council and the Secretariat. With the UN Secretariat forced by its most powerful members (and largest contributors) to downsize and streamline in the name of efficiency and improved management, the developing countries worry that its interests are being given shorter shrift. Unquestionably, the General Assembly needs reform and revitalization—more than just a shorter agenda and fewer resolutions. The difficulty lies in gaining the approval of a majority of member states.

The Security Council. Under Article 24 of the Charter, the Security Council has primary responsibility for maintaining international peace and security and the authority to act on behalf of all members of the UN. Chapter VI deals with the peaceful settlement of disputes and provides a wide range of techniques for investigating disputes and helping parties achieve resolution without using force. Chapter VII specifies the Security Council's authority to identify aggressors and to commit all UN members to take enforcement measures, such as economic sanctions, or to provide military forces for joint action. Prior to 1990, the Security Council used its enforcement powers under Chapter VII on only two occasions. During the Cold War years, it relied on the peaceful settlement mechanisms under Chapter VI to respond to the many conflicts on its agenda; for example, prior to 1992, all UN peacekeeping forces were authorized under Chapter VI. Since then, the Security Council's use of Chapter VII, including its provisions for economic sanctions and military enforcement action, has increased dramatically, and most peacekeeping operations now carry Chapter VII authority, as discussed in Chapter 4.

The Security Council was deliberately designed to be small so that it could facilitate swifter and more efficient decisionmaking in dealing with threats to international peace and security. It is also the only UN body that has permanent

PHOTOGRAPH 2.1. UN Security Council authorizes no-fly zone over Libya, tightens sanctions, March 17, 2011. SOURCE: UN Photo 467078/Paulo Filgueiras.

and nonpermanent members. The five permanent members (P-5)—the United States, Great Britain, France, Russia (successor state to the seat of the Soviet Union in 1992), and the People's Republic of China (PRC, replacing the Republic of China [ROC] in 1971)—are key to Security Council decisionmaking because each has **veto** power. The nonpermanent members, originally six in number and expanded to ten in 1965, are nominated by one of the five regional groups and elected for two-year terms. At least four nonpermanent members must vote in favor of a resolution for it to pass. Under current rules, no country may serve successive terms as a nonpermanent member. Five of the nonpermanent seats go to Africa and Asia, two each to Latin America and Western Europe, and one to Eastern Europe.

The designation of permanent members reflected the distribution of military power in 1945 and the desire to ensure the UN's ability to respond quickly and decisively to aggression. Their veto power reflected the unwillingness of either the United States or the Soviet Union to accept UN membership without such a provision. It also reflected a realistic acceptance by others that the UN could not undertake enforcement action against its strongest members. The veto, however, has always been controversial among small states and middle powers. Today, with the many changes in world politics and the reality that other states contribute more financially than three of the permanent members, there are serious questions about the legitimacy and effectiveness of the composition of permanent membership. The issue of reforming the makeup of the Security Council is discussed later in this chapter.

The Security Council differs from the General Assembly and ECOSOC in that it has no regular schedule of meetings or agenda; historically, it has met and acted only in response to specific conflicts and crises. Any state, including non-UN members, has the right to bring issues before the Security Council, although there is no guarantee of action. The secretary-general can also bring a matter to the council's attention. Beginning in 2000, the Security Council initiated so-called thematic meetings to address broader issues such as HIV/AIDS as a threat to peace, child soldiers, and cooperation between the UN and regional organizations under Chapter VIII of the Charter.

Nonmembers may attend formal meetings and address the council upon request when they have an interest in a particular issue. In practice, nonmembers are often invited to private and informal meetings as well.[9] Also, states contributing peacekeeping troops now regularly participate in informal consultation with the council, as do the heads of the International Committee of the Red Cross (ICRC), other NGOs, and other nonstate actors. In short, "the Security Council is not a sealed chamber, deaf to voices and immune to pressure from beyond its walls."[10]

Much of the diplomacy and negotiation relating to the council's work takes place in various informal consultations such as those of the P-5 and "consultations of the whole."[11] Little, if any, of the bloc or coalition-building activity so common to the General Assembly takes place in the Security Council. None of the P-5 can necessarily count on the support of other permanent or nonpermanent members. The council presidency rotates monthly among the fifteen members, and presidents play an active role in facilitating discussions and consensus building, determining when the members are ready to reach a decision and, hence, to convene a formal meeting. The president also confers regularly with the secretary-general, relevant states, and other actors that are not represented on the council.

In addition to its responsibilities under the Charter for maintaining international security, the council participates in the election of the secretary-general, justices to the International Court of Justice, and new UN members in collaboration with the General Assembly. During the 1940s, it held approximately 130 meetings a year. The Cold War diminished its use, and in 1959, for example, only 5 meetings were held. Since 1990, the frequency of formal and informal meetings has steadily risen. As of early 2011, the council had approved more than 1,900 resolutions since its inception and issued hundreds of Presidential Statements summarizing the outcomes of meetings where no resolutions were acted upon.

The permanent members' veto power, while still controversial, is less of a problem today than during the Cold War when the Soviet Union employed it frequently not only to block action on many peace and security issues but also to block admission of Western-supported new members and nominees for secretary-general. The United States did not exercise its veto until the 1970s, reflecting its early dominance and many friends. Since then, however, the US has used its veto more than any other permanent member, most frequently on resolutions relating to the Arab-Israeli-Palestinian conflict and in defense of Israel. China took advantage of the early precedent that allowed abstentions not to be counted as negative votes (i.e., vetoes) to abstain a total of twenty-seven times between 1990 and 1996 on a series of enforcement measures (including those against Iraq), thus registering its disagreement but not blocking action. (See Table 2.1 for a summary of vetoes cast and note how infrequently the veto has been used since 1995.)

Since the late 1980s, the Security Council has taken action on more armed conflicts, made more decisions under Chapter VII of the UN Charter, authorized more peacekeeping operations, and imposed more types of sanctions in more situations than ever before. It took the unprecedented step of creating war crimes tribunals to prosecute individuals responsible for genocide and war crimes in

TABLE 2.1. Changing Patterns in the Use of the Veto in the Security Council, 1946–2011

Period	China[a]	France	Britain	US	USSR/Russia	Total
1946–1955	1	2	—	—	80	83
1956–1965	0	2	3	—	26	31
1966–1975	2	2	10	12	7	33
1976–1985	0	9	11	34	6	60
1986–1995	0	3	8	24	2	37
1996–2005	2	0	0	10	1	13
2006–2011	2	0	0	3	3	7
Total	7	18	32	83	125	264

[a]Between 1946 and 1971, the Chinese seat on the Security Council was occupied by the Republic of China (Taiwan), which used the veto only once (to block Mongolia's application for membership in 1955). The first veto exercised by the present occupant, the People's Republic of China, was therefore not until August 25, 1972.

SOURCE: www.globalpolicy.org/images/pdfs/Z/Tables_and_Charts/useofveto.pdf; www.un.org/Depts/dhl/resguide/scact2011.htm.

Rwanda, the former Yugoslavia, and Sierra Leone and required all states to cooperate with these tribunals. It authorized NATO bombing against Bosnian Serb forces in Bosnia in 1995 and African Union (AU) peace enforcement in Somalia and Darfur. It authorized UN-administered protectorates in Kosovo and East Timor. It expanded definitions of threats to peace to include terrorism even before the 9/11 attacks and thereafter approved Resolution 1373 that requires all member states to adopt antiterrorism measures in the International Convention for the Suppression of the Financing of Terrorism, which came into effect in 2002. These developments are discussed in detail in Chapter 4.

The Security Council has also created a number of monitoring bodies since 1990. These include sanctions committees, the Counter-Terrorism Committee (CTC), the Peacebuilding Commission (PBC), and the 1540 Committee that was established following the passage of Resolution 1540 (2004) that obligates states to establish domestic controls to prevent proliferation of weapons of mass destruction (WMD) to state or nonstate actors. The use of such authority *over* UN members and the council's intrusive sanctions and weapons inspections regimes for Iraq throughout the 1990s led Canadian diplomat David Malone to call the trend "a movement toward a regulatory approach to international peace and security."[12]

Although the Charter gives the council enormous formal power, it does not give it direct control over the means to use that power. For that the council must depend upon the voluntary cooperation of states willing to provide military and civilian personnel for peacekeeping missions, to enforce sanctions, to pay their dues, and to support enforcement actions either under UN command or by a coalition of the willing. Yet many council Chapter VII decisions since 1990 have proved more ambitious than either the member states were willing to support with resources and troops or the secretariat could effectively manage. As a result, the Security Council damaged its own and the UN's credibility.

The Security Council's activism since 1990 and US decisions in 1999 (Kosovo) and 2003 (Iraq) to undertake military actions without explicit council authorization have provoked vigorous debate among scholars and policymakers about the council's power, authority, and legitimacy.[13] Clearly, the Charter endows the Security Council with a great deal of formal power and authority. Yet the use of that authority would seem problematic given the traditional assumption that international obligations are binding only with states' consent. Key is the widespread acceptance of the Security Council as the international institution that can grant collective legitimacy for the use of armed force. In the case of the 2003 Iraq War, for example, it was recognition of the council's authority that led both supporters and opponents of the US-led invasion to seek approval or to block it. And despite concerns at the time that the council was a "failed" and "debilitated" body,[14] both sides clearly saw the legitimacy of the council's authority at stake. Searching for evidence of the council's authority for the post-9/11 antiterrorism actions mandated in Resolution 1373, for example, Cronin and Hurd note, "It is not the act of issuing these mandatory declarations that offers evidence of increased authority, but, rather, the fact that most member states accepted the *right* of the Council to do so."[15] With the increase in council activity since 1990 and questions over its ability to function effectively, questions remain over its legitimacy—issues we return to in examining reforms below.

The Economic and Social Council. ECOSOC, with its fifty-four members, is the UN's central forum for addressing international economic and social issues, and its purposes range from promoting higher standards of living to identifying solutions to economic, social, and health problems and "encouraging universal respect for human rights and fundamental freedoms." The activities it oversees encompass a majority of human and financial resources of the UN system. The founders of the UN envisaged that the various specialized agencies, ranging from the ILO and WHO to the World Bank and the IMF, would play primary roles in operational activities devoted to economic and social advancement, with ECOSOC responsible for coordinating those activities. Hence, the Charter speaks of ECOSOC's functions in terms of that coordination and also charges it with undertaking research and preparing reports on economic and social issues, making recommendations, preparing conventions, and convening conferences. Of those tasks, coordination has been the most problematic because so many activities lie outside the effective jurisdiction of ECOSOC. It is through consultative status with ECOSOC that many NGOs have official relationships with the UN and its activities. (See Chapter 3 for further discussion.)

ECOSOC's membership has been expanded through two Charter amendments. The original eighteen members were increased to twenty-seven in 1965 and to fifty-four in 1973. Members are elected by the General Assembly to three-year terms based on nominations by the regional blocs. Motivated by recognition that states with the ability to pay should be continuously represented, four of the five permanent members of the Security Council (all but China) and major developed countries have been regularly reelected. ECOSOC acts through decisions and resolutions, many of which are approved by consensus or simple majority votes. None are binding on member states or on the specialized agencies, however. Recommendations and multilateral conventions drafted by ECOSOC require General Assembly approval (and, in the case of conventions, ratification by member states).

ECOSOC holds one four-week substantive meeting each year, alternating between UN headquarters in New York and Geneva where several of the specialized agencies and other programs are headquartered. It also holds many short sessions and preparatory meetings. In 2007 and 2008, respectively, ECOSOC launched two new types of meetings. The first is the Annual Ministerial Review to assess progress toward the Millennium Development Goals and implementation of goals agreed upon at major UN conferences and summits. The second is the biennial Development Cooperation Forum intended to bring together all relevant actors for dialogue on policy issues affecting development cooperation. Both sets of meetings include member states, all relevant UN institutions, civil society, and the private sector.

The economic and social activities that ECOSOC is expected to coordinate are spread among subsidiary bodies (such as expert and working groups), nine functional commissions, five regional commissions, and the nineteen specialized agencies. (See Figure 2.1.) A number of entities created by the General Assembly, such as the UN Development Programme (UNDP), UN Fund for Population Activities (UNFPA), UN Children's Fund (UNICEF), and World Food Programme (WFP), report to both the General Assembly and ECOSOC, compounding the complexity and confusion. The scope of ECOSOC's agenda includes widely diverse topics from housing to narcotic drug control, literacy to refugees, the environment to rights of indigenous peoples. Development is the largest subject area.

Functional and Regional Commissions. Part of ECOSOC's work is done in a set of nine functional commissions: Social Development, Narcotic Drugs, Status of Women, Science and Technology for Development, Sustainable Development, Population and Development, Crime Prevention and Criminal Justice, Statistics, and Forests. The Statistical Commission reflects the importance of statistical studies and analysis for analyzing problems and making national and international social and economic policies. The wide range of data on social and economic conditions that has been gathered over the years is vital to dealing with various world problems.

Two of the most active commissions are the Commission on the Status of Women (CSW), established in 1946 to prepare recommendations and reports concerning women's political, economic, social, and educational rights, and (until 2006) the Commission on Human Rights. All of the UN-initiated declarations and conventions on human rights up to then were products of this body's work. Both of these are discussed further in Chapter 6.

Beginning in 1947, ECOSOC also created five regional commissions to stimulate regional approaches to development with studies and initiatives to promote regional projects based on the rationale that cooperation among countries within a geographic region would benefit all. A 1950 report of the Economic Commission for Latin America, for example, highlighted data on the declining terms of trade of developing countries and influenced many countries to adopt import-substitution policies to reduce their dependence on trade. In the 1960s, the Economic Commission for Africa pioneered the study of population growth and the role of women in development. The regional commissions are discussed further in Chapter 5.

Coordination is inherently difficult within any complex organization, and national governments have their own problems in this regard. Indeed, one analyst argues that ECOSOC's problems are attributable in part to "the absence of coordination at the national level in regard to international policies and programmes."[16] The steady expansion of UN economic and social activities over more than sixty-five years has made ECOSOC's mandate for coordination almost impossible to fulfill. This has led to persistent, but largely unsuccessful, calls for reform since the late 1940s, described below.

The Secretariat. The UN Secretariat is composed of approximately 55,000 professional and support staff based in New York, Geneva, Vienna, Nairobi, Bangkok, and other UN offices around the world. They are individuals who, though nationals of member countries, serve the international community. Early IGO secretariats were established by the Universal Postal Union and International Telegraph Union in the 1860s and 1870s, but their members were not independent of national governments. The League of Nations set the first precedents for a truly international secretariat of individuals who were expected to be impartial in serving the organization as a whole and dedicated to its principles. A complementary principle of an international civil service is for member states to respect the international character and responsibilities of the staff, regardless of their nationality. This practice carried over to the UN and its specialized agencies (which have their own secretariats), with personnel for all but the most senior posts recruited from a broad geographic base and advanced over time on the basis of merit and seniority. Top-level posts do not, however, conform to this civil service model but are appointed by the secretary-general based on nominations and political pressures from member governments. Secretariat members are not expected to give up their national loyalty, but are expected to refrain from promoting national interests—a sometimes difficult task at times in a world of strong nationalisms. Articles 100 and 101 deal with the Secretariat's internationalism and independence.

The Secretary-General. The UN secretary-general's position has been termed "one of the most ill-defined: a combination of chief administrative officer of the United Nations and global diplomat with a fat portfolio whose pages are blank."[17] The secretary-general is the manager of the organization, responsible for providing leadership to the Secretariat, preparing the UN's budget, submitting an annual report to the General Assembly, and overseeing studies conducted at the request of the other major organs. Article 99 of the Charter also authorizes the secretary-general "to bring to the attention of the Security Council any matter which in his opinion may threaten the maintenance of international peace and security." This provides a basis for the secretary-general's authority and ability to be an independent actor.

Over time, secretaries-general have often, but not always, come to play significant political roles as spokespersons for the organization; as conveners of expert groups, commissions, and panels to frame issues, marshal research, and outline choices; and as mediators drawing on the Charter's spirit as the basis for taking initiatives. Yet the secretary-general is simultaneously subject to the demands of two constituencies—member states and the Secretariat itself. States elect the UN's chief administrator and do not want to be either upstaged or publicly opposed by the person in that position. The secretary-general also has to answer to the secretariat personnel working in programs and agencies across the UN system. The balancing act is not always easy. As chief executive officer, the secretary-general also has to have good personnel management and budgetary skills.

The secretary-general holds office for a five-year renewable term on the recommendation of the Security Council and election by two-thirds of the General Assembly. The process of nomination is intensely political, with the P-5 having key input because of their veto power. For example, when the United States opposed the reelection of Boutros Boutros-Ghali in 1996, it forced members to agree on an alternate candidate, Kofi Annan. Efforts to establish a better means of selecting this global leader have not succeeded. Not surprisingly, those elected have all come from relatively small states (see Box 2.1).

BOX 2.1 **UN Secretaries-General (1946–present)**		
Secretary-General	*Nationality*	*Dates of Service*
Trygve Lie	Norway	1946–1953
Dag Hammarskjöld	Sweden	1953–1961
U Thant	Burma	1961–1971
Kurt Waldheim	Austria	1972–1981
Javier Pérez de Cuéllar	Peru	1982–1991
Boutros Boutros-Ghali	Egypt	1992–1996
Kofi Annan	Ghana	1997–2006
Ban Ki-moon	Republic of Korea	2007–present

Because of differences in personality and skills as well as in the challenges faced, each secretary-general has undertaken his tasks in a different way, with varying consequences for the organization. Their personalities and interpretations of the Charter, as well as world events, have combined to increase the power, resources, and importance of the position. More than just a senior civil servant, the UN secretary-general has become an international political figure and even the UN's moral voice. Collectively, then, the secretaries-general have been a key factor in the emergence of the UN as an independent actor in world politics. (We explore the secretary-general's role more fully in Chapter 3.)

Functions of the Secretariat. The UN Secretariat is organized into a series of offices and departments, including the Executive Office of the Secretary-General; the Office of Legal Affairs; the Departments of Political Affairs, Peacekeeping Operations, Disarmament Affairs, and Economic and Social Affairs; and the Office for the Coordination of Humanitarian Affairs. Each of these is headed by an undersecretary-general. Only about one-third of secretariat personnel are based at headquarters in New York or Geneva; others are posted in more than 140 countries. Their work often has little to do with the symbolic politics of the General Assembly, or even with the highly political debates of the Security Council, but it may highlight gaps in policy and contribute ideas for addressing specific problems drawn from outside consultants, NGOs, and expert groups. Most secretariat staff are involved in implementing the economic, humanitarian, and social programs that represent much of the UN's tangible contribution to fulfilling the Charter promises to "save succeeding generations from the scourge of war . . . promoting social progress and better standards of life in larger freedom." Others are supporting UN peacekeeping operations. The Secretariat is also responsible for gathering statistical data, issuing studies and reports, servicing meetings, preparing documentation, and translating speeches, debates, and documents into the UN's six official languages. Service in the UN Secretariat is not without risk. More than 350 civilian staff members have died while in UN service, including Sergio Vieira de Mello, the secretary-general's special representative to Iraq, and 21 others in the August 2003 bombing of UN offices in Baghdad as well as UN Secretary-General Dag Hammarskjöld in a plane crash in the Congo in 1961.

The UN Secretariat staff and the secretariats of the specialized agencies share a number of the characteristics of bureaucracies more generally. They derive authority from their rational-legal character and from their expertise; they derive legitimacy from the moral purposes of the organization and from their claims to neutrality, impartiality, and objectivity; and they derive power from their missions of serving others. Many Secretariat staff are technocrats—individuals with specialized training and knowledge such as the neoliberal economists in the World Bank and IMF and the public health experts in WHO. How they see a problem and how the organizational culture frames an issue may determine what solutions are discussed and the actions taken.

Woman have not occupied key positions in the UN Secretariat. As one scholar comments, "One might have expected the UN to lead in integrating women into work compared with other institutions. The pace has been glacial."[18] The chair of the first World Conference on Women held in Mexico City in 1975 was a man. Still today, only about one-third of the professional and higher ranks of the UN Secretariat's professional staff are women; only at the entry levels has gender balance been achieved. No women have been among the top candidates for secretary-general. Nafis Sadik of Pakistan was the first woman to head a major UN agency when she was appointed head of the UN Fund for Population Activities in 1987. Louise Frechette of Canada was appointed as the first deputy secretary-general in 1998. Five other women have headed UN agencies to date.

The UN Secretariat has been criticized, not only for its failure to hire women, but also for lapses in its neutrality, duplication of tasks, and poor administrative practices. It was tarnished by the scandal over UN mismanagement of the Oil-for-Food Programme (OFFP). Initiated in 1996, this program permitted limited sales of Iraqi oil to finance food supplies and medicine as humanitarian relief. About $67 billion was transferred through the program. In 2004, sources revealed that Saddam Hussein's government had pocketed more than $10 billion from both smuggling and kickbacks. Although control of smuggling and approval of contracts were responsibilities of the P-5, administration of the contracts was a Secretariat task. Among those accused of receiving kickbacks were private companies, European politicians, the Palestine Liberation Organization (PLO), and a handful of UN administrators, including the director of the OFFP. Although the secretary-general was not found guilty, his son was implicated, and others at the UN resigned or were fired. The scandal provided plenty of fuel for UN critics in the United States and elsewhere. It raised major questions about the UN's ability to manage large long-term projects and about who was more responsible for the failures: the P-5 or the Secretariat.

Member states share blame with UN secretaries-general and staff for many of the administrative problems, however. General Assembly and Security Council resolutions may be vague and unrealistic; objectives often depend on member governments' actions, funding commitments, and other factors to be fulfilled; and since the UN is a political organization, the secretariat is subject to interference and pressure from member states. Key positions in the secretary-general's cabinet are, in fact, reserved for nationals nominated by P-5 governments, and other member states have demanded a share of senior posts as well. Although there have been numerous criticisms of secretariat inefficiency over the years, many member states do not necessarily want the UN to have an effective secretariat and secretary-general since that could diminish their own ability to control what the UN does. We discuss issues of secretariat reform later in the chapter.

The International Court of Justice. Although its predecessor, the Permanent Court of International Justice, enjoyed only a loose association with the League of Nations, the International Court of Justice as the judicial arm of the UN, headquartered in The Hague, shares responsibility with the other major organs for ensuring that the principles of the Charter are followed. Its special role is providing states with an impartial body for settling legal disputes in accordance with international law and giving **advisory opinions** on legal questions referred to it by international agencies. All members of the UN are ipso facto parties to the ICJ Statute.

The General Assembly and Security Council play a joint role in electing the fifteen judges who serve nine-year terms (five are elected every three years). Judges must have qualifications befitting appointment to the highest judicial body in their home country and recognized competence in international law. Together they represent the major legal systems of the world, but act independently of their national affiliations, utilizing different sources of law set forth in Article 38 of the ICJ Statute as the basis for judgments. Their deliberations take place in private, their decisions are decided by majority vote, and decisions, including dissents, include the reasons on which they are based.

The ICJ has **noncompulsory jurisdiction**, meaning that parties to a dispute (only states) must all agree to submit a case to the court; it has no executive to enforce its decisions and no police to bring a party to justice. Enforcement therefore depends on the perceived legitimacy of the court's decisions, the voluntary compliance of states, and the "power of shame" if states fail to comply.

The ICJ has had 120 contentious cases brought before it between 1946 and 2011. It has never been heavily burdened, but its caseload has increased significantly in recent years as a result of the Cold War's end and greater trust in the court by developing countries. Also, many newer international legal conventions require the use of the ICJ to resolve disputes. To speed up what is often a lengthy process, the court has instituted the option of using a chamber of five justices to hear and determine cases by summary procedure.

ICJ cases have only rarely reflected the major political issues of the day because few states want to trust a legal judgment for the settlement of a largely political issue. The court has helped states resolve numerous territorial disputes (for example, the *Case Concerning the Land and Maritime Boundary Between Cameroon and Nigeria*), disputes over delimitation of the continental shelf (in the North Sea, for example), and fisheries jurisdiction (such as in the Gulf of Maine case). The ICJ has also ruled on the legality of nuclear tests, hostage taking, the right of asylum, use of force, environmental protection, application of the Genocide Convention in Bosnia, and expropriation of foreign property.

On twenty-five occasions, the ICJ has issued advisory opinions on legal issues at the request of UN organs. Among the more prominent are the *Reparation for Injuries Suffered in the Service of the United Nations* opinion (1949), in which the UN's international legal personality was clarified, and the *Certain Expenses of the United Nations* opinion (1962), which declared peacekeeping expenses part of the fiscal obligations of member states. In the first, for example, the UN was accorded the right to seek payment from a state held responsible for the injury or death of a UN employee. With this case, the ICJ also established that it had the power to interpret the Charter, although no such power was expressly conferred upon it either by the Charter or by the court's own statute or rules. A recent advisory opinion, *Legal Consequences Arising from the Construction of a Wall in the Occupied Palestinian Territories* (2004), represented a more political issue, having been requested by the General Assembly in 2003.

Because only states can bring cases before the ICJ, the court cannot deal with contemporary disputes involving states and nonstate actors such as terrorist and paramilitary groups and private corporations. Furthermore, while judicial decisions are sources of international law under the court's statute, Article 38.1(d) also provides that the "decision of the Court has no binding force except as between the parties and in respect of that particular case." In other words, state sovereignty was intended to limit the applicability of ICJ judgments, unlike national courts that use precedents from prior cases to shape future judgments and, hence, the substance and interpretation of law. In reality, however, the ICJ has used many principles from earlier cases to decide later ones, which has contributed to greater consistency in its decisions and more respect for the court's ability to aid the progressive development of international law.

Assessments of the ICJ often focus on its relatively light caseload and slow processes, but other opinions stress its contributions to "the process of systematizing, consolidating, codifying and progressively developing international law."[19] Furthermore, with the creation of other judicial bodies, the ICJ is no longer the only site for adjudicating disputes, and there are many other ways to settle disputes besides resorting to adjudication. For example, there are a number of other international tribunals within the UN system. Some are tied to specialized agencies, such as the International Labour Organization's Administrative Tribunal and the International Centre for the Settlement of Investment Disputes within the World Bank. Others have been established to adjudicate specific issues such as the Law of the Sea Tribunal and the International Criminal Court (ICC). Still others are temporary bodies designed to deal with a particular problem such as the UN Compensation Commission that dealt with claims against Iraq following its invasion of Kuwait and the ad hoc war crimes tribunals created to adjudicate crimes against humanity and war crimes in the former Yugoslavia, Rwanda, and Sierra Leone. The ICC, in particular, is discussed in Chapter 6.

The Trusteeship Council. This council was originally established to oversee the administration of the non-self-governing trust territories that carried over from the mandate system of the League of Nations. These territories were former German colonies, mostly in Africa, that were placed under the League-supervised control of other powers (Great Britain, France, Belgium, and Japan) because they were deemed unprepared for self-determination or independence. The eleven UN trust territories also included Pacific islands that the United States had liberated from Japan during World War II. The council's supervisory activities include reporting on the status of the people in the territories, making annual reports, and conducting periodic visits to the territories. The council terminated the last trusteeship agreement when the people of the Trust Territory of the Pacific Islands voted in November 1993 for free association with the United States. The Trusteeship Council and its system of supervision had provided a model for the peaceful transition to independence for colonial and dependent peoples, thus playing a role in the remarkable process of decolonization during the 1950s and 1960s. Thus, the very success of the Trusteeship Council spelled its demise.

To avoid amending the UN Charter, the council continues to exist, but it no longer meets in annual sessions. In recent years, there has been discussion about new functions for the Trusteeship Council, though no action has yet been taken. One proposal calls for giving the council responsibility for monitoring conditions that affect the global commons (seas, seabed, and outer space). Another calls for using it to assist "failed states." A third proposal would transform the council into a forum for minority and indigenous peoples.

The Specialized Agencies. A number of specialized agencies, including the ILO and Universal Postal Union, predate the UN itself and were brought into relationship with the UN under Article 57. The founders of the UN envisaged that functional agencies would play key roles, particularly in activities aimed at economic and social advancement. Thus, Articles 57 and 63 of the Charter called for the affiliation with the UN of various organizations established by separate international agreements to deal with issues such as health (WHO): food (Food and Agriculture Organization, or FAO); science, education, and culture (UN Educational, Scientific and Cultural Organization, or UNESCO); and economics (the IMF and World Bank). Today, nineteen specialized agencies are formally affiliated with the UN through agreements with ECOSOC and the General Assembly (see Figure 2.1). Like the UN itself, they have global responsibilities, but separate charters, memberships, budgets, and secretariats, as well as their own interests and constituencies.

Several factors complicate the relationship between ECOSOC and the specialized agencies. One factor is geographical dispersal. Several are headquartered in Geneva; others are in Rome, Paris, Montreal, Washington, London, Vienna, and Berne (Switzerland). In the field, each agency has often had its own separate building and staff. This dispersal affects efficiency, budgets, and coordination.

Another complicating factor is that historically, the specialized agencies have operated quite independently, with ECOSOC having no control over their budgets or secretariats. How can one achieve an integrated international program when different agencies, each with its own administration and objectives, are carrying out similar activities? For example, the ILO's activities include employment promotion, vocational guidance, social security, safety and health, labor laws and relations, and rural institutions. These overlap with FAO's concern with land reform, UNESCO's mandate in education, WHO's focus on health standards, and UN Industrial Development Organization's (UNIDO) concern with manpower in small industries. The result is constant coordination problems. The Bretton Woods institutions—the World Bank, IMF, and former General Agreement on Tariffs and Trade (GATT), now the World Trade Organization—have generally operated quite independently of ECOSOC and the rest of the UN system. The WTO, created in 1995, is not even part of the UN system. Since 1998, however, ECOSOC has hosted annual meetings of finance ministers and World Bank, IMF, WTO, and UNCTAD officials to coordinate financing for development, and one unique feature of the Millennium Development Goals is that they represent goals embraced by all parts of the UN system.

The major economic institutions are discussed further in Chapter 5. We provide a brief overview here of one specialized agency: the ILO; other specialized agencies, such as the WHO and FAO, are discussed in subsequent chapters.

The origins of the ILO can be traced to the nineteenth century, when two industrialists, Welshman Robert Owen and Frenchman Daniel Legrand, advocated an organization to protect labor from abuses of industrialization and the development of the labor movement in Europe and the United States. Labor's growing political importance and Owen and Legrand's ideas led to the adoption of the Constitution of the International Labour Organization in 1919 by the Paris Peace Conference. The constitution was based on the belief that world peace could be accomplished only by attention to social justice. Thus, the ILO became an autonomous organization within the structure of the League of Nations, an institutional model adopted by the United Nations.

The ILO's major activity is setting standards for treatment of workers. Since 1919, more than 200 labor conventions have been signed and 180 recommendations made. In many countries, the international labor codes on such issues as the right to organize and bargain, the ban on slavery and forced labor, the regulation of hours of work, agreements about wages, and workers' compensation and safety are translated directly into domestic law. Among the conventions designated "fundamental" by the ILO are the conventions against forced labor, freedom of association, discrimination, and child labor. Sixty-eight states have ratified all these conventions; the United States has ratified but two, the forced labor and child labor conventions.

Under Article 33, the ILO can take action against states to secure compliance, but in practice, the ILO generally promotes compliance through the less coercive means of gathering member-state reports and hearing complaints of non-compliance. Using peer pressure and persuasion rather than hard sanctions, it makes recommendations to states on how their records can be improved and offers technical assistance programs to facilitate state compliance.

The ILO, headquartered in Geneva, Switzerland, accomplishes its work through three major bodies, each of which includes a tripartite representation structure involving government officials, employers, and workers. This integration of governmental and nongovernmental representatives is a unique approach not duplicated in any other IGO. Nonetheless, the arrangement has been uniquely suited to represent both governmental and societal interests. Much like the General Assembly, the International Labour Conference meets annually; the Governing Body—the executive arm of the ILO—establishes programs, and a Committee of Experts examines governments' reports on compliance with ILO conventions.

Global Conferences and Summits. Multilateral global conferences date back to the period after World War I when the League of Nations convened conferences on economic affairs and disarmament. Since the late 1960s, the UN has sponsored global conferences and summit meetings of heads of state and government on topics ranging from the environment, food supply, population, and women's rights to water supplies, children, and desertification, as shown in Box 2.2. These conferences and summits are ad hoc events, convened at the request of one or more countries, and authorized by the General Assembly or ECOSOC, with all member states eligible to attend. Names can be deceiving particularly for those events since 1990 termed "summits" where the sessions for heads of state and government last one or two days and may or may not be accompanied by a conference running from two to six weeks. There was a large cluster of global conferences in the 1970s and another in the 1990s with a lull in the 1980s and a deliberate effort to scale back since 2000.

UN-sponsored global conferences and summits serve a variety of purposes. They "seek to raise global consciousness about a particular problem, hoping to change the dominant attitudes surrounding the definition of the issue"; to educate publics and government officials; to generate new information; to provide opportunities to develop soft law, new norms, principles, and international standards; to highlight gaps in international institutions by providing new forums for debate and consensus building; and to "set in motion a process whereby governments make commitments and can be held accountable."[20] The environmental conferences and the women's conferences, in particular, have led governments to create appropriate national bodies to address the issues.

Global conferences provide opportunities for developing transnational issue networks by inviting participation and input from scientific and other expert groups, NGOs, and private corporations. Most global conferences have involved two conferences in the same location—the official conference with member states and a parallel NGO-organized conference. Participation has varied widely from the UN Conference on the Human Environment (UNCHE) in Stockholm in 1972, which included 114 UN member states and more than 200 NGOs in the parallel Environment Forum, to the 2002 Johannesburg Summit on Sustainable Development attended by approximately 21,000 people, including representatives of 191 states and some 8,000 representatives of NGOs and other organizations. These conferences have contributed greatly to the growth of NGOs and civil society; they have helped to increase understanding of the links among issues as seemingly disparate as environmental protection, human rights (especially for women), poverty alleviation, and development and trade.

Global conferences typically have involved extensive preparatory processes, including in-depth studies by experts and preparatory meetings convened by committees known as "prepcoms" and involving both NGOs and states. This is where decisions are made on many key agenda items, experts brought in, and NGO roles at the conference itself determined. There may also be regional meetings to help build consensus on proposed conference outcomes. By one estimate, at least

BOX 2.2. UN-Sponsored Global Conferences and Summits

Topic	Global Conference	Summit
Aging	1982, 2002	
Agrarian Reform and Rural Development	1989, 2006	
Children		1990
Climate	1979, 1990, 2007, 2010	2009
Desertification	1977	
Education	1990	
Education for Sustainable Development	2009	
Environment	1972	
Environment and Development	1992, 2012	
Financing for Development		2002, 2008
Food	1974, 2002	1996, 2009
Habitat (Human Settlement)	1976, 1996	
Human Rights	1968, 1993	
Illicit Trade in Small Arms	2001	
Information Society		2003, 2005
Law of the Sea	1958, 1973–1982	
Least-Developed Countries	1981, 1990, 2001, 2011	
Millennium Development Goals	2010	
New and Renewable Sources of Energy	1981	
Population	1974, 1984	
Population and Development	1994	
Racism	1987, 2001, 2009	
Science and Technology for Development	1979	
Social Development		1995
Sustainable Development		2002
Sustainable Development of Small Island States	1994	
UN Reform, New Millennium Challenges		2000, 2005
Water	1977	
Women	1975, 1980, 1985, 1995	

60 percent of the final conference outcomes are negotiated during the preparatory process.[21] The background studies can also serve as wake-up calls to the international community, as, for example, when studies prior to the 1982 World Assembly on Aging showed that developing countries would face challenges of aging populations in fewer than fifty years.

The outcomes of UN-sponsored global conferences and summits generally include declarations and action plans. Several of the conferences in the 1970s also led to new institutions to meet conference goals, including the United Nations Environment Programme (UNEP) and the UN Development Fund for Women (UNIFEM). The 1992 Rio conference on the Environment and Development charged NGOs with key roles in implementing goals. The Platform of Action approved at the 1995 Fourth World Conference on Women in Beijing called for "empowering women" through access to all types of economic resources.

By the late 1990s, the difficulties of monitoring what was actually being done and integrating implementation of conference outcomes with the main UN organs, especially ECOSOC, had become increasingly problematic. The US Congress had joined sides with the critics to impose a moratorium on US participation in UN global conferences except for the Durban antiracism conference scheduled for 2001. Even before that, the UN began a systematic effort in 1995 to focus on crosscutting themes coming out of the conferences. ECOSOC convened a special session in 1998 on the challenge of integrating and coordinating implementation and follow-up to major conferences and summits. In 2003, the General Assembly voted to end the practice of convening follow-up conferences. As a result, a number of subsequent major UN-sponsored gatherings have been "summits," rather than global conferences. For example, the Millennium Summit in 2000 focused on mobilizing agreement on the eight Millennium Development Goals, thus deliberately addressing the need to integrate the development-related goals of various separate conferences. At the 2005 World Summit, various UN reform proposals were the central focus, with Secretary-General Kofi Annan putting forth his own program of action, *In Larger Freedom: Towards Development, Security, and Human Rights for All.* Although leaders failed to act on Security Council reform, they did approve the creation of a new Peacebuilding Commission, a Human Rights Council to replace the Commission on Human Rights, strengthened UN oversight capacity, language endorsing the "responsibility to protect," a condemnation of terrorism "in all its forms and manifestations," and a recognition of the serious challenge posed by climate change.[22]

The bottom line is that UN-sponsored conferences and summits are an integral part of global governance, not just stand-alone events tied to the United Nations. As part of broader political processes, the conferences in particular have mobilized energies and attention in a way that established institutions cannot. They have pushed different parts of the UN system, although the record of implementation is uneven and much depends on NGOs' ability to sustain pressure on governments to live up to commitments they have made and to assist the UN in meeting the demands placed on it. There are, then, mixed opinions on the value of global conferences and summits. In one view, "conferences are one of the main devices . . . that are used to spawn, nurture, and massage new ideas as well as to nudge governments, international secretariats, and international civil service to alter their conceptions and policies."[23] Critics, however, have argued that the large conferences are too unwieldy, often duplicate work of other bodies, and are an inefficient way to identify problems and solutions. They query whether the global conferences are just expensive media events whose declarations and programs of action have little value.[24]

The UN Conference on Law of the Sea (UNCLOS) (1973–1982) illustrates a somewhat different type of UN-sponsored global conference, namely, one used to negotiate a major law-creating treaty for states to subsequently ratify. UNCLOS entailed a nine-year political process involving more than 160 governments in complex negotiations. It was triggered by the need to update the law of the sea following the independence of many new states in the 1960s and the endorsement by the UN General Assembly in 1967 of the principle that the high seas and deep seabed are part of the "common heritage of mankind." The Law of the Sea Convention, concluded in 1982, came into effect in 1994 and has been ratified now by 159 states. Participants in the negotiations were official representatives of states; there was no formal participation by NGOs. Items were negotiated in committees of the whole, and the outcome was a legal document, not statements of goals and aspirations. A similar treaty-negotiating process began in 2009 for a successor agreement to the 1997 Kyoto Protocol on climate change, which expires in 2012. As with UNCLOS, these negotiations are proving to be long and difficult, as discussed in Chapter 7.

PERSISTENT ORGANIZATIONAL PROBLEMS AND THE CHALLENGES OF REFORM

Like any longstanding organization, the UN has long been in need of reform. Indeed, one commentator called this "a constant refrain" at the UN—"never finished, never perfected."[25] Over the UN's history, there have been persistent calls for reform, including Charter revision. In the 1970s, the primary focus was on improving coordination of economic and social programs; in the 1980s, calls for financial reforms dominated the agenda; since the early 1990s, managerial reforms, improvement of the UN's ability to support peace operations, and Security Council reform have been among the major issues. All link directly to the first dilemma—the demands for governance and the UN's capacity to meet those demands.

To be sure, the UN has made many changes over the years, but rarely have these been enough to solve the institutional weaknesses. The UN is still hamstrung by pre–Cold War structures, redundant agencies, inadequate personnel policies, a lack of accountability, and inadequate resources. The membership of the Security Council is particularly problematic since its permanent members reflect the world of 1945, not the world of the twenty-first century.

How can UN reform occur? First, changes in the major organs of the UN require amending the UN Charter. This has happened twice thus far. In 1963, the Security Council membership was increased from eleven to fifteen, its voting majority changed from seven to nine, and ECOSOC was enlarged from eighteen to twenty-seven members. In 1971, ECOSOC was expanded to fifty-four members. Like many constitutions, the UN Charter is designed to be difficult to amend. Under Articles 108 and 109, amendments must be approved and ratified by two-thirds of the UN member states, including all five permanent members of the Security Council. The principal reform that would require Charter amendment is the size and composition of the Security Council. It is also the most controversial.

Many changes, however, can and have been accomplished without amending the UN Charter. This includes the creation of new bodies such as the Commission on Sustainable Development in 1993 to meet new demands, addressing coordination, management, transparency, and accountability issues, and the termination of bodies that have outlived their usefulness. In 1997, for example, Secretary-General Kofi Annan merged three departments into one Department of Economic and Social Affairs, and all the Geneva-based human rights programs into the Office of the High Commissioner for Human Rights. He reduced the size of the Secretariat by almost 4,000, created the post of deputy secretary-general, grouped the central offices into five executive groups (their heads forming a cabinet), and promoted the idea of UN "houses" in developing countries to bring UN development agencies and programs together. In short, incremental changes are easier to effect than revolutionary changes.

The obstacles to UN reform, however, are not procedural but political. There are deep political disagreements among the UN's members and between strong and weak states. All want to steer the organization in directions congruent with their objectives or try to prevent it from infringing on their interests. Everyone agrees that the UN needs reforming, but they disagree about the kind of reform needed and the purpose. Developed countries want more productivity and efficiency from the UN Secretariat, reductions in programs and activities, elimination of overlap, improved management, and better coordination. Developing countries are interested in greater economic and political equity through redistribution of resources and enhanced participation in key decisionmaking. They want more power within the system and more programs oriented toward development. They fear management reforms that would cost them their share of plum secretariat jobs and the loss of favored programs. NGOs want a UN more open and accountable to civil society, allowing them greater input and participation. In short, most reform proposals have hidden political agendas and policy goals. We focus here on three specific sets of issues: Security Council reform, financing, and management. Chapter 8 delves further into the politics and feasibility of future reform.

Security Council Membership and Voting

No UN reform issue is as controversial as the question of changing the Security Council's membership and voting rules. With the P-5 still limited to the five major victor nations of World War II and their veto power over substantive issues, the Security Council has been viewed for many years as something of an anachronism. The P-5 underrepresent the majority of the world's population and the principal financial contributors to the UN; Europe is overrepresented at the expense of Latin America, Africa, and Asia; China is the only Asian and developing country; Germany and Japan contribute more financially than Russia, China, Great Britain, and France.

Should Security Council membership be expanded and diversified to accord more with representative principles? What arrangements can satisfy the criteria of representation and efficiency? Should voting be modified to alter the antidemocratic bias of the veto power? Would the legitimacy of Security Council actions be enhanced by diversifying the geographic representation and altering the voting structure? With the council's greater activity since the Cold War's end, these issues have gained increasing urgency, as the Asian, African, and Latin American states have challenged their exclusion from permanent seats and the disproportionate representation of developed countries, and as some developed countries have challenged their exclusion as well.

Virtually everyone agrees that more states should be added to the Security Council to alleviate the inequities in representation. The trick is to increase the number of members for geographic representation and enhanced legitimacy while maintaining a small enough size to ensure efficiency.[26] A second issue concerns whether the distinction between permanent and nonpermanent members should be kept and whether new permanent members would have veto power. Some proposals would give no veto power to the new permanent members, others would limit veto power to Chapter VII questions, still others would grant veto power comparable to what the P-5 currently enjoy, and some would eliminate the veto entirely on the grounds that it is undemocratic. The latter is a nonstarter for all permanent members, and Britain and France are hardly eager to give up their seats. In reality, as one observer noted, "new veto-wielding permanent members would only increase the likelihood of blockage and still further paralyze the organization."[27] Another noted that "without first tackling working methods [of the council], no real reform is proposed at all."[28] Box 2.3 summarizes the debate over Security Council reform.

Resolving these issues has proved impossible thus far. There is no agreement on what process or formula should be used to determine who would get new permanent seats. There are three likely African candidates for permanent membership

---

BOX 2.3. The Debate over Security Council Reform

Issue

Representation
    Council needs greater representation of Africa, Asia, and Latin America
    Permanent members should better reflect geopolitics and economics
        Proposed additions: Germany and Japan
        One member each from Asia and Latin America, two from Africa, but
            who and how to select?
    No permanent members
    No new permanent members
    Veto power
        Eliminate entirely
        Reduce scope for its use to Chapter VII decisions
        Keep current P-5, but not give new permanent members veto power
        Give all permanent members veto power

Efficiency
    Size should be large enough to allow greater representation, but small
        enough to preserve the ability to act
    Proposed size: 22–26 members

Who Decides

Reform of council membership requires Charter amendment, which takes a vote of two-thirds of the General Assembly members and must be ratified in accordance with their respective constitutional processes by two-thirds of the members of the UN, including all permanent members of the Security Council (Chapter XVIII, Article 108).
    Reforms in methods of work may be made by the Security Council itself.

(Nigeria, Egypt, and South Africa). Countries (such as Pakistan) that know a rival (such as India) is more likely to be a candidate tend to oppose adding any permanent seats. Thus, Italy opposes a seat for Germany, and Argentina challenges Brazil's candidacy. The United States endorsed India for a permanent seat in 2010; China has opposed seats for both India and Japan. The Chinese position is an excellent illustration of how a country's political interests prevent Security Council reform. China champions Latin American and African participation as indicative of its support for developing countries, but opposes more participation from Asia. Not surprisingly, China opposes any reforms linked to democratization. In short, China prefers to keep the size of the council small, to maintain its veto for "historic reasons," and to be the sole representative of a major continent.[29]

In advance of the World Summit in 2005, Secretary-General Kofi Annan and a number of member states pressed hard to get a resolution. Four countries that have quietly and sometimes not so quietly campaigned for permanent seats—Japan, Germany, India, and Brazil—went public on the issue in an effort to line up votes. This Group of Four suggested a twenty-five-member council, including six permanent seats, four of which would be reserved for themselves. The African Union supported a different plan, adding eleven seats, two of which would be reserved for Africa. Still another group of middle powers, including Italy and Pakistan, proposed a twenty-five-member council with ten new rotating seats. The United States has not taken a position on the veto for any new members.

In short, there is no agreement precisely because the issue of Security Council representation is so important. As Luck pointed out, "[It involves] profound and persistent divisions about which and how many countries should sit around the table; whether permanent status should be extended; what the balance among regions and groups should be; whether the veto should be retained, modified, or eliminated; how decisions should be made; and whether its working methods should be further refined. . . . The very fact that none of this has been resolved . . . testifies . . . to the divergent perspectives and interests among member states, and to the value capitals place on the work of the council."[30]

Despite the frustration and disappointment in some quarters when the 2005 discussions came to naught, the issue persists. "It would be a grave error for those who think that Security Council reform will go away," Nirupam Sen of India said. "They believe it would be like the Cheshire cat, where you have the smile without the cat, but they will find that the cat has nine lives."[31] The lesson, however, is that formal reforms such as this are difficult to achieve and likely to come only at glacial speed.

Yet, despite these deep divisions and the widely expressed concerns in 2003 that the feared loss of legitimacy as a result of the debate about Iraq might permanently paralyze the Security Council, new peacekeeping missions have been authorized, such as in the Democratic Republic of the Congo, and others have been expanded, as in Côte d'Ivoire, as discussed in Chapter 4. And when crises break out, such as North Korea's 2010 attack on a South Korean island and Iran's resistance to international pressure to end its nuclear program, the international community turns to the Security Council. States want to be where the action is; states still want to become nonpermanent members. Participation is seen as a mark of status and prestige for a state and its diplomats. States attach symbolic importance to Security Council endorsement of regional peacekeeping operations, such as the African Union's in Somalia. Thus, the Security Council continues to be seen as the most authoritative body in the international community for dealing with threats to peace, and it retains considerable legitimacy despite its unrepresentative composition.

Financing

The UN has had longstanding financial problems because it has no independent source of money and depends almost entirely on its member states for assessed and voluntary contributions. In recent years, partnerships with major philanthropists such as Bill Gates and Ted Turner and some corporations have led to contributions to specific areas such as health, but these are relatively small relative to the UN's total budget and needs. As with Security Council reform, there has been no shortage of proposals for changing structures and methods of financing as well as for enhancing oversight and efficient use of resources. Although reform in UN financing does not require Charter amendment, it does require the support of a majority of members and, most important, support of the UN's major contributing states. If the UN's largest contributor, the United States, opposes adoption of the UN's budget unless changes are made, as happened in the 1980s, 1990s, and again in 2005, it can provoke a financing crisis for the organization unless a compromise is found.

Like the UN system itself, the UN's budget is complex; in fact, it comprises several budgets. The UN's regular budget covers its administrative machinery, major organs, and their auxiliary agencies and programs. It grew from less than $20 million in 1946 to more than $2.4 billion in 2009. Peacekeeping expenses constitute a separate budget (more than $7 billion in 2009), and each specialized agency also has a separate budget. These two types of budget expenditures are funded by member-state assessments according to a formula based on ability to pay. In addition, however, many economic and social programs, including UNICEF, UNDP, WFP, and the UN High Commissioner for Refugees (UNHCR), are funded by states' voluntary contributions, which frequently exceed the amounts of their assessments. Table 2.2 illustrates the relative size of each of these categories of budget expenditure based on assessed and voluntary contributions and changes between 1986 and 2009. The escalation of peacekeeping costs in the early post–Cold War years (1992–1995) and since 2005 is particularly notable.

TABLE 2.2. UN System Expenditures (in $US millions)

| Year | Assessed Contributions | | | | Voluntary Contributions | | | | Grand Total |
	Regular	Peacekeeping	Agencies	Total	Programs	Agencies	Total		
1986	700	242	981	1,923	2,672	953	3,625		5,548
1990	791	464	1,378	2,633	3,970	1,347	5,317		7,950
1995	1,135	3,364	1,720	6,219	5,275	1,151	6,426		12,645
2000	1,089	1,800	1,766	4,655	5,681	1,406	7,087		11,742
2004	1,483	2,934	2,032	6,449	10,641	2,183	12,824		19,273
2007	2,054	5,148	2,141	9,343	13,473	3,225	16,698		26,041
2009	2,499	7,061	2,308	11,868	16,591	3,189	19,780		31,648
Total	9,751	21,013	12,326	43,090	58,303	13,454	71,757		114,847

SOURCE: www.globalpolicy.org/un-finance/tables-and-charts-on-un-finance/un-system-budget/27505.html

The formulas for member states' assessed contributions for the regular budget and for peacekeeping operations are reevaluated every three years. The General Assembly's Committee on Contributions considers national income, per capita income, economic dislocations (such as from war), and members' ability to obtain foreign currencies. Initially, the highest rate (for the United States) was set at 40 percent of the assessed budget and the minimum rate at 0.04 percent for states with the most limited means. Over time, these rates have been adjusted: The US share was reduced to 22 percent, and the minimum dropped to 0.0001. Between 1985 and 2002, for example, Japan's share increased from 11.82 percent to 18.9 percent, but the Soviet/Russian figure declined from 11.98 percent to 1.15 percent, a reflection of Japan's economic strength and Russia's decline. Russia now contributes less than Brazil, South Korea, and Canada. Figure 2.2 shows the scale of assessments for major contributors and the majority of UN members for 2010–2011. Three things are particularly striking: first, Russia's assessment is too small to appear on the chart; second, nine states contribute about 70 percent of the UN's regular budget; and third, the other 182 UN members together contribute 32 percent.[32]

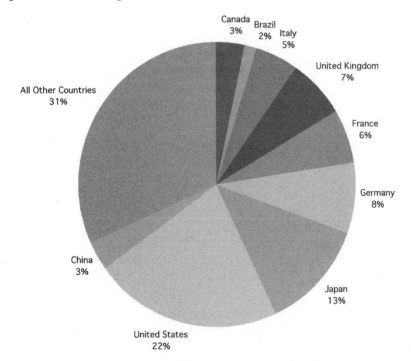

FIGURE 2.2. **UN Members' Contributions Based on Scale of Assessments, 2010–2011**

SOURCE: General Assembly Resolution 64/248

Not surprisingly, the UN has frequently experienced difficulties in getting states to pay their assessments. States fail to fulfill their legal obligations to pay for reasons ranging from technicalities in timing to poverty to politics to unhappiness with the UN in general or with specific programs and activities. The result has been periodic financial crises. The only sanction provided by the Charter in Article 19 is the denial of voting privileges in the General Assembly if a member falls more than two years in arrears, although that has never occurred. Nonetheless, there have been several financial crises. During the early 1960s, the Soviet Union, other Communist countries, and France refused to pay their peacekeeping assessments for operations in the Congo and Middle East. During the 1980s, the United States began withholding part of its dues. Congress and the Reagan administration were unhappy with specific UN policies, the **politicization** of many agencies, and procedures that gave the United States, the largest contributor, little weight in budget decisions. In both cases, changes were negotiated and voting privileges were not suspended.

In the late 1990s, the UN faced its most serious financial crisis, with member states owing more than $2.5 billion for current and past assessments. Only 100 of 185 members had paid in full. The United States, by far the biggest debtor, owed $1.6 billion, or two-thirds of the total due. The financial crisis prompted by these **arrearages** (unpaid assessments or debts) threatened the organization's ability to fulfill the various mandates given it by member states and illustrated the second dilemma: the tension between demands for governance and institutional weakness arising from states' unwillingness (the United States being one example) or inability (the situation of many states in economic difficulties) to pay their assessed contributions. The crisis was partially resolved by an agreement struck in the US Congress and with the UN General Assembly to reduce the US assessments for the regular budget and peacekeeping and for payment of all arrears by 2003, subject to certain conditions.[33] Nonetheless, the financing problem persists. In 2009, arrearages to the UN's regular budget totaled $829 million, with the United States alone owing 93 percent of the total.

Beyond states' assessed and voluntary contributions, the UN is limited in finding ways to finance its activities and programs. It has neither the authority to borrow money nor a history of private fund-raising. Although the short-term financial pressure would be significantly reduced if the United States paid its debts, the long-term problem will persist, namely, how to fund adequately the many economic, social, and security activities that member states have approved. Secretary-General Kofi Annan's millennial report, *We the Peoples*, noted, "When the scope of our responsibilities and the hopes invested in us are measured against our resources, we confront a sobering truth. The budget for our core functions . . . is about 4 percent of New York City's annual budget and

nearly a billion dollars less than the annual cost of running Tokyo's fire department. Our resources are simply not commensurate with our global tasks."[34]

Administration, Management, and Coordination

UN effectiveness has also been plagued by administrative problems. The UN
Secretariat grew almost continuously until the 1990s: from 300 persons in 1946
to a peak of 14,691 in 1994; it was reduced to less than 8,000 in the early years of
the new millennium, but has since grown again. Its growth can be linked to the
proliferation of programs and activities, ranging from peacekeeping missions to
technical assistance, as well as the expansion of the UN's membership. Studies
conducted both under the UN itself and by members such as the United States
came to similar conclusions about the lack of coordination, the expansion of
programs with little consideration of financial commitments, and weak to nonexistent program evaluation. And periodically charges of political bias, mismanagement, and inefficiency surfaced.

The first five secretaries-general paid little attention to internal management
of the Secretariat and also had little incentive for change. Thus, it took the UN
more than fifty years to adopt management systems such as program reviews,
internal audits, performance evaluations for staff members, and effective recruitment and promotion practices. Even then, developed countries were more
concerned about effective management, financial control, and clear objectives
than were many developing countries.

When Kofi Annan became secretary-general in 1997, he was pressured by
the United States in particular to reduce the size of the Secretariat by 25 percent
and implement other reforms as described earlier. In his "quiet revolution," departments were merged, administrative costs cut, and a code of staff conduct
developed. In 2001 and 2002, more reforms were undertaken. In the area of
peacekeeping, the Brahimi Report called for strengthening the secretariat's
ability to support operations, and the General Assembly approved a 50 percent
increase in staff for the Department of Peacekeeping Operations and more flexibility in administration.[35] A new system went into effect in 2001 for recruiting,
placing, and promoting staff that gave more emphasis to merit, competence,
and accountability for results than tenure and precedent. These changes did
not require Charter amendments.

The latter part of Kofi Annan's tenure as secretary-general was marred most
by the highly publicized Oil-for-Food Programme, described earlier. In response to that scandal, the US government conducted six investigations of the
UN and that program. Former US Federal Reserve chairman Paul Volcker
chaired the UN investigation. As Annan admitted, "The inquiry committee has
ripped away the curtain, and shone a harsh light into the most unsightly cor-

ners of our organization. . . . Who among us can now claim that U.N. management is not a problem, or is not in need of reform?"[36] Following the investigations, the Secretariat introduced measures to improve the performance of senior management, including monitoring of individual performance and a new Office of Internal Oversight Services with operational independence. Policies dealing with fraud, corruption, whistle-blower protection, financial disclosure, conflict of interest, and procurement contracts were adopted to prevent the type of personnel abuses found in the oil-for-food scandal.

Secretary-General Ban Ki-moon's follow-through with these reforms has met with criticism. As explained in Chapter 3, the administrator of the Office of Internal Oversight Services has publicly questioned that body's ability to act independently. Clearly, secretariat reform is an ongoing process if the UN's bureaucracy is to grow in capacity, adapt its management and working procedures, and maintain its effectiveness and legitimacy.

The problem of multiple agencies engaged in similar tasks has plagued the UN system from the beginning. The founders designed the organization to be decentralized because this would increase the capacity of different groups to participate while minimizing the potential for politicization, but the lack of coordination in the area of economic and social development and in humanitarian crises has been particularly criticized. Numerous reports and recommendations have sought to improve ECOSOC's effectiveness as the main coordinating agency for economic and social programs, but that requires dialogues with the World Bank and IMF; more effective relationships with the specialized agencies, funds, and programs; and the greater involvement of NGOs in policymaking processes. The Millennium Development Goals approved in 2000 represent a major shift toward greater coordination across the entire UN system (we explore this subject further in Chapter 5).

The problems of coordination and management are also evident in humanitarian crises produced by wars and natural disasters—whether they be crises that unfold over time, such as drought in East Africa or the conflict in Darfur or the Democratic Republic of the Congo, or sudden emergencies, such as the 2004 Indian Ocean tsunami or the 2010 Haitian earthquake. Historically, there has been a functional division of responsibilities among UN agencies: the UNHCR manages refugee camps, UNICEF handles water and sanitation, the WFP is responsible for food supplies and logistics, and WHO handles the health sector. In some situations, peacekeeping forces have safeguarded relief workers and supplies. Yet, as one observer described, "The United Nations did not respond as a system but rather as a series of separate and largely autonomous agencies. Each had its own institutional dynamics, formulated its own priorities, and moved according to a timetable of its own devising."[37]

The problem of coordination in emergencies, however, is compounded by the presence of hundreds of NGOs that vary in size and resources, have different cultures and philosophies, and resist efforts to harmonize activities in order to maximize the predictability and evenness of help for victims. The UN Office for the Coordination of Humanitarian Affairs created in 1998 is headed by an undersecretary-general who is responsible for coordinating all emergency relief within and outside the UN system. Still, UN specialized agencies, private relief contractors, and NGOs frequently resist giving up their independence and compete for a share of the action. Just creating a UN office for coordination does not ensure meaningful coordination, as the Haitian crisis discussed in Chapter 7 shows. Any proposal for change advantages some agencies, states, and NGOs while disadvantaging others. In Chapter 8, we shall explore further the politics of reform and of what is possible along with evaluating where the UN has had its greatest impact and experienced significant failures.

CONCLUSION

The UN was created to promote and protect the interests of states as well as to preserve peace and security in the world and to promote economic and social development and human rights. It is far easier to understand the UN by looking at what it has and has not been able to do in relationship to these different issue areas than just by knowing how it is structured and operates. In subsequent chapters, we shall do just that. First, however, it is important to understand the roles of states and coalitions of states, secretaries-general, and NGOs as actors within the UN. We explore these various actors in the UN system in Chapter 3.

Notes

1. On the League, see F. S. Northledge, *The League of Nations: Its Life and Times, 1920–1946* (New York: Holmes and Meier, 1986); and F. P. Walters, *A History of the League of Nations* (New York: Oxford University Press, 1952).

2. Norman J. Padelford (executive officer for Commission IV of the UN Conference Secretariat), letter to family and friends, June 26, 1945.

3. Paul Taylor and A. J. R. Groom, eds., *The United Nations at the Millennium: The Principal Organs* (New York: Continuum, 2000). Works on the specific organs include Sydney D. Bailey, *The Procedure of the UN Security Council,* 3rd ed. (New York: Oxford University Press, 1999); David M. Malone, ed., *The UN Security Council: From the Cold War to the 21st Century* (Boulder: Lynne Rienner, 2004); M. J. Peterson, *The UN General Assembly* (London: Routledge, 2006); and Simon Chesterman, *Secretary or General? The UN Secretary-General in World Politics* (Cambridge: Cambridge University Press, 2007).

4. The difference is exemplified in the two UN Web sites: one for the central organs, www.UN.org, and one for the system as a whole, www.unsystem.org.

5. Harold K. Jacobson, *Networks of Interdependence: International Organizations and the Global Political System,* 2nd ed. (New York: Random House, 1984), 39.

6. M. J. Peterson, "General Assembly," in *The Oxford Handbook on the United Nations,* ed. Thomas G. Weiss and Sam Daws (Oxford: Oxford University Press, 2007), 98.

7. Courtney B. Smith, *Politics and Process at the United Nations: The Global Dance* (Boulder: Lynne Rienner, 2006), 218.

8. Dutch Permanent Mission to the UN, "General Assembly Reform: The Role and Impact of Resolutions" (November 16, 2005), www.pvnewyorki.org/statements /general_assembly.

9. Ian Hurd, "Legitimacy, Power, and the Symbolic Life of the UN Security Council," *Global Governance* 8, no. 1 (2002): 42.

10. Ian Johnstone, "The Security Council as Legislature," in *The UN Security and the Politics of International Authority,* ed. Bruce Cronin and Ian Hurd (New York: Routledge, 2008), 88–89.

11. See Smith, *Politics and Process,* 238–245.

12. David M. Malone, *The International Struggle over Iraq: Politics in the UN Security Council, 1980–2005* (New York: Oxford University Press, 2006), 173.

13. On the debate on Security Council authority and legitimacy, see Ian Hurd, *After Anarchy: Legitimacy and Power in the United Nations Security Council* (Princeton: Princeton University Press, 2007) and "Theories and Tests of International Authority," in *The UN Security Council and the Politics of International Authority,* ed. Cronin and Hurd, 23–39.

14. Michael J. Glennon, "Why the Security Council Failed," *Foreign Affairs* 82, no. 2 (2003): 16–35.

15. Cronin and Hurd, *The UN Security Council and the Politics of International Authority,* 201.

16. Paul Taylor, "Managing the Economic and Social Activities of the United Nations System: Developing the Role of ECOSOC," in *United Nations at the Millennium,* ed. Taylor and Groom, 108.

17. Brian Hall, "Blue Helmets," *New York Times Magazine,* January 2, 1994, 22.

18. Thomas G. Weiss, "The John W. Holmes Lecture: Reinvigorating the International Civil Service," *Global Governance* 16, no. 1 (2010): 41.

19. B. G. Ramcharan, "The International Court of Justice," in *United Nations at the Millennium,* ed. Taylor and Groom, 177.

20. Michael Schechter, *United Nations Global Conferences* (New York: Routledge, 2005), 9.

21. Michael Schechter, "Making Meaningful UN-Sponsored World Conferences of the 1990s: NGOs to the Rescue?" in *United Nations–Sponsored World Conferences: Focus on Impact and Follow-Up,* ed. Michael G. Schechter (Tokyo: United Nations University Press, 2001), 189.

22. United Nations, *World Summit Outcome,* A/60/L.1, sec. 81 (2005), available at www.un-ngls.org/un-summit-final-doc.pdf.

23. Louis Emmerij, Richard Jolly, and Thomas G. Weiss, *Ahead of the Curve: UN Ideas and Global Challenges* (Bloomington: Indiana University Press, 2001), 89.

24. Jacques Fomerand, "UN Conferences: Media Events or Genuine Diplomacy?" *Global Governance* 2, no. 3 (1996): 361–375.

25. Edward Luck, "Principal Organs," in *Oxford Handbook on the United Nations,* ed. Weiss and Daws, 653.

26. Peter Wallensteen, "Representing the World: A Security Council for the Twenty-first Century," *Security Dialogue* 25, no. 1 (1994): 67.

27. James A. Paul, "Security Council Reform: Arguments about the Future of the United Nations System" (1995), www.globalpolicy.org/security/pubs/secref.htm.

28. Edward C. Luck, "The UN Security Council," in *Irrelevant or Indispensable? The United Nations in the 21st Century,* ed. Paul Heinbecker and Patricia Goff (Waterloo, Canada: Wilfred Laurier Press, 2005), 148.

29. J. Mohan Malik, "Security Council Reform: China Signals Its Veto," *World Policy Journal* (Spring 2005): 19–29.

30. Edward C. Luck, "How Not to Reform the United Nations," *Global Governance* 11, no. 4 (2005): 410.

31. Quoted in Warren Hoge, "U.N. Envoys See Loss of Steam for Expanding Security Council," *New York Times,* November 18, 2005.

32. Excellent data can be found on the Global Policy Web site, www.globalpolicy.org.

33. See Margaret P. Karns and Karen A. Mingst, "The United States as 'Deadbeat'? U.S. Policy and the UN Financial Crisis," in *Multilateralism and U.S. Foreign Policy. Ambivalent Engagement,* ed. Stewart Patrick and Shepard Forman (Boulder: Lynne Rienner, 2002), 267–294.

34. Kofi Annan, *We the Peoples: The Role of the United Nations in the 21st Century* (2000), www.un.org/millennium/sg/report/full.htm.

35. United Nations, *Report of the Panel on United Nations Peace Operations* (Brahimi Report), A/55/305-S/2000/809 (August 21, 2000).

36. Malone, *International Struggle over Iraq,* 133.

37. Larry Minear, "Humanitarian Action in the Former Yugoslavia: The UN's Role, 1991–1993," Occasional Paper no. 18 (Providence: Thomas J. Watson Institute for International Studies, 1994), 28.

3

------<o>------

Actors in the
United Nations System

If the UN is the world's stage, then who are its key actors? The organization was formed by states, it depends on states for its sustenance, and it is directed by states on the supposition that it may be useful to them. The Charter accords special status to five states, giving them permanent membership on the Security Council and veto power. But middle powers, emerging powers, and small states all have historically played important roles, particularly when acting through blocs and coalitions.

If the UN is but a venue for states, or just another diplomatic instrument for states to utilize, that is compatible with a realist view. But if it has become an actor in its own right, and if nonstate actors play influential roles within the UN system, the liberal perspective is more appropriate. In fact, the members of the Secretariat, particularly the secretary-general and other major officials, have acquired authority, influence, and legitimacy that enable them to act at times without the explicit direction of the governing bodies and a majority of member states. Consistent with constructivist views, the UN's professional staff may influence the actions of member states and others because of their expertise and role as important sources of ideas. Our discussion of actors in the UN system, then, must consider not only various member states but also coalitions and blocs, the secretary-general, and the Secretariat.

Increasingly, "the peoples" in whose name the UN Charter was drafted are exerting their voices through NGOs and other civil society groups. External experts, scholars, consultants, committed citizens, and certain NGOs have long worked with UN bodies and the Secretariat, but their roles as actors in the UN system have grown in recent years. This has led to the concept of a **third UN** to complement Inis Claude's distinction between the first UN, consisting of the arenas where member states debate issues and make recommendations and decisions, and the second UN, consisting of the UN and specialized agency secretariats. The roles of the third UN include advocacy, research, policy analysis, and the promotion of ideas. Its members frequently provide new ideas, advocate new policies, and mobilize public support for UN activities.[1]

In examining the roles of various actors in the UN, then, we shall employ this concept of three UNs, particularly for analyzing the Secretariat and NGOs—the second and third UNs.

THE ROLE OF STATES

From a realist perspective, the UN is primarily an instrument of its dominant member states, one among many diplomatic tools used by states to serve their national interests. States may use the UN to gain a collective stamp of approval on specific actions, points of view, principles, and norms; they may seek to create new rules, enforce existing ones, and settle disputes. The UN and many of its agencies serve useful functions. They gather and analyze information, improving the quality of information available to governments. They bring representatives of states together regularly, thereby affording them opportunities to gather information about other governments' attitudes and policies to the benefit of their own decisionmaking. This continuing interaction also enhances the value for states of maintaining a good reputation. The UN's decisionmaking processes encourage states to form coalitions and to link specific issues so as to enhance their bargaining power on those issues. States have used the UN system to create a variety of valuable programs and activities for addressing global problems; these range from development assistance, disease eradication, and aid to refugees to peacekeeping, election monitoring, and human rights promotion.

The UN, however, may be more than just an instrument of its member states. The organization also exercises influence and imposes constraints on its members' policies and the processes by which those policies are formed. Year in and year out, the meetings of the UN General Assembly, and all other bodies, set international, and hence national, agendas and force governments to take positions on issues such as the Middle East, environmental degradation, China's human rights record, and the status of women. These meetings and ongoing data gathering on each state's economy, trade, balance of payments, population, and compliance with treaties also subject states' behavior to international surveillance. UN-approved rules, norms, and principles, whether on human rights, the law of the sea, ozone depletion, or the financing of terrorism, force states to realign their policies if they wish to maintain a reputation for law-abiding behavior and to enjoy the benefits of reciprocity from other states. Many of the ideas that have come out of the UN system over more than sixty years have led governments to change their own thinking about policy approaches to various issues. Particularly in democratic, pluralist societies, norms and rules created by the UN may be used by domestic interest groups to press for changes in national policies.[2] This reflects the liberal institutionalist view that the UN operates through the interaction between state members, coalitions, and groups with a two-way flow of influence between the organization and its member states. And like other IGOs, the UN thereby reduces cheating, increases transparency, and maximizes gains for all parties. In short, the UN and organizations help shape state preferences.

Intergovernmental organizations such as the UN depend on their member states. To be effective and hence relevant, the UN must be able in some ways and to some extent to influence the largest, most powerful states in the system. It must be valued by them as a means of inducing other states to change their behavior, to redefine their interests, and to accept certain constraints. From the very inception of the UN in the 1940s, no state has been more critical than the United States. Yet the United States has a long history of conveying "mixed messages" concerning its support for international organizations, particularly the UN.[3] Over time, notes one scholar, "Relations between the United States and the UN have oscillated between periods of friendship and friction."[4]

The Key Role of the United States

As the dominant power after World War II, the United States played an important role in shaping the international system structure, including the establishment of many IGOs, from the UN to the Bretton Woods institutions, the International Atomic Energy Agency, and the United Nations Environment Programme. The provisions of the UN Charter, for example, were consistent with US interests, and until the 1960s the United States could often count on the support of a majority on most major issues. This enabled the United States to use the UN and its specialized agencies as instruments of its national policies and to create institutions and rules compatible with US interests.

Over time, the United States has used the UN for collective legitimation of its own actions, examples being Korea in 1950, the Cuban missile crisis in 1963, the Iran hostage crisis in 1979, the first Gulf War in 1990–1991, and the terrorist attacks on the World Trade Center and the Pentagon on September 11, 2001.

From the late 1960s to mid-1980s, however, the United States was much more ambivalent about international institutions in general and about parts of the UN system in particular. It withdrew from the ILO in 1978 (rejoining it more than two years later) and from UNESCO in 1984 (rejoining it in 2003), because of politicization and bureaucratic inefficiency. Developing countries' demands in the 1970s for a New International Economic Order, their repeated resolutions linking Zionism with racism, and their criticisms of American policies led Washington to oppose many UN-sponsored development programs and to view the UN as a hostile place. US alienation from the UN was borne out in the steep drop in US voting with majorities in the General Assembly in 1981. In the Security Council, the United States used its veto thirty-four times between 1976 and 1985 (see Table 2.1). In 1985, when Congress imposed conditions on contributions and withheld full payment as a strategy to force change, congressional support for paying UN dues started to decline.[5]

US antipathy to the UN moderated somewhat in the late 1980s. Changes in Soviet policy under Mikhail Gorbachev created opportunities for UN efforts to settle a number of regional conflicts. The UN's success in handling new peacekeeping challenges, and the war against Iraq in 1991, generated widespread optimism about an expanding UN role in the post–Cold War era. Yet US voting with the majority on roll call votes in the UN General Assembly reached its lowest point ever in 1990 (10 percent), and it improved only slightly in subsequent years.

In 1993, the Clinton administration articulated a policy of assertive multilateralism designed to share responsibilities for global peace with other countries by working through an invigorated UN, but the stance was short-lived. The US post–Cold War record on multilateralism has continued to be a mixed one. By the mid-1990s, problems with UN missions in Somalia, Rwanda, and Bosnia overshadowed successes elsewhere. The US experience in Somalia, in particular, had a devastating effect on its relationship with the UN. The United States became unwilling to commit its own military personnel in UN peacekeeping operations and withdrew its support for new types of peacekeeping in general. It lost confidence in then secretary-general Boutros Boutros-Ghali and undertook a unilateral campaign to deny him a second term in 1996. Other unilateralist actions followed, including the convention banning antipersonnel land mines (1997), and the Kyoto Protocol (1997), the International Criminal Court (1998), and the rejection of the Comprehensive Test Ban Treaty (1999). In addition, Congress contributed to the UN's financial crisis by continuing to withhold US dues for the regular budget and for peacekeeping, as discussed in Chapter 2.

Given President George W. Bush's past statements and the records of his close associates, no one expected him to be a strong supporter of multilateralism or of the UN. His unprecedented decision in 2001 to renounce US signature of the Rome Statute and the active campaign against the International Criminal Court provoked widespread condemnation. Still, immediately following the terror attacks of September 11, 2001, the United States turned to the UN and received Security Council support for action. Various measures were passed to restrict the ability of Al Qaeda from raising money and to support counter-terrorism initiatives (discussed in Chapter 4). A year later, the United States undertook protracted negotiations through the UN to address the problem of Iraq and its presumed weapons of mass destruction. Yet when the United States chose to go to war against Iraq in 2003 without authorization from the Security Council, the international community viewed it as evidence that the US did not consider itself bound by the obligations of the UN Charter. Nevertheless, the United States did return to the Security Council to secure help with the challenges of postwar Iraq and Afghanistan.

The administration of President Barack Obama projects the same mixed message. The appointment of Ambassador Susan Rice and the restoration of her position to cabinet status suggested a willingness to take the UN seriously. In 2009, US peacekeeping arrears were paid, and the United States signed the Convention on the Rights of Persons with Disabilities—the first action on an international human rights treaty since 2002. In 2011, the US joined with other P-5 members to protect Libyans against their government with the use of force. US interests can and should be advanced through the UN, whether for national security or poverty alleviation.

Despite its record of ambivalence about the UN, the United States has long supported organizational reform, although its position on particular reforms varies with other member states. Indeed, UN reform has often been a key demand for some US politicians, especially conservative Republicans in Congress.

Several factors have shaped US ambivalence. More than in many other states, US policy is shaped by domestic politics, including presidential leadership (or lack thereof), executive-legislative relations, lobbying by domestic groups, public opinion, and the sharp partisan divide between Democrats and Republicans. In particular, the role of Congress has been critical for the US relationship with the UN, as it controls the budget, an important source of US power in the UN. Although the Obama administration paid all US arrears in 2010, the congressional elections that year returned a Republican majority to the House of Representatives and renewed calls for cutting US contributions to the UN. The divisions within the American public are reflected in poll results. A 2008 poll by the Chicago Council on Foreign Relations reported 79 percent of respondents wanted the UN strengthened to investigate human rights violations, arrest genocidal leaders, and organize a permanent peacekeeping force. Although historically only about 40 percent think the UN is doing a good job, polls in 2010 showed a deep partisan divide, with Democrats twice as likely as Republicans to think the UN was doing a good job.[6]

US policy is also shaped by more general attitudes of American political culture, notably a belief in US **exceptionalism**. America's unique history, its record of democracy, and its support for human rights all give it a special role in international relations. This belief, reinforced in the early years of the twenty-first century by its lone superpower status and by neoconservatives in the Bush administration who championed the use of US power, has contributed to tendencies toward unilateralism. The dilemma is that the UN needs the support of the United States if it is to remain a vital institution.

Despite US mixed messages, historically "American preferences on many issues, embodied in US policies and backed by US power, have explained a great many . . . public policies emanating from the United Nations, its associated specialized agencies, and the managing institutions of the global economy."[7] Yet the UN has "always been and continues to be a Western organization," Puchala argues, because "the 'West' . . . never was, nor is it now, solely the United States."[8] Whether the UN remains a Western organization remains to be seen, as China and other emerging powers exercise increasing influence. As one journalist noted in early 2011, "The United States still has formidable strengths. Its economy will eventually recover. Its military has a global presence and a technological edge that no other country can yet match. But America will never again experience the global dominance it enjoyed in the 17 years between the Soviet Union's collapse in 1991 and the financial crisis of 2008. Those days are over."[9] Still, the main actors in the UN have always included and will continue to include other major powers.

Other Major Powers

Among the major powers in the UN system are the other four permanent members of the Security Council. The Soviet Union (now Russia), France, Great Britain, and China have each had significant roles in shaping the organization's development and, like the United States, have not always been ready to commit themselves to using the UN as the major arena for their foreign policy. Japan and Germany have also been major players in the UN since the 1970s by providing funding.

The Soviet Union/Russia. The Soviet Union played a key (though largely negative) role in the UN during the Cold War period, clashing frequently with the United States and its allies. Between 1945 and 1975, the Soviet Union used its veto 113 times; more than half of the vetoes were on membership applications in the early 1950s, and the impasse over the membership of the divided states of Korea, Vietnam, and Germany continued until the 1970s. In the 1960s and 1970s, the Soviet Union often sided with the newly independent states in the General Assembly, supporting self-determination for colonial peoples, the Palestine Liberation Organization, and the New International Economic Order agenda. This strategy permitted it to vote with the majority in the General Assembly a high percentage of the time. For ideological reasons, the Soviet Union and other bloc members were not part of the Bretton Woods institutions, but did participate in many other specialized agencies.

Significant changes in the actions and attitudes of the Soviet Union became evident in 1987, even before the Cold War's end. After years of opposition to UN peacekeeping, the Soviet Union agreed to having UN peacekeepers monitor and legitimize its troop withdrawal from Afghanistan and end the Iran-Iraq War. In the Gulf War of 1990–1991, the Soviet Union abandoned its former ally Iraq and supported US-UN actions, albeit with reservations about the use of force. The Soviets wished not only to prevent bloodshed but also to assert what little influence they had left and to limit damage to their future interests in the region.[10] The Soviet Union's need for US economic and emergency aid to deal with its own internal problems and its desire for support in dealing with its crumbling empire overrode other considerations.

The speed and thoroughness of the Soviet Union's dismemberment in 1991 brought a number of changes. There was a period during the early 1990s when US-Russian cooperation reached a peak, voting together 89 percent of the time in the General Assembly. That dropped dramatically by the end of the decade, when agreement between the two fell to 40 percent and Russia opposed US and NATO intervention in Kosovo, for example, and endeavored to put together enough votes in the Security Council to condemn the action. Russia was then a much-diminished power with meager economic means and was moving in a different direction than the United States and its allies.[11]

Today, Russia still exercises influence as a major power with its veto power in the Security Council and its influence in parts of the former Yugoslavia, the former Soviet republics, and the Middle East. This was evident during the 2003 debate over Iraq when Russia joined France and Germany in opposing the US invasion of Iraq. Like its European counterparts, Russia preferred to extend UN-mandated inspections of Iraqi sites and a peaceful settlement. Subsequently, however, as violence in Chechnya grew, along with evidence that Islamic militants were entering Russian territory, Russia's then president, Vladimir Putin, assumed a more pragmatic position and gave the United States more latitude.[12] Since 2005, Russia has been a major player in international efforts to deal with Iran's nuclear program. Its veto power gives it influence in the Security Council deliberations over sanctions, and its status as a major nuclear power with long involvement in Iran allows its leaders to offer alternative diplomatic solutions. Yet Russia's UN assessment dropped from 8.7 percent in 1991 to 1.6 percent in 2010–11, showing that it wields relatively limited influence over many other areas of UN activities.

France and Great Britain. France and Great Britain continue to be major actors in the UN and world politics despite their diminished status. As members of the P-5, they hold veto power; both continue to be significant donors, their assessments being between 6 and 8 percent; and both have played active roles in post–Cold War UN peacekeeping and enforcement operations by providing troops in the Gulf War, Bosnia, and Afghanistan. During the Cold War, they played secondary yet important supporting roles on East-West issues in the UN Security Council. Both were placed in a defensive position by pressures in the 1950s to move their colonies to independence. Since 1990, each has also assumed responsibility for a subcontracted enforcement operation—Great Britain in Sierra Leone and France in Rwanda, Côte d'Ivoire, and Congo. As prominent players in the World Bank and International Monetary Fund, both contribute senior personnel and financial resources and vote consistently with other large developed countries. Both have supported such initiatives as the International Criminal Court, the Kyoto Protocol and ongoing climate change negotiations, the land-mines treaty, and the Comprehensive Test Ban Treaty, all of which were rejected by the United States.

In UN politics, however, Great Britain and France have also carved different niches. During the 1970s and 1980s, France's role can best be described as mediator between the South's NIEO agenda and the North's opposition to change. More than other developed countries, France was ready to accept state intervention in regulating commodity markets and financial compensation to developing countries for market failure. It has always been a stronger supporter of UNESCO, which is based in Paris and has traditionally been headed by a Frenchman. On other issues, France's positions have paralleled those of other developed countries—for example, France voted with the United States and Great Britain in opposition to mandatory economic sanctions against South Africa. Yet France has also shown greater interest than Great Britain in developing and enforcing a common European position—that is, a common position on major issues among members of the European Union.

The desire to assert a common EU position in opposition to military action in Iraq in 2003 pitted France against the United States and Great Britain in the UN Security Council. Supporting the IAEA request for more time to conduct UN-led weapons inspections, France opposed any military action against Iraq not approved by the council. During a tense five-month period, President Chirac and President Bush engaged in active lobbying to convince nonpermanent members of the Security Council to support their respective positions. In the end, facing clear opposition, the United States dropped its attempt to get UN authorization; it blamed the failure on French obstructionism and the general incapacity of the UN to enforce its resolutions.[13] The French view is that a Security Council mandate is indispensable for intervention in another country.

Britain, France's partner in the European Union, took a different position on that and other issues. Prime Minister Tony Blair attempted to sell the US position on Iraq to the EU and was a strong member of the US-led coalition. Great Britain has always had a prominent position in the UN, not only as a permanent member of the Security Council, but also as a member of other restricted-member committees, notably the Geneva Group for review of budgets and programs. It is always voted to membership in ECOSOC, and a British jurist has always held a seat on the ICJ. This privileged position also carries over to the specialized agencies: Britain has occupied leadership positions in the ILO and the WHO.[14]

Britain occupies leadership positions for several reasons. First, British delegates and Secretariat members are frequently called on to exercise their skill in drafting. Second, continued ties to Africa and Asia through the Commonwealth give the British established contacts with many of the UN's members. Third, Britain has been a leader, along with the United States, in promoting UN financial reform and accountability. Fourth, through special voluntary contributions, Britain does pay a larger share of expenses than its assessment. Britain wants to keep its privileged position and has opposed, like France, efforts to restructure the Security Council.

Despite its strong involvement in UN peacekeeping operations, its participation in the 1991 Gulf War, 2003 Iraq War, and ongoing NATO operations in Afghanistan, Great Britain has generally been reluctant to send troops outside of Europe. It has preferred a noncombat role, favored humanitarian emergencies, and shied away from placing its troops within the UN command structure.[15]

Continuing ties with their former colonies help both Britain and France retain substantial influence and interests in Africa and in the developing world more generally. Yet both are part of the North, and that limits the extent of their influence. The same cannot be said for China, the only developing and non-Western country among the P-5 whose influence in the world and in the UN has been growing steadily.

China. The fifth permanent member of the Security Council, China, historically was far less active or interested in international institutions generally and the UN in particular, but that pattern has changed since the late 1990s. The Republic of China (ROC) originally held China's Security Council seat, which it continued to occupy long after the Chinese revolution brought the People's Republic of China (PRC) to power in Beijing and sent the ROC government to Taiwan. In 1971, Third World votes granted the PRC the Chinese seat, and Taiwan walked out of the body. Up to that time, the PRC had been a member of only one IGO. As one scholar noted in 2002, "The PRC's newcomer status in the world of international organizations has meant that the last thirty years have involved a steep learning curve, mediated by its own ambitions, changing perceptions, and unique perspectives."[16]

During its first decade of UN membership, the PRC kept a low profile. Although it supported the G-77 and the nonaligned group positions on decolonization and economic development issues and joined a number of UN specialized agencies, it remained uninvolved in security issues and "showed little interest in, or respect for, the norms, principles, and even rules of the international organizations it joined."[17] Only in 1981, when threatened with the loss of voting rights under UN's Article 19, did China begin to pay its share of peacekeeping assessments. In the late 1980s, China's move to a market economy, its subsequent rapid economic growth, and its increasing share of world trade made admission to the IMF, World Bank, and WTO essential. The PRC assumed China's seats in the IMF and World Bank in 1980 and eventually gained its own seat on the Executive Board. In 2001, after fifteen years of negotiations, China was accepted into the WTO.

Over time, China's participation in various UN bodies has led it to redefine its interests and policies. For example, despite its resistance to international human rights norms, it fought hard to host the 1995 Fourth World Conference on Women because it believed that a successful conference would bring prestige to China. Also in the same year, China agreed to accept selected ILO labor standards, and, in doing so, it initiated a process to modify appropriate domestic laws. In 1992, it reversed its previous support for nuclear proliferation and signed the Nuclear Nonproliferation Treaty. Still, adjusting domestic practices to international norms in human rights and the environment has been a slow and incomplete process.

Historically, China has shown strong adherence to the principles of sovereignty and noninterference in the domestic affairs of states. Increasingly, these have created conflicts with its growing desire to be accepted as part of the international community. The 1989 Tiananmen Square massacre highlighted the divergence between the conception of popular sovereignty held by most of the world and China's belief in state sovereignty. Its actions were widely condemned in the UN and in human rights circles. In 1990, China was confronted with a test of its commitment to the principle of collective security. Although it opposed using force to remove Iraq from Kuwait, it did not want to be the "odd country out." This led it to abstain on key votes in the Security Council, a strategy that allowed it to register its objections but not bear responsibility for blocking international action. These same dilemmas came up repeatedly during the 1990s with the advent of more assertive peacekeeping operations under Chapter VII; China abstained on forty-one votes. By threatening to use the veto, then agreeing not to block action, China could exercise influence consistent with its great-power status

China's dramatic economic growth has now greatly bolstered its status as a rising major power. In 2000, its assessment was still only 0.9 percent of the UN budget. In 2010–11, that had risen to 3.0 percent. With a growing sense of national pride, increasing assertiveness, a burgeoning economy, and P-5 membership, China's views have to be taken into account. This has become increasingly evident on both security and economic issues. Threat of a Chinese (as well as Russian) veto led the United States and NATO to intervene in Kosovo in 1999 without seeking Security Council approval. China, in fact, exercised its veto to end the UN's preventive deployment of peacekeepers in Macedonia, albeit on the grounds of that country's ties with Taiwan! In the lead-up to the 2003 Iraq War, China preferred that the dispute be settled peacefully through the UN and quietly joined the coalition against the United States. China did not want to jeopardize its oil supply from the Middle East. Since 2000, China has contributed to UN peacekeeping operations in Liberia, Haiti, DRC, and South Sudan, among others. Its veto power has given it leverage with respect to efforts to deal with the crises in Darfur (Sudan), North Korea, and Iran. In Darfur, China's rapidly rising need for oil along with its antipathy to sanctions and humanitarian interventions led it to oppose Security Council actions under Chapter VII. Only reluctantly has it supported UN forces in Darfur, further sanctions against Iran in 2010, and UN-sanctioned intervention in Libya in 2011.

With respect to economic issues, China has historically supported the G-77 and the nonaligned group positions, pleading for special treatment as a developing nation. Yet as its economy has boomed, China has increasingly had to balance its own interests and representing those of other developing states.[18] Those interests are often more similar to those of other powerful states. Within the Bretton Woods institutions, China's influence is growing. The World Bank was one of the biggest funders of external aid to China in the 1990s; now China is a lender. In 2010, China became the bank's third largest shareholder, ahead of Germany and after the United States and Japan; in the IMF its quota increased to 6.0 percent, putting it third behind the United States and Japan. With the 2007–2008 global financial crisis, China's power in the G-20 expanded, buttressed by its huge foreign currency reserves. Its call for a new international currency to replace the dollar was but one indication of its growing assertiveness. Whether China's economic power will be harnessed within the UN remains unclear. As one scholar notes, China wants "not only to assume a greater stake in international organizations but also to remake the rules of the game."[19]

China's emergence as a major world power with considerable economic prowess will almost guarantee it a greater role on the UN stage. As the most populous state in the world, the only non-Western member of the P-5, a nuclear weapons state with growing nonnuclear military capabilities, the second largest economy behind the United States as of 2010, the largest aid donor to African countries, the largest holder of US government debt, and the world's largest emitter of carbon dioxide, China is a key actor.

Germany and Japan. The ranks of the world's major powers include Germany and Japan, yet neither is a permanent member of the Security Council; indeed, their historical experiences as the defeated World War II powers have had a major impact on their individual willingness and capacity to make certain international commitments. Because of Germany's pivotal geographic position in Cold War Europe, there was a concerted effort to bring it into organizations such as NATO and the European Economic Community (precursor of the EU). Yet it was not until 1973 that the two German states—the Federal Republic of, or West, Germany and the German Democratic Republic, or East Germany— were admitted into the UN.

Japan joined the UN almost twenty years earlier, in 1956. During those early years, Japan kept a low profile; it concentrated on a few selective issues, such as keeping the People's Republic of China out of the UN and supporting the UN as a guarantor of the peace. In the 1970s, Japan's role in UN politics shifted markedly. Japan joined with the less developed countries to uphold the right of self-determination for the Palestinian people, accept the role of the Palestine Liberation Organization in the UN, and support other Arab causes. These positions reflected Japan's national interest given its resource (particularly oil) vulnerability. The UN was just one of the forums where Japan supported the Middle East oil producers.[20]

The decade of the 1990s was pivotal for Germany and Japan in the UN. In both countries, the 1991 Gulf War stimulated debates over their international roles. Both had been asked to make significant monetary contributions to the war, yet neither was a member of the Security Council, nor had they been consulted. Both had constitutional impediments to participation in any collective enforcement or peacekeeping operation. In 1992, the Japanese Diet (Parliament) approved legislation permitting up to 2,000 Japanese troops to be deployed in UN peacekeeping missions under limited conditions. Thus, the Japanese joined the UN operation in Cambodia, known as the United Nations Transitional Authority in Cambodia (UNTAC). This development set a precedent for subsequent Japanese participation in other UN operations, and although it was largely limited to humanitarian tasks, it was an important step toward Japan's full contribution to the UN.

The German Constitutional Court ruled in 1994 that German military forces could participate in UN peacekeeping operations. Germany has now sent more than 7,000 soldiers to UN and UN-mandated operations in Kosovo, Ethiopia,

Georgia, Liberia, Lebanon, Sudan, and Afghanistan. It has played a particularly vital role in the UN-authorized NATO operation in Afghanistan, supporting the reconstruction program, providing security assistance forces, funding humanitarian programs in education and culture, and training police.[21]

Why did Germany and Japan change their constitutions to participate in UN peacekeeping? Both are, after all, major UN financial supporters. Japan is the second largest contributor to the UN, its assessed contribution being set at 13 percent, which is greater than the combined share of Germany and China. Both are major contributors to the IMF, World Bank, and WTO. German and Japanese participation in peacekeeping can best be explained by self-interest. Both seek permanent seats on the UN Security Council, and both realize that participation in peace and security activities is an essential criterion. Thus, it was surprising when Germany abstained in a UN Security Council vote authorizing force to protect Libyan civilians under siege, while its closest European Union and NATO allies supported the measure, as did Libya's Arab neighbors.

Major powers are not the only states that matter in the UN. In fact, multilateral diplomacy in the UN system opens many opportunities for a group of states known as middle powers, as well as small states, to exercise influence. And a number of middle powers are among those countries categorized as rising or emerging powers. Categorizations such as these are always subject to dispute, but they provide a way of identifying and analyzing the roles of different states.

Middle Powers: The Traditional and Emerging Powers

The so-called traditional middle powers have played and continue to play an important role in UN politics. This group of states can be characterized according to the kinds of policies they pursue, including multilateralism, compromise positions in disputes, and coalition building to secure reform in the international system. Canada, Australia, Norway, and Sweden as well as Argentina, Brazil, India, South Africa, and Nigeria have been considered the traditional middle powers. During the Cold War era, they were seen as uniquely able to facilitate UN activity, when disputing parties were wary of great-power involvement, but less so of middle-power mediation. During the 1944 Dumbarton Oaks conference, Prime Minister Mackenzie King of Canada called for a special position in the UN for Canada and others. His argument was that states ought to have a role commensurate with their contribution and that a division between the great powers and the rest was unworkable. Although a provision for special status for middle powers failed to become part of the UN Charter, the notion persisted.

When UN peacekeeping was developed in the 1950s, middle powers became frequent contributors of peacekeeping troops. Canada has played a particularly vital role, providing leadership, helping to train peacekeepers, setting up command structures, and providing communication and linguistic facilities and medical expertise. Its political culture has influenced Canada's preferences in the UN "for pragmatic non-ideological compromise, a belief in pluralism and tolerance, and a commitment to the orderly mediation and resolution of conflicts."[22] During the Cold War, Canada tried to maintain a line between taking independent action through the UN and supporting its neighbor to the south. During the Gulf War, Canada was reluctant to support military action, preferring to give sanctions more time. That was true in 2003 as well, when Canada offered no support to the US position on Iraq, but preferred to continue inspections.

Since the 1990s, Canada's role in the UN has come under greater domestic scrutiny. How could the country support more than one-quarter of its troops in UN peacekeeping when other domestic policy commitments were pressing? Widely publicized misconduct by Canadian troops in Somalia and Yugoslavia, and the subsequent government cover-up, stimulated a public debate over training and racism in the Canadian military and its continued ability and willingness to serve in more expensive and dangerous operations. Canada began to decrease the number of troops in UN peacekeeping operations. Although the country has sent more than 120,000 peacekeepers worldwide, it now ranks only 55 out of 108 countries participating, and its financial share of the UN peacekeeping budget has declined. At the same time, Canada turned its energy to issues of human security. The country managed the negotiations for the convention banning antipersonnel land mines, helped to draft guidelines for humanitarian intervention, and hosted the first conference of parties to the Kyoto Protocol on Climate Change in 2005. Nevertheless, in 2010 Canada failed to win a seat on the UN Security Council, the first time its bid had failed.

Australia is also a strong supporter of the UN, although the extent of its participation has varied according to the exigencies of domestic politics. Its major commitment to peacekeeping has tended to be concentrated on conflicts in Southeast Asia. It played a key diplomatic role in Cambodia and provided the force commander for UNTAC. Closer to home, Australia was involved in Papua New Guinea and East Timor. With respect to the latter, Australia provided military forces, police, and civilian personnel, totaling about one-half of the 11,000-person force.[23]

Beyond peacekeeping, Australia has been a crucial player in leading and supporting coalitions. It helped establish the Cairns Group of Fair Trading Nations to push reform in international agricultural trade during the GATT trade negotiations in the early 1990s, for example. This coalition crossed both divides: East-West and North-South. Australia provided the intellectual leadership and managed the difficult negotiations in support of a freer, more open, and nondiscriminatory international trade regime in agriculture.[24]

India occupies a unique position since it has been seen as a traditional middle power and now is regarded as an emerging power. As a traditional middle power, for example, India's longstanding participation in peacekeeping operations in the Middle East and Africa has served its aspiration for international recognition and for a permanent seat on the Security Council. Indian generals commanded operations in Korea, Congo, Sierra Leone, Bosnia, and the Middle East. Participation in peacekeeping also helped India project its image as a nonaligned state and claim to leadership in the **Nonaligned Movement (NAM)**. India helped create the movement in the 1950s and then used it to reinforce its activist multilateral agenda. In the first UN General Assembly session in 1946 and later in the nonaligned summits, India spoke out about racism in South Africa and led the push to end apartheid and colonialism. However, through its refusal to sign the Treaty on the Non-Proliferation of Nuclear Weapons (1970) and the Comprehensive Nuclear Test Ban Treaty (1996), and by testing a nuclear device in 1998, India has also been a spoiler in UN efforts to curb nuclear nonproliferation. Because of its huge population and rapidly growing economy, it is a major player in climate change negotiations, but has joined with China, Brazil, and others to block commitments to reduce carbon dioxide emissions. India continues to aspire to a permanent seat on the Security Council and was very pleased when President Obama in 2010 endorsed this aspiration.

Since the 1990s, India and other emerging economic powers have played an increasing role in UN politics both on security and on economic issues. In the 1990s, Brazil became a significant contributor to peacekeeping operations, concentrating first on the former Portuguese colonies (Angola and Mozambique) where common language provided a link. Since 2004, Brazil has commanded the UN force in Haiti and provided almost a fifth of its personnel. The Brazilian military's extensive experience in infrastructure building, development, and managing political unrest has made it a valuable partner in Chapter VI operations. Like India, Brazil seeks a permanent seat on the Security Council.

Also in the 1990s, Nigeria orchestrated the Economic Community of West African States' (ECOWAS) intervention in Liberia; later, in Sierra Leone, it provided financing and three-quarters of the manpower for the operations. In 2005, it provided much of the manpower for the UN-authorized African Union peacekeeping force in Darfur (Sudan) and hosted negotiations between the Sudanese government and the rebels.

On economic issues, Brazil, India, Nigeria, Turkey, South Africa, and China have found their voices inside and outside the United Nations. For example, they have played a leading role in the Group of 20 advanced developing countries that have pushed hard for greater concessions on agricultural and other trade in WTO negotiations. During negotiations in 2008, for example, India,

China, and Brazil blocked agreement when they demanded that the United States and European Union reduce farm subsidies. These three and others have successfully pushed for a greater say in the World Bank and IMF where they have been underrepresented. They have been active in pushing for a greater role for the G-20 since the 2007–2008 international financial crisis made evident the need to involve more states in guiding international economic relations. As discussed further in Chapter 6, most of these initiatives are occurring outside of the UN itself, leading many to question the continuing relevance of the UN in economic issues.

The essence of the middle powers' and emerging powers' role lies in the importance of secondary players in international politics; there must be followers as well as leaders. They can be both. Fostering cooperation in the future is likely to require leadership based not only on military capability and economic strength but also on diplomatic skill and policy initiatives—strengths that middle and emerging powers can contribute.

Small and Developing States

For small states everywhere, and for the majority of less developed countries, the UN has facilitated a number of foreign policy objectives. First, membership in the UN is a symbol of statehood and sovereignty. Second, small states in particular use the UN and the specialized agencies as the arena in which they can carry on bilateral and multilateral discussions, even if they concern non-UN matters. With limited diplomatic and economic resources, less developed countries find in the UN a cost-efficient forum where they can forge multilateral ties and conduct bilateral talks on a range of issues. The fall General Assembly sessions are vehicles for conducting other business among representatives and visiting ministers. Third, small states, especially the small European and Latin American states, have used the UN to promote the expansion of international law in an effort to constrain the major powers and protect small-power interests. Fourth, the UN enlarges the "voice" of small states and offers opportunities to set the global agenda. For example, because Kuwait was a UN member, Iraq's invasion and occupation in 1990 immediately gained attention, and there was strong support for sanctions and even the use of force. Yet Georgia was not successful in doing likewise in the face of Russia's intervention in 2008. Costa Rica was influential in the formation of the Commission on Human Rights in the 1940s and the new post of UN High Commissioner for Human Rights in the 1990s, viewing each as essential to the pursuance of its human rights agenda.[25] When it assumed leadership of the Nonaligned Movement and the Organization of the Islamic Conference in 2003, Malaysia assumed a proactive role on a number of issues within the UN. Noted one scholar, "Malaysia's influence in world politics has been far greater than its national power potential, almost approximating to that of a middle power, and in the main this was due to its imaginative foreign policy and high profile diplomacy."[26]

Because small and less powerful states do not have the diplomatic resources to deal with all issues in depth, participation in the UN has tended to force them either to specialize in particular issues or in some cases to follow the lead of larger states within the Group of 77 or other coalitions. Participation in the UN not only aids in achieving foreign policy objectives directly but also provides small states with more avenues. The UN presents opportunities for interest aggregation by facilitating the formation of coalitions to enhance weak states' influence. With the proliferation of UN-related bodies, small states may also seek the body most favorable to their interests—a phenomenon known as "forum shopping."

Small and weak states have been able to bargain with major powers in the UN for their support on certain important issues in return for economic concessions. In the Gulf War, for example, some small states that were nonpermanent members of the Security Council at the time agreed to support US-UN action in return for favors. Ethiopia extracted a promise from the United States to broker a peace between the government and Eritrean rebels. Egypt and Malaysia received financial "rewards." For Yemen, however, the consequence of opposition to the Gulf War was the withdrawal of US aid and commitments. In 2003, the smaller nonpermanent members of the Security Council such as Guinea, Angola, and Cameroon were courted extensively by both sides in the divisive debate over Iraq, but in this instance were not receptive to financial inducements.

Developing countries are the direct major beneficiaries of most UN economic and development programs. They may apply to the World Bank and UN development agencies for project, technical assistance, and structural adjustment funds to augment their economic development plans. They are also the beneficiaries of funds from the UN specialized agencies, including the WHO, the World Food Programme, the International Fund for Agricultural Development, UNHCR's refugee programs, and the UN Disaster Relief Organization's emergency disaster funds.

Although there have long been weak and quasi states in the international system, one of the major developments since the Cold War's end has been the phenomenon of fragile and failing states. Somalia has been a prime example of a failed state since its central government collapsed in 1991; other examples of failing or failed states, some of which have now partially recovered, include the Democratic Republic of the Congo, Sierra Leone, Afghanistan, Haiti, and East Timor. Such "states" have led to two dilemmas. Do they merit representation in international bodies, including the UN? What actions should be taken to rebuild them and by whom? International law assumes that states not only have control of their territory but also have capacity to govern and to comply with international obligations. As discussed further in Chapter 4, the UN has taken on **state-building** tasks in a number of instances, including Kosovo (not yet a state in 2011) and East Timor (a state and UN member since 2002). The dilemmas of what to do about failed and failing states persist.

Although small and developing countries have frequently enhanced their "voice" and influence through coalitions and blocs, all member states participate in one or more such groupings. As in any parliamentary or legislative body, coalition building is a primary strategy for garnering a majority of votes in favor of or opposition to proposals for action.

COALITIONS, BLOCS, AND THE IMPORTANCE OF CONSENSUS

Early in the UN's history, states in the same geographic region, or those sharing economic or political interests, formed coalitions to shape common positions on issues and to control a bloc of votes.[27] The UN Charter itself specified that the General Assembly should give consideration to "equitable geographic distribution" in electing the nonpermanent members of the Security Council and members of ECOSOC, though it offered no guidance about how to do so. By informal agreement, these groups came to correspond roughly to the major regions of the world: Western Europe, Eastern Europe, Africa, Latin America, Asia, and the Middle East. Each region has adopted different rules and procedures for selecting candidates. For the Security Council, the Latin American group tends to give preference to the larger states (Argentina, Brazil, and Colombia), but the African group rotates candidates among the respective member states.

The European Union has developed the most formalized process for continual consultation among its member states and for delegating responsibility to articulate common policies. Members increasingly act as a single unit in the UN, voting as a bloc on social and economic issues. On issues of security, however, the EU members have found it difficult to take common positions, as illustrated in the divisions over the Middle East and the 2003 Iraq War.

Subregional groups often show remarkable unity in the General Assembly as well as in other bodies where they might participate. For example, high cohesion can be found among the five Nordic states and the Caribbean members of the Caribbean Community.

Coalitions are important because the General Assembly body functions like a national parliament, each state having one vote and decisions being made by

---

BOX 3.1. Caucusing Groups in the United Nations (Number of Member States)

Regional Groups

African states (53)
Asian states (52)
Latin American and Caribbean states (33)
Western European states and others (29)
Eastern European states (21)

Other Multilateral Groups

Group of 77 (ca. 132)
Association of Southeast Asian Nations (ASEAN) (10)
Nonaligned Movement (ca. 130)
Organisation of the Islamic Conference (56)
Nordic Group (5)
European Union (27)

---

a majority (either simple or two-thirds under specified circumstances). Just as a majority political party (or a coalition) can control most decisions, so can a stable coalition comprising a majority of UN member states. These coalitions within the UN have tended to persist for long periods; the presence of such groups led to the practice of consensus voting in the General Assembly, as described in Chapter 2.

During the Cold War, two competing coalitions were composed of states aligned with either the United States or the Soviet Union. The Eastern European states could be counted on to vote consistently with the Soviet Union, thus forming a true bloc. Many nonaligned states also voted regularly with the Soviet bloc. Throughout the mid-1950s, the Western European, Latin American, and British Commonwealth states voted closely with the United States on issues that involved Cold War competition and also often on human rights, social concerns, and UN administration. Despite some internal tensions, that US-dominated coalition held a controlling position in UN General Assembly voting until 1955.

Beginning in 1960 with the influx of new African and Asian states, a new coalition emerged, the Group of 77, whose members constituted more than two-thirds of the UN's membership. By 1971, the G-77 had become the dominant coalition, based upon its high level of cohesion on development-related issues.

As such, it was able to set agendas in the General Assembly, ECOSOC, and many specialized agencies. The G-77 was often supported by the Eastern European bloc when the Soviet Union took advantage of opportunities to escape its minority position and accuse the West of being responsible for the problems of developing countries. Once the People's Republic of China held the Chinese seat, it also supported G-77 demands for economic change. The cohesion among the G-77 reached its peak in the mid-1970s. Thereafter, differences in social and economic conditions among Asian, African, and Latin American countries made common policy positions more difficult to forge, and the G-77's influence declined. Instead, the G-20 emerged first in the WTO as a "booming voice" of developing countries.[28] In many UN bodies, including the General Assembly, the developed-developing country divide still shapes coalitions on issues of economic inequality and development. But on many specific policies, cohesion has weakened and differences among coalition members have become more pronounced.

Other interests can also serve as the basis for coalitions in the UN, however. For example, the thirty landlocked countries that first coalesced during the law of the sea negotiations in the 1970s and early 1980s have tended to vote together on specific issues of trade and transportation; they have also convened UN-sponsored meetings to address their particular needs. So, too, have the forty-five small-island states, many affected by climate change. The member states of the Organization of Petroleum Exporting Countries (OPEC) who once provided leadership for the G-77 and a New International Economic Order in the 1970s now play a key role as a group in the international financial institutions.

States sharing particular political interests have used their contacts with each other to influence politics within the UN. For example, the Commonwealth—fifty-four states formerly part of the British Empire—operates as a coalition at the UN as well as at the intergovernmental and societal levels. The Nonaligned Movement, previously a strong bloc of like-minded states opposing colonialism, racism, and Cold War alignments, has refocused its energies since the Cold War's end on representing small non-Western states. The NAM tries to promote common positions within the Security Council and elsewhere, and it works closely with the G-77.

A relatively recent coalition has emerged among the democratic states, the UN Democracy Caucus. That informal group has pushed for inclusion of good governance norms not only in UN development programs but also in the international financial institutions' aid conditions. That group has also urged the adoption of a concerted human rights agenda. The United States, in particular, has favored collaboration with this group of like-minded (and -governed) states.

In addition to coalitions and blocs, UN members also increasingly rely on ad hoc informal groups of states particularly to support UN peace-related actions.

In the late 1970s, the so-called Contact Group on Namibia worked alongside the Security Council in the search for a peaceful solution to the problem of South West Africa, or Namibia, which had been under South African control as a League of Nations mandate since the end of World War I. That group involved high-ranking members of five UN missions (Canada, France, Germany, Great Britain, and the United States) in a decadelong series of negotiations that eventually led to independence for a democratic Namibia. Subsequently, contact groups were formed as part of efforts to settle conflicts in Central America and the former Yugoslavia.

In the 1990s, such groups proliferated. Some states, usually between three and six, organized as "Friends of the Secretary-General" and included at least one interested member of the P-5. The "friends" keep in close contact with the secretary-general and support his efforts to find a peaceful solution to a crisis. The group is kept small so that meetings can be quickly convened. More than one country is used to exert pressure on parties and present a common view to the international community. The purpose is to keep a peace process on track and coordinate the work of mediators, either before reaching a formal agreement or in implementing an agreement. "Friends" groups have been formed, for example, for Haiti (Canada, France, the United States, Venezuela); Georgia (France, Germany, Russia, Great Britain); and Tajikistan (Afghanistan, Iran, Turkey, the United States, Uzbekistan).[29] In an effort to advance peaceful settlement of the Israeli-Palestinian conflict, the UN, the United States, Russia, and the EU make up the so-called Quartet—a further illustration of the value attached to collaborative approaches.

Groups and coalitions, then, provide order and some coherence in a UN of 193 member states and a crowded agenda. Some serve primarily parliamentary-style functions of putting issues on the table, establishing negotiating positions, garnering votes, and engaging in bargaining. Still others have complemented the UN secretary-general's role as a mediator by bringing the assets of several countries to bear on efforts to find a peaceful settlement to a difficult conflict.

THE SECRETARY-GENERAL AND THE UN SECRETARIAT AS KEY ACTORS

The international prominence of the UN's secretary-general has contributed to the emergence of the UN itself as an autonomous actor in world politics. Both the secretary-general and the UN's Secretariat, particularly senior officials, however, wield significant influence within the UN itself and occasionally over member states. They form the so-called second UN. Both command authority to shape agendas and frame issues. Both are often asked to recommend "what is the right thing to do." Both tend to emphasize their "neutrality, impartiality, and objectivity in ways that make essentially moral claims against particularistic self-serving states."[30] Some constructivists have made the argument that international organizations such as the UN have autonomy because they are bureaucracies and their authority is based on impersonal rules. As two scholars described the process, "IOs, through their rules, create new categories of actors, form new interests for actors, define new shared international tasks, and disseminate new models of social organization around the globe."[31] Acting autonomously may mean that the bureaucracy develops its own views and manipulates material and information resources. These characteristics may lead to undesirable outcomes such as tunnel vision, bias, and reluctance to embrace reform.

The Secretary-General

For more than fifty years, a pattern of leadership has evolved: Secretaries-general have taken advantage of opportunities for initiatives, applied flexible interpretations of Charter provisions, and sought mandates from UN policy organs as necessary. Eight successive secretaries-general have contributed to developing their own political roles and that of the institution (see Box 2.1). Their personalities and interpretations of the UN Charter, as well as of world events, have combined to increase the power, resources, and importance of the position. More than just a senior civil servant, the UN secretary-general is an international political figure "subject to the problems and possibilities of political leadership."[32]

The UN secretary-general is well placed to serve as a neutral communications channel and intermediary for the global community. Although she or he represents the institution, she or he can act independently of the policy organs even when resolutions have condemned a party to a dispute, maintaining lines of communication and representing the institution's commitment to peaceful settlement and alleviation of human suffering. Although these tasks call for diplomatic skills, it has become essential for the secretary-general also to have strong managerial and budgetary skills.

The most important resource for UN secretaries-general is the power of persuasion. The "force" of majorities behind resolutions may lend greater legitimacy to initiatives, though it may not ensure any greater degree of success. Autonomy is also a source of the secretary-general's influence. For example, during the Security Council's 2002–2003 debate over Iraq's failure to disarm and cooperate with UN inspections and whether to authorize a US-led war, Kofi Annan steered an independent course by pushing for Iraqi compliance, council unity, and peace. This type of approach facilitates a secretary-general's ability to serve as a neutral intermediary. U Thant stated, "The Secretary-General must always be prepared to take an initiative, no matter what the consequences to him or his office may be, if he sincerely believes that it might make the difference between peace and war."[33] Annan put it more bluntly: "I know some people have accused me of using diplomacy. That's my job."[34]

Dag Hammarskjöld, the second secretary-general, played a key part in shaping the role and the UN during the critical period 1953–1961. Hammarskjöld articulated principles for UN involvement in peacekeeping. He demonstrated the secretary-general's efficacy as an agent for peaceful settlement of disputes, mediating the release of eleven US airmen under the UN command in Korea who had been imprisoned by the Communist Chinese and seeking a solution to the secession of the Congo province of Katanga just before his death in 1961. Hammarskjöld also oversaw the initiation of UN peacekeeping operations with the creation of the United Nations Emergency Force (UNEF) at the time of the 1956 Suez crisis. He is generally credited with inventing the idea of preventive diplomacy.

Javier Pérez de Cuéllar, the fifth secretary-general, presided over the UN's transformation from the brink of irrelevance in the 1980s to an active instrument for resolving conflicts and promoting international peace at the end of the Cold War. In his persistent, patient, low-key approach to Israel's 1982 invasion of Lebanon, the Falklands/Malvinas War, the Iran-Iraq War, and the ongoing problems in Cyprus, Namibia, and Afghanistan, he epitomized the ideal intermediary.

Secretary-General Boutros Boutros-Ghali pushed the boundaries of the office further with the benefit of independent UN information-gathering and analytical capability. He prodded states, including the US, to take action in Somalia. He engaged the UN in civil conflicts in Cambodia, Bosnia, and Haiti. This activism and his antagonistic relationship with the United States led to his defeat for a second term in 1996.

Kofi Annan, a Ghanaian national, became the seventh secretary-general and the first from within the UN bureaucracy. A much quieter individual, Annan pledged change, yet proved even more of an activist than his predecessor. He carried out extensive administrative and budgetary reforms within the UN, including structural changes within the Secretariat, discussed in Chapter 2. He strengthened liaisons between various departments and NGOs and initiated dialogue with business leaders. He built a better relationship with the US Congress, an important step given Congress's failure to fully fund US dues to the UN for much of the 1990s. Having won the Nobel Peace Prize for himself and the organization, a widely respected Annan won reelection in 2001. He used his "bully pulpit" as UN head, including his annual reports to the General Assembly, to speak out on controversial issues such as HIV/AIDS, changing interpretations of state sovereignty, and the emerging norm of humanitarian intervention and to initiate programs such as the Global Compact with private corporations. He took the unprecedented step of publishing reports on the UN's failures in the disastrous massacre in the UN-declared safe area of Srebrenica, in the Rwandan genocide, and in security for UN personnel in Iraq. His prestige and authority were damaged, however, by the oil-for-food scandal discussed in Chapter 2. As one close observer of the UN noted, both Boutros-Ghali and Annan "shared a reputation as proponents of big ideas, bold doctrines, and a generous interpretation of the scope and authority of the office."[35]

Still, even activist secretaries-general can find their influence limited. Mark Malloch Brown, former administrator of UNDP, left that post to serve as deputy secretary-general and *chef de cabinet* to Kofi Annan. He later remarked, "I found when it came to management and budgetary matters that the secretary-general was less influential than I had been as administrator of UNDP. Whereas I had had a cooperative board that was not infected by bitter political confrontation, he was hostage to intergovernmental warfare."[36] This suggests that individual personality is not the only variable affecting the secretary-general's ability to act independently.

Ban Ki-moon, the eighth secretary-general, has had a very different approach to the role from his two immediate predecessors. While he proclaimed climate change to be a high priority early on, he has been unable to translate that general commitment into action. His low-profile approach did work in Myanmar, where he got the government to accept international assistance after the devastation of Cyclone Nargis in 2008. Ban's reluctance to speak out when his words would antagonize the US, Russia, or China, however, has met with sustained criticism, as did his handling of the Sri Lankan war when he selected an inappropriate negotiator with ties to India. Perhaps most critically, Ban's management skills have been widely rebuked.[37] In 2010, the outgoing undersecretary-general of the Office of Internal Oversight Services, Inga-Britt Ahlenius, wrote a scathing critique of Ban's management practices, particularly his efforts to undercut the independence of the internal investigations division. She called Ban secretive, his actions "reprehensible," and his leadership "deplorable," concluding that "the secretariat now is in a process of decay."[38] While that and other criticisms are unlikely to affect the "campaign" for his reelection at the end of 2011, he also has his supporters, particularly for his tough support of UN peacekeepers in Côte d'Ivoire. Nonetheless, evaluation of Ban highlights tensions among those, particularly the United States and other states, who prefer the secretary-general to be an efficient manager and an instrument of members, those who may be content with a weak individual who does not exercise leadership, and those who prefer a more independent figure willing to take initiatives and direct a powerful bureaucracy.

In addition to the secretary-general himself, various special representatives of the secretary-general who are now appointed in conjunction with all UN peacekeeping missions and often serve as mediators can exercise significant indepen-

PHOTOGRAPH 3.1. Secretary-General Ban Ki-moon remarks on the death of Al-Qaida leader Bin Laden, May 2, 2011. SOURCE: UN Photo 471791/Paulo Filgueiras.

dent influence. Among the most notable special representatives have been Sergio Vieira de Mello, the special representative successively in Lebanon, Kosovo, East Timor, and Iraq;[39] Martti Ahtisaari, winner of the 2008 Nobel Peace Prize who served as special representative in Namibia and Kosovo; and Lakhdar Brahimi, who, among his many important UN posts, served as special representative in Haiti, South Africa, Afghanistan, and Iraq.

The directors-general of the specialized agencies also wield considerable power. Diplomatically, they carry the same rank as the secretary-general, historically a factor complicating efforts of the latter to coordinate initiatives across different parts of the UN system. But the role of the second UN extends beyond these high-level officials, and it is to that we turn.

The UN Secretariat as Bureaucracy and Actor

The UN's Secretariat and the secretariats of the specialized agencies share some of the characteristics of bureaucracies more generally. They derive authority in performing "duties of office" from their rational-legal character and from their expertise; they derive legitimacy from the moral purposes of the organization and from their claims to neutrality, impartiality, and objectivity; and they derive power from their missions of serving others. The different agencies within the UN system tend to be staffed by technocrats—individuals with specialized

training and knowledge who shape policy options consistent with that expertise. "In fact," Barnett and Finnemore note, "the organization will not readily
entertain policy options not supported by its expertise. Professional training,
norms, and occupational cultures strongly shape the way experts view the
world. They influence what problems are visible to staff and what range of solutions are entertained."[40]

The Secretariat includes the under- and assistant secretaries-general, the
heads of departments such as peacekeeping and electoral assistance, the high
commissioners for refugees and for human rights, the heads of programs such as
UNDP and UNICEF, and the head of UN Women—the new UN organization
that became operational on January 1, 2011. All UN senior-level officials can potentially be highly influential in building awareness of issues and calling attention to specific problems such as child soldiers, violence against women, refugee
crises, or torture in China. Staff in the field with development or peace operations can significantly shape the success or failure of those operations by their
actions. Chapter 6, for example, examines the leadership that high commissioners for human rights have played.

The UN's bureaucrats play a significant role in shaping the agendas of various
meetings. The ways in which they understand particular conflict situations can
also influence how member states view them. For example, Barnett and
Finnemore show how the UN staff defined the situation in Rwanda in 1994 as a
civil war and failed to see that the unfolding genocide was quite different from
violence against civilians in other ethnic conflicts. "Because Rwanda was a civil
war there was no basis for intervention," they note. "The rules of peacekeeping . . .
[at that time] prohibited peacekeeping in a civil war and in the absence of a stable
cease-fire . . . but also shaped its [the Secretariat's] position on how peacekeepers might be used in this volatile situation."[41] Furthermore, Secretary-General
Boutros-Ghali did not make the argument for intervention. Thus, the UN's failure
to stop the genocide in Rwanda was "the predictable result of an organizational
culture that shaped how the UN evaluated and responded to violent crises."[42]

Examples of such Secretariat influence in defining issues can be drawn from
many other UN agencies. In the mid-1980s, HIV/AIDS, for example, was viewed
as solely a health problem and, hence, the province of the medical professionals
in WHO. Only gradually did other UN agencies demonstrate the scope of the
epidemic's effects and the necessity for interagency collaboration in dealing with
the problem. The influence of liberal economists in the IMF and World Bank has
long been noted as a major factor shaping the way those institutions' bureaucracies think about and address development issues and financial crises.

Yet influence in international institutions is not limited to states, secretaries-
general, directors-general, or bureaucrats. Increasingly, nonstate actors have
come to play leading roles as part of the third UN.

NONSTATE ACTORS: THE THIRD UN

Three types of nonstate actors have been important to the UN from its inception and, therefore, make up the third UN. These include nongovernmental organizations, academics and experts who serve as consultants, and independent commissions of prominent individuals, all of which interact with the first and second UNs and influence thinking and policies. They are characterized by their independence from governments and from the UN Secretariat. None are monolithic. And "deciding who is in or out of the third UN depends on the issue and the period in question."[43]

NGOs as Actors in the UN System

The rapid growth in numbers, roles, and influence of NGOs in global politics generally and within the UN system is one of the striking developments since the Cold War's end. The members of these organizations are private individuals or associations that come together around some common purpose. To some, these groups together form the basis of a global civil society. Some NGOs are formed to advocate a particular cause such as human rights, peace, or environmental protection. Others are established to provide services such as disaster relief, humanitarian aid, or development assistance. Some are in reality government-organized groups (dubbed GONGOs). Scholars and analysts distinguish between not-for-profit groups (the vast majority) and for-profit corporations; it is also common to treat terrorist, criminal, and drug trafficking groups separately.

The estimates of numbers of NGOs vary enormously. The 2008–2009 *Yearbook of International Organizations* identified more than 8,000 nongovernmental organizations that have an international dimension in terms of either membership or commitment to conduct activities in several states. Exclusively national NGOs number in the millions. Many large international NGOs (INGOs) are transnational federations linking a number of national groups. Examples include the International Federation of Red Cross and Red Crescent Societies, Oxfam, Médecins Sans Frontières (Doctors Without Borders), World Wildlife Fund, Human Rights Watch, Amnesty International, and Save the Children.

Article 71 of the UN Charter authorized ECOSOC (but not the General Assembly) to grant consultative status to NGOs. Resolution 1296 adopted in 1968 formalized the arrangements for accrediting NGOs whose influence occurred primarily within ECOSOC's subsidiary bodies, and particularly within the Commissions on Human Rights, Status of Women, and Population. The UN-sponsored global conferences beginning in the 1970s greatly increased the visibility and power of NGOs. In the conferences focusing on women, the environment, human rights, population, and sustainable development, NGOs found valuable new outlets for their activities. In many cases, groups participated in preconference meetings with delegates, organized their own parallel meetings on topics of interest, published materials to increase public awareness of the issues, provided inputs to official conference documents, and developed networks with other NGOs to enhance their influence. At the conferences themselves, the rules for NGO participation have varied. While some conferences permitted NGO lobbying and NGO roles in implementation, others limited participation to informal activities. Those experiences strengthened the NGOs' resolve to gain greater formal access and clearer rules for participation.

ECOSOC Resolution 31 in 1996 granted access to national-level NGOs, enlarging the number of NGOs with consultative status to more than 3,000. Those NGOs have broad access to UN bodies: They may consult with officers from the Secretariat; place items on agendas in ECOSOC, the functional commissions, and other subsidiary bodies; attend meetings; submit statements; and make oral presentations with permission. Still, the Conference of Non-Governmental Organisations in Consultative Status with the United Nations Economic and Social Council (CONGO) has called for clearer procedures for participation, and the 2003 Cardoso Report called for enhanced relationships between the UN and relevant civil society partners.

In the General Assembly, four NGOs—the International Federation of the Red Cross and Red Crescent Societies, the International Committee of the Red Cross (ICRC), the Inter-Parliamentary Union, and the Sovereign Military Order of Malta—have special privileges to participate as observers in all assembly sessions. Since the late 1980s, NGOs have had access as petitioners to some assembly committees, notably the Third Committee (Social, Humanitarian, and Cultural) and the Second Committee (Economic and Financial).

In 1997, NGOs first gained limited access to Security Council meetings. Through the NGO Working Group on the Security Council (organized by Amnesty International, the Global Policy Forum, EarthAction, and the World Council of Churches, among others), NGOs that provide relief aid in humanitarian emergencies have gained a voice in council deliberations. For example, Oxfam, CARE, and Doctors Without Borders have spoken on the Great Lakes crisis in Africa, and discussions on AIDS have included NGO representatives. Informal consultations between NGOs, the Security Council president, and council members are now a common practice.

Whether NGOs are recognized through ECOSOC accreditation is now largely an academic question since they have found various other ways for influencing UN policymaking and implementation. Women's NGOs, which have a long history of networking with women in governments and various UN bodies, have effectively used these informal links and during the four world conferences on women pressed for mainstreaming women's and gender issues. A coalition of NGOs, the Global Call to Action Against Poverty, has promoted the Millennium Development Goals by mobilizing local community leaders and groups.

By contrast, however, the UN Development Programme does not engage systematically with any NGOs, and its advisory committee actually shields UNDP from such interactions. This is particularly troubling since UNDP resident coordinators have been designated by Secretary-General Ban as representing "one UN system" in charge of a single multisector, country-owned program that includes NGO participation. A pilot project in eight countries is being run to test the effectiveness of this effort at centralization.[44]

Several UN specialized agencies and programs have long welcomed the involvement of NGOs. Only the ILO, however, has formalized their participation in the unique tripartite system of representation. UNESCO, for example, has enjoyed an extensive network of national commissions, scientific councils, and more than six hundred NGOs in consultation. UNICEF and the United Nations Development Fund for Women (UNIFEM) also have long histories of recognizing the importance of NGOs. In a number of specialized agencies, though, it has been a long struggle to incorporate NGOs in a meaningful way. In many cases, NGOs are contractors of services the specialized agencies provide rather than stakeholders in programs.

The barriers to NGO participation do not lie just within the UN. A 2004–2005 survey of UN system agencies conducted by the UN-NGLS (UN Non-Governmental Liaison Services) found that NGOs' lack of funding to participate in meetings and follow up was a significant constraint. NGOs themselves acknowledge the difficulty in balancing the interests and desires of groups from the developed with those from the developing world, for example. Even when NGOs participate, they see impact on low policy issues rather than on core economic questions. As one NGO questioned, "We are being listened to but are we being heard."[45]

NGO participation in the loosely UN-related international financial organizations has been quite uneven. Since the late 1970s, women's and environmental NGOs have pressured the World Bank, for example, to adopt a women-in-development and environmental friendly agenda. They often targeted specific bank projects such as big dams. Since 1994, the bank turned to a more participatory development approach, but those results are uneven. Increasingly, the bank has used NGOs to collaborate on and administer projects, but admitted, "CSOs [civil society organizations] invited to consultation meetings were those who were easily accessible and approving of the government and the Bank's preferred strategies. Moreover, CSOs who were invited often did not get enough timely and appropriate information about the issues at stake, the options being considered, and how the PRSP [Poverty Reduction Strategy Papers] process works, thus limiting their ability to effectively participate in the process."[46] The IMF has, likewise, been slow to develop formal contacts with NGOs because its specialized focus on monetary policy has not lent itself easily to NGO input. Yet even the IMF felt NGO influence during the Jubilee 2000 campaign for debt reduction orchestrated by a wide range of NGOs, religious groups, trade unions, and business associations.

For several decades, there have been proposals to give civil society actors a forum of their own. The People's Millennium Assembly held in 2000 was an ad hoc version of such a forum that brought together representatives of more than one hundred NGOs. Although the names have varied—a UN Parliamentary Assembly, a Forum of Civil Society, a Second Assembly—the ideas are basically the same. To proponents, nonstate actors—including NGOs—should have a venue for consultations among themselves and should be given standing within the UN system. Such an assembly would give voice to heretofore unrepresented groups, add transparency to the international political process, and potentially add accountability. It would also require UN Charter reform.

Yet there are deep divisions among member states, the UN Secretariat, as well as NGOs and other nonstate actors themselves over greater nonstate participation. Many governments have mixed or even negative feelings about NGOs. For example, governments in Africa, Asia, and Latin America often feel threatened by the pressures of human rights NGOs, developed countries do not always welcome NGO pressure for economic justice, the Nonaligned Movement and small countries oppose expanded NGO access to the General Assembly, and the UN Secretariat fears that greater NGO involvement would be costly both in stretching material resources and in complicating procedures already deemed cumbersome.

NGOs do not speak with one voice on the issue of participation within the UN system or on any other issue. There are differences in interest and perspective, often leading to conflict among NGOs, the not-for-profit business associations, and private companies. The not-for-profit business associations have been included within the NGO sector by the UN, even though their individual members are businesses. NGOs have been especially upset by the ease with which businesses and MNCs have acquired status and participatory rights by their presence on national delegations and through the Global Compact, while NGOs are typically not represented on national delegations and have to undergo strenuous examination to gain consultative status. Even among the NGOs themselves, there are significant divisions, between the traditional NGOs (which they say represent the people) and growing social movements like indigenous people and between the larger more established NGOs and smaller local ones.

Academic and Expert Consultants

Almost from its inception, the UN has drawn on the knowledge of outside experts to study specific issues and prepare reports. These have in a number of cases included individuals who later were awarded Nobel Prizes for their work in economics such as Jan Tinbergen, W. Arthur Lewis, Gunnar Myrdal, and Amartya Sen. Much of this work took place in the 1950s and 1960s and contributed to early understandings of economic development. The UN System of National Accounts was the product of a committee of experts convened by the UN Statistical Office. Similarly, measures for full employment, economic development, and international economic stability were developed by outside experts. Sen, for example, wrote both for the ILO World Employment Programme in the 1970s and for UNDP's Human Development Reports in the 1990s.

Independent Commissions

The third UN also includes independent commissions composed of prominent individuals such as former foreign ministers, heads of government, and ambassadors. The commission may be established by the UN, a government, or others; often, there is a team of academic researchers who provide study papers for the commission that typically presents its report to the UN secretary-general. Since the late 1960s, when a commission led by former Canadian prime minister Lester Pearson produced the report *Partners in Development* (1969), there have been a large number of other commissions, several of which are discussed in later chapters. These include the Commission on Environment and Development chaired by Norwegian prime minister Gro Harlem Brundtland in the 1980s, the Commission on Global Governance whose 1995 report *Our Global Neighborhood* helped to make the concept of global governance more widely known, and the Commission on Civil Society led by former Brazilian president Fernando Henrique Cardoso whose 2004 report was mentioned above. In 2004, Secretary-General Kofi Annan convened the High-level Panel on Threats, Challenges, and Change as part of the preparation for the World Summit planned in conjunction with the UN's sixtieth anniversary in 2005.

What differentiates the independent commissions from the academic and expert consultants is the collective weight they bring to their recommendations. With high-level individuals from different parts of the world participating in deliberations, lending their names to its report, and, in many cases, advocating adoption of a commission's recommendations, they combine "knowledge with political punch and access to decisionmakers." Thus, independent commissions have been a major factor in "nourishing ideas"—a major contribution of the UN overall. They have also been important vehicles for the prominent participants to "voice criticisms at higher decibel levels and make more controversial recommendations than when they occupied official positions."[47]

CONCLUSION

States remain major actors in the UN system, although their sovereignty may be eroding and their centrality may be diminished by the activism of the UN bureaucracy, NGOs, and other nonstate actors. Across the years, they have used the United Nations for foreign policy purposes and have been affected in turn by the organization's actions. Since the Cold War's end, there have been proliferating demands for UN action on security, economic, human rights, and other issues. The political will, or commitment, of member states remains a critical factor in determining whether sufficient action is taken and sufficient resources are made available. Yet ideas for what to do and resources in the field for implementing economic and social problems have increasingly come from NGOs and other nonstate actors. The third dilemma—the dilemma of who provides leadership—is not necessarily resolved by the wealthiest and most powerful states. As we have discussed, the United States has continued to send "mixed messages" about its willingness and ability to provide leadership and funding. The willingness of other powerful states to share financial burdens, to participate in UN peace operations, and to provide other kinds of leadership and of middle powers to be leaders or followers is essential. Likewise, the ability and willingness of small states to support global initiatives and to fulfill their own commitments are part of the picture. The proliferation of NGOs and other nonstate actors, the emergence of global civil society, and the roles of the secretary-general and UN bureaucracy as actors are developments that complicate and enrich the cast of characters on the UN's stage.

Notes

1. Thomas G. Weiss, Tatiana Carayannis, and Richard Jolly, "The 'Third' United Nations," *Global Governance* 15, no. 1 (2009): 123.

2. Margaret P. Karns and Karen A. Mingst, eds., *The United States and Multilateral Institutions: Patterns of Changing Instrumentality and Influence* (Boston: Unwin Hyman, 1990).

3. Edward C. Luck, *Mixed Messages: American Politics and International Organization, 1919–1999* (Washington, DC: Brookings Institution Press, 1999).

4. Lise Morjé Howard, "Sources of Change in United States–United Nations Relations," *Global Governance* 16, no. 4 (2010): 485.

5. Margaret P. Karns and Karen A. Mingst, "The United States as 'Deadbeat'? U.S. Policy and the UN Financial Crisis," in *Multilateralism and U.S. Foreign Policy: Ambivalent Engagement,* ed. Stewart Patrick and Shepard Forman (Boulder: Lynne Rienner, 2002), 267–294.

6. John Washburn, UNAUSA "World Bulletin," March 3, 2010, www.unausa.org /worldbulletin/030310.

7. Donald J. Puchala, "World Hegemony and the United Nations," *International Studies Review* 7, no. 4 (2005): 575.

8. Ibid., 576.

9. Gideon Rachman, "Think Again: American Decline," *Foreign Policy* (January–February 2011): 63.

10. See Ken Matthews, *The Gulf Conflict and International Relations* (London: Routledge, 1993), 81.

11. Michael Grossman, "Role Theory and Foreign Policy Change: The Transformation of Russian Foreign Policy in the 1990s," *International Politics* 42, no. 3 (2005): 334–351.

12. Dmitry Shlapentokh, "Outside View: Russian Troops in Iraq," *Washington Times* (2004), www.washingtontimes.com/upi-breaking/2004.

13. B. Gregory Marfleet and Colleen Miller, "Failure After 1441: Bush and Chirac in the UN Security Council," *Foreign Policy Analysis* 1, no. 3 (2005): 333–360.

14. For extensive treatment of the British position, see A. J. R. Groom and Paul Taylor, "The United Kingdom and the United Nations," in *The United Nations System and the Politics of Member States,* ed. Chadwick F. Alger, Gene M. Lyons, and John E. Trent (Tokyo: United Nations University Press, 1995), 376–409.

15. Tom Woodhouse and Alexander Ramsbotham, "The United Kingdom," in *The Politics of Peacekeeping in the Post–Cold War Era,* ed. David S. Sorenson and Pia Christina Wood (London: Frank Cass, 2005), 100–103.

16. Ann Kent, "China's International Socialization: The Role of International Organizations," *Global Governance* 8, no. 3 (2002): 345.

17. Ann Kent, *Beyond Compliance: China, International Organizations, and Global Security* (Stanford: Stanford University Press, 2007), 63.

18. Kent, "China's International Socialization," 349.

19. Elizabeth G. Economy, "The Game Changer: Coping with China's Foreign Policy Revolution," *Foreign Affairs* 89, no. 6 (2010): 143.

20. See Sadako Ogata, "Japan's Policy Towards the United Nations," in *United Nations System and the Politics of Member States,* ed. Alger, Lyons, and Trent, 231–270. See also Reinhard Drifte, *Japan's Quest for a Permanent Security Council Seat: A Matter of Pride or Justice?* (New York: St. Martin's Press, 2000).

21. Mary N. Hampton, "Germany," in *Politics of Peacekeeping in the Post–Cold War Era,* ed. Sorenson and Wood, 43–44.

22. Keith Krause, David Dewitt, and W. Andy Knight, "Canada, the United Nations, and the Reform of International Institutions," in *The United Nations System and the Politics of Member States,* ed. Alger, Lyons, and Trent, 171.

23. Hugh Smith, "Australia," in *Politics of Peacekeeping in the Post–Cold War Era,* ed. Sorenson and Wood, 9–13.

24. Andrew F. Cooper, Richard A. Higgott, and Kim Richard Nossal, *Relocating Middle Powers: Australia and Canada in a Changing World Order* (Vancouver: University of British Columbia Press, 1993).

25. Alison Brysk, "Global Good Samaritans? Human Rights Foreign Policy in Costa Rica," *Global Governance* 11, no. 4 (2005): 445–466.

26. Quoted in Sally Morphet, "Multilateralism and the Non-Aligned Movement: What Is the Global South Doing and Where Is It Going?" *Global Governance* 10, no. 4 (2004): 533.

27. Courtney B. Smith, *Politics and Process at the United Nations: The Global Dance* (Boulder: Lynne Rienner, 2006). See especially chap. 3.

28. Greg Hitt and Scott Miller, "Booming Voice for New Bloc," *Wall Street Journal,* December 17–18, 2005.

29. See Teresa Whitfield, *Friends Indeed? The United Nations, Groups of Friends, and Resolution of Conflict* (Washington, DC: United States Institute of Peace Press, 2007).

30. Michael Barnett and Martha Finnemore, "The Power of Liberal Organizations," in *Power in Global Governance,* ed. Michael Barnett and Raymond Duvall (New York: Cambridge University Press, 2005), 170, 173.

31. Michael Barnett and Martha Finnemore, *Rules for the World: International Organizations in Global Politics* (Ithaca: Cornell University Press, 2004), 3.

32. Oran R. Young, *The Intermediaries: Third Parties in International Crises* (Princeton: Princeton University Press, 1967), 283.

33. Ibid., 284.

34. Barbara Crossette, "Kofi Annan Unsettles People, as He Believes U.N. Should Do," *New York Times,* December 31, 1999.

35. Edward C. Luck, "The Secretary-General in a Unipolar World," in *Secretary or General? The UN Secretary-General in World Politics,* ed. Simon Chesterman (Cambridge: Cambridge University Press, 2007), 202.

36. Mark Malloch Brown, "The John W. Holmes Lecture: Can the UN Be Reformed?" *Global Governance* 14, no. 1 (2008): 10.

37. See "The Score at Half-Time," *Economist* (June 11, 2009), available at www.economist.com/node/13825201/print.

38. Quoted in Colum Lynch, "Departing U.N. Official Calls Ban's Leadership 'Deplorable' in 50-Page Memo," *Washington Post,* July 20, 2010, A14.

39. Samantha Power, *Chasing the Flame: One Man's Fight to Save the World* (New York: Penguin, 2008).

40. Barnett and Finnemore, "The Power of Liberal International Organizations," 174. The ideas in this section draw heavily from pages 171–178.

41. Barnett and Finnemore, *Rules for the World,* 151–152.

42. Ibid., 155.

43. Weiss, Carayannis, and Jolly, "The 'Third' United Nations," 127.

44. See Nora McKeon, *The United Nations and Civil Society: Legitimating Global Governance—Whose Voice?* (London: Zed Books, 2009), 151–160.

45. Quoted in ibid., 132.

46. World Bank, *World Bank–Civil Society Global Policy Dialogue Forum,* Washington, DC, April 20–22, 2005, Summary Report.

47. Weiss, Carayannis, and Jolly, "The 'Third' United Nations," 133.

4

◄◦►

Maintaining International
Peace and Security

> We acknowledge that we are living in an interdependent
> and global world and that many of today's threats
> recognize no national boundaries, are interlinked and
> must be tackled at the global, regional, and national levels
> in accordance with the Charter and international law.
> —2005 World Summit Outcome

War, *the* fundamental problem in international politics, has been the primary factor motivating the creation of IGOs from the Concert of Europe in the nineteenth century to the League of Nations and the United Nations in the twentieth century. Despite being the most destructive century in human history, the twentieth century was also the century of creating ways to prevent wars.

The nature of wars and conflicts has changed in significant ways in the past sixty years. There has been a sharp decrease in the incidence of interstate war. The number of intrastate (internal) armed conflicts resulting from the collapse of an already weak state such as Somalia, ethnic conflict as in the former Yugoslavia, civil war such as the North-South civil war in Sudan (1983–2005), or civil wars internationalized through the intervention of other states or groups such as in the Democratic Republic of the Congo (1996–2001) more than doubled in the 1990s. Yet because there were actually more wars terminated, there was a net decline in conflicts. That trend has reversed since 2005, although most new conflicts are relatively minor and kill few people.[1] These developments are the result of three major political changes: the end of colonialism, the

97

Cold War's end, and the end of the superpower rivalry that paralyzed many efforts to deal with threats to peace and increased international activities, especially by the United Nations, to stop ongoing wars and prevent new ones.

The primary threats to peace and security that the UN's Charter was designed to deal with were interstate wars. Even though the majority of all conflicts since 1945 have been within states, with only a few exceptions, until the Cold War's end, the Security Council rarely determined that civil wars were threats to international peace and security. Since 1990, however, conflicts within states have been the council's primary focus, and the UN's member states have empowered it to play a much more active role in dealing with them and with postconflict peacebuilding efforts. Many post–Cold War conflicts have been accompanied by humanitarian disasters resulting from the fighting, ethnic cleansing or genocide, the collapse of governmental authority (failed states), or famine and disease. The numbers of refugees and internally displaced persons have risen dramatically—and often in a very short period of time. These have provoked debates about the legitimacy of international armed intervention under UN auspices to protect human beings—that is, humanitarian intervention, or R2P.

Traditionally, security meant *state* security—the security of borders, control over population, and freedom from interference in the government's sovereignty over its internal affairs. With the body of internationally recognized human rights norms steadily expanding in the second half of the twentieth century, the balance between the rights of sovereign states and the rights of people began to shift. Increasingly, it was argued that *human* security should take precedence over security of governments or states. This shift has provided support for the new norm of a responsibility to protect populations at risk and legitimacy for armed intervention to protect human beings against the violence of governments, paramilitary forces, militias, and police. This was dramatically illustrated in the rapid convergence of international opinion on the need for action against the Qaddafi regime in Libya in early 2011 that contrasted with the slow responses to genocide in Rwanda in 1994 and Darfur in 2004, as discussed below.

The changing nature of conflicts and complex humanitarian crises then are two challenges to peace and security in the twenty-first century. Other threats include the spread of weapons of mass destruction, particularly nuclear weapons, and terrorism. These threats are not new, but the linkages between them are, and they present major challenges to the UN and international efforts to maintain peace and security.

LINKING INTERNATIONAL RELATIONS THEORIES

International relations theorists differ sharply in their views of the causes of war and whether and how international institutions can respond to the use of armed force and conflicts. Realists come in "hard" and "soft" varieties when dealing with threats of force, breaches of the peace, and conflict resolution. The "hard" variety hold firm to traditional realist views about states' likely use of force and the role of power struggles among states in prompting conflict. They don't see many differences between the dynamics that give rise to interstate and intrastate conflicts. Security dilemmas affect parties to both. In realists' eyes, balance-of-power politics, alliances, and force itself are key means to resolve conflicts since IGOs do not provide effective mechanisms. Should any consideration be given to intervention by a third party, only major powers have the resources to influence the parties or intervene effectively, but their incentives to do so are often limited.

The "soft" variety of realists comes closer to liberals in some respects, as they envisage a broader range of options and actors. Diplomacy and mediation are among the options "soft" realists consider valuable for dealing with conflicts and use of force, in order to change parties' cost-benefit analyses in favor of peaceful settlement versus war. They also recognize the role of IGOs as interveners.

Liberals have traditionally supported international law and organization as approaches to peace, and, hence, the concepts embodied in the UN Charter reflect liberal theory. They also believe that economic interdependence and the spread of democracy will reduce the incidence of armed conflicts. This so-called liberal democratic peace is a basis for contemporary postconflict peacebuilding activities. Liberalism also sees NGOs and IGOs, as well as individuals, states, and ad hoc groups, among the actors that may play roles as third parties in peaceful efforts to settle disputes, stop fighting once it has started, secure a settlement, and build conditions for peace. Thus, while liberals don't oppose the use of force when necessary, they prefer to use nonmilitary means, including sanctions and diplomacy, to avert or end armed conflicts.

Since the mid-1990s, constructivism has contributed substantially to understanding the evolution and role of norms as well as to reconceptualizing security itself. Constructivists have examined how norms on the use of force and which groups should be protected have changed.[2] They have shown how norms against specific weapons such as the taboos on the use of chemical and nuclear weapons have evolved over time. They have traced the emergence of the R2P norm and the role of NGOs in the conventions banning land mines and cluster munitions.

Much of the rich recent literature on interstate and civil wars as well as on conflict resolution draws on multiple schools of thought so that there is no definitive theory setting forth clear conditions under which wars will occur or peace will be secured—and by whom. The contextual factors shaping human choices—the choice for war and the choice to settle a dispute peacefully—defy tidy theorizing. In short, we know a lot about both, but not enough to lay out a single theory to guide the maintenance of international peace and security.

MAINTAINING PEACE AND SECURITY:
THE UN CHARTER AND ITS EVOLUTION

Maintaining peace and security has always been the primary purpose of the UN, but how the UN undertakes this task has changed over time in ways never envisaged by the founders. Many provisions of the Charter that lay largely unused during the forty years of the Cold War have seen far more use since 1989. Over time, the UN has also created new ways of addressing security threats and seeking to secure peace—demonstrating the flexibility of the UN Charter.

The United Nations Charter in Article 2 (sections 3, 4, and 5) obligates all members to settle disputes by peaceful means, to refrain from the threat or use of force, and to cooperate with UN-sponsored actions. This normative prohibition was a direct outgrowth of the Kellogg-Briand Pact, concluded in 1928. The use of force for territorial annexation is now widely accepted as illegitimate—witness the broad condemnation of Iraq's invasion of Kuwait in 1990 and the large number of states that contributed to the US-led multilateral effort to reverse that occupation. The use of force in self-defense against armed attack is accepted and was the basis for the Security Council's authorization of US military action after the September 2001 terrorist attacks. International norms prescribe, however, that the response must be proportional to the provocation—the basis for widespread condemnation of Israel's large-scale military responses in 2006 and 2009 to rockets fired by Hezbollah and Hamas from Lebanon and Gaza, respectively. A large majority of states accept the legitimacy of using force to promote self-determination, replace illegitimate regimes, and correct past injustices. The UN Security Council refused in 2003, however, to authorize use of force against Iraq, leading the United States to form an ad hoc coalition to remove Saddam Hussein from power. In 2011, however, the council authorized "all necessary means" to stop the Libyan government from using force against its citizens. As discussed in Chapter 2, the Security Council has primary responsibility for maintenance of international peace and security (Article 24), and there is a strong consensus on its authority to (de)legitimize the use of force.

Chapter VI specifies the ways in which the Security Council can promote **peaceful settlement** of disputes. For example, under Article 34, the Security Council may investigate disputes that threaten international peace and security. Throughout the Cold War years, the Security Council relied on the Charter's peaceful settlement mechanisms in responding to the many situations placed on its agenda. And, as discussed below, when peacekeeping—peace operations with lightly armed troops to maintain a truce or cease-fire agreement—was first undertaken in the late 1940s and 1950s, it was under Chapter VI since there is no provision in the Charter for this.

Chapter VII—what some would call the "teeth" of the Charter—specifies actions the UN can take with respect to threats to the peace, breaches of the peace, and acts of aggression. The Security Council can identify aggressors (Articles 39 and 40), decide what enforcement measures should be taken (Articles 41, 42, 48, and 49), and call on members to make military forces available, subject to special agreements (Articles 43–45). Because the Cold War made concurrence among the Security Council's permanent members almost impossible to achieve, Chapter VII was invoked on only two occasions during this period. Since 1989, however, the situation has changed dramatically, and Chapter VII has been invoked on many occasions to authorize the use of force and various types of sanctions by the UN alone, by a regional organization, or by a **coalition of the willing** led by a particular country such as the United States (Haiti), Australia (East Timor), and Great Britain (Sierra Leone). Today, it is common for most UN peace operations to have a mandate under Chapter VII.

Chapter VIII recognizes the rights and responsibilities of regional organizations to "make every effort to achieve peaceful settlement of local disputes" before referring them to the Security Council. When a regional organization seeks to use force, however, Security Council authorization is required to maintain the UN's primacy with respect to international enforcement. In some cases, a regional IGO has acted first and sought Security Council authority retroactively. Since 2003, NATO, the EU, and the African Union have emerged as the primary regional organizations involved in peace operations, often in partnerships with the UN (and each other)—as exemplified by the AU/UN Hybrid Mission in Darfur.

Because the UN's founders did not envision a major role for the UN with respect to arms control and disarmament, the UN Charter contains only two short references to this aspect of maintaining international peace and security. In Article 11, the General Assembly is authorized to consider principles governing disarmament and the regulation of armaments and may make recommendations to the Security Council or member states. In Article 26, the Security Council, with the assistance of the Military Staff Committee, which has been moribund from the beginning, is charged with formulating plans for "the establishment of a system for the regulation of armaments." Nonetheless, the advent of nuclear weapons in 1945 put disarmament and arms control on the UN's agenda, with the General Assembly's very first resolution calling for the creation of the Atomic Energy Commission to propose how to ensure that atomic energy was used only for peaceful purposes. Over time, the UN General Assembly has played a key role in developing arms control and disarmament norms and international law, although the most fruitful negotiations have often taken place outside the UN.

Over its history, the UN has addressed security threats in a variety of ways, utilizing the provisions of Chapters VI, VII, and VIII of the Charter, and also creating new approaches such as **preventive diplomacy** and deployment, mediation by the secretary-general, both traditional and complex peace operations, targeted sanctions, and enhanced monitoring procedures. With shifting norms, the changing nature of conflicts, and large-scale humanitarian crises since the Cold War's end, and the innovations of postconflict peacebuilding and statebuilding, the Security Council has become the centerpiece of the UN. Other innovations include the creation of ad hoc criminal tribunals to prosecute war crimes and crimes against humanity, a variety of counterterrorism measures, condemnation of sexual violence and rape as tools of war, and mandated gender-sensitive elements of UN activities relating to peace and security. These newer approaches illustrate how the UN has evolved as an institution.

MECHANISMS FOR PEACEFUL SETTLEMENT AND PREVENTIVE DIPLOMACY

From ancient times, there has been agreement about the desirability of settling disputes peacefully. The 1899 and 1908 Hague Conferences laid the foundations for mechanisms still in use today with the Convention for the Pacific Settlement of International Disputes. The assumption is that war is a deliberate choice for settling a dispute and that it is possible to create mechanisms that will influence actors' choices. They call for third-party roles variously labeled good offices, inquiry, mediation, conciliation, adjudication, and arbitration. The mechanisms were incorporated into both the League of Nations Covenant and Chapter VI of the UN Charter.

Among the peaceful settlement approaches, the UN has been most involved through good offices and mediation led by the secretary-general, a special representative of the secretary-general, or an ad hoc group of states (usually including at least one permanent member of the Security Council) such as a "contact group" or "Friends of the Secretary-General," as discussed in Chapter 3. Secretary-General Javier Pérez de Cuéllar secured agreement on the Soviet Union's withdrawal from Afghanistan, and Alvaro de Soto, his special representative, for example, mediated an end to the conflicts in Central America in the late 1980s. With the advent of more complex peace operations since the Cold War's end, special representatives of the UN secretary-general not only have been responsible for securing an end to armed conflict (a peacemaking role) but also often head peacekeeping and peacebuilding operations (coordination and managerial roles). They must engage in ongoing mediation among the parties to the conflict, contributors to the peace operation, UN agencies, regional organizations, key regional states, and NGOs involved in the postconflict environment. Most special representatives are career UN diplomats who have both close personal relationships with the secretary-general and other high-level UN officials as well as the ability to be effective diplomats outside the UN.[3]

Adjudication and arbitration of conflicts relating to peace and security may take place in the International Court of Justice, ad hoc war crimes tribunals, the International Criminal Court, and arbitration panels. The Permanent Court of Arbitration, for example, has ruled on a number of border disputes such as between Ethiopia and Eritrea (2002) and between northern and southern Sudan (2009). Several ICJ contentious cases have involved peace and security issues, among them the case concerning US intervention in Nicaragua in the 1980s and cases involving French nuclear testing in the South Pacific. The former, however, demonstrated the limitations of adjudication for dealing with peace and security issues. Despite the fact that the court found that the US mining of Nicaragua's harbors, attacks on port installations, and support for the Contras infringed upon the prohibition against the use of force, the United States rejected the ICJ's jurisdiction in the case, and it had little impact on the conflicts in Central America. It remains to be seen whether the work of the ad hoc war crimes tribunals and ICC has any deterrent effect on future conflicts.

Preventive diplomacy, an innovative approach to peaceful settlement introduced by Secretary-General Dag Hammarskjöld in the late 1950s, is "action to prevent disputes from arising between parties, to prevent existing disputes from escalating into conflicts and to limit the spread of the latter when they occur."[4] Most often, preventive diplomacy takes the form of diplomatic efforts, sometimes coupled with economic sanctions or arms embargoes. Preventive deployment is intended to change the calculus of parties regarding the purposes to be served by political violence and to deter them from choosing to escalate the level of conflict. It is estimated that the UN's deployment of 1,000 peacekeeping troops to Macedonia from late 1992 to 2001 cost $0.3 billion as opposed to an estimated $15 billion had the violence in other regions of the former Yugoslavia spread to Macedonia.[5] Successful preventive diplomacy depends on timeliness, which has provoked debate within the UN about early warning systems; indeed, the costs of waiting tend to be much higher than those for preventive action. But preventing conflicts is rarely easy, and opportunities are frequently missed. Since the 1990s, the International Crisis Group has emerged as an important actor providing early crisis warnings and actively helping policymakers in the UN, regional IGOs, donor countries, and countries at risk to better prevent and manage conflicts.

Preventive diplomacy is widely recognized today as an area in need of greater attention. The 2005 UN World Summit Outcome stressed the importance of preventing armed conflict, promoting a "culture of prevention," and developing "a coherent and integrated approach."[6] In 2008, the UN created the Mediation Standby Team—a mobile "SWAT team" for preventive diplomacy, consisting of six individuals from around the world with expertise on key issues such as cease-fires, transitional justice, constitution writing, security arrangements, and power sharing—to help address crises. Because peaceful settlement efforts are not always successful, however, the founders of the UN recognized the importance of provisions for collective security and enforcement actions.

COLLECTIVE SECURITY, ENFORCEMENT, AND SANCTIONS

The concept of collective security was at the heart of President Woodrow Wilson's proposal for the League of Nations as an alternative to the traditional balance-of-power politics that had frequently led to wars. Collective security is based on the conviction that peace is indivisible and that all states have a collective interest in countering aggression whenever and wherever it may occur. It assumes that potential aggressors will be deterred by the united threat of counterforce mobilized through an international organization such as the League or the UN. If enforcement is required, then a wide range of economic and diplomatic sanctions as well as armed force may be utilized.

Chapter VII of the UN Charter provides the legal basis for the UN's collective security role and for enforcement decisions that bind all UN members, specifying actions the UN can take with respect to threats to the peace, breaches of the peace, and acts of aggression. Because of the P-5's veto power in the Security Council, the UN is a limited collective security organization. Korea in 1950 and the 1990 Gulf War in response to Iraq's invasion of Kuwait come the closest to being collective security actions. Bosnia and Kosovo, Afghanistan, and Iraq II are cases that illustrate the controversies surrounding collective security. They each involved application of Chapter VII enforcement action, employing both armed forces and sanctions.

Collective Security Efforts Involving Armed Force

Korea. The sanctioning of UN forces to counter the North Korean invasion of South Korea in 1950 was made possible by the temporary absence of the Soviet Union from the Security Council in protest against the UN's refusal to seat the newly established Communist government of the People's Republic of China. Thus, the UN provided the framework for legitimizing US efforts to defend the Republic of Korea and mobilizing other states' assistance. An American general was designated the UN commander, but he took orders directly from Washington. Some fifteen states contributed troops during the three-year war.

The Gulf War. The end of the Cold War led many to speculate that now the UN Security Council could function as a collective security body. The first test of that belief came with Iraq's invasion of Kuwait in the summer of 1990. That triggered a period of unprecedented activity by the UN Security Council. Unity among the P-5, including the Soviet Union (despite its longstanding relationship with Iraq), facilitated the passage of twelve successive resolutions during a four-month period, activating Chapter VII of the Charter. These included, most importantly, Resolution 678 of November 1990, which authorized member states "to use all necessary means" to reverse the occupation of Kuwait.

The military operation launched under the umbrella of Resolution 678 was a US-led multinational effort resembling a subcontract on behalf of the organization. US commanders did not regularly report to the secretary-general, nor did senior UN personnel participate in military decisionmaking. Coalition forces did not use the UN flag or insignia. After the fighting ceased in late February 1991, a traditional lightly armed peacekeeping force known as the United Nations Iraq-Kuwait Observer Mission (UNIKOM) was organized to monitor the demilitarized zone between Iraq and Kuwait.

The US-led military action in the Gulf coming right at the end of the Cold War was widely regarded as exemplifying a new and stronger post–Cold War UN. But it also came under critical scrutiny.[7] Germany and Japan, which contributed substantial monetary resources, were excluded from decisions on the Security Council because they were not members; consequently, they became interested in securing permanent membership on the council, as discussed in Chapter 3. Many developing countries supported the action, but they were also troubled by the autonomy of the US-led operation. The Gulf War marked only the beginning, however, of efforts to deal with Iraq's threats to regional peace.

Bosnia and Kosovo. In 1992, the UN Security Council again invoked Chapter VII, calling on member states to "take all necessary measures" nationally or through regional organizations to facilitate delivery of humanitarian aid in war-torn Yugoslavia. This action came after various peacemaking efforts and the UN peacekeeping force (UN Protection Force for Yugoslavia or UNPROFOR) had failed to stop the escalating fighting in Bosnia-Herzegovina, one breakaway province. The resolution authorized the creation of UN "safe areas" in six Bosnian cities and enforcement of a "no-fly zone" over Bosnia, removal of heavy weapons from urban centers, economic sanctions on Serbia and Montenegro, and air strikes against Bosnian Serb forces attacking the "safe areas." US and European forces under NATO auspices, implemented the no-fly zone over Bosnia and, eventually, in 1995, conducted air strikes against Bosnian Serb positions that helped create conditions for negotiating a peace agreement. Not only was this the first time the UN had ever cooperated with a regional alliance, but it was also NATO's first-ever enforcement action.

NATO's second enforcement action, however, occurred in another part of the former Yugoslavia, the province of Kosovo, where the ethnic Albanian majority sought independence. It was extremely controversial because it occurred without prior authorization from the UN Security Council. In March 1999, NATO began more than two months of aerial bombing in Kosovo and parts of former Yugoslavia itself after Yugoslav (Serbian) rejection of a negotiated settlement for Kosovo and growing evidence of ethnic cleansing. Secretary-General Kofi Annan captured the dilemma Kosovo posed when he stated, "It is indeed tragic that diplomacy has failed, but there are times when the use of force may be legitimate in the pursuit of peace. . . . [But] the Council should be involved in any decision to resort to the use of force."[8] Russia, China, and other countries loudly protested the illegality of NATO intervention, but Great Britain maintained a Security Council resolution was not necessary when there was "overwhelming humanitarian necessity."[9] Yet the debate over NATO's military action reflected concerns that it worsened the humanitarian crisis by prompting the huge refugee outflow, civilian casualties of bombing, and destruction of infrastructure such as power plants and bridges on the Danube River.

The NATO-led action in Kosovo brought to the fore a major issue relating to the UN's collective security and enforcement role, namely, whether and when a regional organization or individual member states, including major powers such as the United States, must obtain authorization from the Security Council to use force. The issue arose again after September 11, 2001, when the United States intervened in Afghanistan on the grounds of self-defense to bring down the Taliban government that had harbored Al Qaeda training camps for terrorists. The issue was most sharply debated in 2002–2003 when the United States pushed for Security Council endorsement of military action to bring down the government of Saddam Hussein on the grounds that Iraq had repeatedly failed to implement Security Council resolutions, had ousted UN weapons inspectors, and was developing weapons of mass destruction.

Afghanistan. Within twenty-four hours of the September 11, 2001, terrorist attacks on the US, the UN Security Council approved Resolution 1368, which, among other things, recognized the US right to self-defense under Article 51. The US interpreted the resolution as providing an international legal basis for its military action against the Taliban regime and Al Qaeda camps in Afghanistan one month later. Following the Bonn Conference establishing the Afghan Interim Authority in December 2001, Security Council Resolution 1386 authorized a British-led International Security Assistance Force (ISAF) with enforcement power under Chapter VII to help the Afghan transitional authority maintain security.

In 2003, NATO took control of ISAF, with the US continuing combat operations against Al Qaeda and the Taliban under Operation Enduring Freedom. Under UN Security Council Resolution 1776 (2007), ISAF is mandated to disarm militias, reform the justice system, train a national police force and army, provide security for elections, and combat the narcotics industry. Given the growth of Taliban attacks from 2006 on, the distinction between US-led combat operations and NATO-ISAF actions blurred, as the latter took on more offensive operations. In early 2011, ISAF had more than 130,000 troops from forty-eight countries, with the US, UK, Germany, and Italy contributing the bulk of the force. Beyond its authorizing role, the UN is involved in humanitarian assistance, human rights, and peacebuilding tasks in Afghanistan.

The greatest problems regarding the legitimacy of the use of force arise when it is neither a clear case of self-defense (individual or collective) in response to an armed attack nor authorized by the Security Council. Hence, the story of US efforts to secure Security Council authorization for enforcement actions against Iraq in late 2002 and 2003—Iraq II—is a very different and controversial one.

Iraq II. During the fall and winter of 2002–2003, the United States expended a great deal of diplomatic effort in trying to muster Security Council support for a Chapter VII operation against Iraq. President George W. Bush warned Iraq that force would be used to uphold the objectives set by the Security Council unless it agreed to be peacefully disarmed of all weapons of mass destruction and accept the return of UN weapons inspectors. In October of that year, the US Congress authorized the president to use armed forces if necessary. In November, the Security Council unanimously passed a new resolution (1441) reinforcing the inspections regime and giving Iraq a last opportunity to provide full information on its WMD and missile programs. Although unwilling to authorize states in advance to use force against Iraq, the council did state that lack of cooperation, lies, and omissions would constitute a material breach that could lead to action. Despite UN and International Atomic Energy Agency reports showing that Iraq was cooperating with the strengthened inspections regime, the United States and Great Britain sought Security Council authorization in early 2003 for military action to disarm Iraq. They were forced to withdraw their draft resolution in the face of opposition from three other P-5 members (France, Russia, and China), as well as most nonpermanent members, including Germany. As one analyst has noted, this was "a resolution too far," and their skepticism or opposition was "not

surprising, given their different interests, their different views of war, their different assessments of any threat posed by Iraq, and their stated concerns about U.S.
dominance."[10]

By deciding to go to war in Iraq in March 2003 in defiance of the majority of
the Security Council, however, the United States, Great Britain, and their coalition allies posed a serious challenge to the authority of the council to authorize
the use of force. And because a major argument for military action involved what
has been called "anticipatory self-defense"—or preventive action—the question
was one of whether military action can be taken unilaterally in response to non-
imminent threats. In short, the war in Iraq raised a host of questions of principle
and practice concerning the UN's role in enforcement, including the fundamental question of the UN's relevance. Did the Security Council's failure to support
the US action in Iraq illustrate the UN's ineffectiveness and confirm its waning
legitimacy, especially in the face of a superpower with overwhelming military
power and a willingness to pursue its own agenda without Security Council authority, as some have argued? Or did the Security Council work as its founders
envisioned, not supporting UN involvement unless all the P-5 members and a
majority of nonpermanent council members concurred? The debate was an intense one, with the supporters of the US position deriding the UN for its lack of
follow-up to the sanctions, and opponents of the US-led war applauding the
UN's stance and appreciative of the UN role in postconflict peacebuilding.[11] Yet
as the debate over UN relevance raged, "the occupying powers soon realized . . .
that *some* form of UN involvement was essential to help overcome the difficulties
created by the occupation's lack of legitimacy and public support."[12] In both Iraq
and Afghanistan, the UN became involved in peacebuilding activities, as discussed later.

Anti-Piracy Enforcement. In a further illustration of the changing nature of
security threats, piracy—an ancient problem—has become a major contemporary problem. Although piracy had been a problem in Southeast Asia, particularly in waters of the Indonesian archipelago, it was brought under reasonable
control through regional efforts after 2000. More than one hundred pirate attacks were launched on ships in the Gulf of Aden and off the coast of Somalia
in 2008, however, significantly disrupting major shipping routes. For the first
time, in December 2008, the UN Security Council unanimously authorized the
use under Chapter VII of "all necessary means" against piracy and armed rob-
bery at sea by states and regional and international organizations. NATO and
EU member countries have sent ships for a multinational naval task force, as
have many other countries, including India, Russia, Japan, South Korea, and
China. Between 2008 and early 2011, more than four hundred ships were hi-

jacked, boarded, or fired upon by pirates operating from Somalia. Additional efforts have been directed to creating an international tribunal to try pirates, to strengthening local courts, and to addressing Somalia's own problems that fuel piracy as a lucrative endeavor.

Since 1990, use of armed forces authorized under Chapter VII has become more frequent, but so too have sanctions become integral to the UN's enforcement efforts.

Enforcement Through Sanctions

Sanctions have long been a favorite tool in states' efforts to get others to do what they wanted them to do. Unilateral sanctions, however, have always been problematic because they do not close off alternative markets and sources of supply for the target state(s). Organizing multilateral sanctions without a multilateral forum or organization through which to reduce the diplomatic transaction costs of securing other states' cooperation is a difficult undertaking. Hence, beginning with the League of Nations, the potential for using sanctions as an instrument of security governance was significantly enhanced.

Until 1990, the UN imposed mandatory sanctions under Chapter VII only twice: economic sanctions against the white minority regime in Southern Rhodesia after it unilaterally declared its independence from Great Britain in 1965 and an arms embargo on South Africa in 1977. Since the Cold War's end, sanctions have become a key enforcement instrument. Beginning with the sanctions imposed on Iraq in 1990, the UN Security Council utilized different forms of sanctions in fourteen situations over the next eleven years, leading one study to dub the 1990s "the sanctions decade."[13]

The range of sanctions has included not only comprehensive economic and trade restrictions but also more targeted measures such as arms embargoes against Yugoslavia, Angola, the Sudan, Iran, and Afghanistan. In an effort to hurt those most responsible for conflicts rather than ordinary people, the Security Council has frozen the assets of governments and specific individuals (e.g., Libya, the Taliban, Al Qaeda, Iran, North Korea), imposed travel bans for government and rebel leaders and their families (e.g., Sudan, Liberia, Iran), and established import-export bans for specific commodities such as oil, tropical timber, and diamonds (e.g., Liberia, Sierra Leone) (see Table 4.1). The purposes for which these sanctions were employed have steadily broadened. Sanctions have been employed to counter aggression (Iraq), to restore a democratically elected government (Haiti, Côte d'Ivoire), to respond to human rights violations (Yugoslavia, Rwanda), to end wars (Angola, Ethiopia, Eritrea, Democratic Republic of the Congo), to end state sponsorship and support of terrorism (Libya, Sudan, Taliban, Al Qaeda), and to halt nuclear weapons proliferation (Iraq, Iran, North Korea).

TABLE 4.1. Selected UN Sanctions

Type of Sanction	Target Country	Years
Arms Embargo	South Africa	1978–1994
	Iraq	1990–2004
	Afghanistan	1990–2000
	Yugoslavia	1991–1996, 1998–2001
	Somalia	1992–
	Libya	1992–2003, 2011–
	Angola and UNITA	1993–2002
	Sierra Leone (rebels only)	1998–2010
	Al Qaeda and Taliban	1999
	DRC	2003–2008
	Liberia	2003–
	Côte d'Ivoire	2004
	Sudan (Militias)	2004–
	Iran	2006–
	North Korea	2006–
	DRC (Militias)	2008–
	DRC (Targeted)	2008–
Export or Import Limits (ban exports of selected technologies, diamonds, timber, etc., or place embargo on imports of oil, etc.)	Cambodia (logs, oil)	1992–1994
	Angola (diamonds)	1993, 1998–2002
	Sierra Leone (oil, diamonds)	1997–1998, 2000–2003
	Liberia (diamonds)	2001–2007
	Liberia (timber)	2003–2006
	Côte d'Ivoire (diamonds)	2004–
Asset Freeze	Yugoslavia	1992–1995, 1998–2000
	Libya	1993–1999, 2011–
	Angola (UNITA only)	1998–2002
	Afghanistan	1999–2001
	Al Qaeda and Taliban	1999–
	DRC (Militias)	2003–
	Liberia	2003–
	Côte d'Ivoire (Targeted)	2004–
	Sudan (Targeted)	2004–
	Lebanon (Targeted)	2005–
	Iran (Targeted)	2006–
	North Korea (Targeted)	2006–
	DRC (Targeted)	2008–
Denial of Visas (travel bans)	Libya	1992–1999, 2011–
	Angola (UNITA only)	1997–2002
	Sudan	1998–
	Al Qaeda and Taliban	1999–2001–
	Afghanistan	2001–2003
	Liberia (Targeted)	2003–

(continues)

TABLE 4.1. *(continued)*

Type of Sanction	Target Country	Years
Denial of Visas (travel bans)	DRC (Militias)	2004–
continued	Côte d'Ivoire (Targeted)	2004–
	Sudan (Targeted)	2004–
	Iran (Targeted)	2006–
	North Korea (Targeted)	2006–
	DRC (Targeted)	2008–
	Iran (Targeted)	2010–
	Libya (Targeted)	2011–
Cancellation of Air Links	Libya	1992–1999
	Afghanistan	1999–2001
Comprehensive Sanctions	Southern Rhodesia	1965–1980
	Iraq	1990–2003
	Yugoslavia	1992–1995
	Haiti	1993–1994

Iraq and the Problems with Comprehensive Sanctions. When Iraq invaded Kuwait in August 1990, the Security Council immediately invoked Chapter VII to condemn the invasion and demand withdrawal. Subsequent resolutions imposed economic and transport sanctions against Iraq and established a sanctions committee to monitor implementation. Following the Gulf War, on April 3, 1991, the council passed Resolution 687, enumerating terms of the cease-fire agreement and a far-reaching plan for dismantling Iraq's weapons of mass destruction. The earlier comprehensive sanctions were to continue until all the provisions were carried out to the Security Council's satisfaction. The only exception was oil sales authorized under the 1995 Oil-for-Food Programme to pay for food and medical supplies.

The Iraq sanctions became highly controversial as they produced a mounting humanitarian crisis among ordinary Iraqis (aggravated by the government's diversion of funds from the Oil-for-Food Programme). Evidence of malnutrition, contaminated water supplies, infectious disease, and high infant and child mortality rates generated widespread sympathy and calls for ending sanctions. The Iraqi government also exacerbated the crisis for political purposes and rejected international proposals to alleviate it. Over time, sanction fatigue grew among neighboring and other nations that had traditionally relied on trade with Iraq, and compliance eroded as unauthorized trade and transport links multiplied. The United States and Great Britain, however, insisted on complete compliance before the sanctions could be lifted and rejected proposals by Russia, France, and other countries to reward Iraq's cooperation and encourage further progress by partially lifting sanctions. The result was a stalemate, since Saddam Hussein was widely thought to believe that the US and UK would be satisfied only with his ouster; hence, he had no incentive to cooperate.[14]

The sanctions were finally lifted in May 2003 following the US invasion of Iraq. In retrospect, former Canadian UN ambassador David Malone concludes, "On many levels, the Program worked: it saved many lives, it drove the disarmament process, and it prevented rearmament by keeping the lion's share of Iraq's oil wealth and imports—which could be used to produce WMD—out of the hands of Saddam Hussein. . . . [T]he Iraqi military and weapon programs had, in fact, steadily eroded under the weight of sanctions."[15] Still, the sanctions created broad resentment of the US and its allies who were seen as the key supporters of sanctions.

Applying Lessons About Sanctions. Sanctions were among several approaches used by the UN in the 1990s to end a bitter civil war in Angola that began in 1974. Next to the Iraq sanctions, by 2002 the Angolan sanctions were the longest in effect, but they had little impact until 1999, however, because there had been almost no monitoring to ensure compliance. That changed when an independent panel of experts was created by the Security Council to investigate sanctions violations and recommend ways to enhance compliance. By mid-2001, the monitoring group reported that arms deliveries were greatly reduced, countries were no longer providing safe havens to officials of the rebel National Union for the Total Independence of Angola (UNITA), and diamond export revenues (targeted by the sanctions) had dropped. Long considered a failure, Angola became "one of the most important developments in sanctions policy in recent years."[16]

The Security Council drew three important lessons from the experience with comprehensive sanctions on Iraq and the experience with sanctions on Angola. The first is the importance of tailoring what and who are sanctioned to the specific situation to reduce ambiguity, close loopholes, and avoid unacceptable humanitarian costs. The second is the importance of monitoring compliance. Third, in intrastate conflicts and failed states, generalized sanctions are largely ineffective against the leaders of armed factions or in an environment absent normal governmental controls over taxation or borders. Since 2000, independent expert panels have gathered data on violators, supply routes, networks, and transactions in conjunction with all UN-imposed sanctions; the Security Council has named and shamed violators by publicly identifying them; and regional IGOs and NGOs as well as private corporations have been recruited as partners in implementing and monitoring sanctions. Still, as one group of scholars concludes, "Smart sanctions may satisfy the need . . . to 'do something,' . . . and they may serve to unify fraying coalitions and isolate a rogue regime. But they are not a magic bullet for achieving foreign policy goals."[17] Nevertheless, sanctions continue to be a major tool in UN enforcement efforts.

Although the UN has used the enforcement powers embodied in Chapter VII extensively since 1990, its conflict-management role before and after 1990 has been most notable in the evolution of peacekeeping and the complex activities related to peacebuilding. Despite the debate over the UN's continuing relevance and effectiveness following the US intervention in Iraq and deep Security Council divisions, there has been a dramatic increase in UN peace operations of various types since 2003. This illustrates the continuing vitality of these approaches to conflict management.

PEACEKEEPING

Peacekeeping, first developed to provide observer groups for cease-fires in Kashmir and Palestine in the late 1940s, was formally proposed by Lester B. Pearson, the Canadian secretary of state for external affairs, at the height of the Suez crisis in 1956 as a means for securing the withdrawal of British, French, and Israeli forces from Egypt, pending a political settlement. Its development enabled the UN to play a positive role in dealing with regional conflicts at a time when hostility between East and West prevented the use of the Chapter VII provisions for sanctions and collective security. Since the Cold War's end, peacekeeping's use has broadened to include a variety of tasks, sometimes blurring the line with enforcement. The UN and some regional IGOs have deployed various types of peace operations to help maintain cease-fire agreements, stabilize conflict situations to create an environment conducive to peaceful settlement, help implement peace agreements, protect civilian populations at risk in humanitarian crises, and/or to assist in laying the foundations for durable peace. With more than sixty operations since 1948, the majority of them initiated since 1990, peacekeeping in various forms has become "one of the most visible symbols of the UN role in international peace and security."[18]

Distinguishing Between Enforcement and Peacekeeping

The UN traditionally defined peacekeeping as "an operation involving military personnel, but without enforcement powers, undertaken by the United Nations to help maintain or restore international peace and security in areas of conflict."[19] Since there is no Charter provision for peacekeeping, it lies in a "grey zone" between the peaceful settlement provisions of Chapter VI and the military enforcement provisions of Chapter VII and is sometimes referred to as Chapter VI and a half. Some operations in the 1990s crossed that "grey zone" and more closely resembled enforcement, creating controversy and operational problems that we address below. Since the Cold War's end, the UN has noted more recently, "peacekeeping has evolved from a primarily military model of observing cease-fires and the separation of forces after inter-state wars, to incorporate a complex model of many elements—military, police and civilian—working together to help lay the foundations for sustainable peace."[20] It has become common, therefore, to distinguish between traditional peacekeeping and complex, multidimensional peacekeeping and peacebuilding operations. Thus, peacekeepers' tasks have varied significantly over time and with the Security Council mandates for different types of peace operations, as outlined in Box 4.1.

The key distinction between enforcement and peacekeeping lies in three principles that guide UN peacekeepers: consent of the parties to the conflict, impartiality, and use of military force only as a last resort and in self-defense or in defense of the mandate. All three have become more problematic with different types of post–Cold War operations, particularly those in intrastate conflicts. In more "muscular" operations, that is, operations with more troops, more heavily equipped than traditional peacekeepers, and with a mandate that permits the use of force other than in self-defense, the line between peacekeeping and enforcement has clearly been blurred, for in many situations there has been no peace to keep, no cease-fire to monitor, and no consent for the mission from the local parties who are not states or include a failed state, such as in Somalia and the Democratic Republic of the Congo. Therefore, the resolutions for most UN peace operations now invoke Chapter VII, not only to provide the legal basis for a range of actions, but also to show the council's political resolve and remind member states of their obligations to give effect to council decisions.

In principle, peacekeeping has numerous advantages over enforcement. First, no aggressor need be identified, so no one party to the conflict is singled out for blame—making it easier to get approval for an operation. This is also why it is important for UN peacekeepers to maintain credibility as an impartial force; otherwise, they can be perceived as favoring one or more parties and become a target themselves, as has happened in several situations since 1990, including Somalia, Bosnia, and Côte d'Ivoire.

Second, in peacekeeping, there is at least nominal consent to cooperate with peacekeepers. Yet consent is problematic when various armed rebel and militia groups operate quite independently, as they do in the DRC. Having given consent, states may prohibit certain actions impeding the operation, as Eritrea did by denying UN peacekeepers permission to use helicopters and land patrols to monitor the cease-fire line with Ethiopia, leading to the UN's withdrawal. Or governments may call for premature withdrawal of a mission (that is, before the mandate has been fulfilled). In two extreme cases, peacekeepers in both Bosnia and Sierra Leone found themselves taken hostage. But one scholar

BOX 4.1. **Types of Peace Operations Tasks**

Traditional Operations

These include the following:

Observation, Monitoring, and Reporting
    cease-fires and withdrawal of forces
    investigating complaints of violations

Separation of Combatant Forces
    establish buffer zones
    use of force only for self-defense

Complex, Multidimensional Operations

The above tasks, plus many of the following:

Observation and Monitoring
    democratic elections
    human rights
    arms control

Limited Use of Force
    maintain or restore civil law and order
    disarm combatants
    demining

Humanitarian Assistance and Intervention
    open food and medical supply lines; guard supplies
    protect aid workers
    protect refugees
    create safe havens

Peacebuilding
    rebuild and train police and judiciary
    organize elections and promote civil society
    repatriate refugees

Statebuilding
    security sector reform (military and police)
    strengthen rule of law, rebuild judiciary
    reform bureaucracy, reduce corruption
    promote market-led development
    provide interim civil administration

warned, "Peacekeeping operations are increasingly being tested by deteriorating consent. . . . [Yet] consent should not be understood to require absolute deference to the wishes of the host government, or scaling back the more intrusive aspects of the peacebuilding agenda at the first sign of resistance."[21]

A third advantage of peacekeeping over enforcement is that most operations have required relatively small numbers of troops from contributing states, a critical factor since peacekeeping operations rely on ad hoc military units, or subcontracting to a coalition of states or regional IGO. The size of peacekeeping forces has varied from small monitoring missions numbering fewer than 100 to UN peacekeeping missions on the Golan Heights between Israel and Syria (UN Disengagement Observer Force, or UNDOF) that remained relatively constant at just over 1,000 troops, to major operations requiring 20,000 or more troops, such as in Cambodia, Somalia, and Bosnia in the early 1990s and the DRC and Darfur since 2004. During the Cold War, peacekeepers were drawn almost exclusively from the armed forces of nonpermanent members of the Security Council, often nonaligned members, small states, or middle powers such as Canada, India, Sweden, Ghana, and Nepal.

Since the end of the Cold War with multidimensional operations, military, police, and civilians are needed. The majority of peacekeeping contingents continue to come from countries other than the P-5, but there has been a major shift in where they come from. Most come from countries in the Global South, with the top five contributors in 2011 being Bangladesh, Pakistan, India, Egypt, and Nigeria. China first made personnel (civilian police) available for the stabilization mission deployed in Haiti in 2004. Sweden and Canada now contribute no troops for peacekeeping. For the much larger operations, the "muscle" of major military powers (e.g., the United States, Britain, and France), with their logistical capability, large numbers of trained personnel, heavy equipment, and airpower, may be needed. In a number of situations, however, the requisite "muscle" has not always been readily forthcoming because states were reluctant to provide sufficient military forces to back up a Security Council mandate and were unwilling to risk casualties when no major national interests were stake. It is not uncommon for the number of troops and police, however, to be significantly lower than the numbers authorized by the Security Council. For example, the joint AU/UN mission in Darfur, authorized in 2007, was still at barely 85 percent of authorized troop strength at the end of 2010. Few UN missions have succeeded in securing adequate numbers of police.

Traditional Peacekeeping
All of the conflicts where traditional peacekeeping has been used have been between states. Peacekeepers' purpose was to contain fighting and monitor a cease-fire agreement until negotiations could produce a lasting peace agreement.

The peacekeepers were either unarmed or lightly armed and often stationed between hostile forces to monitor truces and troop withdrawals, provide a buffer zone, and report violations, and they were authorized to use force only in self-defense. Their size and limited capacity mean that they cannot stop a party determined to mount an offensive, as Israel has repeatedly shown in attacking Lebanon despite the presence of the United Nations Interim Force in Lebanon (UNIFIL).

Kashmir and Cyprus provide two examples of longstanding traditional peacekeeping missions. In Kashmir, UN observers have monitored a cease-fire line between Indian and Pakistani forces in the disputed area of Kashmir since 1948 with little movement toward a settlement. The United Nations Force in Cyprus (UNFICYP) was established in 1964 to monitor a cease-fire between local Greek and Turkish Cypriot forces. UNFICYP remained in place even during the Turkish invasion in 1974 and continues to patrol a buffer zone between the two communities today. The presence of UN peacekeepers and a variety of diplomatic initiatives have failed, however, to produce a settlement of the Cyprus conflict.

In the late 1980s, traditional peacekeepers facilitated the withdrawal of Soviet troops from Afghanistan and supervised the cease-fire in the eight-year war between Iran and Iraq. These actions resulted from changes in Soviet foreign policy initiated by General Secretary Mikhail Gorbachev and also quiet diplomacy by Secretary-General Pérez de Cuéllar. The Nobel Peace Prize for 1988 was awarded to UN peacekeeping forces in recognition of their "decisive contribution toward the initiation of actual peace negotiations."

Traditional peacekeeping is still important in the Middle East where UN forces remain in place in Lebanon and on the Syrian-Israeli border. It was used to monitor cease-fires along the Iraq-Kuwait border after the Gulf War in 1991 and between Ethiopia and Eritrea (2000–2008).

Traditional peacekeeping is primarily useful in interstate conflicts where there is a cease-fire or peace agreement and a limited mandate. Most peacekeeping operations since the Cold War's end, however, have been complex ones with broader mandates, often with Chapter VII authorization to use "all necessary means," and a variety of tasks intended to lay the foundations for long-term stability in internal or civil conflicts. The guiding principles of peacekeeping—consent, impartiality, and limited use of force—still hold, however.

Complex, Multidimensional Peacekeeping

The Cold War's end, the UN's successful experience with peacekeeping in the late 1980s, and its active role in responding to Iraq's invasion of Kuwait increased world leaders' enthusiasm for employing UN peacekeepers in still more missions. Peace agreements ending conflicts in Central America, southern Africa, and Southeast Asia called for new types of missions. Weak state institutions, the rise in civil wars, and complex humanitarian emergencies in the former Yugoslavia,

Angola, Mozambique, Somalia, Rwanda, Congo, and Sierra Leone demanded larger, more muscular, and more complex operations. While troop contingents in such operations have engaged in observer activities characteristic of traditional operations, they have also been called on to monitor the cantonment, disarmament, and demobilization of military forces and clear land mines. Other military personnel, civilians, and police along with NGOs and UN agencies such as UNHCR, UNICEF, and UNDP have been involved in restoring law and order, repatriating and resettling refugees, organizing and supervising democratic elections, human rights monitoring and promotion, and rebuilding the police and judiciary. In four cases (Namibia, Cambodia, Kosovo, and East Timor), the UN has also provided interim or transitional civil administration. (See Table 4.2.)

Many of these tasks are associated with the concept of postconflict **peacebuilding**—which can be defined as "external interventions that are intended to reduce the risk that a state will erupt into or return to war."[22] Of the fifty-one peacekeeping operations the UN has undertaken since 1988, the majority have involved peacebuilding tasks, some of which the UN and other actors may initiate even before a conflict is fully ended. The specific contours of a peace operation whose mandate includes peacebuilding depend on the nature of the conflict situation as well as the consensus and political will among the Security Council members. Regional organizations, including ECOWAS, EU, AU, and NATO, have all been involved in these operations since 1990, often in partnership with the UN (and each other). The task of coordinating all the actors and activities can be a significant challenge. Typically, this falls to the special representative of the secretary-general.

UN missions in Somalia, the former Yugoslavia, and the DRC illustrate dilemmas in peacekeeping operations where there is no peace to be kept; Namibia and Cambodia illustrate peacebuilding missions; and Kosovo and East Timor exemplify statebuilding exercises. The AU/UN Hybrid Mission in Darfur (UNAMID), discussed later, illustrates the effort to combine a regional organization's capabilities with those of the UN.

No Peace to Keep: Somalia, Former Yugoslavia, and Democratic Republic of the Congo. *Somalia.* Almost twenty years after conflicts first erupted in Somalia and the former Yugoslavia, the problems these two situations posed for UN peacekeepers still exemplify some of the major dilemmas the UN faces. In 1992, civil order had totally collapsed, and warring clans had seized control of Somalia. Widespread famine and chaos accompanied the fighting. The control of food was a vital political resource for the Somali warlords and supplies of food a currency with which to pay the mercenary militias. The Security Council was initially slow to react, assuming it needed the consent of the Somali warlords to provide humanitarian assistance, consistent with the norms of traditional peacekeeping. A

TABLE 4.2. Complex UN Peacekeeping Operations (Representative Cases)

Country	Somalia	Cambodia	E. Timor	E. Timor	Bosnia/Croatia	DR Congo	Sudan-Darfur	DR Congo	Côte d'Ivoire
Mission	UNOSOM II	UNTAC	UNTAET	UNMIT	UNPROFOR	MONUC	UNAMID	MONUSCO	UNOCI
Dates	5/93-5/95	7/91-4/95	10/99-5/02	8/06-	2/92-12/95	11/99-7/10	7/07-	5/10-	2/04-
Maximum Strength:									
Troops	28,000	15,900	6,281		38,599	19,815	17,711	19,815	9,600
Police		3,600	1,288	1,608	803	1,229	5,109	1,270	1,350
Observers			118		684	760	235	760	200
Civilians	2,800	2,400	2,482	1,266	4,632	3,756	3,876	3,769	1,126
Military Liaisons				34					
Chapter VII Authority	✓		✓		✓	✓	✓	✓	✓
Military Tasks									
Monitor Cease fire	✓	✓	✓		✓	✓	✓		✓
Peace Enforcement	✓	✓	✓		✓	✓	✓		✓
Disarmament	✓	✓				✓			✓
Demining	✓	✓				✓			
Refugee & Humanitarian Aid									
Refugee Return	✓	✓	✓		✓	✓			✓
Assist Civilians	✓	✓	✓		✓	✓	✓		✓
Protect Intl. Workers						✓	✓		✓
Civil Policing									
Police Retraining		✓	✓	✓		✓		✓	✓
Electoral Assistance									
Monitor Elections		✓	✓	✓		✓			✓
Legal Affairs									
Constitution/Judicial Reform	✓	✓	✓	✓		✓		✓	✓
Human Rights Oversight		✓	✓	✓		✓	✓	✓	✓
Administrative Authority		✓	✓						

small contingent of five hundred lightly armed Pakistani troops (the UN Operation in Somalia, or UNOSOM I) was finally deployed in August 1992 with a mandate to protect relief workers, but was inadequate for the task at hand.

Finally, in December 1992, faced with a mounting humanitarian crisis, the Security Council authorized a large US-led military-humanitarian intervention (Unified Task Force, or UNITAF, known to the American public as Operation Restore Hope) to secure ports and airfields, protect relief shipments and workers, and assist humanitarian relief efforts. The secretary-general also wanted UNITAF to impose a cease-fire and disarm the factions, but neither the outgoing Bush nor the incoming Clinton administration would agree to enlarge the mission's objectives, and the result was prolonged disagreement about the mission.

Despite these problems, UNITAF was largely successful in achieving its humanitarian objectives, supplying food to those in need and imposing a de facto cease-fire in specific areas. In 1993, the Security Council created UNOSOM II—a larger and more heavily armed force than a traditional peacekeeping contingent but smaller than UNITAF and lacking much of the heavy equipment and airpower the United States had brought to Somalia. UNOSOM II, with 20,000 troops and 8,000 logistical personnel from thirty-three countries, included 5,000 US soldiers (as compared to 26,000 in UNITAF) and was authorized to use force when disarming the factions. When 23 Pakistani soldiers were killed in June 1993, UNOSOM II gave up all pretense of impartiality and targeted General Mohamed Farah Aidid for elimination. Thus, the UN became one of the players in the Somali conflict. Four months later, 18 American soldiers were killed by Aidid's soldiers—an episode captured in the film *Blackhawk Down*—leading President Clinton to announce that the US contingent would be withdrawn by March 1994 and that future American participation in UN peacekeeping operations would be reevaluated. UN operations in Somalia ceased in March 1995, having successfully ended the humanitarian emergency (famine), but not having helped the Somalis to establish an effective government or end their internal strife.

UNOSOM remains a controversial undertaking.[23] Although begun at the height of the post–Cold War enthusiasm for UN peacekeeping, UNOSOM's difficulties led to reluctance, especially on the part of the United States, to undertake such activities in the future. It had major implications for the UN's handling of the conflict that broke out almost simultaneously in the former Yugoslavia and of the 1994 genocide in Rwanda. The UN largely ignored the continuing problems in Somalia until 2007 when the Security Council authorized an African Union peace operation to stabilize the situation and, ostensibly, lay the foundation for transitioning to a future UN role.

Former Yugoslavia/Bosnia and Herzegovina. Yugoslavia's disintegration into five separate states in the early 1990s unleashed the fiercest fighting in Bosnia-

Herzegovina, where Muslim Bosnians, Croats, and Serbs were heavily inter-mingled. Nationalist leaders of each group fueled ancient suspicions and hostil-ities; each group's military and paramilitary forces attempted to enlarge and ethnically cleanse its territorial holdings. The resulting war killed more than 200,000 people, produced millions of refugees, and subjected thousands to con-centration camps, rape, torture, and genocide.

Between 1991 and 1996, the Security Council devoted a record number of meetings to debates over whether to intervene, to what end, and with what means in the former Yugoslavia. Initially in 1991, consistent with Chapter VIII of the Charter, the UN deferred to European Union diplomatic efforts first to find a peaceful settlement and then to negotiate repeated cease-fire agreements. The mandate of the peacekeeping mission (UNPROFOR) organized in 1992 was gradually broadened from maintaining a cease-fire in Croatia, disbanding and demilitarizing regular and paramilitary forces, and delivering humanitarian as-sistance to creating safe areas for refugees in Bosnia, relieving the besieged city of Sarajevo, protecting basic human rights, and using NATO to enforce sanctions, a "no-fly zone," and safe areas, as well as conduct air strikes. In short, what began as a traditional peacekeeping mission was transformed into a much more com-plex one involving use of force bordering on enforcement, as explained earlier. The lightly armed UN peacekeepers encountered massive and systematic viola-tions of human rights, a situation demanding more vigorous military action, and very little interest by the parties in making peace.

By late 1992, the Security Council had invoked Chapter VII, calling on mem-ber states to "take all necessary measures," and repeatedly invoked it to expand UNPROFOR's mandate. Yet Security Council resolutions did not produce the manpower or logistical, financial, or military resources needed to fulfill the man-dates. All sides interfered with relief efforts and targeted UN peacekeepers and international aid personnel. UN personnel were reluctant to use the authority given them to call for NATO air strikes. The UN "safe areas" were anything but safe for the civilians who had taken refuge in them. Srebrenica, in particular, be-came a humiliating defeat when UN peacekeepers failed to prevent the massacre of more than 7,000 Bosnian Muslim men and boys by Bosnian Serbs in July 1995.[24] The International Criminal Tribunal for the Former Yugoslavia (ICTY) was established in 1993, but UN members lacked the political will for a full-scale enforcement action against the Bosnian Serbs and their Serbian backers.

The UN's peacekeeping role in Bosnia and Croatia ended with the US-brokered Dayton Peace Accords of November 1995, and UN blue helmets were replaced by the NATO Implementation Force (IFOR) of 60,000 combat troops; these included 20,000 Americans and units from almost twenty non-NATO countries, including Russia. (It subsequently was replaced by a smaller NATO

Stabilization Force, or SFOR, and, in 2005, by an EU peacekeeping force.) Along-side NATO, many IGOs and NGOs have been involved since 1995 in implement-ing different parts of the Dayton Accords and dealing with Bosnia's extensive needs. The UN itself was charged with monitoring and reforming Bosnia's police forces—a difficult task because of the shortage of international police personnel and high levels of distrust among the three Bosnian groups. UN specialized agen-cies have been responsible for aiding children (UNICEF), promoting develop-ment projects (UNDP and the World Bank), and refugee return and resettlement (UNHCR), among other tasks.[25]

The Bosnian experience demonstrates the dangers of complex peacekeeping operations that require greater use of force without the parties' consent and with-out the political will to turn them into full-blown enforcement operations. Since the late 1990s, the UN has confronted similar challenges in a number of conflict situations, including Liberia, Sierra Leone, Côte d'Ivoire, Haiti, and the Demo-cratic Republic of the Congo. None is as complex or as deadly as the DRC.

Democratic Republic of the Congo: The "Infinite Crisis." The UN's involvement in the Democratic Republic of the Congo that we examine next exemplifies most clearly a multidimensional peace mission operating in a situation of international-ized civil war with multiple belligerents, continuing violence, large-scale humani-tarian crisis, lootable resources to fuel the fire, and a weak, failing state. The DRC has ten times more people and fifty times more territory than Bosnia; the conflict there has been far more violent and complex at times. Only after more than five years of fighting (and a peace agreement) did the UN peacekeeping force there reach one-sixth the size of IFOR and receive Chapter VII authority. It has been the UN's largest operation in recent years.

Crises in the Congo have threatened international peace and security in several different periods. The first occurred when the Congo gained independence from Belgium in 1960 and civil order collapsed, leading to a four-year UN peace oper-ation that presaged many post–Cold War complex operations and failed to create much stability. The second followed the genocide in Rwanda in 1994 when Hutu extremists responsible for the genocide fled to UN-run refugee camps in Eastern Zaire, as it was then called, but no peacekeeping force was established to disarm or prevent them from regrouping and carrying out attacks inside Rwanda. The third began with a 1996 rebellion against longtime Zairian dictator Col. Joseph Mobutu backed by Uganda and Rwanda. Following Mobutu's ouster, a wider war erupted in 1998. Laurent Kabila, the new leader of the renamed Democratic Re-public of the Congo, antagonized Rwanda and Uganda as well as powerful Con-golese figures and ethnic groups, leading the two countries to intervene on behalf of antigovernment groups. Angolan and Zimbabwean forces intervened on the side of the DRC government along with troops from Namibia, Chad, Eritrea, and

FIGURE 4.1. Democratic Republic of the Congo

Sudan; the Rwandan Hutu militia; and other militias that supported government forces as well as their own agendas.

Dubbed "Africa's First World War," the 1998–2002 war was incredibly complex, with the various rebel and militia groups and troops from eight other African countries competing for political power and access to Congo's vast mineral deposits. It was also disastrous for civilians, millions of whom were displaced and died of war-related diseases and starvation. A peace agreement was signed in late 2002, but smaller-scale violence has persisted, as has the massive humanitarian crisis, with large population displacements, extremely violent systematic rapes, and collapse of the health and food systems. The death toll since 1998 and 2010 is more than 5.4 million people, making this the world's deadliest conflict since World War II. The economic interests of neighboring states and various militias in Congo's resources have been central to the conflict's persistence and a major impediment to peacemaking efforts. The inability or unwillingness of the

Congolese government to control its own troops has contributed to the humanitarian crisis. The UN force has been tarnished by failure to protect civilians adequately and by widespread sexual exploitation and abuse by its peacekeepers—a problem that led to organizational changes within the UN, disciplinary proceedings, new policies, and training procedures.

Initial efforts to halt fighting in the DRC were led by African countries in the Southern African Development Community (SADC), which mediated the Lusaka Agreement that provided the basis for the UN's initial action in 1999. The Security Council authorized the UN Organization Mission in the Democratic Republic of the Congo (MONUC) as a small observer force of 4,900 designed to monitor a cease-fire. It took three years, however, to reach that strength, and there were numerous cease-fire violations. The situation began to improve in 2001 when the Security Council condemned Rwanda's and Uganda's continuing presence and demanded their withdrawal, while approving changes in MONUC's operation. With SADC and Organization of African Unity mediation, the DRC government and various rebel groups reached agreement in 2002 to form a transitional government, with MONUC tasked to help disarm the militias, albeit still without enforcement power.

In 2003, an upsurge of ethnic violence in Ituri Province in the east led the Security Council to authorize deployment under Chapter VII of an interim emergency multinational force formed by the EU. Operation Artemis was the EU's first military operation. Mandated to reinforce MONUC and halt the rapidly deteriorating humanitarian situation in the city of Bunia, troops from five EU countries were on the ground within a week, but the operation was limited in duration (three months) and scope (securing the situation only in Bunia itself, not the Ituri region). In 2004, the Security Council strengthened MONUC's mandate, authorizing the use of force to protect civilians, assist the transitional government, fill the security vacuum, and disarm and repatriate former armed militias, including the Rwandan Hutu *genocidaires*. It also authorized an increase in number of troops to 16,700—if fully staffed. In short, it took four years for MONUC's mandate to evolve from traditional peacekeeping as an observer force to a complex, multidimensional operation involving peace enforcement and protection of civilians. Although the largest UN operation, not only was the force understaffed for its mission, but with its more aggressive tactics, the UN peacekeepers became targets themselves—just as in Somalia.

Following the 2002 peace agreement, some peacebuilding activities were begun to support the DRC's national unity government: protection of human rights; disarmament, demobilization, and reintegration; security sector reform; and a political transition process, including elections and legislative reform. In 2006, with support of an EU rapid-reaction force and EU funding, the Congo held its first multiparty presidential and parliamentary elections in forty years. MONUC itself was deployed throughout the country during the election period. Remarkably, the elections were considered reasonably free and fair and brought a degree of democracy to the Congo's long history of dictatorial politics. To many, this appeared to signal the success of UN-led peacebuilding efforts. MONUC had also succeeded in ending the fighting between regional and national groups. Living conditions for the majority of Congolese improved, international donors increased funding for the DRC, violence against civilians disappeared, displaced persons returned to their villages, trade resumed within the country, and humanitarian organizations gained access to much of the country.[26]

Despite these signs of progress, however, violence persisted and, since 2008, has worsened in Congo's eastern provinces, particularly North and South Kivu, and elsewhere. The Hutu militias are still active along with various Congolese militias, the Rwandan and Ugandan governments, and the Uganda-based Lord's Resistance Army. Illegal exploitation and looting of the DRC's rich natural resources continue to support the various armed groups, and the humanitarian crises continue, with communal violence and the worst instances of sexual violence in the world committed by militias and Congolese government troops alike engaging in widespread rape. The elections also did not produce democracy or any improvement in the DRC's socioeconomic indicators.

Although most UN member states had hoped that MONUC would be withdrawn after the 2006 elections, the Security Council successively increased the size and mandate of the force over the next three years in an effort to address the persistent violence in the east and continue the various peacebuilding activities. In 2009, MONUC undertook more robust efforts to stabilize the eastern Congo in conjunction with Congolese national troops. These operations, however, proved controversial because of the army's record of human rights abuses and the UN peacekeepers' failure to protect civilians. They also led to tensions with the government and, finally, to a request that the UN withdraw all peacekeeping forces by mid-2011. Under diplomatic pressure, the DRC government softened its position, and agreement was reached on reconfiguring the UN operation as a stabilization mission (UN Organization Stabilization Mission in the Democratic Republic of the Congo or MONUSCO after its French name). The Security Council also authorized the withdrawal of up to 2,000 troops from MONUC's peak number of 18,650 (not including police and civilian staff). The military force remained concentrated in eastern Congo at the beginning of 2011, and further withdrawal is linked to conditions on the ground and joint assessment with the DRC government. Elections scheduled for 2011 will provide a major test of progress in peacebuilding.

This conflict is far more complex than either Somalia or Bosnia. While the UN and other international actors have largely focused on national and regional causes of the violence, there are longstanding local conflicts over land, resources, and political power that need to be addressed. One scholar who has worked in the DRC for extended periods since 2001 has found that the international actors have viewed the extensive grassroots violence as "a normal feature of life in a peaceful Congo" and not as a problem that they could or should address. She faults the dominant peacebuilding culture in the UN and other agencies, along with various Congolese actors; Rwandan, Ugandan, and Burundian leaders; as well as those involved in arms trafficking and illegal looting of DRC resources for the failure of the peace process.[27]

The Congo case underscores the Security Council's difficulty in crafting an overall strategy for dealing with complex threats to peace that include local violence and intrastate and interstate conflict, coordinating diplomatic and military activities rather than just responding to events on the ground and crisis situations, and providing the people and material necessary to accomplish a multidimensional operation's goals. The Congo case also underscores logistical and operational difficulties. Congo's huge size presents enormous difficulties that magnify the cost of peace operations since roads and railroads are virtually unusable, requiring the use of more expensive air transport. The peacekeepers themselves have exacerbated the problems, failing to protect civilians from rape and abuse, engaging in sexual exploits themselves (more than 200 recorded cases since 2000), and participating in corrupt practices. The UN has responded by pressuring the national contingencies to repatriate offending soldiers, and the UN Office of Internal Oversight Services investigated the Pakistani peacekeepers for buying gold from the militias and trading weapons for gold. That investigation proved so controversial that it was finally stopped in order not to anger Pakistan, one of the largest contributors of troops to UN peacekeeping.[28] Longer term solutions include better training for peacekeeping, hiring more women peacekeepers, and changing the culture of impunity that pervades MONUSCO.

Because it is in the heart of Africa and has immense resources, the stability of the DRC has implications for that continent and for resource-poor states and corporations. But it has been of limited importance to the major Western powers, especially the United States. This raises the difficult question of whether it is better to undertake a weak operation or none at all when there isn't the will for a robust one. A weak operation still raises expectations that civilians will be protected and peace kept, but hundreds of thousands have died and thousands more have suffered rape and other major human rights abuses, despite the presence of UN peacekeepers. The operation has tarnished the UN's reputation. UN experimentation with peacebuilding has met with better results.

Experiments in Peacebuilding: Namibia and Cambodia. To understand the roots of post–Cold War peacebuilding, we look at two of the first missions the UN undertook—in Namibia and Cambodia. Both were essentially experiments for the UN in undertaking new types of activities. Both took place in the wake of international agreements.

Namibia. A former German colony (South West Africa) that was administered by South Africa as a League of Nations mandate after World War I, Namibia became the object of intense international efforts through the UN to secure its independence. In the late 1970s, the Security Council approved a plan setting the terms for this with the approval of South Africa and the main Namibian liberation group. Implementation stalled, however, for a decade until there was agreement on the withdrawal of both Cuban and South African troops from neighboring Angola. The UN Transition Assistance Group (UNTAG), in Namibia, deployed in April 1989, had the most ambitious and diverse mandate of any UN mission to that time. It included the supervision of the cease-fire between South African and rebel forces (known as the South West Africa People's Organization, or SWAPO), monitoring the withdrawal of South African forces from Namibia and the confinement of SWAPO forces to a series of bases, supervising the civil police force, securing the repeal of discriminatory and restrictive legislation, arranging for the release of political prisoners and the return of exiles, and creating conditions for free and fair elections, which were subsequently conducted by South Africa under UN supervision. With military and civilian personnel provided by 109 countries, UNTAG played a vital role in managing the process by which Namibia moved step by step from war to a cease-fire, full independence, and political stability. This success led the UN to undertake other multidimensional peace-building missions, not all of which enjoyed the same success. Among them was the Cambodian peace operation.

Cambodia. In 1991, following the twenty-year civil war in Cambodia, the Agreements on a Comprehensive Political Settlement of the Cambodia Conflict were signed in Paris with US, Soviet, Chinese, and Vietnamese support. They included a cease-fire among the rival forces and a UN mandate to demobilize the armies, repatriate refugees, organize elections, and assume responsibility for administering the country for an eighteen-month transition period. In essence, the agreements "charged the UN—for the first time in its history—with the political and economic restructuring of a member state as part of the building of peace under which the parties were to institutionalize their reconciliation."[29]

A small advance mission helped the four Cambodian parties implement the cease-fire. The UN Transition Authority in Cambodia (UNTAC) was deployed in 1992. The Security Council mandate called for up to 22,000 military and civilian personnel. UNTAC's military component was charged with supervising the cease-fire and disarming and demobilizing forces. Civilian personnel had responsibility for Cambodia's foreign affairs, defense, finance, and public security. UN personnel also monitored the police, promoted respect for human rights, assisted in the return of 370,000 Cambodian refugees from camps in

Thailand, organized the 1993 elections that returned civil authority to Cambo-dians, and rehabilitated basic infrastructure and public utilities. According to Boutros Boutros-Ghali, then secretary-general, "Nothing the UN has ever done can match this operation."[30]

UNTAC helped end the civil war and bring a peace of sorts to most of the country, although it was unable to achieve a complete cease-fire, demobilize all forces, or complete its civil mission. Cambodia, therefore, illustrates the difficulty of carrying out all aspects of a complex peacekeeping and peacebuilding mission. Although the UN conducted a successful election in 1993, Cambodia was not a stable state, as UNTAC's mandate had not included building an effective legal system and constitutional process or promoting economic development.

In two other post–Cold War situations, the UN built on its experience in Namibia and Cambodia when it undertook more extensive statebuilding re-sponsibilities in Kosovo and East Timor. Statebuilding can be an even more am-bitious undertaking than peacebuilding, as it involves efforts to create, reform, or strengthen the institutions of government. In neither Kosovo nor East Timor, however, was there a prior peace agreement or an existing state; both were prov-inces of other countries (Yugoslavia and Indonesia); both involved the use of force by a coalition of the willing—the United States and NATO for Kosovo and a UN-authorized Australian-led force for East Timor. And in the case of Kosovo, its international legal status was among the questions to be determined.

The UN and Statebuilding. *Kosovo.* Following NATO bombing of Serbia and intervention to protect Kosovar Albanians in 1999 from ethnic cleansing by Serbian-Yugoslav military forces, the Security Council authorized the UN Mis-sion in Kosovo (UNMIK) to undertake wide-ranging civilian administrative functions in conjunction with a NATO peacekeeping force (known as KFOR); these duties included maintaining civil law and order, aiding the return of refugees, coordinating humanitarian relief, supporting the reconstruction of key infrastructure, promoting Kosovo's autonomy and self-government, and helping determine Kosovo's future legal status. The head of UNMIK, a special repre-sentative of the secretary-general, coordinated the work of several non-UN or-ganizations, among which various functions were divided. The UN had chief responsibility for police, justice, and civil administration; the Organization for Security and Cooperation in Europe (OSCE) handled democratization and insti-tution building; the EU was responsible for reconstruction and development; and the UNHCR was responsible for all humanitarian matters. The Kosovo mission was pathbreaking in its nature and scope.

There have, however, been a number of problems with the Kosovo mission. First, the Albanian Kosovars clearly sought independence, but the mandate called for the respect of Yugoslavia's sovereignty and the protection of Serbs living in Kosovo who wanted to be part of Yugoslavia (now Serbia). Thus, it has been unclear when and how the UN's interim administration could end since Serbia, supported by Russia and others, has vigorously opposed independence. Second, it proved particularly difficult to recruit adequate numbers of police for UNMIK. Third, coordination among the partner organizations has been hampered by different organizational objectives and cultures, and the UN has no authority to impose coordination. Fourth, the economy has become extensively criminalized, with little done by UNMIK to curb transnational drug, organ, and human trafficking. Over time, Kosovars also complained that "the quality of the UN international staff has declined and is constituted primarily of nationals from countries less democratic than Kosovo."[31] All these difficulties contributed to skepticism about the long-term outcome of this international effort at statebuilding.

In 2006, the UN special envoy for Kosovo, Martti Ahtisaari, initiated a diplomatic process to determine Kosovo's final status, which led to a proposal for self-government under EU supervision. This would have perpetuated international supervision and Kosovo's uncertain legal status. In February 2008, the Kosovo Provisional Self-Government declared the country's independence. Despite recognition from sixty-nine UN members, including the United States and many, but not all, EU members, and an ICJ advisory opinion in 2010 declaring that Kosovo's independence was not a violation of international law, Kosovo remains in limbo. NATO continues to maintain troops there, and UNMIK, along with the UN special representative of the secretary-general, continues to hold executive authority. When and how the situation will be resolved and the UN's statebuilding role terminated are unclear.

East Timor. Similarly, the UN statebuilding effort in East Timor that also began in 1999 continues in 2011, although it is hoped that there can be a transition process after national elections scheduled in 2012. Unlike Kosovo, where its future status was unspecified, the UN's charge was unequivocal in East Timor: to lead the territory to statehood.

The UN began its peace operation in 1999 after almost fifteen years of diplomatic efforts to resolve the status of East Timor—a former Portuguese colony seized by Indonesia in the mid-1970s. Violence had broken out, Indonesian troops failed to restore order, and almost a half-million East Timorese were displaced. The Security Council initially authorized Australia to lead a multilateral force to restore order; later it created the UN Transitional Administration in East Timor (UNTAET), a multidimensional mission with a mandate to exercise all judicial, legislative, and executive powers to assist in the development of civil and social services, provide security, ensure the delivery of humanitarian aid, promote sustainable development, and build the foundation for stable liberal democracy. As in Kosovo, the UN's role involved collaboration with other IGOs as well as with NGOs. The task was not easy because there was no road map to follow. Sergio Vieira de Mello, the special representative of the secretary-general who went to East Timor from Kosovo, noted, "We had to feel our way, somewhat blindly, towards [the two-phased strategy of devolving executive power] wasting several months in doing."[32]

Yet despite Timorese complaints of delay and insufficient empowerment, after just three years, elections were held in 2002 and an independent Timor-Leste recognized. A small UN operation continued to provide support for stability, democracy, justice, law enforcement, and external security until 2005 when it was terminated despite Timor's lack of economic development and still shaky political institutions. With riots and renewed political instability in 2006, it was clear that the UN had left too soon. The Security Council authorized the new UN Integrated Mission in Timor (UNMIT) with a mandate to support the state and relevant institutions to ensure stability and security. But the 2006 crisis revealed "the weakness of government institutions, police and military, rivalries among leaders, regional differences, and a culture of violence," in short, in the view of the International Crisis Group, a "failed state in the making."[33] Like most contemporary UN missions, UNMIT has operated with twelve-month renewal; in 2011, transition planning was under way.

Evaluating Success and Failure in Peacekeeping and Peacebuilding

What defines success in peacekeeping and peacebuilding? An end to fighting? A political solution in the form of a peace agreement? A period of years (two, five, ten?) without renewed violence? The establishment of a functioning government? The successful holding of free elections? A democratic state? The completion of a mandate? In reality, because the mandates of different types of missions differ significantly, the answer to the question of success must be linked to the mandates. Also, the various stakeholders in peace operations may well have different standards for judging success. The local population may define success in terms of returning to their homes; troop-contributing states may see success in terms of mission termination; the Secretariat may link it to mandate completion; for the Security Council, success may be defined in terms of long-term stability.

With respect to interstate wars, there is strong evidence that traditional peacekeeping missions reduce the risk of another war.[34] The first UN Emergency Force averted war between the Arab states and Israel for eleven years, and the UN Disengagement Observer Force has kept peace between Israel and Syria on the Golan Heights since 1974. The UN Force in Cyprus has averted overt hostilities between the Greek and Turkish communities on Cyprus, although it could not prevent the 1974 invasion by Turkish forces. There has been no renewal of hostilities either between Iraq and Iran or between Iraq and Kuwait, and for years UN monitors' presence helped India and Pakistan to avoid war and contain intermittent hostilities along the line of control in disputed Kashmir.

Yet experience demonstrates that having international monitors for a truce does not resolve the underlying conflict. Fighting may resume, even with UN monitors in place, especially as the UN has historically been reluctant to condemn states for violations for fear of jeopardizing its impartiality. "This unfortunately undermined the organization's ability to use the spotlight of international attention to help maintain peace," noted one scholar.[35] The tension, however, between credibility and impartiality is a dilemma for the UN, with the Security Council's greater willingness to condemn belligerents and even to take military action against those who threaten peace.

Research on peace operations in civil wars and peacemaking efforts has shown that peacekeeping has little or no significant effect on mediation or negotiation success, while failed peacekeeping efforts have a negative effect on diplomatic initiatives in both interstate and civil wars.[36] Studies also show that UN peacekeepers are most likely to be deployed in the most difficult conflicts, where there is no decisive military outcome, where belligerents have a long history of conflict, where governments are weak, and, hence, where peace is most fragile (if it exists at all). And it is noteworthy that more than half of all UN peace operations have been in Africa, including seven of the fifteen missions in 2011.

The majority of UN peace operations since 1990 have been multidimensional missions charged with containing conflicts, preventing their resumption, and undertaking a variety of tasks to create the conditions for durable peace. Research shows that such multidimensional operations have reduced the risk of war by half, whereas enforcement missions have been more associated with unstable peace.[37] Yet there is a disturbing rate of conflict recurrence within five years, despite negotiated agreements and the presence of peacekeepers.[38]

Precisely because complex peacekeeping missions combine different types of tasks as well as civilian and military components, the assessment of these operations may be mixed. In Somalia, UN and US forces were successful in achieving the humanitarian tasks, but they failed in the pacification and nation-building tasks. Cambodia is regarded as a short-run success with longer term mixed reviews. Likewise, Timor-Leste achieved independence, but the UN left too soon, had to return, and the long-term prognosis is uncertain. The long-term outcome also remains in doubt in several of the African conflicts in which the UN has been involved, including Sierra Leone, Liberia, Côte d'Ivoire, the DRC, and Sudan. Some tasks such as arms control verification, human rights monitoring, and election supervision tend to be successful because they are most similar to traditional peacekeeping. They are generally linked to a peace agreement and, hence, involve consent of the parties.

Studies of various types of peace operations have yielded many insights into the situational difficulties that can affect success and failure, particularly in civil wars. These include factors relating to the conflict itself and factors relating to the mission. Clearly, the desire of combatants for peace makes a huge difference, along with their consent and cooperation with the mission. The number and coherence of belligerents, the deadliness of the conflict, the roles of neighboring states, the presence of spoilers, a coerced peace, and the availability of lootable natural resources such as diamonds, tropical timber, and oil can affect the potential success or failure of peace operations. As one scholar has observed, "If peacekeepers tend to deploy only to relatively easy cases . . . [s]uch a policy would help the UN and the international community to avoid embarrassing failures, but . . . it will also ensure the irrelevance of peacekeeping." In fact, peacekeepers are more likely to be deployed after wars that end in a stalemate, especially long wars, and where there are three or more parties; they are less likely to be where access to primary commodities is at stake.[39]

With regard to factors relating to the mission, the political will of UN member states to make necessary resources available (including sufficient forces and authority to use them) is key. The difficulty of a peace operation's mission as well

PHOTOGRAPH 4.1. Bangladeshi all-female police unit arrives in Haiti, June 1, 2010. SOURCE: UN Photo 438559/Marco Dormino.

as the clarity and feasibility of the mandate set forth in one or more Security Council resolutions are important variables. So are the leadership, command structure, and quality of personnel, including the energy, skill, and improvisation of the secretary-general's special representative heading the mission. The timing of both deployment and withdrawal is critical. Many critiques of the Cambodian mission note the long delay in deployment, for example, reflecting the UN's average deployment timetable of four to six months during the 1990s. The Brahimi Report on UN peace operations in 2000 concluded that the first twelve weeks after a cease-fire or agreement were key.[40] After that, peace may begin to unravel and the parties lose confidence in the process. With improved military planning following that report, the UN succeeded in deploying approximately 6,000 troops each to four operations in Burundi, Haiti, Eastern Congo, and Côte d'Ivoire within a few weeks in 2004.

In multidimensional operations, other factors in success include the demobilization and demilitarization of soldiers; the wide deployment of police monitors along with police and judicial reform; the extensive training of election monitors; gender training for peacekeeping troops, appointment of women protection advisers in missions where sexual violence has been a feature of the conflict, and the deployment of women peacekeepers; and, most critically, continuous political support. Studies have also shown that learning and adaptation by UN personnel both in the field and at UN Headquarters in New York make a critical difference.[41]

Peacebuilding and statebuilding missions clearly take time to achieve results. "Fixed timelines, often designed to reassure skeptical domestic audiences in troop-contributing countries," one analyst concludes, "work only if all local parties are committed to peace and will therefore do worse if the operation leaves than if it stays."[42] In short, there is no formula for peacebuilding and statebuilding. Each situation is unique and requires getting the implementation environment right. The UN and other international actors involved in such efforts have often paid insufficient attention to local dynamics and whether local actors are truly interested in the liberal democratic type of state that peacebuilders typically seek to create.[43] Whereas Kosovo and Bosnia show that lengthy stays do not guarantee success, East Timor shows that early ones almost always link to failure (or the need to return). Sustained attention, political will, and resources are clearly crucial, including the support of neighboring states and major powers.

Improving the UN's Operational Capability

The UN itself cannot ensure that all the factors making for a successful operation are met; that depends also on the commitments of states and, most especially, the major powers, as well as participating regional organizations. Nevertheless, the UN has had to take a number of steps in response to the increased demand for peacekeeping to bolster its capacity to manage a large number of complex operations and to address the difficulties and failures it has encountered.

Improving Capacity: Department of Peacekeeping Operations. Major reforms of the Department of Peacekeeping Operations (DPKO) were undertaken during the 1990s, notably a 50 percent increase in staff, the addition of military staff from member states, and experts in demining, training, and civilian police. Secretary-General Ban Ki-moon restructured DPKO again in 2007, creating a separate Department of Field Support; the two departments then embarked on an ongoing reform process to improve the planning, management, and conduct of UN peacekeeping operations. Many of the suggestions have been drawn from the Brahimi Report. That report called for strengthening the planning and management of complex peace operations, the Secretariat's information-gathering and analysis capacity in order to improve conflict prevention, as well as staff levels. Those changes were essential to prepare for more robust peacekeeping.[44] Some of its recommendations have been implemented, including the creation of strategic deployment stocks and the use of rapid-deployment teams.

Improving Support for Peacebuilding: The Peacebuilding Commission. In various forms and degrees, postconflict peacebuilding activities are an integral part of most complex, multidimensional UN peace operations today. They have also become part of the activities of many UN agencies and other organizations, both IGOs and NGOs. Although no other operations have been undertaken with statebuilding mandates such as those for Kosovo and East Timor, the UN has endeavored to utilize lessons from these and other missions to strengthen its ability to coordinate and sustain such endeavors. Central to this is the Peacebuilding Commission (PBC) created in 2006 to bring together all the relevant actors to address the need for integrated strategies and sustained attention for postconflict peacebuilding and recovery.

The PBC is composed of thirty-one UN member states, including the P-5, top providers of assessed and voluntary contributions, military personnel, and civilian police, and serves as an intergovernmental advisory body to bring together all relevant actors within and outside the UN, marshal resources, and advise on strategies for reconstruction, institution building, and sustainable development. The UN General Assembly also approved a multiyear standing Peacebuilding Fund for postconflict reconstruction to be financed by voluntary contributions and a small Peacebuilding Support Office within the Secretariat. The first two countries referred to the PBC by the Security Council were Burundi and Sierra Leone; subsequently, the Central African Republic, Liberia, and Guinea-Bissau have been added. In each of the countries on its agenda, consultations between the PBC and government identify critical areas for consolidating peace, such as strengthening the rule of law, security sector reform, promoting good governance, and youth employment and specific projects for funding by the Peacebuilding Fund and international and national donors. The fund also supports projects in non-PBC countries to avert the risk of relapse into conflict, help implement peace agreements, or strengthen peacebuilding efforts.

Whether the PBC truly improves the UN's ability to build on the lessons of the complex operations to create and sustain more integrated missions remains to be seen. Peacebuilding is expensive; for example, in Bosnia, the international community expended more than $5 billion in aid for a country of four million people, and still the results are "disappointing," revealing "severe limitations in the international community's capacity to keep and build peace after civil wars."[45] This level of international engagement is unlikely to be replicated elsewhere, especially if the interests of key states are absent. Tellingly, while there are more than 120,000 personnel in fifteen UN missions in 2011, no new mission had been mandated since the AU/UN Hybrid Mission in Darfur in 2007, and "peacekeeping operations, especially the UN's, were under tremendous operational, political, and financial pressure to scale down."[46] UN capacities are stretched, as are member states' willingness to contribute troops, provide funding, and sustain support for those missions.

Many post–Cold War complex peacekeeping operations have also involved major humanitarian emergencies. These crises have called for international responses to human suffering, despite the longstanding norm of noninterference in states' domestic affairs. This triggered debate about an emerging norm of humanitarian intervention based on the evolution of humanitarian and human rights norms, the new concept of a "responsibility to protect," and the emerging concept of "human security."

HUMANITARIAN INTERVENTION— R2P—PROVIDING HUMAN SECURITY

Horrific as some earlier twentieth-century conflicts had been, many post–Cold War conflicts were marked by the humanitarian disasters they produced: displaced populations, refugees, mass starvation, deliberate targeting of civilians, rape as a tool of ethnic cleansing, widespread abuses of human rights, and genocide. In the last decade of the twentieth century, it is estimated that 35 million people faced humanitarian crises. In this "revolutionary decade for humanitarian action . . . the Security Council authorized more than a dozen Chapter VII operations in response to conscience-shocking human catastrophes; regional organizations were seized with these issues and responded; militaries and humanitarian agencies adopted new policies and practices . . . [and]

the lives of literally hundreds of thousands were saved."[47] This marked a sea change, as during the Cold War, not one Security Council resolution mentioned humanitarian intervention.

While the UN Charter precludes the United Nations from intervening in matters within states' domestic jurisdiction (Article 2, section 7), the once-rigid distinction between domestic and international issues has weakened. Because human rights are often abrogated, citizens are made refugees, and weapons are moved across borders, civil wars have increasingly been viewed as threatening international peace, thereby justifying UN action. In April 1991, after the Gulf War's end, Western powers created safe havens and no-fly zones to protect Iraqi Kurds in northern Iraq and Shiites in the south. The UN's intervention in Somalia was initiated for humanitarian reasons, as was NATO's in Kosovo. Other interventions motivated in part by humanitarian crises included Haiti, Bosnia, Sierra Leone, East Timor, and DRC. Yet the UN is more known for its failures than its successes in humanitarian intervention. Rwanda offers the most striking example.

Rwanda: A Failure of Political Will. The UN was still engaged in Somalia when humanitarian disaster on a massive scale erupted in yet another small African country, Rwanda. In April 1994, following the death of President Juvenal Habyarimana (a Hutu) in a mysterious plane crash, Hutu extremists in the Rwandan military and police began slaughtering the minority Tutsi as well as moderate Hutus. In a ten-week period, more than 750,000 men, women, and children were killed out of a total Rwandan population of 7 million. When the Tutsi-dominated Rwandan Patriotic Front (RPF) seized the capital of Kigali, approximately 2 million Rwandans fled their homes in the largest and most rapid migration of the twentieth century. Media reports led to a public outcry to "do something." Yet the UN's experience in Somalia produced a pattern of paralysis, halfhearted action, and then belated intervention, spearheaded by France.

The roots of the Rwandan conflict between the Hutu and the Tutsi go back to colonial times when first German and then Belgian rulers favored the minority Tutsi over the majority Hutu. Periodic outbreaks of devastating ethnic violence gave way to open fighting in 1990 between the Hutu-dominated government and the RPF, based in neighboring Uganda. A 1993 peace agreement led to establishment of the UN Assistance Mission in Rwanda (UNAMIR) to monitor the cease-fire and investigate allegations of noncompliance. Initially, the UN Secretariat saw the violence in April 1994 as a renewal of civil war.[48] Despite the reports of massacres and pleas from the UN commander for reinforcements, in a bizarre move, the Security Council voted to reduce UNAMIR's strength from 2,539 to 270. Four weeks later, responding to public pressure for action and finally acknowledging the genocide taking place, the council voted to deploy

5,500 troops to protect civilians and the delivery of humanitarian aid. Few countries were willing to volunteer troops, however, and the human tragedy mounted, as is graphically shown in the film *Hotel Rwanda*.

Ten weeks after the massacres began, the Security Council finally invoked Chapter VII to authorize member states (led by France) to set up a temporary multinational operation in Rwanda and pave the way for a reconstituted UNAMIR. Only then, under an onslaught of media coverage, did the United States itself finally send in charter flights bearing personnel, supplies, and equipment to aid the refugees (but not the victims of genocide within Rwanda). UNAMIR belatedly established a humanitarian protection zone in southeastern Rwanda in an attempt to ensure the safety of threatened civilians. It provided security for relief supply depots and escorts for aid convoys. Its personnel restored roads, bridges, power supplies, and other infrastructure destroyed by the civil war. The mission ended in April 1996, not because peace had been restored or humanitarian needs fulfilled but because the new (Tutsi-led) government requested the departure of UN troops.

Because it became apparent that Rwanda's massacres were the product of a planned campaign of genocide by Hutu extremists, the Security Council established the International Criminal Tribunal for Rwanda (ICTR) in 1995. Earlier action by the Security Council, however, could almost certainly have reduced the scale of humanitarian disaster. The Independent Inquiry on Rwanda reported that "the responsibility for the failings of the United Nations to prevent and stop the genocide in Rwanda lies with a number of different actors, in particular the Secretary-General [then Boutros Boutros-Ghali], the Secretariat [in which Annan was head of the Department of Peacekeeping Operations at the time], the Security Council, UNAMIR and the broader membership of the United Nations."[49] All agreed that "never again" would they fail to respond to genocide.

As Rwanda illustrated, force may be the only way to halt genocide, ethnic cleansing, and other crimes against humanity. Given their colonial experiences, however, many Asian and African countries are skeptical about altruistic claims by Western countries. Along with Russia and China, they have insisted on Security Council authorization as a prerequisite for intervention. The controversy over NATO's intervention in Kosovo in 1999 led Secretary-General Kofi Annan to call for a new international consensus on how to approach the issues of humanitarian intervention. In response, the government of Canada along with major foundations created the International Commission on Intervention and State Sovereignty to examine the legal, moral, operational, and political questions relating to humanitarian intervention. Its 2001 report endorsed the "responsibility to protect" and set forth criteria for military intervention dealing with right authority, just cause, right intention, last resort, proportional means, and reasonable prospects.[50] Annan himself vowed in accepting the report, "Of all my aims as Secretary-General, there is none to which I feel more deeply committed than that

of enabling the United Nations never again to fail in protecting a civilian population from genocide or mass slaughter."[51] The collective political will of UN members to intervene for humanitarian purposes was first tested in the Darfur region
of the Sudan.

Darfur. Beginning in 2003, the western region of Darfur in the Sudan presented
yet another horrific humanitarian disaster. Fighting between government forces
and rebels from the Sudanese Liberation Army and the Justice and Equality
Movement forced thousands to flee their homes after attacks from government-
backed Arab militias (known as Janjaweed), many seeking shelter in neighboring
Chad. During the next year, the humanitarian disaster grew to 100,000 refugees
and more than 1 million internally displaced persons; estimates of those killed
started at 10,000. Although various UN specialized agencies were active in providing food, establishing refugee camps, initiating a massive vaccination program, and warning of human rights abuses, their efforts were frequently blocked
by the Sudanese government. It was May 2004, however, before the Security
Council addressed the issue, and then it merely called for the Sudan to disarm the
Janjaweed and cease fighting. That toothless action was followed by promises to
aid the African Union's deployment of cease-fire monitors. Secretary-General
Annan pushed for more concerted action, supported by US Secretary of State
Colin Powell, who labeled Darfur a clear case of genocide in mid-2004.[52] With
both China and Russia opposing coercive measures, the Security Council in 2005,
acting under Chapter VII, referred the Darfur crisis to the new International
Criminal Court for action against those responsible for the genocide. By that
time, between 180,000 and 300,000 people had died and 2.4 million individuals
had been displaced, and the Sudanese government announced it would not cooperate with the ICC. The "never again" promise following Rwanda's genocide
again looked hollow.

By the end of 2006, the AU monitoring force in Darfur had expanded to
more than 7,000, but its mandate and capabilities were limited, and it had had
little success in protecting the targeted population in Darfur. NATO assistance
with airlift and training of African troops and EU provision of civilian and military police, funding, and logistics, which began in mid-2005, did not make a
significant difference in the situation, yet were critical to supporting the AU
operation. Secretary-General Annan noted that it was "dwarfed by the size of
the challenge," even with outside assistance.[53]

Finally, in 2006, the Security Council authorized the creation of a larger, more
muscular UN force to replace the AU force, but specified that the force could be
deployed only with Sudan's consent. Because neither the UN nor the AU was
successful in persuading the Sudanese government to accept UN peacekeepers
despite many months of negotiations, the two decided to create a hybrid UN/AU

force in Darfur. Only in spring 2007 did Sudan accept the proposed force of some 21,000 troops to be deployed in three stages, with a preponderance of the forces and the commanders to come from Africa.[54] Negotiations still dragged on for months, with the Sudanese government even refusing to grant visas to the UN team tasked with assessing the possible mission.

On July 31, 2007, the Security Council passed Resolution 1769, which authorized the hybrid UN/AU mission under Chapter VII to protect civilians, provide security for humanitarian aid, monitor compliance with cease-fire agreements, and monitor the security situation along the borders with Chad and the Central African Republic. The force has an African commander and an African civilian serving as the joint UN/AU special representative, taking his orders from the AU peace and security commissioner and the UN secretary-general. The two organizations have set up mechanisms to facilitate communication between their secretariats. The mission, however, was plagued by delays, some caused by Sudanese obstruction, others by the difficulty of securing sufficient commitments of troops, helicopters, and ground support. When initially deployed in January 2008, it was composed largely of AU personnel rehatted, still undermanned and equipped. In mid-2011, UNAMID had more than 17,000 troops, more than 4,000 police, and an international civilian staff of more than 1,000, in addition to local civilians and UN volunteers. (It was second only in size to the NATO operation in Afghanistan.) It has faced major logistic challenges, given the remoteness of the Darfur region and lack of roads and other infrastructure.

Although the violence in Darfur has abated, the conflict is ongoing, and UNAMID has continued to face obstruction from the Sudanese armed forces as well as rebel groups. It has been able to make only a marginal difference in the security and humanitarian situation and faced attacks, ambushes, and kidnappings aimed at UNAMID personnel and humanitarian aid workers; indeed, more than thirty have been killed since 2008. Both peace negotiations and cease-fire talks have been intermittent and unsuccessful as of mid-2011. The situation is complicated by the ICC's indictment of Sudan's president, Omar al-Bashir, for war crimes committed in Darfur and by the independence of South Sudan. Another humanitarian intervention—Libya—illustrates some of the same dilemmas.

Libya. A Tunisian street vendor setting himself aflame to protest police brutality in December 2010 ushered in what has become known as the Arab Spring. Mass demonstrations protesting longstanding authoritarian rule in Egypt, Tunisia, Egypt, Bahrain, Yemen, Syria, Jordan, and Libya in 2011 stirred national and international debates. Yet only one has resulted in an international enforcement action—Libya. In that country, what began as nonviolent protests became an all-out secession and civil war, as the eastern half of the state declared autonomy and factions in the military and government defected from the government ruled by Col. Muammar el-Qaddafi for more than forty years. Qaddafi publicly predicted "rivers of blood" and "hundreds of thousands of dead"; he expressed his willingness to use all weapons available "to cleanse Libya house by house," and he referred to the protesters as "cockroaches," the same term used by Hutus to dehumanize the Tutsi during the Rwandan genocide.[55]

The international community feared a humanitarian crisis out of the chaos. How could people be protected from their own government's violence? How could the large number of foreign nationals from many African states, China, Bangladesh, Egypt, and Tunisia be protected? This time, the UN Security Council was listening. Resolution 1970 (February 26, 2011) imposed targeted sanctions on Libya: freezing assets, imposing an arms embargo, and referring the matter to the International Criminal Court. Citing "widespread and systematic attacks," the council stated that government actions "may amount to crimes against humanity." It stated clearly that Libyan authorities had a responsibility to protect the population, only the second time the council had invoked the doctrine.

Only three weeks later (March 17, 2011), amid mounting violence, the Security Council passed Resolution 1973, authorizing the members to "to take all necessary measures" to protect civilians, establish a no-fly zone, enforce the arms embargo, and permit air strikes and military action, short of landing troops. This marked the first Security Council approval of force on behalf of R2P. The resolution was approved by ten affirmative votes and five abstentions (Russia, China, India, Germany, and Brazil). Russia and China generally oppose UN measures occurring within sovereign states, Russia questioning who would carry out enforcement and what the end would look like and China bowing to the wishes of the Organisation of the Islamic Conference and the Arab League that had called for the Security Council to act.

Like other UN-authorized operations requiring strong military assets, enforcement began with US air strikes designed to protect civilian supporters of the secessionists and the establishment of a no-fly zone. NATO subsequently took over the bulk of military operations, aided by the US military. The authorization of intervention in Libya showed that R2P had gained remarkably wide acceptance in a short period of time, even if it reignited some critical issues and was applied selectively. Yet as the war in Libya dragged on in 2011, concerns even among R2P's advocates grew that it had become a justification for war.[56]

The Dilemmas of R2P. These three cases highlight four essential problems that the UN and international community face with humanitarian intervention. The first is selectivity. Why did the UN authorize a humanitarian mission in Somalia, but ignore the long-running civil war in Sudan in the early 1990s when there was large-scale loss of life as a result of deliberate starvation, forced migrations, and massive human rights abuses? Why did the international community mobilize so rapidly to aid the victims of the 2004 Indian Ocean tsunami yet fail to respond more promptly to the humanitarian crises in Darfur or the genocide in Rwanda? In 2011, the same questions were being asked about the Middle East. Why did the Security Council authorize military action to protect civilians under attack from the government in Libya, but not take action in Yemen, Bahrain, or Syria?

Second is the problem of timely action. International action was too little and too late to save thousands of human lives in Somalia, Srebrenica, Rwanda, Sierra Leone, the DRC, and Darfur. Mobilizing a force takes time—unless one or more major powers (or a coalition such as NATO) deem it in their national interest to act. That is one of the reasons there have been repeated recommendations for some type of small rapid-reaction force available to the UN secretary-general to protect civilians caught in humanitarian disasters. Still, learning from peacekeepers' experience, the best such a force might do is to draw international attention to a crisis and hope that a larger response will be forthcoming.

Third, application of R2P requires political will. When the major powers have no strategic interests, they are apt not to respond, as Rwanda illustrates. When P-5 states have conflicting interests, it is more difficult to apply R2P, and the response may be too little or too late. Both Russia and China have traditionally opposed using enforcement measures for internal disputes. Both Russia and China had economic interests in the Sudan and preferred not to jeopardize their ties with Sudan's government to support Darfur. Likewise, the EU and the US put priority on the 2005 peace accord ending the long civil war in southern Sudan and on cooperation with the Sudanese government in the war against terrorism, resulting in a very delayed response. Islamic countries have not supported sanctions against an Islamic state prior to the crisis in Libya. "Major and minor powers alike are committed only to stopping killing that harms their national interests," a *Washington Post* article concluded. "Why take political, financial and potential military risks when there is no strategic or domestic cost to remaining on the sidelines?"[57]

Finally, R2P brings up the tension between legality and legitimacy. The UN Charter (Art. 2, section 7) precludes UN intervention "in matters which are essentially within the domestic jurisdiction of any state." NATO's intervention in Kosovo to protect civilians from ethnic cleansing was not authorized by the UN Security Council. Thus, technically, it was illegal, but deemed ethically justifiable or legitimate. The Libyan intervention was authorized by the Security Council, hence legal. But was it legitimate? Was it really to protect civilians? As

Michael Doyle asks, "Will the interveners brush aside the restrictions of the Security Council resolution and topple Qaddafi—and thereby discredit the legal authorization of RtoP? Regardless, the intervention in Libya is sure to shape how RtoP is applied in the future."[58]

Regardless of selectivity, egregious errors, and continuing controversy, the very fact that debate has been taking place over the legitimacy of humanitarian intervention for more than a decade now and that the Security Council has repeatedly referred to humanitarian crises as threats to international peace and security under Chapter VII marks a huge change. Not only did the 2005 World Summit endorse R2P, but in 2006, the Security Council approved Resolution 1674, which called for the protection of civilians in armed conflict.

Humanitarian concerns have long motivated advocates of arms control and disarmament who see particular weapons as inhumane or who want to eliminate wars entirely by eliminating the weapons of war. The history of disarmament and arms control efforts is a mixed one, however. Advocates have been highly successful in getting the subject established permanently on the UN's agenda. But Claude notes that "it is important to avoid confusing long hours of international debate, vast piles of printed documents, and elaborate charts of institutional structure with meaningful accomplishment."[59] Still, there have been some notable achievements, particularly with regard to controlling chemical, biological, and nuclear weapons of mass destruction.

ARMS CONTROL AND DISARMAMENT

The UN Charter did not envision a major role for the UN with respect to arms control and disarmament, although Article 26 did give the Security Council responsibility for formulating plans for regulation of armaments. Disarmament had been discredited during the interwar era because it had failed to avert the outbreak of World War II. The Charter had just been signed, however, when the use of two atomic bombs on Japan on August 6 and 10, 1945, signaled the advent of nuclear weapons. This immediately put disarmament and arms control on the UN's agenda, with the General Assembly's very first resolution calling for the creation of the Atomic Energy Commission to propose how to ensure that atomic energy was used for only peaceful purposes. Hence, the nuclear threat not only transformed world politics but also made the UN a key place for pursuing disarmament and arms control agreements. As with all international treaties, the UN is the depository for such agreements.

Although nuclear weapons are the highest-profile issue, arms control and disarmament efforts have also been directed at chemical and biological weapons, conventional weapons, missile technology, small arms, antipersonnel land mines and, most recently, cluster munitions. The primary goal has been to conclude international conventions limiting or banning various categories of weapons; reducing arms expenditures, arms transfers, and sales; and establishing mechanisms for monitoring and enforcing states' compliance. Since the 1990s, an added challenge has been limiting nonstate actors' access to arms and, in particular, preventing terrorist and other groups from gaining access to WMD.

Over time, the UN General Assembly has played a key role in developing arms control and disarmament norms and international law, including the Treaty on Nuclear Non-Proliferation and the Comprehensive Test Ban Treaty. It also created various bodies to deal with arms control and disarmament issues, including the Disarmament Commission in 1952 and the Conference on Disarmament in 1979 to serve as the primary multilateral disarmament negotiating forum. There have been several reorganizations with accompanying name changes, reflecting a debate about which countries should participate in disarmament negotiations. In reality, the most fruitful negotiations on most issues have often taken place outside the UN among the relevant major powers. The recent cases of land mines and cluster munitions have demonstrated the ability of middle powers and coalitions of NGOs to provide leadership for diverse groups of states to pursue arms control initiatives without major power participation in view of "a widespread sense that the UN [particularly the Conference on Disarmament] has become dysfunctional and moribund as a forum for negotiating arms control and disarmament treaties."[60]

The Challenges of Limiting Proliferation of Nuclear Weapon Capability

Even at the height of the Cold War, following President Dwight D. Eisenhower's Atoms for Peace proposal in 1954, the United States and the Soviet Union collaborated in creating an international agency to help spread information about the peaceful uses of atomic energy and to provide a system of safeguards designed to prevent the diversion of fissionable material. The International Atomic Energy Agency was established in 1957 as a specialized agency of the UN. The Cuban missile crisis in 1963 provided impetus for the two superpowers to sign the Partial Test Ban Treaty. They then participated in UN-organized negotiations for a treaty banning the spread of nuclear weapons. The Treaty on the Non-Proliferation of Nuclear Weapons (NPT) was signed by the two superpowers in 1967 and then opened to other nations to sign. It entered into force in 1970. Currently, 189 UN member states are parties to the NPT.

The essence of the NPT is a bargain that in return for the pledge of non–nuclear weapon states (NNWS) not to develop weapons, they will be aided in gaining access to peaceful nuclear technologies. In addition, the declared nuclear weapon states (NWS) promised to give up their weapons at some future time. In essence, the NPT created a two-class system of five declared nuclear weapon states (the United States, the Soviet Union/Russia, Britain, France, and China) and everyone else as non–nuclear weapon states. Although accepted by most states, this two-class system has always been offensive to some, most notably India, which conducted a peaceful nuclear test in 1974 and five weapons tests in 1998. All but five states (North Korea, which withdrew in 2004, India, Pakistan, Cuba, and Israel) are now parties to the NPT. Three states that previously had nuclear weapons programs (South Africa, Brazil, and Argentina) became parties in the 1990s along with three states (Belarus, Kazakhstan, and Ukraine) that gave up nuclear weapons left on their territory after the dissolution of the Soviet Union. In 1995, the UN NPT Review Conference approved an indefinite extension of the treaty, conditioned on renewed efforts toward disarmament and a pledge by the nuclear weapon states to conclude a Comprehensive Test Ban Treaty. The latter was drafted under UN auspices in 1996, but ratification stalled in 1998 when the US Senate rejected the treaty and India and Pakistan conducted weapons tests.

The IAEA is a critical part of the nuclear nonproliferation regime, especially its safeguard system of inspections that provides transparency about the security of non–nuclear weapon states' nuclear power plants—that is, that nuclear fuel is not being diverted from peaceful to weapons purposes. The IAEA system is supplemented by the export control agreements of the forty-four-member Nuclear Suppliers Group.

Although the IAEA system appeared operational and reliable for many years, the discovery of a secret Iraqi nuclear weapons program in 1991—in direct violation of Iraq's IAEA safeguard agreements and its obligations under the NPT—brought the entire system under scrutiny. It also drew the UN Security Council into discussion of arms control issues for the first time. The Gulf War cease-fire resolution (Security Council Resolution 687) created the Iraq disarmament regime with the most intrusive international inspections ever established. To oversee the destruction of Iraq's chemical and biological weapons and missiles as well as production and storage facilities, and to monitor its long-term compliance, the Security Council created the UN Special Commission for the Disarmament of Iraq (UNSCOM). The IAEA was responsible for inspecting and destroying Iraq's nuclear weapon program. The extensive sanctions imposed on Iraq following its invasion of Kuwait remained in place to enforce compliance with the disarmament regime as well as other provisions of the cease-fire.

Between 1991 and 1998, inspectors moved all over Iraq, carrying out surprise inspections of suspected storage and production facilities, destroying stocks of materials, and checking documents. Iraq continually thwarted UNSCOM and IAEA inspectors, removing equipment, claiming to have destroyed material without adequate verification, arguing that some sites were off-limits, and complaining about the makeup of the commission. It severed all cooperation in November 1998, and inspectors were withdrawn. The successor to UNSCOM, the UN Monitoring, Verification, and Inspection Commission (UNMOVIC) was allowed to begin inspections anew in November 2002. Along with the IAEA, it was able "to verify the non-existence of a reconstituted Iraqi programme and rebuff various misleading allegations," only to have its work cut short by US military action against Iraq in March 2003.[61]

The problems that the IAEA and UNSCOM encountered in Iraq mirror the broader problems with international enforcement and with two other states with nuclear programs—North Korea and Iran. As a consequence of the revelations about Iraq's nuclear program in 1991, the IAEA Board of Governors strengthened nuclear safeguards. The Security Council has also been actively involved in efforts to enforce North Korea's and Iran's compliance with the NPT, while ad hoc groups of states have managed diplomatic initiatives. In 1993, North Korea refused to admit inspectors to suspected sites and threatened to withdraw from the NPT. In 2002, it abrogated a 1994 agreement that renewed inspections and expelled the IAEA's inspectors, then withdrew from the NPT, produced additional plutonium for bombs, tested its first device (2006), declared itself an NWS, and refined its missile technology. In response, the Security Council approved targeted sanctions on North Korea (see Table 4.1).

Iran remains a major concern despite its announced intention to develop nuclear capacity only for peaceful purposes. The extent of its nuclear program eluded IAEA inspectors until 2003. Indeed, many of Iran's activities are permissible under the NPT, but because they have been carried out surreptitiously, the United States and Europeans in particular worry that it actually seeks to develop the capacity to build and deliver nuclear weapons.

With respect to Iran (or any other country that is party to the NPT), when the IAEA determines that it is not in compliance with its treaty obligations with respect to full inspections, uranium enrichment, or potential weapon development, the issue may be referred to the Security Council for enforcement action. The EU initially led negotiations with Iran to try to secure an agreement that would bring it into compliance. China and Russia, as well as some nonpermanent council members, opposed the use of sanctions. Nonetheless, in September 2005, the IAEA's board voted twenty-two to one, with twelve abstentions, to report Iran's "many failures and breaches of its [NPT] obligations" to the Security Council.[62] When the council took up the issue in 2006, Iran threatened to withdraw from the NPT and to retaliate if sanctions were imposed. Nonetheless, the Security Council has approved and extended sanctions on Iran under Chapter VII repeatedly since 2006 (see Table 4.1). The 2008 resolution (1747), for example, authorized inspections of sea and air cargo to and from Iran, tightened monitoring of Iranian financial institutions, extended travel bans and asset freezes, and enlarged the list of targeted individuals and companies. Mindful of the lessons from the 1990s sanctions on Iraq, the Security Council created a monitoring committee and clearly spelled out humanitarian exemptions as well as the actions Iran must take for the sanctions to be suspended or terminated.

The danger if the international community fails to halt North Korea's and Iran's nuclear programs is threefold: first, the greater risk of weapons being used; second, the risk that other countries in both regions will feel pressured to reconsider their nonnuclear status; and third, that one or both will supply nuclear weapons to Al Qaeda or some other nonstate group. These risks clearly threaten the entire NPT regime. Similarly, with the discovery in early 2004 that Pakistan's chief nuclear scientist, Dr. A. Q. Khan, ran a secret global network of nuclear suppliers, it became clear that new IAEA safeguard strategies were needed to prevent proliferation, especially to Al Qaeda, which has declared its interest in acquiring WMD. In response, the Security Council approved Resolution 1540 (April 2004), which affirmed WMD proliferation as a threat to international peace and directed states to enact and enforce domestic legislation to protect materials and block illicit trafficking in WMD material—an action that some member states and NGOs thought represented an "unprecedented intrusion into national lawmaking authority" because of its legislative character.[63] The Security Council's 1540 Committee is charged with reviewing member states' reports on their compliance. That 129 states submitted reports by April 2006 was seen by experts as a measure of initial success.[64] The reporting requirement in Resolution 1540 can be a burden on many countries, especially smaller developing ones, yet fewer than 30 states had not submitted any reports as of 2011.

The key difference between the conventions dealing with chemical and biological weapons and the NPT is the acceptance by all parties of a total ban on the possession, development, and use of these weapons of mass destruction. In other words, there is no two-class system. Yet the failure of the NWS under the NPT's two-class system to move in the direction of disarmament continues to rankle. The US invasion of Iraq in 2003 on the grounds that its supposed WMD programs threatened regional and global security appears to have led North Korea and Iran, for example, to conclude that their only defense or leverage against the world's sole superpower would come through the acquisition of nuclear weapons. Thus, the challenge of preventing nuclear proliferation has become more, not less, serious since the Cold War's end. The fear that nuclear as well as chemical and biological weapons could be acquired and used by terrorist groups is likewise very real.

COPING WITH TERRORISM

Terrorism is an old threat to individual, state, and regional security that is now almost universally recognized as a threat also to international peace and security. Since the 1967 Arab-Israeli War and Israeli occupation of the West Bank and Gaza, much of the terrorist activity has originated in the Middle East, from the Palestinians' quest for self-determination, rivalries among various Islamic groups, and the rise of Islamic fundamentalism. Since 1980, religious-based groups (Islamic and others such as Hindu nationalists) as a proportion of active terrorist groups have increased significantly. Of particular importance was the development of Al Qaeda—the shadowy network of Islamic fundamentalist groups in many countries—led by Osama bin Laden that has been linked to the 1993 New York World Trade Center bombing, the 1998 attack on US embassies in Africa, the 1999 attack on the USS *Cole*, and the 9/11 attacks as well as the Madrid, London, and other bombings. The increased ease of international travel and telecommunications have made transnational terrorism less confined to a particular geographic place and enabled terrorist groups not only to form global networks but also to move money, weapons, and people easily from one area to another—thus creating a global problem. Weak or failed states such as Somalia are important because they create gaps in international efforts to control borders and the flow of people, money, and arms as well as to deny terrorists sanctuaries for training camps and operations.

The tactics of terrorists and whether the actions were local or global have tended to drive international responses. From the late 1960s through the 1970s, airline hijackings were a popular terrorist method for projecting a message. Hostage taking has been another tactic used by terrorist groups. The most common terrorist incidents involve the use of bombs on airplanes, trucks, cars, and ships or suicide bombers. Prominent examples include Pan American Flight 103 that blew up over Lockerbee, Scotland, in 1988 and the simultaneous attacks on the US embassies in Kenya and Tanzania in 1998. In addition, although the four planes involved in the 9/11 attacks were initially hijacked, they were turned into lethal weapons of mass destruction in a new twist on the old car-bomb strategy. Suicide bombings were pioneered by young members of the Tamil Tigers in Sri Lanka and then adopted by young Palestinians during the second Intifada, the 9/11 hijackers, as well as groups in Iraq, Afghanistan, and Pakistan. Concerns about terrorist groups gaining control of WMD or the materials to produce them magnify the importance of controlling these weapons, particularly nuclear materials, as discussed above.

International efforts to address terrorism have long been hobbled by the inability to agree on a definition. The problem is "how to formulate the term without criminalizing all armed resistance to oppressive regimes[,] . . . how to distinguish legitimate armed struggle from terrorism and how much emphasis to place on identifying root causes of grievances that lead individuals and groups to adopt terrorist methods."[65] This is often cast as the problem of distinguishing "freedom fighters" from terrorists.

The UN system has become the hub for many counterterrorism efforts because of its global reach, legitimacy, and legal authority, although limited resources and operational capacity mean that a number of counterterrorism activities take place elsewhere. Currently, twenty-three bodies within the UN system are engaged in counterterrorism efforts.

Since 1972, the UN General Assembly has played a major role in developing the normative framework defining terrorism as a common problem (without agreeing on a definition of terrorism itself) and concluding a series of thirteen international law-creating treaties and three protocols. They create norms outlawing terrorist acts against civil aviation, airports, shipping, diplomats, and nuclear materials. The most recent conventions address the problems of terrorist bombings, financing, and nuclear terrorism. Only since the 9/11 attacks has there been a concerted effort to secure universal ratification, with technical assistance provided to countries whose legal systems are weak. According to some experts, the dramatic increase in ratifications since 2001 shows that "the United Nations has been successful in creating a stronger legal foundation among states for institutionalizing the battle against terrorism," with more than one hundred states having acceded to or ratified at least ten of these conventions.[66] None of the UN conventions and protocols on terrorism has a treaty-monitoring mechanism, however.

In 1996, the UN General Assembly drafted the Comprehensive International Convention on Terrorism, but differences about how to define terrorism held up adoption. In 2004, the secretary-general's High-level Panel on Threats, Challenges, and Change proposed a definition and called on the General Assembly to conclude the convention.[67] The 2005 World Summit Outcome endorsed these recommendations, including language that condemned terrorism "in all its forms and manifestations, committed by whomever, wherever and for whatever purposes, as it constitutes one of the most serious threats to international peace and security."[68] This is seen as a major step toward a consensus definition, but still not sufficient to allow conclusion of the convention.

The Security Council began to address the question of terrorism only in the 1990s, led by the US push for sanctions against Libya, the Sudan, Afghanistan, and Al Qaeda for their roles in supporting terrorism. In 1992, the Security Council invoked Chapter VII to condemn terrorist acts and Libya's role. To pressure Libya into giving up the two men indicted for the bombings of Pan American Flight 103, the Security Council imposed travel and diplomatic sanctions, flight bans, and an embargo on aircraft parts in 1992 and 1993. In 1999, after a 1998 ICJ ruling opened the way to an agreement for trial in the Netherlands and for Libya to pay compensation to the families of those killed, Libya delivered the two suspects in the Pan Am case, and the UN suspended many of the sanctions. The remainder were lifted in 2003, but the United States did not lift its own sanctions on Libya until 2006.

Sanctions were imposed on the Taliban regime in Afghanistan in 1999, including an arms embargo, aviation and financial sanctions, a ban on the sale of acetic anhydride (which is used in processing opium into heroin), diplomatic restrictions, and a travel ban. UN members had concluded that it was impossible for the UN to maintain neutrality in Afghanistan's civil war and only the Taliban's removal would end its support for terrorism (including harboring Osama bin Laden after he fled Sudan), its role in the heroin trade, and its harsh treatment of women. The Security Council set up an office for sanctions-monitoring assistance for the six neighboring countries. Although diplomatic isolation was effective, other sanctions did not persuade the Taliban to end its support for terrorism until after the US intervention in October 2001 led to regime change.

Sanctions, then, have been one major approach for the Security Council in responding to terrorism. The global legal regime to counter terrorism also includes several UN Security Council resolutions adopted under Chapter VII authority that impose other types of legal obligations on member states. The first and most important is Resolution 1373 (2001), adopted following the 9/11 attacks. It was unprecedented in obliging all states to block the financing and weapon supply of terrorist groups, freeze their assets, prevent recruitment, deny them safe haven, and cooperate in information sharing and criminal prosecution. It also urged member states to sign and ratify the twelve antiterrorism conventions existing at the time. In addition, Resolution 1373 established the Counter-Terrorism Committee, a committee of the whole Security Council discussed in Chapter 2, which monitors states' capabilities to deny funding or haven to terrorists. In 2004, the council established the Counter-Terrorism Executive Directorate (CTED) to provide it with more permanent staff.

A key aspect of Resolution 1373 is its reporting requirements. The CTED assists the CTC members in reviewing and analyzing reports from member states concerning their counterterrorism actions. In an extraordinary show of compliance, every UN member state submitted a report for the first round, leading one group of experts to state, "Member state compliance with CTC reporting requests has been greater than for any previous Security Council mandate."[69] The reports provide a large body of information on the counterterrorism capabilities of most UN members, but they pose a significant burden for processing. As of early 2009, the CTC had received more than six hundred reports, but it has so far refrained from "naming and shaming" those states that are resisting compliance and no longer makes the reports available to the public. Irregular and delayed submissions of reports by states have increased, suggestive of reporting fatigue. Between 2005 and 2010, the CTED also conducted fifty-five site visits. As these visits have expanded, the CTC seems to be "maximizing the functionality and minimizing the politics, bringing enhanced legitimacy to the CTC's engagement with member states."[70]

The CTED is specifically designed to strengthen the counterterrorism capabilities of member states through technical assistance and training for bureaucrats. It has assisted states in drafting legislation, adapting money-laundering laws and controls on informal banking systems, and provided training in counterterrorism standards. Half of CTED's forty staff members are legal experts specialized in legislative drafting, border and customs controls, and policy and law enforcement. The need for their services has never been greater. In addition, the UN Office on Drugs and Crime's Terrorism Prevention Branch assists states in ratifying and implementing the conventions and strengthening national criminal justice systems.

Resolutions 1373 and 1540 (discussed above) along with their respective committees and professional staff have not only expanded the UN's counterterrorism activities but also shifted responsibility from the General Assembly to the Security Council as the primary body dealing with the issue. In 2006, however, the General Assembly adopted the United Nations Global Counter-Terrorism Strategy (A/RES/60/288)—the first attempt to provide a comprehensive global framework for addressing the problem of terrorism. That strategy is built around four pillars: addressing conditions conducive to the spread of terrorism, preventing and combating terrorism, building state capacity, and defending human rights while combating terrorism. A task force composed of representatives from various specialized agencies, DPKO, CTED, the 1540 Committee, many other UN offices, and Interpol works to ensure overall coordination of activities throughout the UN system. Whether it succeeds in bringing greater coherence remains to be seen. There are clear limits to what the UN can do in fighting terrorism, given its limited operational capacities in relevant areas and nonexistent intelligence-gathering capacity.

FUTURE CHALLENGES FOR THE
UN'S ROLE IN PEACE AND SECURITY

The UN's experience in dealing with changing threats to international peace and security has highlighted a number of lessons that represent important issues for the future. These tie directly to the three dilemmas around which this book is organized.

Dilemma 1: Changing Threats Versus the Limits on the UN's Role

A major lesson of sixty-five years of UN efforts to provide collective security and enforcement, and especially of the peace operations since 1990, is that although international military action (in contrast to sanctions) should be authorized by the Security Council, the actual work of applying force has to be subcontracted to a coalition of the willing led by one or more major powers with sufficient military capabilities. States never have and never will empower the UN with the means to exercise coercion. "The U.N. itself can no more conduct military operations on a large scale on its own than a trade association of hospitals can conduct heart surgery," Michael Mandelbaum has noted.[71]

In peace operations where the line between peacekeeping and enforcement is blurred and the situation requires some use of military force, UN-appointed commanders need clear operational mandates from the Security Council and DPKO spelling out how they can use force other than in self-defense to disarm local militias, deliver humanitarian relief, and protect civilians. More than this, they require sufficient military strength and the continuing political support of member states to carry out their tasks under circumstances of adversity. When UN peacekeepers use force, they give up the UN's impartial position to confront one or more belligerent groups. They also run a greater risk that peacekeepers will lose their lives. Even so, ambitious objectives and substantial support cannot guarantee desired outcomes, as the seeming impotence of the UN force in the eastern DRC demonstrated in the face of mass rapes in 2010.

What is often referred to as the problem of political will of member states has several dimensions. First, it is important to emphasize that as an IGO, the UN depends on its members' support to act. When the necessary political will is lacking, (1) the Security Council may not address or act on a given issue (for example, ignoring the crisis in Darfur for almost two years); (2) member states may fail to provide the personnel, financial, or logistical support necessary to implement resolutions passed by the council; or both. Although much has been made in recent years of the need to prevent outbreaks of violence and horrendous crimes against humanity, prevention is more easily said than done. Member states have been reluctant to provide the UN Secretariat with significant early-warning capability that would aid preventive efforts.

Funding for peacekeeping operations has long been a problem. Observer missions are generally funded from the UN's regular budget, whereas full-scale peace operations are funded through special peacekeeping assessments. Yet member states, large and small, are frequently in arrears, and as more and larger peace operations have been mounted, the financial strains have increased. In 1987, the cost of peacekeeping was $240 million; in 1995, it reached $3.36 billion; after dropping for several years, it passed the $7 billion mark in 2010. Total arrearages in early 2011 were $2.4 billion—with the United States alone owing the largest share.[72]

The recruitment of forces for UN peacekeeping continues to be a significant problem. As peacekeeping demands have increased, military units have been drawn from many more countries. For poor developing countries, there are financial benefits because UN pay scales are far higher than their own (but arrearages of richer countries can make payments slow in coming). The greater risks of casualties, however, in post–Cold War operations made many developed countries more reluctant to participate. This raises "major ethical and operational questions," in the words of David Malone. "The industrialized countries," he said, "need to think hard about their attitudes toward Africa."[73] The possibility of "subcontracting" various peacekeeping tasks to a regional organization, such as the African Union, may seem logical and consistent with Chapter VIII of the UN Charter, but there are significant limits on the capacity of most regional organizations other than NATO. As noted earlier, the EU has been reluctant to make long-term commitments. The Darfur experiment in a hybrid operation has yet to be repeated, and the Security Council has shown no eagerness to replace the current AU force in Somalia with a UN-led force, as was expected. Police units are particularly difficult to recruit in sufficient numbers, and now that the UN is making use of female peacekeepers, it remains to be seen how easily it can meet needs for them.

Finally, the UN's managerial capacity, especially with respect to peacekeeping operations, has been an increasingly contentious issue as operations have become larger, more complex, and more expensive and have involved coordination among military and civilian components, various UN agencies, regional organizations, and NGOs. Although the UN peacekeeping reform initiatives since the mid-1990s have improved coordination and management of peace operations, much could still be done in this regard. Accusations of sexual abuse and corruption involving UN peacekeepers in the Democratic Republic of the Congo highlight the UN's inability to exert adequate control over field operations, despite efforts to impose greater discipline.

For many, however, the most serious issue relating to the UN's ability to address changing threats to international peace is the very composition and operation of the Security Council, as discussed in Chapter 2. Although the legitimacy of Security Council authority is still high, there is widespread recognition of the need for change. The challenge is getting agreement on how to accomplish that not only among the P-5 but also among the majority of the UN's membership.

Dilemma 2: Changing Norms and Challenges to Sovereignty

Although consent of parties remains key to traditional and complex peacekeeping, the emergence of R2P reflects significant shifts in recognizing that sovereignty carries responsibilities, including the responsibility to protect persons. "Surely," Secretary-General Annan concluded in 1999, "no legal principle—not even sovereignty—can ever shield crimes against humanity."[74] Indeed, the UN Charter itself makes clear that sovereignty cannot stand in the way of responses to aggression and threats to peace or states' obligations to meet their commitments under the Charter. International customary and treaty law also limits sovereignty. Thus, Iraq could not use sovereignty as a defense against the intrusive arms control inspections and sanctions after the Gulf War. Nor did states raise objections on the grounds of sovereignty to the extensive reporting requirements of Resolution 1373 and the CTC or the more recent requirements of Resolution 1540 to prevent nuclear materials from falling into the wrong hands.

Changing norms, however, do not ensure that responses to all humanitarian crises and conflicts will be uniform. As the discussion on humanitarian intervention makes clear, selectivity, timing, political will, and legality have been and are likely to be ongoing problems. These issues touch directly on sovereignty, which may justify a state's unwillingness to carry out Security Council decisions or to accept UN involvement in certain conflicts.

Dilemma 3: The Need for Leadership Versus US Dominance

As Kosovo and the US invasion of Iraq in 2003 illustrate, although international legitimacy matters, a sole superpower determined to take action will not be deterred by the absence of Security Council authorization. The acrimonious, divisive debate in the UN about the war in Iraq was widely regarded as raising serious issues about the future effectiveness of the UN, and especially of the Security Council. It was "at least as much about American power and its role in the world as about the risks posed by Iraq's weapons."[75] With the rise of China, India, and Brazil since 2005 and the increased constraints on the United States, however, these fears have not been borne out. And, as the 2011 action in Libya showed, the United States under President Obama has been more inclined to forge international consensus and limit its role in international interventions. Yet a major dilemma for the UN is that when security threats have required more complex and more coercive responses, only the United States, some of its NATO allies, and a few other developed states have the capability to carry out Security Council mandates involving the use of force.

As discussed in Chapter 3, the US record on multilateralism in general and the UN in particular has been one of "mixed messages" throughout the twentieth century and into the first decade of the twenty-first. Historically, the United States was supportive of traditional UN peacekeeping and provided logistical support and equipment to most operations. But as its involvement deepened with more complex and muscular operations, the US has imposed on itself more restrictions, particularly in operations outside of its direct national interest. Yet President George W. Bush turned to the UN after 9/11 for authorization to intervene in Afghanistan, he expended great diplomatic effort in difficult negotiations on a resolution about how to deal with Iraq, and President Obama was reluctant to support humanitarian intervention in Libya until a coalition had been forged and the Security Council authorized action. These actions affirm that even for the United States, the UN has a unique capacity to confer legitimacy. Still, the US military predominance and worldwide geopolitical interests make other states wary of US power and intentions. This has consequences for the US ability and willingness to provide the necessary leadership in the UN for issues of peace and security.

CONCLUSION

Traditionally, international peace and security have meant states' security and the defense of states' territorial integrity from external threats or attack. As suggested by our discussion of humanitarian intervention and the R2P norm, the concept of human security—the security of human beings in the face of many different kinds of threats—has begun to take hold. These concerns are reflected in the discussions in Chapters 5, 6, and 7 about the need to eradicate poverty and reduce the inequalities exacerbated by globalization, promote sustainable development and greater respect for human rights norms, and address the growing security threats posed by poor health and environmental degradation.

Notes

1. For these and other data, see *The Human Security Report, 2009/2010* (New York: Oxford University Press, 2010), www.hrsgroup.info.

2. Martha Finnemore, *The Purpose of Intervention: Changing Beliefs About the Use of Force* (Ithaca: Cornell University Press, 2003).

3. On the role of SRSGs, see Timothy D. Sisk, "Introduction: The SRSGs and the Management of Civil Wars," *Global Governance* 16, no. 2 (2010): 237–242, and other articles in the Special Focus section of this issue of the journal.

4. Boutros Boutros-Ghali, *An Agenda for Peace: Preventive Diplomacy, Peacemaking, and Peacekeeping* (New York: United Nations, 1992), 45.

5. Michael E. Brown and Richard N. Rosecrance, *The Costs of Conflict: Prevention and Cure in the Global Arena* (Lanham, MD: Rowman and Littlefield, 1999), 225.

6. UN, *World Summit Outcome*, A/60/L.1, sec. 81, 22.

7. Two helpful sources are Abram Chayes, "The Use of Force in the Persian Gulf," in *Law and Force in the New International Order*, ed. Lori Fisler Damrosch and David J. Scheffer (Boulder: Westview Press, 1991), 3–11; and Ken Matthews, *The Gulf Conflict in International Relations* (London: Routledge, 1993).

8. United Nations Press release, SG/SM/7263, AFR/196, December 16, 1999, available at www.un.org/docs/sg/sgsm.htm.

9. Adam Roberts, "NATO's 'Humanitarian War' over Kosovo," *Survival* 41, no. 2 (1999): 106.

10. Adam Roberts, "The Use of Force," in *The UN Security Council: From the Cold War to the 21st Century*, ed. David M. Malone (Boulder: Lynne Rienner, 2004), 141.

11. See Michael J. Glennon, "Why the Security Council Failed," *Foreign Affairs* 82, no. 3 (2003): 16–35; and responses, Edward C. Luck, "The End of an Illusion," Anne-Marie Slaughter, "Misreading the Record," and Ian Hurd, "Too Legit to Quit," all published in *Foreign Affairs* 82, no. 4 (2003): 201–205. See also the debate, "The United Nations Has Become Irrelevant," *Foreign Policy*, no. 138 (September–October 2003): 16–24.

12. Mats Berdal, "The UN after Iraq," *Survival* 46, no. 3 (2004): 82.

13. For a set of excellent studies of the "sanctions decade," see David Cortright and George A. Lopez, *The Sanctions Decade: Assessing UN Strategies in the 1990s* (Boulder: Lynne Rienner, 2000).

14. Ramesh Thakur, *The United Nations, Peace, and Security* (New York: Cambridge University Press, 2006), 145.

15. David M. Malone, *The International Struggle over Iraq: Politics in the UN Security Council, 1980–2005* (New York: Oxford University Press, 2006), 135.

16. David Cortright and George A. Lopez, *Sanctions and the Search for Security* (Boulder: Lynne Rienner, 2002), 71.

17. Gary Clyde Hufbauer et al., *Economic Sanctions Reconsidered,* 3rd ed. (Washington, DC: Peterson Institute for International Economics, 2007), 141.

18. Thakur, *The United Nations, Peace, and Security,* 37.

19. United Nations, *The Blue Helmets: A Review of United Nations Peace-Keeping,* 3rd ed. (New York: UN Department of Public Information, 1996), 4. This is an excellent resource on peacekeeping operations up to the mid-1990s. The UN Web site is a valuable resource on all past and current UN operations: www.un.org/Depts /dpko/home.htm. See also the *Annual Review of Global Peace Operations,* a project of the Center on International Cooperation at New York University since 2006 and published by Lynne Rienner Publishers, as well as articles and data published in the journal International Peacekeeping.

20. United Nations, *Peacekeeping Operations: Principles and Guidelines* (New York: UN Department of Peacekeeping Operations, Department of Field Support, 2008), 18.

21. Ian Johnstone, "Managing Consent in Contemporary Peacekeeping Operations," *International Peacekeeping* 18, no. 2 (2011): 172.

22. Michael Barnett et al., "Peacebuilding: What Is in a Name?" *Global Governance* 13, no. 1 (2007): 37. The authors' central point is that the different agencies involved in peacebuilding define and use this term in very different ways

23. For further discussion, see Walter Clarke and Jeffrey Herbst, "Somalia and the Future of Humanitarian Intervention," *Foreign Affairs* 75, no. 2 (1996): 70–85; and Enrico Augelli and Craig N. Murphy, "Lessons of Somalia for Future Multilateral Humanitarian Assistance Operations," *Global Governance* 1, no. 3 (1995): 339–366.

24. United Nations, *Report of the Secretary-General Pursuant to General Assembly Resolution 53/35: The Fall of Srebrenica,* UN Doc. No. A/54/549, November 15, 1999, www.un.org/peace/srebrenica.pdf.

25. See Georgios Kostakos, "Division of Labor Among International Organizations: The Bosnian Experience," *Global Governance* 4, no. 4 (1998): 461–484.

26. Séverine Autesserre, *The Trouble with the Congo: Local Violence and the Failure of International Peacebuilding* (New York: Cambridge University Press, 2010).

27. Ibid. In addition to the time Autesserre spent as an ethnographer in the Congo, she conducted extensive interviews with UN officials, Western and African diplomats, NGO staff members, victims and perpetrators of violence, and Congolese political, military, diplomatic, and civil society actors. She has also analyzed a wide variety of documents, including agency memoranda and confidential reports. Her research, therefore, incorporates extensive original data on the DRC conflict. See also Jason K. Stearns, *Dancing in the Glory of Monsters* (New York: PublicAffairs, 2011).

28. M. Plaut, "Trading Guns for Gold: Pakistani Peacekeepers in the Congo," *Review of African Political Economy* 34, no. 113 (2007): 585.

29. Michael W. Doyle, *UN Peacekeeping in Cambodia: UNTAC's Civil Mandate* (Boulder: Lynne Rienner, 1995), 26.

30. "The 'Second Generation': Cambodia Elections 'Free and Fair,' but Challenges Remain," *United Nations Chronicle* (November–December 1993): 26.

31. Quoted in Andrea Kathryn Talentino, "Perceptions of Peacebuilding: The Dynamic of Imposer and Imposed Upon," *International Studies Perspectives* 3, no. 2 (2007): 163. For an earlier assessment of the UN mission in Kosovo, see Alexandras Yannis, "The UN as Government in Kosovo," *Global Governance* 10, no. 1 (2004): 67–81.

32. Sergio Vieira de Mello, "Message to the UNITAR-IPS-JIIA Conference." See also Sergio Vieira de Mello, "How Not to Run a Country: Lessons from Kosovo and East Timor," UNITAR-IPS-JIIA Conference to Assess the Report on UN Peace Operations, Singapore, February 2001.

33. International Crisis Group, "Timor-Leste: Security Sector Reform," *Asia Report* no. 143 (January 17, 2008): 1.

34. Paul F. Diehl, "Forks in the Road: Theoretical and Policy Concerns for 21st Century Peacekeeping," *Global Society* 14, no. 3 (2001): 337–360.

35. Virginia Page Fortna, "Interstate Peacekeeping: Causal Mechanisms and Empirical Effects," *World Politics* 56 (July 2004): 510.

36. J. Michael Greig and Paul F. Diehl, "The Peacekeeping-Peacemaking Dilemma," *International Studies Quarterly* 49, no. 4 (2005): 621–645.

37. Virginia Page Fortna, *Peace Time: Cease-Fire Arrangements and the Durability of Peace* (Princeton: Princeton University Press, 2004), 283–285.

38. Paul Collier et al., *Breaking the Conflict Trap: Civil War and Development Policy* (Washington, DC: World Bank and Oxford University Press, 2003).

39. Virginia Page Fortna, "Does Peacekeeping Keep Peace? International Intervention and the Duration of Peace After Civil War," *International Studies Quarterly* 48, no. 2 (2004): 283. For other studies, see Fortna, *Peace Time;* Virginia Page Fortna, *Does Peacekeeping Work? Shaping Belligerents' Choices After Civil War* (Princeton: Princeton University Press, 2008); M. Gilligan and Stephen J. Stedman, "Where Do the Peacekeepers Go?" *International Studies Review* 5, no. 4 (2003): 37–54; Stephen J. Stedman, Donald Rothchild, and Elizabeth M. Cousens, *Ending Civil Wars: The Implementation of Peace Agreements* (Boulder: Lynne Rienner, 2002); and James Cockayne, Christoph Mikulaschek, and Chris Perry, *The United Nations Security Council and Civil War: First Insights from a New Dataset* (New York: International Peace Institute, September 2010).

40. United Nations, *The Report of the Panel on United Nations Peace Operations* (Brahimi Report), A/55/305-S/2000/809 (August 21, 2000).

41. See Lise Morjé Howard, *UN Peacekeeping in Civil Wars* (New York: Cambridge University Press, 2008); James Dobbins et al., *The UN's Role in Nation-Building: From the Congo to Iraq* (Santa Monica: Rand, 2005).

42. William J. Durch, "Are We Learning Yet? The Long Road to Applying Best Practices," in *Twenty-First-Century Peace Operations,* ed. William J. Durch (Washington, DC: United States Institute of Peace Press, 2006), 594.

43. Stein Sundstøl Eriksen, "The Liberal Peace Is Neither: Peacebuilding, State Building, and the Reproduction of Conflict in the Democratic Republic of Congo," *International Peacekeeping* 16, no. 5 (2009): 652–666.

44. United Nations General Assembly and Security Council, *Report of the Panel on United Nations Peace Operations,* A/55/305-S/2000/809 (August 21, 2000), www.un.org/peace/reports/peace_operations/.

45. Elizabeth Cousens and David Harland, "Post-Dayton Bosnia and Herzegovina," in *Twenty-First-Century Peace Operations,* ed. Durch, 121.

46. Center on International Cooperation, *Annual Review of Global Peace Operations, 2011* (Boulder: Lynne Rienner, 2011), 4.

47. International Commission on Intervention and State Sovereignty (ICISS), *The Responsibility to Protect: Research, Bibliography, Background—Supplementary Volume to the Report* (Ottawa: International Development Research Centre for ICISS, 2001), 220. The report and supplementary volume are available online at www.iciss-cisse.gc.ca.

48. Michael Barnett, *Eyewitness to a Genocide: The United Nations and Rwanda* (Ithaca: Cornell University Press, 2002).

49. United Nations, *Report of the Independent Inquiry into the Actions of the United Nations During the 1994 Genocide in Rwanda,* S/1999/1257 (December 15, 1999), www.un.org./news/ossg/rwanda_report.htm.

50. ICISS, *The Responsibility to Protect: Report of the International Commission on Intervention and State Sovereignty* (Ottawa: International Development Research Centre for ICISS, 2001), 32.

51. United Nations press release, SG/SM/7263, AFR/196 (December 16, 1999), www.un.org/Docs/SG/sgsm.htm.

52. Secretary Powell's remarks were contained in testimony before the US Senate Foreign Relations Committee and reported in the news. See www.washingtonpost.com/wp-dyn/articles/A8364–2004Sep9.html.

53. Kofi Annan, *A More Secure World: The Future Role of the United Nations,* 41st Munich Conference, February 13, 2005.

54. United Nations, *UNAMID Deployment: Background Fact Sheet* (New York: Department of Public Information, September 2007).

55. Jonas Claes, *Libya and the "Responsibility to Protect"* (Washington, DC: United States Institute of Peace, March 1, 2011).

56. "The Lessons of Libya," *Economist* (May 21, 2011).

57. Morton Abramowitz and Samantha Power, "A Broken System," *Washington Post,* September 13, 2004.

58. Michael W. Doyle, "The Folly of Protection," *Foreign Affairs*, snapshot (March 20, 2011), available at www.foreignaffairs.com/print/67503.

59. Inis L. Claude Jr., *Swords into Plowshares: The Problems and Progress of International Organization*, 3rd ed. (New York: Random House, 1964), 267.

60. Thakur, *The United Nations, Peace, and Security*, 165.

61. Trevor Findlay, "Weapons of Mass Destruction," in *Multilateralism Under Challenge? Power, International Order, and Structural Change*, ed. Edward Newman, Ramesh Thakur, and John Tirman (New York: UN University Press, 2006), 228.

62. Mark Landler, "Nuclear Agency Votes to Report Iran to U.N. Security Council for Treaty Violations," *New York Times*, September 25, 2005.

63. Thakur, *The United Nations, Peace, and Security*, 169. On the legislative character, see also Ian Johnstone, "The Security Council as Legislature," in *The UN Security Council and the Politics of International Authority*, ed. Bruce Cronin and Ian Hurd (New York: Routledge, 2008), 80–104.

64. Olivia Bosch and Peter van Ham, "UNSCR 1540: Its Future and Contribution to Global Non-Proliferation and Counter-Terrorism," in *Global Non-Proliferation and Counter-Terrorism: The Impact of UNSCR 1540*, ed. Olivia Bosch and Peter van Ham (London: Chatham, 2007), 212.

65. M. J. Peterson, "Using the General Assembly," in *Terrorism and the UN: Before and After September 11*, ed. Jane Boulden and Thomas G. Weiss (Bloomington: Indiana University Press, 2004), 178.

66. David Cortright et al., "Global Cooperation Against Terrorism: Evaluating the United Nations Counter-Terrorism Committee," in *Uniting Against Terror: Cooperative Nonmilitary Responses to the Global Terrorist Threat*, ed. David Cortright and George Lopez (Cambridge: MIT Press, 2007), 27.

67. See the High-level Panel's report, *A More Secure World*, www.un.org/secure world/.

68. 2005 World Summit Outcome, General Assembly A/60/L.1, section 81, www.un-ngls.org/un-summit-FINAL-DOC.pdf.

69. Cortright et al., "Global Cooperation Against Terror," 29.

70. J. Cockayne, A. Millar, and J. Ipe, "An Opportunity for Renewal: Revitalizing the United Nations Counterterrorism Program," *Center for Global Counterterrorism Cooperation* (September 2010), available at www.globalct.org/resources_publications.php.

71. Michael Mandelbaum, "The Reluctance to Intervene," *Foreign Policy*, no. 93 (Summer 1994): 11.

72. See www.globalpolicy.org/finance/tables/inxpckp.htm.

73. David M. Malone, "Conclusion," in *The UN Security Council: From the Cold War to the 21st Century*, ed. David M. Malone (Boulder: Lynne Rienner, 2004), 640.

74. Kofi Annan, *Annual Report of the Secretary-General to the General Assembly*, SG/SM7136 GA/9596 (September 20, 1999).

75. Jane Boulden and Thomas G. Weiss, "Whither Terrorism and the United Nations?" in *Terrorism and the UN: Before and After September 11*, ed. Jane Boulden and Thomas G. Weiss (Bloomington: Indiana University Press, 2004), 17.

5

Economic Development and Sustainability

A world not advancing towards the Millennium Development Goals will not be a world at peace. And a world awash in violence and conflict will have little chance of achieving the goals. . . . We need to consider whether the United Nations itself is well-suited to the challenges ahead.

—Kofi Annan, Message to the Conference on Global Economic Governance and Challenges of Multilateralism, Dhaka, January 17, 2004

Since the UN's founding, fundamental changes have taken place in international economic relations and in understandings of development. The global economy has been reshaped by many dichotomies, including globalization tempered by state fragmentation, unprecedented wealth in some locations coupled with the deepening of poverty in others, and major advances in technology complicated by the unanticipated, sometimes unwanted, consequences of technological advancement.

The paradigms used to explain these global economic trends are also changing. Where once development was conceived largely in terms of national economic growth and measured by changes in aggregate and per capita income, a more holistic view has emerged in the broad concept of **human development**: the notion that the general improvement in human well-being and **poverty alleviation** is a primary development objective—an objective that cannot be reached by increasing gross national product (GNP) alone. Much of the activity related to managing international economic relations more generally has taken place historically in what are called the **Bretton Woods institutions** (the World Bank, International Monetary Fund, and General Agreement on Tariffs and Trade, now the World Trade Organization) and, since the mid-1970s, in the Group of 7, which is composed of the major industrialized countries, not in the UN. And, although the World Bank and IMF are UN specialized agencies, they have traditionally operated largely outside the UN system. Nonetheless, the UN and UN-sponsored global conferences have provided much of the intellectual leadership in developing key ideas and frameworks for thinking about development, and UN programs and the specialized agencies have undertaken major development tasks and worked with other actors in partnerships for development.

THE ORGANIZATION OF THE UN SYSTEM FOR PROMOTING ECONOMIC DEVELOPMENT

The UN Charter

The UN Charter's provisions on economic and social development reflected a liberal vision of building institutions and programs to promote prosperity and peace through international cooperation and industrial change. These were also strongly influenced by European social democracy and the American New Deal of the 1930s that envisioned expanding the role of government to deal with social and economic problems. Thus, achieving "international co-operation in solving international problems of an economic, social, cultural, or humanitarian character" is among the provisions of Chapter I and is described in Article 55 as "necessary for peaceful and friendly relations among nations." Yet the specific provisions for carrying out this broad mandate are limited, particularly when contrasted with the extensive sections on managing threats to international peace and security.

In Article 13, the General Assembly is given responsibility for providing general direction, coordination, and supervision for economic and social activities through its Second Committee. Chapter X empowers ECOSOC specifically to undertake studies and prepare reports, make recommendations, prepare conventions, convene conferences, create specialized agencies, and make recommendations for their coordination. And, as discussed in Chapter 2, the founders of the UN envisaged that the specialized agencies affiliated with the UN would play key roles in carrying out operational activities aimed at economic and social advancement, coordinated through ECOSOC. One group of scholars describes ECOSOC as "something of a mailbox between the General Assembly and the rest of the socioeconomic agencies."[1]

Indeed, there was never the expectation that economic activities would be centralized in an "economic security council." Instead, authority on economic issues was dispersed all over the UN system. One could argue that the very characteristics of the issue area of economics—many subissues affecting everyone differently—mean that authority will always be divided and should be, just as it is in most national governments.[2] Over time, the UN has established organizations to address various economic issues and developed several approaches to fulfilling the operational side of its mandate to promote economic and social advancement. These include the commitment to technical assistance; educational and training programs; the creation of regional commissions to decentralize planning and programs; information-gathering, especially by the functional commissions; setting international goals for development; the work of the Bretton Woods institutions; seeking to redress the imbalance in less developed countries' international trade relationships; and the activities of various specialized agencies and programs as well as partnerships with other international organizations and NGOs in promotion of development.

UN Approaches to Development

Technical Assistance and the UN Development Program. In the late 1940s, experts realized that less developed countries lacked the necessary capital for infrastructure development. Discussion on how investment could be channeled grew out of a 1948 General Assembly mandate and US president Harry Truman's 1949 inaugural address. The World Bank, which had already been established, was concentrating on the rehabilitation of war-torn Europe; its strict terms made borrowing problematic for developing countries. Debate between the developed and developing countries was intense, with the latter arguing for a large fund to finance all types of investment, while the former envisaged a much smaller fund to establish research institutes, finance regional training centers, conduct natural resources surveys, and support other preinvestment projects.

The developed countries won the debate. What emerged in 1950 was the UN Expanded Programme of Technical Assistance (EPTA), which, by later in the same decade, had become the primary UN development agency.[3] Through that program, the UN awarded fellowships for advanced training, supplied equipment for training purposes, and provided project experts recruited from around the world. Many projects were jointly funded by the UN and the specialized agencies, such as WHO, the FAO, UNESCO, or one of the regional economic commissions discussed below. EPTA pioneered the approach of asking governments to review their needs and develop plans and administrative machinery for country programs to establish the principle of country owner-ship and control. Today, regular UN budget funds for technical assistance are frequently augmented by voluntary contributions from member states. This development assistance consists of grant aid, not loans; hence, it does not cre-ate future burdens for recipient countries.

In 1965, the General Assembly approved the new United Nations Develop-ment Programme (UNDP) to enhance coordination of the various types of tech-nical assistance programs within the UN system. As noted above, UNDP reports to the UN General Assembly, not ECOSOC—illustrating again the decentral-ized UN approach. And over the years, UNDP itself has become more decen-tralized. One scholar who has conducted extensive field observations of UNDP's work describes UNDP as a "decentralized complex of relatively autonomous (and creative) people and organizations involving independent experts, short-term alliances, and joint projects."[4]

Working in 166 countries, UNDP's contribution can be seen in three areas. First, UNDP focuses UN activities in recipient countries through a resident representative. These representatives are expected to assess local needs and pri-orities, coordinate technical assistance programs, serve as representatives for some of the specialized agencies, and generally link the United Nations with the recipient government. Although the resident representative positions have grown in significance, the resources at their disposal are still dwarfed by those of the World Bank and major bilateral aid donors, let alone private investors. This limits their power to coordinate country-based activities. And the relative autonomy of the specialized agencies makes coordination even more difficult.

Second, UNDP has played an important role in developing and institutional-izing core development ideas. Among the most influential is the annual publi-cation of the *Human Development Report*, beginning in 1990. The reports call attention to new development dimensions and new policies and provide annual updates of the Human Development Index (HDI) for all countries. Based on a composite of indicators for health, education, and income, the HDI helps deci-sionmakers set priorities for development assistance. In addition, UNDP en-courages and supports national and regional reports on human development, thus enabling specific countries and groups to choose additional culturally ap-propriate indicators for both economic development and political governance. The most well known of these regional reports is the *Arab Human Develop-ment Report*, published annually since 2002. The 2004 edition was particularly noteworthy for singling out repressive Arab governments as responsible for the poor development record in the region.[5] Thus, over time UNDP has acquired a "special voice and pulpit and authority to develop alternative ideas."[6]

Third, UNDP's expanded mission calls for stimulating institutional capacities not just in states, its original focus, but within civil society organizations, regional institutions, and other stakeholders. This broad-based institutional focus is consistent with the idea that institutions are critical for sustainability and that partnerships among institutions are necessary. Thus, UNDP provides technical assistance in collaboration with other donors and supports various state and civil society activities.

Regional Commissions. One key ECOSOC innovation was the establishment of regional economic commissions. In 1947, two of what became a network of five regional commissions were formed: the Economic Commission for Europe (ECE) and the Economic Commission for Asia and the Far East (renamed in the 1970s the Economic and Social Commission for Asia and the Pacific, or ESCAP, after the Commission for Western Asia was formed). Shortly thereafter, in 1948, the Economic Commission for Latin America (ECLA) came into being, and ten years later, the Economic Commission for Africa (ECA) was formed. These commissions are designed to stimulate independent regional approaches to development with studies and initiatives to promote regional projects. In both 1977 and 1979, the UN General Assembly expanded the tasks of the commissions to become coordinating agencies for intersectoral, subregional, regional, and interregional UN-related projects.[7]

The UN's regional approach has met with considerable success in articulating new approaches to economic development and in promoting regional and subregional institutions. The European commission under the leadership of the Swedish development economist Gunnar Myrdal provided early impetus to European integration. The Latin American group played an important role during the 1950s in critiquing the liberal economic model's applicability to dependent states. Under the leadership of Raul Prebisch, ECLA encouraged states to adopt import substitution policies to escape economic dependency. Many of its ideas formed the theoretical basis for the New International Economic Order proposals of the 1970s, especially in the area of commodity policy. The Economic Commission for Africa in the late 1960s helped draw attention to women's roles in development when it organized the first regional workshop on the topic. And the ECA through its role in the Lagos Plan of Action for Economic Development of Africa, 1980–2000, spearheaded an alternative economic view with its goals of self-reliance, sustainability, and democratizing the development process.

In terms of institution building, the regional commissions have been responsible for laying the groundwork for a plethora of other regional arrangements, either by directly proposing a new institution, giving financial impetus to new organizations, or actively supporting their creation. ECLA contributed to the establishment of the Central American Common Market (CACM) and the Inter-American Development Bank (IDB), pushing regional industrialization projects. ECA was instrumental in support of the African Development Bank.

Sometimes, the success of those regional organizations, such as ASEAN, has led to a weakening of the regional commission. ESCAP has become less powerful, more ceremonial, and turned its attention away from economic issues.

All the commissions produce high-quality economic surveys of their respective regions, as well as country plans used by national governments and other multilateral institutions. All address the diverse issues of trade, industry, energy, and transportation. Yet disputes among members, such as Arab versus non-Arab states in the Commission for Western Asia, and the lack of resources and expertise in Africa have hampered the work of some commissions.

Information-Gathering: The Functional Commissions. The functional commissions reporting to ECOSOC cover a wide range of responsibilities, but among their most important is gathering, analyzing, and disseminating different types of information. Several have played instrumental roles in development. Here we focus on the Statistical Commission, while the Commission on the Status of Women is discussed below. Two are discussed in later chapters—the now defunct Commission on Human Rights (Chapter 6) and the Commission on Sustainable Development (Chapter 7). The work of the Commission on Transnational Corporations has since been incorporated into UNCTAD.

The UN's seminal role in the evolution of development thinking owed much to what in the late 1940s and 1950s was a very small community of development scholars as well as to the organization's growing research capacity. That included new ways of measuring and quantifying different types of indicators for development. Creating that statistical system was, in the words of one scholar, "one of the great and mostly unsung successes of the UN Organization."[8]

Beginning in 1945, the UN Statistical Commission worked to set international standards for gathering and reporting statistics. In the early years, this meant establishing standards for national accounts, for example. Then, as new ideas permeated the system, various UN agencies recognized the need to collect data that had not previously been collected by member states, let alone analyzed and disseminated worldwide. This included trends in world trade, population growth, food, and industrial production.

In the 1970s and 1980s, the UN emphasis turned to standardizing social statistics on such issues as fertility, hunger, and nutrition. As more attention was being paid to the roles of women in development and the status of women generally, there was a recognized need to collect data by gender. As a result, the UN Commission on the Status of Women compiled and published *The World's Women: Trends and Statistics, 1970–1990*, the first such compilation—an invaluable resource that is updated every five years.[9] In addition to the HDI developed by UNDP in the early 1990s, several other indexes have since been developed, including the Gender Development Index, the Gender Empowerment Measure, the Human Poverty Index, and the Worldwide Governance Indicators. The latter is unique because it measures dimensions of governance, including accountability, political stability, effectiveness, rule of law, and control of corruption.

In short, the information-gathering and analyses undertaken by various UN agencies, including the Statistical Commission, are critical for member states' development planning and for UN policy debates. They have also contributed to another major approach: setting goals.

Setting Goals. By the early 1960s, decolonization had produced the demographic shift in UN membership that dramatically changed the focus of the organization's agenda. With a push from President John F. Kennedy's address to the General Assembly in 1961, that body proclaimed the 1960s as the "United Nations Development Decade." This marked a new role: setting internationally agreed upon goals and targets as a way of mobilizing support for the steps both developed and developing nations needed to take to accelerate progress. The first decade succeeded in spurring attention to development issues, adoption of national planning as a development tool, new studies of links between trade and development, and efforts to increase capacity to adapt science and technology to developing countries' needs. In addition, it saw the creation of new institutions, including UNDP, the World Food Programme, the United Nations Conference on Trade and Development, and the United Nations Industrial Development Organization.

The first development decade was followed by three subsequent decades. In each, there were clearly articulated goals: targets for annual aid to developing states and targets for increases in the average annual growth rates of developing countries, as well as their exports, domestic savings, and agricultural production.

The development decades, however, are not the only examples of UN goal setting to provide guidelines for economic and social development. Other goals have included the eradication of smallpox, expansion of education, reductions in child mortality, increases in life expectancy, and expansion of development. Significant progress has been achieved for many goals in many countries, and the goal of smallpox was completely achieved. Not surprisingly, the greatest shortfalls have been in sub-Saharan Africa and the least-developed countries. One group of analysts notes that "expectations about performance in the 1960s raised the stakes in later decades, and economic performance increasingly fell below the more ambitious economic targets."[10]

The most recent UN goal-setting initiative involves the Millennium Development Goals established in 2000. They constitute a new approach—one that endeavors to bring together much of what has been learned over the past sixty years of development efforts and one that for the first time ever brought together all parts of the UN system. For that reason, they are discussed separately below. Some of the most important UN system economic activities, however, especially in terms of leadership and funding, are found in the Bretton Woods institutions, which have long been viewed as outside the UN system.

The Bretton Woods Institutions. The origins of the Bretton Woods institutions can be found in the worldwide Great Depression of the 1930s, predating the founding of the UN itself. Not only were millions of people impoverished, but the prices of most raw materials also plummeted, causing the people in Europe's African and Asian colonies and the independent countries of Latin America to suffer. Countries adopted "beggar thy neighbor" policies, raising barriers to imports and causing world trade to collapse. With that collapse, US and British economists realized that international institutions were needed to help countries with balance-of-payments difficulties, provide stable exchange rates and economic assistance, and promote nondiscrimination in and reciprocal lowering of barriers to trade. The lesson was confirmed by the realization in 1944–1945 that recovery and rebuilding after World War II would require more capital than war-ravaged countries alone could expect to provide. Hence, in 1944, a meeting at Bretton Woods established the International Bank for Reconstruction and Development (IBRD), the International Monetary Fund, and a nascent trade arrangement. When the UN was subsequently established, these institutions became specialized UN agencies reporting to ECOSOC. Yet having overwhelming economic resources and a high degree of legal autonomy, they have become the centerpiece of multilateral development and economic cooperation.

   The International Bank for Reconstruction and Development, or World Bank. The World Bank's initial task was to facilitate reconstruction in post–World War II Europe. In fact, because the task proved so great, the United States financed the bulk of it bilaterally through the European Recovery Program (or Marshall Plan) rather than multilaterally through the bank. During the 1950s, the bank shifted focus from reconstruction to development. Unlike the UN, where member assessments provide the financing, the bank generates capital funds largely from the international financial markets and, to a lesser extent, from member states. Unlike the UN, which offers grants, the bank lends money at market interest rates to states for major economic development projects. Its lending is not designed to replace private capital but to facilitate its operation by funding projects that private banks would not support, such as infrastructure (dams, bridges, highways), primary education, and health. Unlike private banks, the World Bank attaches conditions to its loans in the form of policy changes it would like to see states make to promote economic development and alleviate poverty.

To aid the World Bank in meeting the needs of developing countries, the International Finance Corporation (IFC) and the International Development Association (IDA) were created in 1956 and 1960, respectively. IDA provides capital to the poorest countries, usually in the form of no-interest ("soft" or concessional) loans with long repayment schedules (fifty years), to allow the least-developed countries more time to reach "takeoff," sustain growth, and hence develop economically. Such funds have to be continually "replenished" or added to by major donor countries. The creation of IDA was a direct response to pressure from the developing countries for concessional loans. The IFC provides loans to promote the growth of private enterprises in developing countries. In 1988, the Multilateral Investment Guarantee Agency (MIGA) was added to the World Bank group. This agency's goal—to augment the flow of private equity capital to less developed countries—is met by insuring investments against losses. Such losses may include expropriation, government currency restrictions, and losses stemming from civil war or ethnic conflict. The World Bank family of institutions now also incorporates the International Centre for Settlement of Investment Disputes (ICSID). Like the UN, the bank group has added new institutions and mechanisms to meet new needs and to service new approaches to economic development. The World Bank, like the other development organizations, the UN itself, and major donor governments, provides funding for development projects, working with both governments and other donors to establish priorities. What the bank has funded, whom those funds are given to, and the conditions attached have changed over time, reflecting new thinking about development itself.

During the 1950s and early 1960s, the emphasis was on funding major infrastructural projects, with funds allocated only to governments; such projects (dams, hydroelectric plants, highways, airports) were viewed as vital to jump-start the development process. There was in the later 1960s and early 1970s a move to fund projects meeting **basic human needs**, programs in education, the social sectors, and health. And beginning in the 1980s, the bank moved to support private-sector participation and greater NGO voice and participation in projects. With the bank and its sister institution, the IMF, the bank pushed a staunchly neoliberal economic agenda of **privatization**, opening markets for capital and trade flow, and **structural adjustment programs**, as explained below.

While the UN itself was increasingly marginalized in economic matters, it continued to serve as a forum for critics of the effects of these priorities. And it offered new ideas and approaches. Most notable were the linkages between women and development and between the environment and development and poverty alleviation, as shown below. Thus, by the 1990s, when the bank added environmentally sustainable development, good governance, and poverty alleviation to its priorities, it was the result of influences from elsewhere within the UN system as well as from NGOs.[11] Though their initial mandates differed, the bank now works closely with the IMF.

The International Monetary Fund. The IMF's chief function at the outset was to stabilize currency exchange rates by providing short-term loans for member states with "temporary" **balance-of-payments** difficulties. Funds to meet such needs were contributed by members according to quotas negotiated every five years and payable both in gold and in local currency. Members could borrow up to the amount they had contributed. Stable currency values and currency convertibility facilitate trade, and trade was viewed as a critical engine for development. At the outset, it was thought that states' balance-of-payments shortfalls would be temporary, and the IMF was to fill the gap.

Increasingly, developing states were experiencing long-term structural economic problems, plagued by persistent high debts and continual balance-of-payments disequilibrium. States could not develop under those conditions. Thus, beginning with the 1982 Mexican debt crisis, the IMF took on the role of intermediary in negotiations between creditors and debtor countries, and also became involved in dictating policy changes as conditions of lending. The IMF came to believe, as did the World Bank, that such changes were essential prerequisites to development. As a result, although the IMF was never intended to be a development institution, its responsibilities have increasingly overlapped with those of the bank and its activities extended into areas of economic activity that the UN has never touched.

Beginning in the 1980s, the IMF insisted on structural adjustment programs, requiring countries to institute economic policy reforms or achieve certain conditions, often referred to as conditionality, in return for economic assistance from both multilateral and bilateral lenders. Labeled the Washington Consensus, consistent with liberal economic theory, the imposed conditions included trade liberalization, economic reforms to eliminate subsidies and introduce user fees, and government reforms such as cutting waste and privatizing public enterprises. The IMF monitored the adjustment programs and determined whether performance criteria were met. During the 1997–1998 financial crisis in Asia, for example, the fund pushed Indonesia to change its entire economic system. In the 1990s, the IMF was also instrumental in the transitions of Russia and other former Communist countries to market economies. The very large size of IMF aid packages for several countries, including Mexico, Russia, and South Korea, effectively placed the IMF in the position of "bailing out" countries on the verge of economic collapse where there were concerns about contagion to other countries. The World Bank and the IMF were both involved in structural adjustment lending (the fund through short-term emergency loans and its negotiating and monitoring roles, the bank through aid for long-term structural reforms).

For almost three decades since the 1980s, vehement criticisms have focused on structural adjustment programs and the imposition of conditionality. Many believe these exact too high social and economic costs and represent a "cookie-cutter" approach to complex problems taken without regard for particular local situations. In this view, bank and fund programs disproportionately affect the already disadvantaged sectors of the population: the unskilled, women, and the poor. Some have been especially outraged by intrusions of these institutions into areas of domestic policy traditionally protected by state sovereignty.[12] Criticism even emerged from within the institutions themselves, some noting that the bank and fund have not followed their own procedures, that bailouts have gone to countries making unwise economic decisions, and that states have been pushed too soon to open their economies to the risks in volatile international financial flows.[13]

Beginning in 2009, the IMF discontinued structural performance criteria for loans, even for loans to low-income countries, in response to both its critics and the 2008 global financial crisis. This represents a substantial overhaul of the IMF lending framework. The amount of the loans can be greater, and loans are to be tailored according to the respective state's needs, a direct response to the criticism of the "cookie-cutter" approach of structural adjustment lending. Monitoring of the loans will be done more quietly to reduce the stigma attached to conditionality. Also in response to previous criticism, the IMF has urged lending to programs that encourage social safety nets for the most vulnerable within the populations. Ideas that were previously unacceptable to the IMF—that capital flows may need regulation and that states might take a proactive role in coordinating economic development—became more acceptable in response to the market failures of the global financial crisis.[14] In all these new emphases, the fund is working closely with the World Bank and other donors.

Governance within the bank and fund has come under increasing scrutiny. By convention, the IMF managing director has always been a European and the World Bank president an American. Both positions carry wide-ranging power and authority. Everyday policies are made by limited-member executive boards operating under **weighted voting systems** that guarantee the voting power of the major donors commensurate with their contributions. Domination by the few opens both institutions to criticism from developing countries that have little power within the two institutions. In the IMF, for example, the United States commands 16.7 percent of shares (and votes), Japan 6.01 percent, Germany 5.87 percent, and France and the United Kingdom each 4.85 percent. Beginning in 2010, China gained a separate executive director for its increased share and Russia, India, and Brazil have also had increases in their quotas and votes, as have low-income countries.

CARTOON 5.1. "BRICS Want Reform," by Paresh Nath. *Reproduced with permission of Cagle Cartoons, Inc. All rights reserved.*

Although changing economic power is reflected in the bank and fund, key Western power is still reflected in the two bureaucracies that employ economists trained largely in Western countries in the same liberal economic tradition as US decisionmakers. Both institutions are also criticized for being secretive and lacking transparency, even though the establishment of the Independent Evaluation Office and more extensive use of the Internet in the IMF have improved the situation. For these reasons, the least-developed countries have traditionally supported the UN's development-related institutions and ideas, where they enjoy a louder voice.

The global financial crisis of 2008–2009 brought out both the strengths and the weaknesses of the bank and the fund. The IMF, the crisis manager, sharply increased its concessional lending and provided policy advice. Emergency loans were made to Pakistan, Guatemala, numerous African countries, Iceland (the first to a developed country), and Hungary. The fund established new credit lines with expanded flexibility for programs and attached fewer conditions. That led the *Economist* to conclude, "The IMF's star has risen steadily through the global economic crisis. Contributions from its members have tripled its firepower. It has rescued economies from Hungary to Pakistan."[15]

Critics wonder, however, why the IMF with its surveillance system didn't see the crisis coming. Why was it unable to convince the largest states (the United States and China) of the need to make changes to redress the imbalance between creditors and debtors? Why didn't the organizations forecast the implications for neighboring countries in the interlinked financial system? Couldn't the bank and the fund have done more to stop the contagion and be better managers? The same questions arose during the Euro crisis of 2010–2011. The IMF and the European Union cofunded the massive bailouts of Greece, Portugal, and Ireland, thus helping to prop up these weaker members. Yet for some observers, these economic crises confirmed that the IMF and bank are increasingly irrelevant, as the G-20 and states such as China, Brazil, and India have sought political power consistent with their emerging economic strength.

Trade Issues and the GATT, UNCTAD, and the WTO. Initially, the Bretton Woods institutions were to include the International Trade Organization. That organization was expected to provide a general framework for trade rules and a forum for ongoing trade discussions. Lack of support in the US Senate, however, killed the proposed organization in 1948. In its place, the General Agreement on Tariffs and Trade was established "temporarily" to provide a framework for trade negotiations. GATT provided an approach to international trade based on principles of trade liberalization, nondiscrimination in trade, and reciprocity. With only a loose link to the UN, GATT and its small staff oversaw trade negotiations in eight successive multilateral rounds of negotiations. During those rounds, most decisions were taken bilaterally, then multilateralized. Each successive round produced tariff cuts on an increasing volume of trade. Gradually, beginning in the late 1960s, treatment for the developing countries was improved, with preferential access to developed-country markets and the elimination of subsidies and rules governing nontariff trade barriers such as government procurement and technical barriers.

Yet within GATT, the interests of the industrialized countries took precedence. Through the 1950s, many less developed countries grew increasingly dissatisfied with GATT's emphasis on trade in manufactured products and its lack of interest in the commodity problem and in trade as a way to transfer economic resources from the rich to the poor countries. Frustrated by the slow response of the Bretton Woods institutions generally to their development needs and by the developed countries' dominance of these institutions, developing countries proposed an international conference to establish principles and policies to govern international trade relations and to guide trade policies. Thus, in 1964, the UN Conference on Trade and Development became a permanent body reporting to the General Assembly, but with its own secretary-general. UNCTAD supporters resisted becoming a separate specialized UN agency, preferring to draw strength from the General Assembly where developing countries commanded a majority of votes.

UNCTAD. UNCTAD's founding conference in 1964 recommended a number of general principles to govern international trade relations as well as recognizing the need for a system of **trade preferences**. Reciprocity, a core GATT principle, was viewed as serving only to perpetuate dependency and underdevelopment. The inherently unequal international liberal trading system could not be made more equal without major changes. Thus, the developing countries argued that they needed special concessions—including preferential access to developed-country markets—to improve their trade. UNCTAD emphasized that the developed countries had a major role to play in addressing the problems of trade affecting developing countries. And it brought into the open the growing split—which persists today—between developed and developing countries over issues relating to trade and development.

UNCTAD continues to meet every four years, and the Trade and Development Board, its permanent governing organ, meets annually. The UNCTAD secretariat has been important in shaping its work because of its close ties with the G-77; it also provides research, analysis, and training for government officials to remedy the limited expertise of many developing countries' governments on complex international trade issues. UNCTAD's dynamics were long shaped by a pattern of group bargaining, prompted by the G-77's high degree of unity and the one-state/one-vote mode of majority decisionmaking. Despite efforts to develop operational responsibilities, it has functioned largely as a forum for debate, negotiation, and legitimation of new norms. It was the primary forum for articulating the major challenges to the predominant liberal thinking about economic development, including the New International Economic Order, discussed below.[16] It has failed to win support, however, from major donor countries and from many mainstream professional economists.[17]

Currently, UNCTAD meetings address such issues as commodity diversification, trade and commercial negotiations, transportation, macroeconomic policies, multinational corporations, and debt financing. Although it sponsors programs for the least-developed countries, including the landlocked and small-island developing countries, its activities have diminished. And, although the interests of developing countries have increasingly diverged, many still view UNCTAD positively as a forum for their voice, even though an evaluation of its almost fifty years of efforts shows few substantial achievements.

The World Trade Organization. Although the interests of the industrialized countries took precedence in GATT, gradually, under pressure from the G-77 and UNCTAD, more favorable, preferential treatment for less developed countries was achieved. The eighth or Uruguay Round of GATT negotiations concluded in December 1993 with the establishment of a true global trade organization—the

World Trade Organization. The agreement also addressed two topics previously excluded from the GATT rules but critical for developing countries: agriculture and textiles.

Although the WTO has no formal relationship with the UN, it does provide a unified organizational structure for managing the growing complexity of global trade issues. WTO membership now stands at 153, with members conducting 97 percent of the world's trade. Like GATT before it, it is based on a contractual framework. Previously negotiated trade agreements are still valid, but joining the WTO involves negotiating the terms of a country's accession to those agreements. For example, when China became a member in 2001 after fifteen years of negotiations, the document setting forth the terms of accession was nine hundred pages long, and China's government had to revise many laws that restricted foreign access to its economy. To assist states in becoming liberalized, the WTO and UNCTAD secretariats jointly operate the International Trade Centre in Geneva to provide technical cooperation to developing and transitional countries in trade promotion and export development.

The WTO has been subject to many of the same criticisms as the bank and fund, particularly from those who see the organization as still representing more the interests of the developed world. Yet it functions very differently. Although it is a one-state/one-vote organization, decisionmaking is generally by consensus, and states' market share is the primary source of influence. The most recent Doha round of trade negotiations—labeled the Development Round—began in 2001 and reached an impasse in 2008, with the United States and European Union on one side and the G-20 emerging countries led by India, Brazil, and China on the other. The latter insisted on the opening up of developed-country agricultural markets, while the United States and EU resisted. Efforts to move forward in 2011 showed new areas of disagreement. In fact, the *Economist* noted that the passage of almost ten years since the outset of the Doha negotiations has seen major changes in the interests of both developed and emerging markets, with the majority of economic growth now taking place in developing countries.[18]

Less developed countries have often turned to the UN specialized agencies and programs for development assistance, seeing them as more attuned to their interests. To illustrate the work of UN specialized agencies as well as UN programs and partnerships, we look at agricultural development and emergency food aid.

The Specialized Agencies, Programs, and Partnerships. The nineteen specialized agencies are an integral part of the UN's approaches to international development and trade (see Figure 2.1). While, as shown above, the World Bank provides capital investment, the IMF ensures financial and monetary stability, and GATT and the WTO foster the opening of markets for trade, development involves a plethora of other particular activities. Trade, for example, cannot occur without a physical means to transport goods, hence the need for ocean shipping and air transport, hence the International Maritime Organization (IMO), the International Civil Aviation Organization (ICAO), the International Association of Transport Airlines (IATA), and the International Telecommunications Union (ITU). Industrial development depends on specific skills, with the UN Industrial Development Organization supplying the expertise. Agricultural development has been promoted through a group of UN-related organizations, the Food and Agriculture Organization and the International Fund for Agricultural Development (IFAD), both UN specialized agencies. They are complemented by the World Food Programme created in 1963 and the Consultative Group on International Agricultural Research (CGIAR) established in 1972, among others. We examine briefly the role of the food agencies in promoting development.

Agricultural Development. The core organization of the international food regime, the FAO, was established in 1945 with the objective of increasing agricultural productivity to eliminate hunger and improve nutrition. Its experts provide policy and technical assistance to improve agriculture generally consistent with free trade principles. Based in Rome, it serves as a knowledge and information center for agricultural activities, including fishing and forestry. During the 1960s, the FAO supported the development and dissemination of high-yield strains of grain and rice that produced the "green revolution" for developing countries. In the 1980s and 1990s, sustainable agriculture and rural development became the organization's primary focus, in keeping with the changing ideas about development.

The rural extreme poor are the target population for the International Fund for Agricultural Development established in 1977 following the 1974 World Food Conference. IFAD finances and cofinances projects to improve agricultural methods in rural areas, including critical ancillary activities such as financial services and off-farm employment. Because East Asia rural poverty rates have dropped dramatically since the 1980s, worldwide rural poverty rates have been reduced from 48 percent to 34 percent, but the persistence of African rural poverty means that 50 percent of IFAD funding goes to that continent.

Emergency Food Aid. In the international headlines responding to food emergencies during natural disasters, war, or famine is the World Food Programme with its operational capacities to deliver food aid to food-deficit countries. Each year, on average, the WFP feeds more than 90 million people in 70 countries; in 2009, those figures were 101.8 million in 75 countries. That represents about 90 percent of the WFP's budget. More than 10,000 employees direct the various field activities, including delivering food supplies, running food-for-work programs where individuals build roads or irrigation systems in exchange for food, and providing school-based feeding programs so that children remain in school. The WFP partners with more than 3,000 local NGOs and community-based organizations to actually distribute the food. Food used for emergency aid is generally donated by developed countries, often from agricultural surpluses. A new approach with funding from private foundations is testing whether the WFP can buy surplus crops from poor farmers in Africa and Central America to feed WFP recipients facing hunger. That "purchase for progress" project is intended to both help food-deficit populations and stimulate production by developing-country farmers.

Partnerships. Increasingly, the WFP partners with private donors like MNCs. Citi, for example, provides cash and in-kind services in advance of emergencies, and Unilever is working to improve the nutrition content of the food delivered, indicative of emerging public-private partnerships. CGIAR, a consortium of fifteen research centers like the International Rice Research Institute (Philippines) and the International Institute of Tropical Agriculture (Nigeria), also exemplifies partnerships among various donors, including the UN's FAO and IFAD, the World Bank, the European Commission, the Bill and Melinda Gates Foundation, and state donors. The scientific research is focused on crops in developing countries.

Many of the relationships among the UN agencies, NGOs, and the private sector were established during the UN-sponsored world food conferences in 1974, 1996, and 2002, which brought together the various constituencies and called attention to a variety of agricultural and food problems. At the 2002 World Food Summit, for example, many traditional issues filled the agenda: food aid to end hunger, emergencies, food safety and phytosanitary regulations, and securing food under conditions of limited water supplies. Among the new issues were the New Partnership for Africa's Development (NEPAD) and the International Treaty on Plant Genetic Resources for Food and Agriculture that engaged the debate on genetic engineering of food crops. More than 650 labor, human rights, and farmer groups participated in the conference, along with 180 countries. This was a clear signal that collaboration with NGOs would increase along with partnerships with multinational corporations such as the Italian food giant Parmalat, which provided funding for the summit.

The specialized agencies illustrate the UN's tendency, in common with many governments, to create new agencies and programs. Some institutions have been established because thinking about development has changed and new institutions meet new needs more readily than old institutions can be reformed. Thus, the UN system has evolved over time in its efforts to meet its mandate to foster cooperation for economic and social development. The result, however, can be problems of duplication, inefficiency, and lack of coordination, as discussed in

Chapter 2. The newer challenges of globalization and the persistence of poverty heighten the need for economic governance and for better coordination of the different parts of the UN system, yet they do not lessen the value of the UN's longtime role in the development of norms and ideas.

THE UN AND EVOLVING IDEAS ABOUT DEVELOPMENT

In contrast to issues of peace and security, as well as thinking about the role of the UN and its Secretariat more generally, traditional international relations theories for the most part do not help us understand what has shaped the UN system in dealing with development. For that, we turn to ideas rooted in economic liberalism. The institutions discussed above, including the Bretton Woods institutions and most of the specialized agencies, were heavily shaped by development thinking in the immediate post–World War II period, particularly in Western Europe and North America, and, hence, by economic liberalism.

Economic Liberalism

Based on ideas from Adam Smith to contemporary thinkers, **economic liberalism** asserts that human beings are rational and acquisitive and will seek to improve their condition in the most expeditious manner possible. Markets develop to ensure that individuals are able to carry out the necessary transactions to improve their well-being. To maximize economic welfare and efficiency and to stimulate individual (and therefore collective) economic growth, markets must operate freely, economics and politics must be separated as much as possible, and governments must permit the free flow of trade and economic intercourse. If they do not interfere in the efficient allocation of resources provided by markets, the increasing interdependence between domestic economies will lead to greater cooperation and aggregate economic development.

Since multinational corporations expanded dramatically beginning in the 1960s, liberals have viewed them as key engines of growth. Economic development, it was thought, could best be achieved through open markets for goods and capital, with international agencies providing limited amounts of assistance in order for development to get off the ground. The private sector would be the engine of development. Yet very quickly, it was recognized that economic development did not just happen; planning was important, as was the development of needed skills, education, health, hygiene, and national administrative services. These were the roots of the initial UN technical assistance programs to develop states' capacity for growth. The Bretton Woods agencies would provide capital for specific infrastructure, address short-term balance-of-payments programs, and provide a forum to negotiate freer trade. FAO programs would be designed to enhance agricultural productivity. Enhanced productivity would lead to surpluses used to invest in growth opportunities across all sectors. But from shortly after the founding of the Bretton Woods system and the establishment of the UN, these liberal economic ideas were challenged by some groups and programs within the UN itself.

Challenges to Economic Liberalism

Belief in the capacity of economic liberalism to meet development challenges was first questioned in the ECLA in the early 1950s and then in UNCTAD in the 1970s. Both in the UN Secretariat and ECLA, academic economists from Latin America argued that development could not take place without fundamental changes in international economic relations to redress the inequalities of power and wealth. Their position was embedded in Marxist thinking: that is, capitalist economic systems are inherently deterministic and expansionary, and they require new resources and the colonization of less developed regions to generate necessary profits. These economists saw the need for radical change in the distribution of international political and economic power if the disadvantaged position of developing countries was to be altered.[19] This view, known as **dependency theory**, posits that the capitalist international system divides states into two groups: those on the periphery and those at the core. Those on the periphery are locked into a permanent state of dependency. This dependency stems from the observation that the prices of primary commodity exports from the developing world do not keep pace with the prices of manufacturing goods imported by the same countries. This inequality was perceived to be relatively permanent, irrespective of the domestic policies pursued or external assistance they received. Multinational corporations with extensive operations within such peripheral states were criticized for exacerbating the dependency, making these companies targets for nationalization.

In essence, dependency theory has argued that development could not take place without fundamental changes in international economic relations to redress the inequalities of power and wealth. These views had strong appeal and came to undergird much of the agenda of developing countries in the UN in the 1960s and 1970s.

The Debate over the New International Order. During 1973 and 1974, the G-77, impatient with the slow progress toward development and bolstered by support from OPEC members—whom the developing countries admired for their challenge to the major oil companies and the developed world—increased its pressure for restructuring international economic relations. In two successive special sessions of the UN General Assembly in 1974–1975, in global conferences on food, population, and women, as well as in UNCTAD, the G-77 used its wide majority and strong solidarity to secure the adoption of the Declaration on the Establishment of a New International Economic Order and the Charter of Economic Rights and Duties of States. The 1975 Seventh Special Session of the UN General Assembly marked the peak of confrontation between developed North and developing South that dominated not only UNCTAD but much of the UN system, including the specialized agencies, in the 1970s.

Through the proposed NIEO, the G-77 sought changes in six major areas of international economic relations with the goal of altering the relationship of dependency between the developed and the developing countries. It sought changes in international trade, including adjustment in the **terms of trade**, to stabilize the prices of such commodities as coffee, cocoa, bauxite, tin, and sugar, and to link those prices with the price of finished products imported from developed countries. The G-77 also demanded greater authority over natural resources and foreign investment in developing countries, particularly through the regulation of MNCs. It wanted improved means of technology transfer to make it cheaper and more appropriate for the local needs. To propel development, the South also demanded increased foreign aid and improved terms and conditions.

Although the G-77 won adoption of the Generalized System of Preferences (GSP) in GATT in 1967, waiving the nondiscrimination rule, GSP schemes were applied unilaterally by the European Community, the United States, and others. They could be withdrawn at any time. Still, this was a step toward establishing the principle of preferential treatment for developing-country exports. The G-77 also won more favorable terms for commodity-price stabilization. On most other issues, however, the North refused to negotiate. No common fund was established to stabilize commodity prices. No regulations on MNCs were concluded. There were no dramatic increases in development assistance. In fact, by the late 1980s, "donor fatigue" had set in, and levels of official development assistance had steadily decreased.

Two other issues pushed by the G-77 remain on the agenda today—restructuring the international financial institutions and debt relief. As discussed above, changes in voting power have occurred in the bank and fund, and in the WTO emerging countries have become much more skilled at exercising leverage. For example, before the Doha round of trade negotiations stalled, rich countries agreed to major concessions eliminating all tariffs and quotas on 97 percent of goods from the fifty poorest countries and to end their agricultural export subsidies by 2013.[20]

Debt Reduction. The issue of excessive debt in developing countries has also been much debated since the early 1970s. Excessive debt in developing countries has led some to spend as much as four times more for debt servicing than on social services or education. When repayment crowds out opportunities for investment in the economy, sectors such as infrastructure, health care, and education suffer. Poverty increases. The debt burden has increased the dependence of developing countries on foreign creditors and on the international financial institutions as well as reduced the ability of their citizens to control their own development policies.

Almost twenty years after the NIEO debate dominated UN agendas, a popular movement known as Jubilee 2000—a coalition of development-oriented NGOs, church groups, and labor groups—launched a campaign advocating debt cancellation. To overcome injustice and poverty, "Breaking the Chains of Debt" became its rallying cry. The movement attracted a broad following, with more than 60 national Jubilee campaigns. They demonstrated, sponsored forums, and lobbied UN regional groups, simplifying a complex issue and spurring action.

In 1996, the IMF and World Bank undertook a major policy shift called the Heavily Indebted Poor Countries Initiative (HIPC), an initiative that was accelerated in 1999 and in 2005, permitting 100 percent debt relief from the IMF and World Bank, among others. States seeking relief are required to submit a Poverty Reduction Strategy Paper and implement it. To be developed in consultation with groups from civil society and UN agencies like UNDP, UNICEF, and WFP, the plan details how the debt relief funds will be channeled to social spending and how management reforms will be implemented to avoid future debt crises. By the end of 2010, thirty-two states had received complete debt relief (out of forty eligible), most of them in Africa. About 45 percent of the funding comes from the IMF and other multilateral institutions, with the rest from bilateral creditors. The bank and fund rely on moral suasion to encourage creditors to cooperate. Jubilee itself splintered after 2000, with its position vindicated by the HIPC.

The founding of UNCTAD coming out of dependency theory and subsequent actions by the G-77 coalescing in the NIEO provided a fundamental, sustained challenge to the dominant liberal economic thinking. More than four decades since the NIEO was first proposed and many of its key elements rejected, some elements such as debt relief and trade preferences for developing countries have been implemented. This has occurred despite the fact that there is now even wider acceptance (some say triumph) of economic liberalism. Yet there have also been modifications of liberalism to incorporate changes in development thinking.

Modifying Economic Liberalism

While NIEO proponents were challenging the fundamental tenets of liberal economic development, some UN agencies recognized the need to modify economic liberalism in view of its perceived failure to eliminate poverty, hunger, illiteracy, and growing income inequality. Collaboration between development scholars and various UN agencies, including the World Bank, produced new approaches oriented to basic human needs and the redistribution of income from growth to the needs of the poorest and to groups left out of the development process.

Women and Development. UN agencies and liberal economic theorists had long believed that as development occurred, women's economic status would inevitably improve. During the early years of the UN, the Commission on the Status of Women, one of the original six functional commissions of ECOSOC, focused on ensuring that women had the right to vote, hold office, and enjoy equal legal rights. There was no special reason to target women as actors in the development process, as all groups would benefit as economic development occurred.

In the 1970s, Esther Boserup, an activist, academic, and UN consultant, found otherwise. In her landmark book, *Women's Role in Economic Development*, she argued that as technology improves, men benefit economically, but women become increasingly marginalized economically.[21] Thus, by 1975, when the UN-sponsored International Women's Year was launched with the first World Conference on Women in Mexico City, the idea emerged that women needed special attention if they were to become participants and active agents in development. Programs should be designed to reduce women's traditional activities and to expand new activities into economically productive roles for them in agriculture, small business, and industry.

The women-in-development agenda (WID), the International Decade for Women, and the first three UN women's conferences in 1975, 1980, and 1985 were all heavily affected by the North-South conflict of that period and by debates over the proposed NIEO. But with governments in the lead at the UN-sponsored conferences, and women's groups working only from the sidelines of parallel NGO meetings, the central issues of women's economic roles and social status were often lost in the process.

Following the approval in 1979 of the Convention on the Elimination of All Forms of Discrimination Against Women (CEDAW), the UN in 1982 established the International Research and Training Institute for the Advancement of Women (INSTRAW) to implement the women-in-development agenda. Funded by voluntary contributions, INSTRAW's goals are to provide training to integrate and mobilize women in the development process and to act as a catalyst in promoting the role of women. The UN Development Fund for Women (UNIFEM), established in 1975, supports projects run by women. The World Bank established the post of adviser on women in 1977. And now virtually all of the UN specialized agencies have integrated women's concerns into their programs.

That integration has been bolstered by the activities of women's groups in the 1990s and by global conferences on the environment, population, human rights, social development, and, of course, women. Women's NGOs pushed for language in the conference declarations and programs of action affirming the centrality of women's roles in sustainable development;[22] for example, the 1994 Cairo Conference on Population and Development declared that the key to population growth and economic development lies in the empowerment of women through education and economic opportunity. It enshrined a new concept of population that gives women more control over their lives by promoting education for girls, a range of choices for family planning and health care, and greater involvement of women in development planning.

Three global women's conferences and the publication in 1990 of *The World's Women*, discussed above, contributed to a major attitudinal shift within the UN system that has linked the social status and political empowerment of women to poverty, violence, the environment, sustainable development, and population control. The Platform of Action unanimously approved by the 1995 Fourth World Conference on Women in Beijing reaffirmed this connection by calling for the "empowerment of all women" through ensuring "women's equal access to economic resources including land, credit, science and technology, vocational training, information, communication, and markets."[23] This was reiterated at the "Beijing Plus Five" and "Beijing Plus Ten" meetings in 2000 and 2005.

The MDGs specifically call for promoting gender equality and empowering women through promoting women's education and improving the health status of women and children. Those goals are needed, for, as Devaki Jain reminds us, "the situation on the ground for many women, especially those living in poverty and in conflict-ridden situations, seems to have worsened, despite the fact that it has been addressed specifically by both the UN and development thought."[24]

In 2010, in an effort to improve the effectiveness of women's programs, the UN General Assembly created UN Women, the United Nations Entity for Gender Equality and the Empowerment of Women. The goal was to merge and build on the work of the different parts of the UN, including INSTRAW, UNIFEM, the Division for the Advancement of Women, and the Office of the Special Adviser on Gender Issues and Advancement of Women. UN Women brings together the human rights dimension (gender equality as a basic human right), the political (underrepresentation in political decisionmaking), and the economic (empowering women fuels thriving economies, spurring productivity and growth). It is designed to help UN bodies formulate policy and standards, advise states with technical and financial support, and monitor the progress of each. Michelle Bachelet, the former president of Chile, was named the first undersecretary-general and executive director. She is in charge of the forty-one-member board and the annual budget of about $500 million.

The issue of women and development illustrates the ways in which NGOs, UN-sponsored global conferences, and UN Secretariat studies—in short, all three UNs—have contributed to reshaping thinking about development and the roles of women and had an impact throughout the UN system, including the World Bank and IMF. It also influenced the human development–centered thinking that emerged in the 1990s along with the concept of **sustainable development**, two other modifications of liberal economic thinking.

The Reconceptualization of Development: Sustainability and Human Development. Another modification of economic liberalism emerged out of recognition that development defined as economic growth was too narrowly construed, leading to unintended and unanticipated side effects, including the marginalization of women. But what if development as conventionally practiced also led to environmental degradation or growth that was unsustainable into the future?

In 1980, the UN General Assembly adopted the World Conservation Strategy advocating the new but poorly defined concept of sustainable development. In 1983, the assembly established the World Commission on Environment and Development (WCED), headed by Prime Minister Gro Harlem Brundtland of Norway and composed of eminent persons from many parts of the world. WCED's task was to formulate a new development approach around the concept of sustainable development. This approach proved politically astute because it recognized that dealing with environmental problems would be ineffective if global poverty and economic inequalities were not addressed. The 1987 Brundtland Commission Report (*Our Common Future*) called for "development that meets the needs of the present without compromising the ability of future generations to meet their own needs."[25] It sought to balance ecological concerns with the economic growth necessary to reduce poverty. (That idea and its implementation are examined further in Chapter 7.) The evolution of the idea of sustainable development provides another example of the major role that the UN has had in the promotion of ideas. It also represents an important modification of liberal economic theory concerning development by linking the management and use of natural resources to their economic, social, and environmental consequences. The concept of sustainable development also created a way to link population and environmental problems.

A further modification occurred in the 1990s with UNDP's introduction of the concept of human development and the annual *Human Development Reports* and HDI, as discussed above. By putting "people at the centre of development," the concept provided "an integrated intellectual framework for catalyzing a new system-wide approach to economic and social development."[26] UNDP's motivation had much to do with the Bretton Woods institutions' harsh structural adjustment policies in the 1980s and the adverse effects on people in many developing countries. Thus, the concept of human development provided an alternative to neoliberal economic policies and a new paradigm.

Two distinguished economists from South Asian countries conceived of the idea and of the *Human Development Reports*—Mahbub ul Haq and Amartya Sen. In the first report, human development was defined as "a process of enlarging people's choices. The most critical of these wide-ranging choices are to live a long and healthy life, to be educated and to have access to resources needed for a decent standard of living. Additional choices include political freedom, guaranteed human rights and personal self-respect."[27] Subsequent reports, all issued by individual authors, refined and expanded these ideas, adding among other things the notion of strengthening capabilities. Thus, the concept of human development underscores a point made in the first UN Development Decade that state economic growth and prosperity measured by GNP and GNP per capita do not automatically translate into human advancement. Studies have in fact shown that countries may make progress on human development even with slow economic growth.

In sum, the importance of human development is that it has provided a framework for integrating activities across the UN system. Together with the outcomes of the global conferences of the 1970s, 1980s, and 1990s, it provided the basis for the MDGs.

Creating a Comprehensive Approach to Development: The Millennium Development Goals

The Millennium Declaration adopted at the UN's Millennium Summit in September 2001 incorporated the set of eight Millennium Development Goals. These represent a conceptual convergence, or what the *Human Development Report 2003* calls a "compact among nations," about reducing poverty and promoting sustainable human development in response to globalization. The mutually reinforcing and intertwined MDGs include halving world poverty and hunger by 2015, reducing infant mortality by two-thirds, and achieving universal primary education. The eighth goal deals with partnerships among UN agencies, governments, civil society organizations, and the private sector as a means to achieving the other seven goals. (See Box 5.1 for the complete list.) The goals are disaggregated into eighteen specific targets, specific time frames, and forty-eight performance indicators with an elaborate implementation plan involving ten global task forces, MDG report cards for each developing country, regular monitoring, and a public information campaign to keep pressure on governments and international agencies.

With the MDGs, "the UN had returned once again to make distinct and pioneering contributions," notes a group of scholars, "by organizing an unprecedented millennium consensus in defining global goals for poverty reduction and mobilizing commitments in support of those goals."[28] What is also most remarkable about the MDGs, Ruggie notes, is that "it is unprecedented for the UN

184

BOX 5.1. The Millennium Development Goals and Targets for 2015

Goal 1: Eradicate Extreme Poverty and Hunger
Halve the proportion of people living on less than one dollar a day (later changed to $1.25 a day) and those who suffer from hunger.

Goal 2: Achieve Universal Primary Education
Ensure that all boys and girls complete primary school.

Goal 3: Promote Gender Equality and Empower Women
Eliminate gender disparities in primary and secondary education preferably by 2005, and at all levels by 2015.

Goal 4: Reduce Child Mortality
Reduce by two-thirds the mortality rate among children under five.

Goal 5: Improve Maternal Health
Reduce by three-quarters the ratio of women dying in childbirth.

Goal 6: Combat HIV/AIDS, Malaria, and Other Diseases
Halt and begin to reverse the spread of HIV/AIDS and the incidence of malaria and other major diseases.

Goal 7: Ensure Environmental Sustainability
Integrate the principles of sustainable development into country policies and programs and reverse the loss of environmental resources.

Reduce by half the proportion of people without access to safe drinking water.

By 2020, achieve significant improvement in the lives of at least 100 million slum dwellers.

Goal 8: Develop a Global Partnership for Development
Develop further an open trading and financial system that includes a commitment to good governance, development, and poverty reduction, nationally and internationally.

Address the special needs of least-developed, landlocked, and small-island developing states.

Deal comprehensively with developing countries' debt problems.

and its agencies, let alone also the Bretton Woods institutions, to align their operational activities behind a unifying substantive framework."[29] The bank and fund produce the *Global Monitoring Report*, which focuses on evaluating the progress of the MDGs.

But articulating goals and monitoring are easier than implementing the necessary policies. On some indicators, the trends are positive; on others, they are not.[30] (See Figure 5.1 for the global trends.) Extreme poverty (living on less than $1.25 a day) has fallen rapidly, and thus the global target of reducing income more than half by 2015 will be met, but that figure represents an improvement since 1990, well before the MDGs were passed. China and East Asia have made the most significant gains, Africa much less significant. Universal primary education is also within reach. The number of children not in school fell by 14 million between 2002 and 2007, even considering population growth, although sub-Saharan Africa and South Asia remain behind. The overall target for gender parity in completing primary school is also likely to be met. Even by 2005, almost two-thirds of the developing countries had met that target. At that rate, by 2015, the target is likely to be met. Likewise, with expansion of infrastructure, access to safe drinking water is on track to be met globally and in most regions, with seventy-six developing countries likely to succeed.

On other MDGs, the assessment is not as positive, with the worst results relating to health and the persistence of hunger. The target least likely to be met is that of reducing maternal deaths, with more than half of the deaths concentrated in six countries (the DRC, Ethiopia, India, Nigeria, Afghanistan, and Pakistan). The data has been widely questioned, however, and major improvements noted. Under-five child mortality, too, has fallen, but not fast enough to meet the MDG target, with sub-Saharan Africa and South Asia falling very short once again. Neither are targets to be reached in reducing hunger or in providing access to basic sanitation, areas that negatively affect health status. The spread of HIV and HIV-related deaths has begun to slow, but the number of people living with HIV/AIDS continues to rise, and mortality from malaria remains high, especially in Africa.

The 2008–2009 global financial crisis clearly was a setback to the attainment of the MDGs and particularly vexing since the overall assessment of the MDGs has been positive. Yet the crisis did not affect all states in the same way. Many emerging and developing states actually did better than expected, with those in Asia achieving more than 6 percent growth rates in 2009 and in Africa more than 2 percent. Southeast Asia, Latin America, and the Caribbean are poised to meet targets, whereas sub-Saharan Africa and South Asia are unlikely to make theirs. The states labeled by the World Bank as "fragile states," states mired in conflict and poor governance, are in the worst position. In 2011, twenty-seven states were so identified in Africa, Asia, and Haiti in Latin America. Furthermore, those states

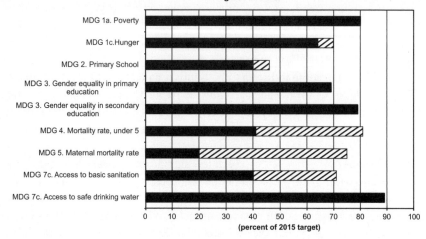

FIGURE 5.1. Progress in Parts: The Millenium Development Goals

SOURCE: *Finance and Development*, September 2010, p. 7.

lack reliable data, making assessments and predictions problematic. In 2008, the World Bank established a special fund, the State and Peace-Building Fund, to address the special needs of this group, establishing partnerships with UNDP, the EU, and major donors. A 2010 UN report asserted that donor investment was falling $35 billion short on an annual basis, well short of the $150 billion goal.[31]

One experiment incorporating the MDGs in an integrated and intensive fashion is the Millennium Village project. Launched in 2004, the project has identified fourteen villages in ten African countries, clustered in distinct agro-ecological zones. Assistance is based on the notion that inexpensive changes in health (such as HIV testing and insecticide-treated bed nets), infrastructure (water, electricity lines, roads, piped irrigation), and business (microfinance, fertilizer) can lift the 400,000 people in these villages out of severe poverty in five years. The project is a joint collaboration between UNDP, Columbia University's Earth Institute, and Millennium Promise, an NGO founded in 2005 for this purpose. Sixty percent of the funding comes from external sources (Japan and the philanthropist George Soros), and 40 percent from indigenous sources. Total cost of the intervention is $150 per villager per year over the five years, essentially the size of the entire local economies.

During 2010, efforts were made to evaluate the Millennium Village project using both systematic empirical evidence and anecdotal evidence. Anecdotal evidence suggests that life for people in these villages had improved: each had a school, a health clinic, and markets to sell surplus generated by better crop yields, although poverty had not been abolished.[32] More systematic analysis found that the intervention sites were performing better than the surrounding areas. But in the absence of baseline data in the comparison villages, we cannot know if the project is actually responsible for the changes. Indeed, on many of the MDG indicators, states like Ghana, Kenya, and Nigeria, where some of the villages are located, have made significant improvements. Would these village-level changes have occurred without the intervention?[33] Most critically, can these improvements be sustained without continued infusion of external resources? We can only speculate. The experiment continues.

Finally, it is important to note that the MDGs are not without their critics. Some have asked why specific MDGs were selected rather than other ones that might, in fact, be better choices. Why were uniform targets set for all countries rather than recognizing that some countries are more handicapped than others in meeting targets for poverty reduction or other goals and that there are different ways of achieving targets? As noted economist Jagdish Bhagwati says, "A more serious problem with the MDG approach, however, is that the central task in development is not the specification of desirable targets . . . but rather the specification of policy instruments that achieve these targets."[34] He and others are also critical of MDG 8 concerning partnerships, because partnerships may and do often involve major corporations of which they are critics.

Even outside the MDGs, the UN has increasingly interacted with other types of actors in addressing economic development issues. Historically, outside consultants and experts have been a primary source of research, advice, and some of the UN's most important ideas. Since the 1990s, MNCs and NGOs have formed a variety of partnerships with the UN.

THE UN AND OTHER ACTORS

MNCs and the Global Compact

As liberal economic theory predicts, private capital has played a key role in economic growth in many parts of the world, and this growth is a prerequisite for development. MNCs produce 25 percent of the world's wealth, and the top 1,000 produce 80 percent of the world's industrial output. Motivated by profit, they have the ability to raise enormous sums of capital and invest in projects around the world that offer employment, thus stimulating growth and raising standards of living. Since the mid-1980s, foreign direct investment has increased dramatically and, in many places, far exceeded multilateral and bilateral lending in stimulating economic growth. For example, from 2000 to 2008, foreign direct investment to less developed countries grew at a more rapid pace than any other kind of external financial resources, increasing from \$4.1 billion in 2000 to \$32.4 billion in 2008. That represented more than 41 percent of capital infusion in thirty-three less developed African countries. Still, the share of worldwide foreign direct investment going to less developed countries is very small, just 1.8 percent of the total, and much of that investment goes to a few oil- and mineral-rich countries.[35]

By the mid-1980s, under strong US influence, the World Bank and IMF included privatization and deregulation of business among conditions for lending in order to support private foreign investment. And, with the growth of private investment, especially in Asia, as a source of development capital, UNDP in collaboration with major donors began to provide governments interested in attracting foreign investment with the support to do so by publishing investment guides.

Yet critics of the liberal economic model have long been dissatisfied with the role international private capital and especially multinational corporations play in economic affairs, believing that they occupy a position of preeminence without being subject to adequate international or national controls. Their goal has been to develop ways of regulating MNCs' activities, and, in fact, such regulation was a goal of the NIEO, described above. The search within the UN for an international code of conduct officially terminated when the Commission on Transnational Corporations was eliminated in 1994, twenty years after it was established. What remained of its work was integrated into UNCTAD.[36] Yet the pressure on MNCs from NGO-led grassroots campaigns has continued, leading many major corporations to implement their own codes of conduct and monitoring mechanisms.

The break from the historical approach to MNCs within the UN, however, was solidified officially in 1999 when Secretary-General Kofi Annan proposed a global compact at the World Economic Forum in Davos, Switzerland. He hoped to join the UN, relevant UN agencies, research centers, corporations, environmental groups, human rights groups, and labor NGOs (represented by the International Confederation of Free Trade Unions) into a partnership committed to providing the social foundations of a sustainable global economy, encouraging private-sector investment in developing countries and promoting good corporate practices.

The **Global Compact** on Corporate Responsibility revolves around nine principles that participating companies agree to uphold. These include adherence to international human rights law, rejection of child and forced labor, abolition of discrimination in employment, and promotion of greater environmental responsibility. Several of these principles reflect earlier work of both the ILO and the Office of the High Commissioner for Human Rights. More than 8,700 companies had signed the Global Compact by 2010, with stakeholders in 130 countries. Ruggie, the father of the Global Compact within the UN Secretariat, describes it as a set of nested networks where parties learn what works and what fails, enhancing corporate social responsibility.[37]

One 2010 empirical study of the effects of the Global Compact on MNC behavior found that firms that sign on will follow up by reporting on their activities. Some companies have actually made policy statements establishing better human rights practices. Over time, others have begun to notice more responsible MNC behavior. By participating in that exercise and practice, the reputation of particular MNCs has been enhanced.[38] Yet measuring what MNCs do compared to what they say is difficult. Hence, the compact is not without its critics. Some point to the fact that companies have joined that previously opposed standard setting. Perhaps, they contend, joining is nothing more than a publicity ploy, as the above empirical study suggests. Others, including many economists, doubt the effectiveness of voluntary mechanisms. Still others point to the fact that the approach does not include any remedies for MNC policies that run counter to the principles.

The Global Compact has not eliminated other efforts to regulate MNCs. UNCTAD still addresses issues of restrictive business practices. WHO has targeted specific MNCs and their marketing practices, most notably the tobacco and pharmaceutical companies. (These issues are addressed in Chapter 7.) Yet, in general, there has been a shift, with the UN seeking to work with MNCs, often in partnership arrangements with NGOs and states and, through those partnerships, to hold them accountable.

NGOs and the Third UN

NGOs are a critical part of the development puzzle, once economically weak and ignored by the UN system, the World Bank, the IMF, and MNCs. Since the 1980s, NGOs have participated in shaping the discourse and pushed for new approaches to development. During the 1990s, they lobbied for a voice in the global conferences that made the critical links between women and development, the environment and development, population and development, and, as shown in the next chapter, development and human rights. And NGOs took on more responsibilities in terms of delivery of services funded by both states and multilateral donor organizations like the UN and the bank.

Some NGOs acquired their expertise in development work by first responding to humanitarian emergencies. The complex emergencies in Somalia, Kosovo, Bosnia, the DRC, Liberia, Sudan, and Haiti drew NGOs in to provide humanitarian assistance, working with UN agencies like the World Food Programme and UNHCR. But as Save the Children, CARE, and World Vision increasingly recognized, their short-term relief work was becoming long term. Recovering from humanitarian emergencies required supporting longer term development objectives—stimulating agricultural development to curb food shortages and forestation to enhance soil productivity and improving local skills for village development. At the same time, states, the UN system, and even the World Bank realized that they could benefit from the local-level expertise of the NGOs who often provide service delivery at a lower cost than the bank's high-cost professional staff. Such are the origins of the development partnerships, now an essential part of the development system, where NGOs implement UN and bank projects. In a few cases, NGOs are even performing services that governments generally perform where weak states such as Bangladesh, Somalia, or the Sudan are either unable or unwilling to provide public services.

As NGOs become the implementers of the programs of others, however, they risk losing the very advantages for which they are attractive. Like all organizations, they become agents of the funders, having to prove themselves with each contract, and thus less willing to risk taking new positions and trying new approaches.

LESSONS LEARNED

The United Nations and its specialized agencies have struggled to be relevant to the major contemporary economic issues, including the imperative for economic development. The complexities of globalization, the strength of MNCs and volume of international private capital, the preeminence of the Bretton Woods institutions, the growth of emerging markets, and the activities of NGOs have made the UN institutions and programs just another set of actors, among many. Still, the UN remains in the forefront of developing new ideas and thinking about economic development and serving as a forum for policy debates on the balance between economic growth and economic equity. The UN has played the role of critic, constructive to some and obstructionist to others. And now, we ask, what lessons have been learned along the way?

First, the UN, along with the rest of the development community, has learned that international involvement in countries should be based on individual countries' needs. Thus, for example, where countries have experienced lengthy periods of civil conflict, as in Namibia, Cambodia, and Mozambique, the UN's development cooperation activities are part of its wider engagement in political and humanitarian areas. The establishment of the Peacebuilding Commission is designed to support continuing engagement after conflict has ended. In other situations, the UN's activities are more limited to technical assistance. In countries in transition from socialist economies in the 1990s, more attention was paid to formalizing accountability and increasing transparency, as well as providing technical assistance for banking reforms and formulating property laws. And the move by the IMF and World Bank away from the Washington Consensus and structural adjustment demonstrates their acknowledgment that one strategy cannot fit all. There are now special programs aimed at states emerging from conflict as well as at states at the lowest level of economic development.

Second, the value of coordinating efforts at the grassroots level has been recognized. To overcome what was often a fragmented approach by various UN programs and agencies, UNDP is now charged with playing a coordinating role within each recipient country, whether that involves a central location, a UN House, where the individual agencies and UNDP are located, giving added power to resident coordinators. The move to require that the Poverty Reduction Strategy Papers be a product of local NGOs as well as various UN agencies, the bank, and fund provides another effort at wider coordination at the grassroots level. Yet as more actors, including bilateral and multilateral donors, participate, coordination becomes even more difficult. A country may have more than twenty-five different donors, each with its own preferences and procedures. Does such fragmentation promote diversity in approaches that may bring more effective results, or does fragmentation lead to chaos and ineffectiveness? That debate continues.

Third, at the substantive level, the UN has incorporated the liberal economic approach, the necessity of market-opening steps for expanding people's choices and ability to help themselves in a sustainable way. Thus, UNDP works with other donors and local officials to develop manuals for countries to use in attracting foreign investment. As part of that strategy, UNDP conducts surveys of what people in different countries want. The bank and fund increasingly listen to governments' desire to provide social safety nets or coordinate their own development policy.

Fourth, more than sixty years of UN development cooperation have shown that poverty is not reduced by general development and economic growth alone. For one thing, the 2011 *World Development Report* issued by the World Bank shows that violence—civil war, ethnic conflict, and organized crime—has become the primary cause of poverty, creating not just a poverty trap, but a violence trap that kills growth and from which countries have difficulty escaping. The legitimacy of government matters along with efforts to prevent violence and to build the conditions for stable peace over the long term. It is impossible, in short, to separate development, statebuilding, and peacebuilding. Bilateral and multilateral aid donors must work with the nonstate sector, including foreign direct investors, to promote poverty reduction and with the government to develop capacity for good governance. Aid workers must work with diplomats, peacekeepers, and human rights advocates. Hence, working in partnerships has become the norm. UNDP has learned also that "the value of educating and training many individuals will remain limited unless the overall policy and institutional environment within which these individuals live and work," and the capacity of the country as a whole, is strengthened.[39] Hence, the UN and other development institutions are now more likely to critique government policies and make investment and aid contingent on meeting certain governance criteria. This represents a broader view of development, one that potentially infringes on state sovereignty.

Fifth, development is no longer seen as unidimensional. The concept of sustainable development has been firmly established so that development means attention to economic distribution, gender equity, and environmental concerns. Yet broadening the meaning of development and elucidating goals such as the MDGs and various governance indicators has not always produced the desired results. Financial and human resources, commitment, and follow-through by national policymakers and the UN are all essential if those goals are to be met.

THE PERSISTENT DILEMMAS

Dilemma 1: Expanding Needs Versus the UN's Limited Capacity

The UN has been an important advocate for the international economic issues that have proliferated in this era of globalization. It has shaped thinking about the requirements for development; introduced new issues to the international agenda; facilitated the mobilization of various constituencies, particularly through the global conferences of the 1970s and 1990s; and provided various institutional responses. The capacity of the UN, the specialized agencies, and the Bretton Woods institutions to respond to the UN Charter's broad mandate for economic and social cooperation has developed in fits and spurts, often in an ad hoc and decentralized manner. New programs and agencies have created a largely unmanageable complex of organizations. With such proliferation inevitably come duplication, contradictory goals, and confusion for donors and recipients alike. Small wonder that coordination has long been an issue for UN economic and social activities and that ECOSOC has never been up to the task.

The main question for the twenty-first century is whether the UN is suited to meet these challenges. Can a decentralized, often redundant system that includes not only the various parts of the UN but also the regional organizations, bilateral donors, the specialized agencies, the Bretton Woods institutions, MNCs, and NGOs become more cohesive? Can the current chaos of development aid lead to sustainable development? Several incremental changes have been made to further UN system coordination for sustainable development. For example, in 2002, the Administrative Committee on Coordination was reorganized into the UN Chief Executives Board for Coordination. This body provides a forum for twenty-eight heads of organizations and programs to meet. Included are the heads of the World Bank, IMF, WTO, WHO, WFP, UNEP, UNDP, FAO,

UNIDO, and IAEA, among others, along with a permanent coordinating committee. This change did bring the Bretton Woods institutions together with other UN agencies and facilitated the global consensus on fighting poverty embodied in the MDGs. But that coordination has not resulted in overall UN leadership on economic issues. Whether the reforms discussed in Chapter 2 will enhance the UN's leadership capacity is an open question.

Dilemma 2: The Persistence of and Challenges to Sovereignty

Efforts by UN system institutions to address economic issues and developmental issues increasingly confront the dilemma of respecting state sovereignty versus intervention in the domestic affairs of states. IMF and World Bank structural adjustment programs clearly required that states adjust their economic and fiscal policies in return for assistance. Indeed, the IMF's power to shape the domestic economic policies of countries receiving aid borders on supranational authority and has been soundly criticized as such. Although the UN has been critical of such policies, UN programs, too, increasingly intrude into areas traditionally reserved for the state, pushing governments to accept a particular economic philosophy and condemning corruption among state officials. Providing technical assistance on issues such as creating a legal system, often with a view about how that system should be constructed, deeply impinges on an area traditionally reserved for states. Coupling economic assistance with calls for both reforms of governance and critiquing sitting governments threatens state sovereignty. This is a trend that is likely to continue in the future. Because of that, the space between the international and the domestic will continue to be a contested one and the boundary between the two less clearly delineated.

Dilemma 3: The Need for Leadership

Unlike security issues, where the United States is still the undisputed dominant power, economic power is increasingly dispersed and the economic system multipolar. Material resources count, but so do intellectual leadership and the strength of numbers in international economic relations. Japan, the EU, India, Brazil, and China are all economic powers whose involvement is critical for the success of development and trade efforts. The United States, for one, has been notably lukewarm on the MDGs and the Global Compact, with few US companies participating. The US preoccupation since 2001 with the war on terrorism, including the wars in Afghanistan and Iraq as well as the economic constraints posed by the 2008–2009 global financial crisis and rising budget deficits, has made it less likely to be a prime mover against poverty. In a striking development, developing countries have become the "engines of the world economy" and contributed most of what economic growth has taken place, according to

the World Bank. Furthermore, trade between developing countries and between them and the BRICS is growing at a rate twice that of world trade. And
"while growth has headed south, debt has headed north."[40] This goes a long way
toward explaining why the third dilemma of leadership is far more of a
dilemma today than even five years ago.

As noted earlier, the World Bank and IMF have begun to accommodate
these shifts. The rapid emergence of the G-20 as a forum in international economic relations is yet another indicator. For meaningful change to occur in
leadership of UN development efforts, however, it is not just a matter of who
are the most powerful states. Successful leadership in development also needs
broad-based participation by people and grassroots organizations in decisionmaking as well as implementation at the lowest possible levels. Hence, there is
greater recognition of the importance of nonstate actors, including NGOs and
MNCs, within the UN system. Partnerships are the modus operandi of the
twenty-first century. Implicitly and, increasingly, explicitly, development is also
linked to human rights, as we see in Chapter 6.

Notes

1. Thomas G. Weiss, David P. Forsythe, Roger A. Coate, and Kelly-Kate Pease,
The United Nations and Changing World Politics, 6th ed. (Boulder: Westview Press,
2010), 282.

2. Karen A. Mingst, "Decentralized, Often Disjointed: The UN and Regional Or-
ganizations in Economic Development," in *The United Nations: Past, Present, and
Future: Proceedings of the 2007 Francis Marion University UN Symposium*, ed. Scott
Kaufman and Alissa Warters (New York: Nova Science, 2009), 147–161.

3. For an extended discussion of the debate, see Richard Jolly et al., *UN Contributions to Development Thinking and Practice* (Bloomington: Indiana University Press,
2004), 66–83. This volume is invaluable for understanding the evolution of development thinking and the UN's contributions.

4. Craig N. Murphy, *The United Nations Development Programme: A Better Way?*
(Cambridge: Cambridge University Press, 2006), 18.

5. Ibid., 242.

6. Mark Malloch Brown, quoted in Weiss et al., *The United Nations and Changing
World Politics*, 285.

7. Yves Berthelot, "Unity and Diversity of Development: The Regional Commis-
sions' Experience," in *Unity and Diversity in Development Ideas: Perspectives from the
UN Regional Commissions*, ed. Yves Berthelot (Bloomington: Indiana University
Press, 2004), 1, 13.

8. Michael Ward, *Quantifying the World: UN Contributions to Statistics* (Bloomington: Indiana University Press, 2004), 2.

9. United Nations, *The World's Women: Trends and Statistics, 1970–1990* (New
York: United Nations, 1991).

10. Richard Jolly, Louis Emmerij, and Thomas G. Weiss, *UN Ideas That Changed the World* (Bloomington: Indiana University Press, 2009), 44.

11. Michelle Miller-Adams, *The World Bank: New Agendas in a Changing World* (London: Routledge, 1999).

12. See Michael Goldman, *Imperial Nature: The World Bank and Struggles for Social Justice in the Age of Globalization* (New Haven: Yale University Press, 2005); and Michel Chossudovsky, *The Globalisation of Poverty: Impacts of IMF and World Bank Reforms* (London: Zed Books, 1997).

13. Joseph E. Stiglitz, *Globalization and Its Discontents* (New York: W. W. Norton, 2002); William Easterly, *The Elusive Quest for Growth: Economists' Adventures and Misadventures in the Tropics* (Cambridge: MIT Press, 2001).

14. Nancy Birdsall and Francis Fukuyama, "The Post-Washington Consensus: Development After the Crisis," *Foreign Affairs* 90, no. 2 (2011): 45–53.

15. "High Stakes," *Economist* (May 15, 2010): 85.

16. See Marc Williams, *Third World Cooperation: The Group of 77 in UNCTAD* (New York: St. Martin's Press, 1991); and Craig N. Murphy, *The Emergence of the NIEO Ideology* (Boulder: Westview Press, 1984).

17. Jolly, Emmerij, and Weiss, *UN Ideas That Changed the World*, 46.

18. "The Doha Round: Dead Man Talking," *Economist* (April 30, 2011).

19. For early illustrations of the Latin American dependency approach, see Teotonio Dos Santos, "The Structure of Dependence," *American Economic Review* 60, no. 5 (1970): 235–246; and Celso Furtado, *Development and Underdevelopment: A Structural View of the Problems of Developed and Underdeveloped Countries* (Berkeley and Los Angeles: University of California Press, 1964).

20. Keith Bradsher, "Trade Officials Agree to End Subsidies for Agricultural Exports," *New York Times,* December 19, 2005.

21. Esther Boserup, *Women's Role in Economic Development* (London: George Allen and Unwin, 1970).

22. See Elisabeth Jay Friedman, Kathryn Hochstetler, and Ann Marie Clark, *Sovereignty, Democracy, and Global Civil Society: State-Society Relations at UN World Conferences* (Albany: State University of New York Press, 2005).

23. "Platform for Action," in *An Agenda for Women's Empowerment: Report of the Fourth World Conference on Women* (A/Conf.177/20). This report also contains the Beijing Declaration.

24. Devaki Jain, *Women, Development, and the UN: A Sixty-Year Quest for Equality and Justice* (Bloomington: Indiana University Press, 2005), 159.

25. World Commission on Environment and Development (Brundtland Commission Report), *Our Common Future* (Oxford: Oxford University Press, 1987), 8.

26. Jolly, Emmerij, and Weiss, *UN Ideas That Changed the World*, 186.

27. UNDP, *Human Development Report, 1990: Concept and Measurement of Human Development* (Oxford: Oxford University Press, 1990), 1.

28. Ibid., 299.

29. John Ruggie, "The United Nations and Globalization: Patterns and Limits of Institutional Adaptation," *Global Governance* 9, no. 3 (2003): 305.

30. See Delfin S. Go, Richard Harmsen, and Hans Timmer, "Regaining Momentum," *Finance and Development* 47, no. 3 (2010): 6–10.

31. Reported in Philippe Douste-Blazy, "The UN Millennium Development Goals Can Be Put Back on Track," *Guardian,* September 5, 2010, www.guardian.co.uk /commentisfree/2010/sep/05/un-millennium-development-goal.

32. See Jeff Marlow, "Progress Report of a Millennium Village," *New York Times,* January 15, 2010, kristof.blogs.nytimes.com/2010/01/15/progress-report-of-a-millennium -village/.

33. See Michael A. Clemens and Gabriel Demombynes, "When Does Rigorous Impact Evaluation Make a Difference? The Case of the Millennium Villages," Working Paper 225, Center for Global Development (October 2010), available at www.cgdev.org.

34. Jagdish Bhagwati, "Time for a Rethink," *Finance and Development* (September 2010): 15–16.

35. Data provided by the UN Office of the High Representative for Least Developed Countries, Landlocked Countries, and Small Island Developing States, in "External Investments More Central in Least Developed Countries," *Africa Renewal* (April 1011): 15.

36. For this history, see Tagi Sagafi-nejad with John Dunning, *The UN and Transnationals: From Code to Compact* (Bloomington: Indiana University Press, 2006).

37. John Gerard Ruggie, "Global-governance.net: The Global Compact as Learning Network," *Global Governance* 7, no. 4 (2001): 371–378.

38. Patrick Bernhagen and Neil J. Mitchell, "The Private Provision of Public Goods: Corporate Commitments and the United Nations Global Compact," *International Studies Quarterly* 54, no. 4 (2010): 1175–1187.

39. UN Development Program, "UNDP in Vietnam: Some Lessons Learned in Supporting the Transition from Poverty to Prosperity" staff paper (September 1997), 18.

40. "Seeing the World Differently," *Economist* (June 12, 2010): 65–66.q

6

Human Rights

Today's human rights violations are the causes of
tomorrow's conflicts.
—Mary Robinson, UN High Commissioner
for Human Rights (1998)

Since the end of World War II, human rights have become a major issue in
world politics and "the single most magnetic political idea of the contemporary
time," in the words of Zbigniew Brzezinski, the former US national security adviser.[1] This trend is best explained not by realism or liberalism but by constructivism. With the spread of the idea that the protection of human rights knows
no boundaries and the international community has an obligation to ensure
that governments guarantee internationally recognized rights, state sovereignty
has been diminished. The end of **apartheid** in South Africa, the recognition of
women's rights as human rights, the spread of democracy, and the emerging
norm of humanitarian intervention all provide evidence of the trend. At the
same time, news headlines regularly remind us that political, civil, social, and
economic rights of individuals and groups are often violated, whether in Syria,
the Sudan, Uganda, or China.

The UN has played an important role in the process of globalizing human
rights. It has been central to establishing the norms, institutions, and activities for
giving effect to this powerful idea that certain rights are universal. States have sel-
dom been prime movers in this process, although their acceptance and support
for human rights is critical. The international human rights movement—a growing network of human-rights-oriented NGOs—and dedicated individuals have
been responsible for drafting much of the language of human rights conventions

and for mounting transnational campaigns to promote human rights norms. The role of these groups and individuals and the processes by which they have persuaded policymakers to adopt human rights policies demonstrate the power of ideas to reshape definitions of national interests, consistent with constructivism.[2] Before we examine the UN and other actors' roles in this process, however, let us look at the historical antecedents in the League of Nations, the International Labour Organization, and key events.

FROM THE LEAGUE OF NATIONS TO THE UNITED NATIONS

Although the League of Nations Covenant made little mention of human rights as such, it nonetheless addressed rights-related issues and set important precedents. For example, the covenant did include specific provision for the protection of minorities and, through the Mandate System, for dependent peoples in colonies of the defeated powers of World War I (Turkey and Germany). A designated victor nation would administer the territory under the league's supervision and so provide a degree of protection from abuses. And, although the Mandates Commission itself did not have rights to inspect, it did acquire a reputation for neutrality in administration. This reflected the growing sentiment that the international community had responsibilities over dependent peoples, the eventual goal being self-determination.

The 1919 Paris Peace Conference also produced five agreements, known as the Minority Treaties, that required beneficiaries of the peace settlement (such as Poland, Czechoslovakia, and Greece) to provide protection to all inhabitants regardless of nationality, language, race, or religion. Similar obligations for civil and political rights were imposed on the defeated states. Minority rights became a major agenda item for the League Council, Assembly, and committees, the admission of new members being contingent on a pledge to protect minority rights; special mechanisms were established for monitoring implementation. In addition, the League established principles on assisting refugees and the Refugee Organization. This step marked the first recognition that the international community has responsibility for protecting those forced to flee their homelands because of repression or war. The League also devoted attention to women's and children's rights, as well as the rights to a minimum level of health. And in the 1930s, the League's assembly discussed the possibility of an international human rights document, but it took no action.

The ILO's mandate to work for the improvement of workers' living conditions, health, safety, and livelihood was consistent with the concepts of economic and social rights. Between 1919 and 1939, the ILO approved sixty-seven conventions that covered such issues as hours of work, maternity protection, minimum age, and old-age insurance; in 1926, it was the first IGO to introduce a procedure for supervising the standards established. This procedure provided an important model for the UN and continues to be a key part of the international human rights regime.

The precedents established by the League and ILO influenced the drafting of the UN Charter's provisions at the end of World War II. In addition, however, the drafters were influenced by wartime Allied goals, the Holocaust, and human rights advocates. First, President Franklin D. Roosevelt's famous "Four Freedoms" speech in 1941 called for "a world founded upon four essential freedoms" and together with his vision of "the moral order" formed a normative base for the Allies in their fight against Germany and Japan.[3] The liberation of Nazi concentration camps in the closing weeks of World War II revealed the full extent of the Holocaust and the deaths of 6 million Jews, gypsies, and other "undesirables." This was a second powerful impetus for seeing human rights as an international issue that required more than talk, though there is debate today over the impact that the Holocaust had on international human rights.[4] In addition, at the UN's founding conference in San Francisco in 1945, a broad spectrum of groups from churches to peace societies, along with delegates from various small states, pushed for the inclusion of human rights language in the Charter. Although they were more weakly worded than these advocates had hoped, seven references to human rights were scattered throughout the final document. Thus, the UN Charter placed the promotion of human rights among the central purposes of the new organization.[5] Over time, the UN's actions changed the public discourse, cemented the idea of human rights for all, and provided an arena for international action.[6]

UN CHARTER PRINCIPLES AND ORGANIZATIONAL STRUCTURES

One of the primary purposes of the UN, as set forth in Chapter I, Article 1, is international cooperation in solving various international problems, including those of a "humanitarian character," and "in promoting and encouraging respect for human rights and for fundamental freedoms for all without distinction as to race, sex, language, or religion." Articles 55(c) and 56 amplify the UN's responsibility to promote "universal respect for, and observance of, human rights and fundamental freedoms for all" and the obligation of member states to "take joint and separate action in cooperation with the Organization for the achievement of the purposes set forth in Article 55."

These provisions did not define what was meant by "human rights and fundamental freedoms," but they established that human rights were a matter of international concern and that states had assumed an as yet undefined international obligation relating to them. They also contradicted the Charter's affirmation of state sovereignty and the principle of nonintervention in the domestic affairs of states contained in Article 2(7). They provided the UN with the legal authority, however, to undertake the definition and codification of these rights. The foundation for that effort was laid by the General Assembly's passage on December 10, 1948, of the Universal Declaration of Human Rights to "serve as a common standard of achievement for all peoples of all nations."[7] Taken together, the UN Charter and the Universal Declaration of Human Rights represented a watershed in the revolution that placed human rights at the center of world politics.

The General Assembly

The General Assembly's broad mandate to discuss any issue within the scope of the UN Charter led states to use this forum to raise specific human rights issues almost from the beginning. In its first session in 1946, India and other countries introduced the issue of South Africa's treatment of its sizable Indian population; thus began the UN's longest-running human rights issue: apartheid in South Africa. Debates concerning colonial issues, and particularly the right to self-determination of colonial and dependent peoples, occupied a major share of General Assembly agendas in the 1950s and 1960s.[8] During the Cold War, some Western countries pushed issues such as forced labor under communism. Over the years, the General Assembly and almost every other UN body have been pressed by Arab states and their allies to condemn Israel's treatment of the Palestinian people in the Occupied Territories. In 2000, for example, the assembly adopted more than twenty resolutions on Israeli-related issues. In the late 1990s, the assembly repeatedly condemned the Taliban government in Afghanistan for its appalling human rights record. In short, the General Assembly's attention to human rights issues has reflected the majority at any given time. These debates have often spilled over into other organs and specialized agencies, leading to charges of politicization. Yet because the assembly is the primary global forum, its debates and resolutions draw attention to issues and, in naming specific states, may shame them into taking action.

The assembly's power under Article 13(1) "to conduct studies and make recommendations for the purpose of . . . assisting in the realizing of human rights and fundamental freedoms for all without distinction as to race, sex, language, or religion" has been used with respect to a variety of issues. Thus, for example, the General Assembly established the UN Decade for Women (1975–1985) and the UN Decade for Human Rights Education (1995–2005). It has approved rights-related declarations such as the 1959 Declaration on the Right of the Child, the 1967 Declaration on the Elimination of Discrimination Against Women, the 1993 Declaration on the Elimination of Violence Against Women, and the 2007 Declaration on the Rights of Indigenous Peoples. Such declarations often form the basis for binding international conventions. In 2008, after contentious debate,

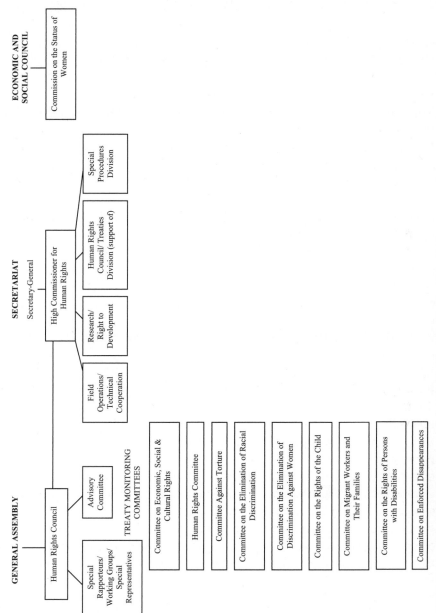

FIGURE 6.1. UN Human Rights Organizational Structure (Selected Bodies)

the General Assembly approved a declaration seeking to decriminalize homosexuality, breaking the taboo on the subject of homosexual rights in UN bodies. Two of the assembly's main committees contribute to the drafting of human rights treaties—the Social, Humanitarian, and Cultural (or Third) Committee and the Legal (or Sixth) Committee. The General Assembly itself must then approve all UN human rights conventions.

Two other types of human rights bodies report to the General Assembly. These include the nine treaty bodies established by the parties to select human rights treaties to monitor implementation. Their members are independent experts (see Figure 6.1). Also reporting to the assembly now is the Human Rights Council (HRC), created in 2006 to replace the former Commission on Human Rights.

Human Rights Council. In 2006, the General Assembly overwhelmingly approved the creation of a new forty-seven-member Human Rights Council to report to the assembly. HRC members are selected in a secret ballot by a majority of the assembly's members for three-year renewable terms with seats distributed among the five recognized regional groups. All council members' human rights records are subject to scrutiny, and the council can suspend members suspected of abuses with a two-thirds vote. The HRC meets for at least ten weeks throughout the year. In 2011, it met in an emergency session to condemn the Libyan government's attacks on its own people.

The Human Rights Council replaced the Commission on Human Rights, which between 1946 and 2006 had been the hub of the UN system's human rights activity and reported to ECOSOC. The commission had drafted most of the major documents that elaborate and define human rights norms, including the Universal Declaration on Human Rights, the two international human rights covenants, and treaties on a range of issues from torture to the rights of the child and the rights of migrant workers. After 1970, its responsibilities had expanded to include procedures for investigating gross violations such as racism and violations in Israeli-occupied Arab territories as well as individual complaints (through what are known as 1235 and 1503 procedures). An empirical study of the commission's actions from 1979 to 2001 found that "targeting and punishment were driven to a considerable degree by the actual human rights records of potential targets."[9] By the mid-1990s, some 60 percent of the more egregious violators had been examined by the commission, a finding that remained consistent in the 2002–2005 period. The commission was criticized, however, for singling out some for human rights abuses and not others and for having among its elected members well-known abusers such as the Sudan, Zimbabwe, Saudi Arabia, Pakistan, Cuba, Nepal, and Libya. Widespread public attention was drawn to the commission in 2001 when the United States lost its seat for the first time. Those who voted against the United States, including some of its allies, did so because of perceived US lack of support for the UN, its continued support of Israel, and its efforts to single out China and Cuba for their human rights abuses.

By creating the Human Rights Council, the General Assembly hoped to improve the credibility of the organization's primary human rights body. The fact that states like Libya were elected to the council has caused many to question, however, whether the council is different. That question was partially addressed in 2011 when the HRC denounced the armed attacks on civilians, killings, arrests, and detentions committed by the Libyan government. The General Assembly subsequently removed Libya from its seat on the HRC.

The HRC has retained many of the same responsibilities and mechanisms as the commission, including the use of special procedures whereby it can mandate a special rapporteur, a special representative of the secretary-general, or a working group of independent experts (usually five members, one from each region) to address specific country situations or thematic issues. The Office of the High Commissioner for Human Rights (discussed below) provides personnel, research, and logistical support for these HRC-appointed special rapporteurs and working groups who may serve no longer than six years.

In 2008, the HRC established a new Advisory Committee made up of eighteen human rights experts who form a think tank for the council. They conduct studies and provide research-based advice at the request of the HRC, drawing on information from NGOs with ECOSOC consultative status, specialized agencies, states that are not HRC members, other IGOs, member states, and observers. The Advisory Committee is clearly intended to be more subordinate to the HRC than its predecessor, the former Sub-Commission on the Promotion and Protection of Human Rights.

An important HRC innovation is the Universal Periodic Review (UPR), where each member state is reviewed by three separate sources: by the state itself, by the Office of the High Commissioner for Human Rights with input from other UN bodies, and by international human rights groups. The reviews along with the monitoring role of the treaty bodies are discussed below.

The Security Council

The UN Charter left the Security Council free to define what constitutes a threat to international peace and security. Throughout the Cold War years, the council did not link security with human rights violations. Like the General Assembly, it did address issues such as the rights of colonial peoples to self-determination, of the Palestinians in the Occupied Territories, and of black majorities under apartheid in South Africa and in Southern Rhodesia because these were seen as situations that threatened international peace and security. The Cold War's end, greater emphasis on human rights issues, and egregious human rights violations in various conflicts made it increasingly difficult to separate human rights abuses and threats to peace. In addition, beginning with Secretary-General Pérez de Cuéllar's 1991 report to the General Assembly, each secretary-general has played an active role in urging the Security Council to address the links between human rights and security. As discussed in Chapter 4, the Security Council has repeatedly found itself faced with humanitarian crises and demands for intervention under Chapter VII of the Charter. Ethnic cleansing, genocide, and other crimes against humanity led it to create ad hoc war crimes tribunals for the former Yugoslavia, Rwanda, and Sierra Leone. Peacebuilding operations are often needed to address human rights protection.

By the end of the 1990s, the Security Council had definitely embraced human rights and was routinely issuing declarations on issues ranging from child soldiers to the role of women in promoting international peace and stability. For example, it adopted Resolution 1325 in 2000, mandating gender training in peacekeeping operations and urging stronger participation by women in field operations. Human rights activities have also been incorporated into the mandates for several peacekeeping operations. In late 2005, the council took the further step of agreeing to hear a report from Secretary-General Kofi Annan on human rights violations in Myanmar. Later in 2007, however, China and Russia vetoed a resolution on those violations, claiming that they had nothing to do with international peace and security. In 2008, the United States and others pushed the council to impose international sanctions on Zimbabwe for its government's human rights violations, but once again both China and Russia vetoed the action, explaining that the measure represented excessive interference in that country's domestic affairs.

As discussed in Chapter 4, the Security Council has a mixed record in responding to complex humanitarian emergencies since the Cold War's end. Its actions in crises from Haiti to Bosnia, Somalia, the DRC, East Timor, Darfur, and Libya reflect mixtures of traditional concerns about threats to international peace and security, greater attention to human rights, and the evolving notion of human security, discussed in Chapter 7.

ECOSOC

The Economic and Social Council was given authority under Article 62 to conduct studies, issue reports, and make recommendations "for the purpose of promoting respect for, and observance of, human rights and fundamental freedoms for all." It has used this authority to address a number of issues such as genocide, the protection of minorities, and, with the ILO, the prevention of forced labor. In addition, Article 68 gave ECOSOC the specific mandate of setting up commissions in the area of human rights, and in 1946 and 1947 it established the Commission on Human Rights, the Commission on the Status of Women, and the Sub-Commission on Prevention of Discrimination and Protection of Minorities (renamed the Sub-Commission on the Protection and Promotion of Human Rights in 1999, but replaced in 2008 by the HRC's Advisory Committee as discussed earlier). Until the establishment of Office of the High Commissioner for Human Rights (discussed below) and the Human Rights Council (discussed above), these commissions had borne the major responsibility for human rights activities in the UN system. With the creation of the HRC, ECOSOC clearly has much less involvement with human rights issues.

Secretariat: The UN High Commissioner for Human Rights

An important addition to the UN organizational structure relating to human rights is the Office of the High Commissioner for Human Rights (OHCHR), established in 1993. It provides a visible international advocate for human rights in the same way that the UN High Commissioner for Refugees focuses international attention on that problem. The office is responsible for promotion and coordination, for mainstreaming human rights into the UN system, and for furnishing information to and supporting the work of relevant UN bodies. It serves as the secretariat for the Human Rights Council and supports the work of special procedures—special rapporteurs, independent experts, and working groups—appointed by the HRC to monitor specific human rights situations and problems.

Increasingly, OHCHR has assumed an operational role, providing technical assistance to countries in the form of training courses for judges and prison officials, electoral assistance, and advisory services on constitutional and legislative reform, among other things.[10] With field offices in many countries, OHCHR is able not only to help strengthen domestic institutions but also to promote compliance with international human rights standards and to report directly to the high commissioner on abuses. The high commissioner sits on the UN Secretary-General's Senior Management Group that effectively serves as a cabinet. The office, however, is handicapped by its small budget allocation (just 2.8 percent of the total UN budget). Although the amount of funding from the UN's regular budget has increased gradually since 2005, more than two-thirds of OHCHR's funding comes from voluntary contributions. It also oversees three humanitarian trust funds that were established by the General Assembly to support activities advancing specific human rights issues. The funds are the Voluntary Fund for Victims of Torture, the Voluntary Trust Fund on Contemporary Forms of Slavery, and the Voluntary Fund for Indigenous Populations.

The office depends in part on the legitimacy, personality, leadership skills, and initiative of the individual commissioner. Three of the six commissioners to date have been women. Mary Robinson, former president of Ireland, and Louise Arbour, Canadian judge and former prosecutor for the Yugoslav and

Rwandan ad hoc criminal tribunals, clearly elevated the effectiveness and prestige of the office. The appointment in 2008 of Navanethem (Navi) Pillay, former judge on the South African High Court, the Rwandan tribunal, and the International Criminal Court, also enhanced credibility of the office. Her active participation in human rights NGOs has solidified critical ties with that community. Her call for an independent investigation into human rights abuses in Sri Lanka after the end of that country's civil war in 2009 and her support for international protection of civilians in the 2011 Libyan conflict is evidence of a strong human rights voice.

The International Court of Justice

The ICJ's role in human rights has generally been minimal. It did confirm the principle of self-determination in the Western Sahara case (1975), and it concluded in a 1971 opinion that South Africa had violated its obligations toward South West Africa (Namibia) under the Universal Declaration of Human Rights. In 2007, the court ruled on the question of whether Serbia had committed genocide in Bosnia-Herzegovina.[11] The lack of attention to human rights by the ICJ has to do primarily with the fact that only states can bring contentious cases to the court, while the General Assembly and Security Council can seek advisory opinions. This tells us more about the limitations of the court itself rather than about the UN and human rights.

To see how the UN organs and bodies have addressed human rights issues, we focus first on how the UN has helped to set the norms, then examine how monitoring, promotional, and enforcement activities occur. Thereafter, we use a series of case studies to illustrate the UN's role.

THE ROLE OF THE UN IN HUMAN RIGHTS

Defining Human Rights: Setting Standards and Norms

The UN's role in setting human rights standards began with the General Assembly's unanimous approval of the Universal Declaration of Human Rights on December 9, 1948, and the passage one day earlier of the Convention on the Prevention and Punishment of the Crime of Genocide. Under the tireless leadership of Eleanor Roosevelt, the wife of the late president Franklin D. Roosevelt and chair of the UN Commission on Human Rights, these documents articulated a far-reaching human rights agenda for the UN.

The Universal Declaration, called by some the most important document of the twentieth century,[12] drew on ideas dating from the French and American revolutions and earlier bills of rights as well as principles of natural rights. Among its catalog of thirty principles, it elucidated rights critical for the exercise of political

PHOTOGRAPH 6.1. Eleanor Roosevelt holds the Universal Declaration of Human Rights, November 1949. *Source*: UN Photo 23783.

freedom, rights essential for the preservation of a civil society, and the social and economic rights of individuals. The declaration listed those claims as a first step toward the articulation of international human rights standards. Since the declaration was only a General Assembly resolution, the expectation was that these rights would be set forth in a covenant (or treaty) that would bind states to respect them. It took until 1966 for the General Assembly to approve the International Covenant on Civil and Political Rights and the International Covenant on Economic, Social, and Cultural Rights, with both entering into force in 1976. Together with the Universal Declaration, they are known as the **International Bill of Rights**.

The two international covenants took so long to ratify because they reflected very different perspectives about what rights are deemed to be universal. The first covenant emerged from so-called **first-generation human rights**, those rights associated with political and civil liberties. They were the first rights to be incorporated into national constitutions and are "negative rights" in that they are intended to block government authorities from interfering with private individuals in civil society. They are linked to Western liberalism and include the right to free speech, freedom of religion, a free press, and the right to congregate at will. The second covenant encompasses **second-generation human rights**, building upon the socialist view that emphasizes economic and social rights such as the right to employment, to health care, and to social security. Referred to as "positive rights," these are the basic material benefits that the state must provide to individuals. While the Universal Declaration incorporated both sets of rights, conflict between Western and socialist views blocked conclusion of a single treaty and resulted ultimately in two treaties. The fact that the United States has yet to ratify the Covenant on Economic, Social, and Cultural Rights indicates that the difference in views persists.

Both prior to and following the approval of the covenants, the UN has brought into being an array of other human rights treaties that systematically define a variety of first- and second-generation rights—including treaties on genocide, slavery and forced labor, refugees, racial discrimination, and discrimination against women. Some of these evolved from the work of UN specialized agencies, particularly the ILO; most were drafted by the Commission on Human Rights. Still other conventions include what many call **third-generation human rights** that protect designated groups, including children, the disabled, indigenous peoples, and migrant workers. Although more controversial, many human rights activists also advocate for collective rights to a safe environment, peace, democracy, and development, for example. A list of selected UN human rights conventions is found in Table 6.1.

Disagreements about the relative priority of the three generations of rights are a major reason for the lack of political will for the enforcement of international human rights. Just as the West has dominated international economic relations, it has tried to dominate the setting of standards for human rights. Thus, the strongest global and regional human rights mechanisms protect civil and political rights, but the other two generations have received less attention. It is also far more difficult to establish standards of compliance for economic and social rights and politically far more difficult to secure agreement on third-generation rights, as the General Assembly's failure to approve the draft convention on indigenous peoples demonstrates.

There is also lingering controversy over whether human rights are truly universal, applicable to all peoples, in all states, religions, and cultures, or whether those rights depend on the cultural setting. In the 1990s, a number of Asian states argued that many of the human rights documents represented Western values and that the West was interfering in their internal affairs with its own definition of human rights. Particularly sensitive has been the debate relating to issues of religion, women's status, child protection, family planning, and practices such as female circumcision. As legal scholar and activist Abdullahi An-Na'im, argues, "Detailed and credible knowledge of local culture is essential for the effective promotion and protection of human rights in any society."[13]

TABLE 6.1. Selected UN Human Rights Conventions

Convention	Opened for ratification	Entered into force	Ratifications, (as of 2011)
General Human Rights			
International Covenant on Civil and Political Rights	1966	1976	167
International Covenant on Economic, Social and Rights	1966	1976	160
Racial Discrimination			
International Convention on the Elimination of All Forms of Racial Discrimination	1966	1969	174
International Convention on the Suppression and Punishment of the Crime of Apartheid	1973	1976	107
Rights of Women			
Convention on the Elimination of All Forms of Discrimination Against Women	1979	1981	186
Human Trafficking and Other Slave-Like Practices			
UN Convention for the Suppression of the Traffic in Persons and of the Exploitation of the Prostitution of Others	1949	1951	81
Supplementary Convention on the Abolition of Slavery, the Slave Trade, and Institutions and Practices Similar to Slavery	1956	1957	123
UN Convention Against Transnational Organized Crime: Protocol to Prevent, Suppress and Punish Trafficking in Persons, Especially Women and Children	2000	2003	143
Refugees and Stateless Persons			
Convention Relating to the Status of Refugees	1951	1954	144

(continues)

TABLE 6.1. Selected UN Human Rights Conventions *(continued)*

Convention	Opened for ratification	Entered into force	Ratifications, (as of 2011)
Children			
Convention on the Rights of the Child	1989	1990	192
Optional Protocol to the Convention on the Rights of the Child on the Involvement of Children in Armed Conflict	2000	2002	139
Optional Protocol to the Convention on the Rights of the Child on the Sale of Children, Child Prostitution and Child Pornography	2000	2002	142
Other			
Convention on the Prevention and Punishment of the Crime of Genocide	1948	1951	141
Optional Protocol to the Convention Against Torture and Other Cruel, Inhuman or Degrading Treatment or Punishment	2002	2006	57
Convention Concerning Indigenous and Tribal Peoples in Independent Countries	1989	1991	20
International Convention on the Protection of the Rights of All Migrant Workers and Members of Their Families	1990	2003	44
Convention on the Rights of Persons with Disabilities	2007	2008	98
International Convention for the Protection of All Persons from Enforced Disappearance	2006	2010	23

SOURCES: University of Minnesota Human Rights Library and UN High Commissioner for Human Rights.

The Final Declaration and Programme of Action of the Vienna World Conference on Human Rights, issued on June 24, 1993, stated: "All human rights are universal, indivisible and interdependent and interrelated." Regional arrangements, the declaration stated, "should reinforce universal human rights standards, as contained in international human rights instruments, and their protection." Yet as former secretary-general Kofi Annan noted, "It was never the people who complained of the universality of human rights, nor did the people consider human rights as a Western or Northern imposition. It was often their leaders who did so."[14]

"Getting countries to toe the mark is only possible when there is a mark to toe."[15] Clearly, the UN has played a major role in establishing those marks. Yet setting standards is only the first step in protecting human rights norms. There must be effective actions by states. Thus, the UN has moved in bits and pieces from articulating norms to monitoring, promoting, and enforcing the standards.[16]

From Articulating Human Rights Norms to Monitoring

Monitoring the implementation of human rights norms requires procedures for receiving complaints of violations from affected individuals or interested groups as well as reports of state practice. It may also be accompanied by the power to comment on reports, make recommendations to states, appoint working groups or special rapporteurs, and vote on resolutions of condemnation. Publicity and public "shaming" are key tools of multilateral monitoring of state compliance.

The ILO was the first international organization to establish procedures for monitoring human rights within states—in this instance, workers' rights—beginning in 1926. Acclaimed as having the most effective monitoring system, the ILO compiles reports from governments about practices under various ILO conventions. ILO staff then prepares comments for the Committee of Experts using a variety of sources: direct contacts, reports of other UN bodies, and reports from employers' and workers' groups to supplement government reports. The findings of the Committee of Experts, while not binding on states, are conveyed to a conference committee for a final report. In some cases, the ILO actually investigates allegations of state noncompliance through its Commission of Inquiry. Although ILO procedures can lead to enforcement under Article 33 of the organization's constitution, the norm is not to utilize coercive measures, but to work with the country in question and offer technical assistance programs to facilitate compliance.

With only governments represented in the UN and in both the former Commission on Human Rights and the Human Rights Council, however, monitoring is much more problematic than standard setting. Nevertheless, developments in the 1970s outside of the UN provided a major impetus for the further evolution of international human rights protection. First, the number of human rights

NGOs increased dramatically; they emerged as a powerful political force, publicizing information on human rights violations and pressing for action by governments, the UN, and regional organizations. Second, events in several parts of the world fueled activists' efforts. Among these were the repressive military regimes that came to power in Chile and Argentina, apartheid's deepening repressiveness in South Africa, and the 1975 Helsinki Accords between the Soviet Union, Eastern European countries, Western Europe, and the United States, which opened the Communist countries to scrutiny and pressure for political liberalization. Third, several countries, including the United States, introduced human rights into their foreign policies in the 1970s. President Jimmy Carter's public support for human rights provided a major boost. Fourth, a broad coalition of West, East, and nonaligned states helped bring much greater attention to UN human rights activities. Most states then found it impossible politically not to give at least some token support to international human rights efforts.

In 1967, the UN Commission on Human Rights was empowered for the first time to examine gross violations of human rights in South Africa and Southern Rhodesia. Further investigations against specific states followed, setting precedents for monitoring. In 1970, ECOSOC Resolution 1503 authorized the commission to undertake confidential investigations of individual complaints that suggest "a consistent pattern of gross and reliably attested violations." This 1503 Procedure, however, only provided for examination of complaints in private and terminated with a report to the commission. Nonetheless, the commission significantly expanded its activities during the 1970s, creating working groups to study specific civil rights problems such as forced disappearances, torture, religious discrimination, and the situation in Chile after the 1973 coup.[17]

In 2008, the Human Rights Council completed a review of the special procedures system, including all existing mandates for special rapporteurs and working groups. In early 2011, there were thirty-three thematic and eight country mandates, ranging from issues such as the Palestinian territories, involuntary detentions, torture, and contemporary forms of slavery to disappearances. The special procedures mandates typically call for the mandate holders (who serve voluntarily, without pay, in order to remain impartial) to examine, monitor, advise, and publicly report on the human rights situation in a given country or a major worldwide problem of violations. Special rapporteurs may respond to individual complaints, conduct studies, and make country visits to investigate the situation. Although the 1503 special procedure can handle only a fraction of the complaints received each year, it does provide means for placing pressure on offending governments as well as encouraging dialogue to address the complaints.

The other primary mode for UN monitoring is through the nine treaty bodies created in connection with specific human rights treaties (see Figure 6.1).[18] Two are linked to the two covenants: The Human Rights Committee provided for by the Covenant on Civil and Political Rights and the Committee on Economic, Social, and Cultural Rights; others are linked to the conventions on the rights of the child, migrant workers, and disabled persons and on the elimination of racial discrimination, torture, discrimination against women, and forced disappearances. Each requires states to submit periodic reports of their progress toward implementation of the treaty. Committees of independent experts elected by the parties to each treaty review the reports, engage in dialogue with governments, and issue concluding comments. Human rights NGOs frequently prepare their own "shadow reports," which provide the committees with an independent assessment of whether governments are fulfilling their commitments and put additional pressure on governments. Other UN agencies such as UNICEF in the case of the Committee on the Rights of the Child may also be important sources of information, while the OHCHR assists with follow-up and regional meetings for each treaty body to assist with the cumbersome reporting processes.

The human rights treaties vary in their provision for individual or group petitions and complaints. Even where there is such a provision, states themselves are generally reluctant to accept it. For example, only about one-third of the states that are party to the International Covenant on Civil and Political Rights have accepted the optional provision that allows individual petitions, and the same is true for the Convention Against Torture. The record is even worse with respect to the Convention on the Elimination of Racial Discrimination: Only a dozen of the parties permit petitions, and of those only a few are African states. No Asian states have accepted this provision. A further problem arises from the limited number of petitions that can be handled in a given year. Of the thousands of complaints relating to civil and political rights filed with the secretary-general each year, only a small fraction can be considered by the Human Rights Committee.

Most scholars agree that further reforms are needed. The treaty bodies are overburdened with work, making effective follow-up impossible. States are bogged down by multiple reporting requirements; late and incomplete reports remain a persistent problem. And even if reports are adequate, many of the UN monitoring systems lack the mandate and capacity to push implementation to the next level.

This leads us to ask whether UN investigations, reports, and resolutions make a difference. One argument contends that, over time, repeated condemnations (often referred to as "naming and shaming") can produce change; this was true to some extent in South Africa, as discussed below. Yet in that case, the repeated condemnations were subsequently coupled with more coercive sanctions. Another point of view holds that public condemnations can antagonize states and harden their position—the opposite of the intended effect. For example, sixteen years of General Assembly resolutions linking Zionism with racism only antagonized Israel and the United States, and it had no effect on the rights of Palestinians in Israel or the Occupied Territories.

So do human rights standards and treaties change state behavior? The evidence is mixed. One study found that if issues within the treaties are taken up by civil society groups, then the state's actual human rights practices are improved. In other words, NGO mobilization can effectively pressure governments.[19] Another study of the effectiveness of monitoring by the UN, NGOs, and the media between 1975 and 2000, however, found "governments put in the global spotlight for violations often adopt better protections for political rights afterward, but they rarely stop or appear to lessen acts of terror. Worse, terror sometimes increases after publicity."[20] That same study also found that when NGOs subsequently took up those human rights issues, the state's human rights practices improved.

In short, although UN human rights monitoring has improved over the years, it has also remained limited in its measurable impact. It is one thing to point to complex procedures, quite another to link those procedures to changes in attitudes and behavior. Some states have opposed aggressive monitoring of their activities. Following the 1989 Tiananmen Square massacre in China, for example, the Sub-Commission on the Prevention of Discrimination approved resolutions criticizing human rights in China—the first condemnations against a major power. China fought back, challenging the aggressive monitoring actions and drawing support from many developing countries. Together, they challenged the extent of NGO involvement, the independence of the subcommission members, the open proceedings, and the secret voting. Beginning in 1993, China successfully blocked all action on US-introduced resolutions dealing with its human rights situation, thereby demonstrating the limits of UN monitoring of ongoing systematic abuse of human rights by a powerful state.[21] Only in 2005, after ten years of effort, did the special rapporteur on torture, for example, secure China's agreement for an official visit. He found abuse "still widespread" and accused the Chinese authorities of obstructing his work.[22] China, in turn, attempted to get the rapporteur to alter the report. Similar to China's attempt to prevent damaging reports from being published, Rwanda attempted unsuccessfully to suppress the publication in 2010 of a report ordered by OHCHR that implicated it in genocide in the Democratic Republic of the Congo.[23] If states believed that such reports did not have an impact, they would not object to publication of the findings.

Translating norms and rhetoric into actions that go beyond stopping violations to change long-term attitudes and behavior is the challenge of promoting human rights. UN efforts in this sphere have been scattered throughout the UN system.

From Monitoring to Promotion

Monitoring activities and evaluating successes and failures over time are not enough in themselves. There are various ways in which efforts are made through the UN system to promote the implementation and observance of international human rights norms. The OHCHR as the secretariat for the Human Rights Council plays a key role in the process and is considered one of the main focal points for promotional activities. As part of their mandates, special rapporteurs, independent experts, and working groups may provide technical assistance to governments and local groups and issue urgent appeals to governments. In 2010, for example, 604 communications were sent to 110 governments.

As noted earlier, the Human Rights Council has initiated the practice of Universal Periodic Reviews. To ensure equal treatment for all, every member state participates in evaluating the strengths and weaknesses of its human rights record every four years. The reviews are conducted by the UPR Working Group (the forty-seven council members) and any other state that wishes to participate. The group reviews national reports compiled by the state under review, information from the independent human rights groups and experts within the UN system compiled by OHCHR, and information provided by other stakeholders, namely, national human rights institutions and nongovernmental organizations. During a three-hour interactive dialogue, states participate and stakeholders can attend, but the latter can speak only when the HRC convenes in regular session. The ultimate goal of the exercise is to design activities and programs to support and expand the promotion of human rights in member countries. States themselves are responsible for implementing the recommendations and are held accountable for progress when reviewed four years later.

A key OHCHR responsibility is to promote mainstreaming of human rights throughout the UN system. Since the early 1990s, the language of second- and third-generation human rights has increasingly been linked to development activities and programs across the entire UN system. Secretary-General Boutros-Ghali's *Agenda for Development* (1995) helped to make this connection through its emphasis on the right to development that had been endorsed by the General Assembly in 1986 (A/41/128). Now the World Bank promotes "good governance," including political and civil rights, among its aid recipients, along with the empowerment of women and participation by civil society. UNDP's annual *Human Development Report* includes numerous indexes that measure gender empowerment, life expectancy, literacy, well-being, and other variables linked to "human," not just economic, development. The Millennium Development Goals discussed in Chapter 5 join all three generations of rights to the goals of eradicating poverty; promoting human dignity; achieving peace, democracy, and environmental sustainability; and involving people in decisions affecting them and their communities. OHCHR has linked each MDG goal to relevant provisions of existing human rights treaties.

The shift in UNICEF's activities since the 1980s illustrates how the incorporation of rights-based language has been influential. UNICEF was pressured by NGOs who saw the ethical and pragmatic justification for rights-based language protecting children. The bureaucracy recognized that such an approach was in its interest as it moved into new activities like its program on "children in especially difficult circumstances," that is, children in natural disasters, wars, or generally at risk. UNICEF became an active participant in the writing of the Convention on the Rights of the Child, then mobilized to promote its adoption. The convention has since served as a motivator for UNICEF programming both under its traditional activities (education, medical care, and nutrition for children) as well as its newer activities (political and civil rights for children, child trafficking, and protection against abuse). As one scholar notes, "UNICEF consistently argues that it now takes a more 'holistic' approach to children in need, looking at all their needs, rather than narrowly focusing on survival and basic development."[24]

Rights-based approaches and programming have also infused the UN's work in promoting democracy. Since the end of the 1980s, the UN has promoted democratization through its electoral assistance programs in conjunction with peacebuilding missions such as those in Namibia, Nicaragua, Cambodia, Kosovo, East Timor, the DRC, Iraq, and Afghanistan. Many of these missions have also involved drafting constitutional, judicial, and security reforms consistent with democratic systems.

The UN Electoral Assistance Division, created in 1992, plays a key role in promoting political and civil rights and democracy by providing technical assistance regarding political rights and democratization to states requesting such assistance. More than one hundred member states have requested assistance on the legal, technical, administrative, and human rights aspects of organizing and conducting democratic elections. The role the UN plays varies according to the wishes of the state. Sometimes that activity entails certifying electoral processes, as it did in the contested Côte d'Ivoire election in 2010. At other times, it involves expert monitoring and reporting back to the secretary-general, using personnel from the UN as well as regional organizations like the Organization for Security and Cooperation in Europe (OSCE) and Organization of American States (OAS), and from NGOs like the Carter Center and the National Endowment for Democracy. In a few cases, the UN has been fully in charge of organizing elections (Cambodia in 1992–1993 and East Timor in 2001–2002), or the UN shares that responsibility with states by providing technical assistance (Afghanistan in 2004–2005, Iraq in 2005, and South Sudan in 2011). Sometimes the UN role can be controversial. In the 2009 Afghan election, for example, the Independent Election Commission was responsible for the conduct of the election, but one top UN official in Afghanistan reported "widespread" fraud, while another suggested the UN permitted the irregularities to occur, politicizing an already divisive situation.

From Promotion to Enforcement

As noted in Chapter 4, the foundation for UN enforcement actions is found in the Charter's Chapter VII. On the two occasions during the Cold War when the council authorized enforcement, it was in response to the persistent gross violations of the rights of black majorities by white minority governments, first in the breakaway British colony of Southern Rhodesia (1966–1980) and then in South Africa (1978–1993). In neither case, however, did the council make an explicit linkage between human rights violations and security threats. Since 1989, however, the UN's member states have been much more willing to link international peace and security with human rights and to consider multilateral intervention. For example, when the Security Council authorized a US-led peacekeeping operation to restore the democratically elected government of Haiti in 1993, it signaled a willingness to enforce the emerging right to democracy—one of the third-generation rights. The sanctions imposed on Libya in 2011 were clearly linked to the Qaddafi government's deliberate targeting of civilians in the fighting with rebel forces.

Since 1990, a series of enforcement actions have been authorized under Chapter VII to deal with humanitarian emergencies in northern Iraq after the Gulf War, Somalia, Bosnia, Rwanda, Sierra Leone, East Timor, and Haiti. In *select* cases, under the norm of humanitarian intervention, the Security Council has explicitly linked egregious human rights violations that result in large-scale humanitarian crises to security threats and authorized enforcement action without the consent of the states concerned. From a human rights point of view, these actions represented a substantial step beyond the kind of humanitarian relief the UN has long provided for refugees through UNHCR and the UN Relief and Works Agency for Palestine Refugees in the Near East. These humanitarian interventions have employed UN peacekeeping forces or coalitions of the willing to protect relief workers, guard medical and food supplies, run convoys, and shield civilians from further violence and suffering in so-called safe areas that often were far from safe due to inadequate numbers of UN troops and unwillingness to employ armed force.

Many governments are suspicious of strengthening the UN's power to intervene in what many still regard as their domestic jurisdiction. Still, the evolution of complex peacebuilding missions and the debate over the R2P norm of humanitarian intervention have set some important precedents for UN enforcement action in the human rights field since the Cold War's end.

We cannot understand the UN's roles in setting standards and in monitoring, promoting, and even enforcing human rights in specific cases, however, without taking a look first at the roles of NGOs involved in human rights and humanitarian activities. It was the increasingly influential activity of NGOs more than political events that produced the shift in UN responses from the 1970s to the 1990s.

THE ROLE OF
NONGOVERNMENTAL ORGANIZATIONS

Much of the UN's success in defining human rights norms, monitoring respect for human rights, and promoting human rights has depended on the activities of the growing international human rights network of NGOs—the third UN. They perform a variety of functions and roles: providing information and expertise in drafting human rights conventions, monitoring violations, implementing human rights norms, mobilizing public support within countries for changes in national policies, mounting publicity campaigns and protests, lobbying, and bringing petitions before international bodies. Human rights advocates have been instrumental in getting governments to incorporate human rights norms into their concepts of national interest. Networks of advocates, and the NGOs of which they are a part, have gotten international responses to human rights violations by motivating governments to cooperate. Humanitarian NGOs not only perform similar roles in calling attention to humanitarian crises but also deliver relief aid to refugees and victims.

Many human rights NGOs were established in the late 1970s after the two international covenants went into effect and after the 1975 Helsinki Accords were signed. The Helsinki Accords gave Western governments and NGOs a basis for monitoring human rights in Eastern Europe and the Soviet Union. This helped weaken Communist regimes in those states and contributed to political and social liberalization. Similarly, the large number of disappearances and other human rights abuses under dictatorships in Chile, Argentina, and other Latin American countries in the 1970s spurred the growth of human rights NGOs. This converged with a greater interest among members of the US Congress in linking human rights with US foreign policy, including foreign economic assistance. They, in turn, relied on NGOs for expertise and information. In the late 1970s and 1980s, many of those same NGOs gained experience in mobilizing and lobbying when they sought to change US policies in Central America.

The number of international human rights NGOs has grown exponentially since the 1970s. Their activities cover an increasingly diverse range: from mere reporting and publicizing violations to promotion, supervisory, and enforcement activities. Although the larger and more well known of the human rights

NGOs have ECOSOC consultative status, that status no longer provides the sole avenue of access. As discussed in Chapter 3, NGOs increasingly utilize other formal and informal opportunities, drawing on their expertise, information, and grassroots connections to legitimize their participation within the UN system, such as in the Universal Periodic Review, explained above. As one UN official noted, "Eighty-five percent of our information came from NGOs. We did not have the resources or staff to collect information ourselves."[25]

NGOs provided much of the momentum for the 1993 World Conference on Human Rights in Vienna and the 1995 Fourth World Conference on Women in Beijing. Their activities were directed at both shaping the official conference outcomes and organizing the parallel NGO conferences. NGOs provided information for official delegates, lobbied governments and international policymakers, and networked with delegates and other NGOs. Some NGOs were also represented on official delegations. Yet because human rights NGOs, like groups in other issue areas, have traditionally been enormously diverse and diffuse in their efforts, coordinated initiatives were difficult.

NGOs also provide much of the information for the UN treaty bodies since many state reports are self-serving and rarely disclose treaty violations. NGOs have undertaken the task of evaluating such reports, gathering additional information, pushing states for compliance, and publicizing abuses. The relationships between NGOs and the treaty bodies vary, however. The Committee on the Rights of the Child enjoys the closest working relationship with NGOs, which regularly review state reports, maintain dialogue with local NGOs, and disseminate information. The Committee Against Torture, however, calls upon concerned NGOs only on an ad hoc basis. So while NGOs have a unique capacity to engage in monitoring, their ability to carry out this function depends on the political space provided by each separate treaty body.

The best-known international human rights NGO is Amnesty International (AI), founded in 1961. AI gained attention for identifying specific political prisoners in countries without respect to political ideology and for conducting publicity and letter-writing campaigns to pressure governments on their behalf. This was a new tool in the human rights arsenal, one that the UN itself could not exercise. AI earned a reputation for scrupulous neutrality by investigating and censuring governments of all types. AI has subsequently moved to support campaigns on broader cross-national issues, like torture, the death penalty, violence against women, and discrimination based on sexual orientation. In these situations, AI has acted strategically, finding issues and states where there is reasonable likelihood of success for its campaigns, based on dissemination of information.[26] But like the Commission on Human Rights, criticisms have been leveled against AI for its differential treatment. One empirical study of AI's background reports and press releases covering 148 countries between 1986 and 2000 found the organization concentrated on powerful countries like China, Russia, and the United States, while some of the most repressive states like Afghanistan, Somalia, and Myanmar received considerably less attention.[27] This is troubling particularly since AI has been especially valuable as an information source for the UN's human rights institutions.

Other key human rights NGOs include the International Commission of Jurists and Human Rights Watch (HRW). It was Aryeh Neier, executive director of Human Rights Watch, who in 1992 proposed creating the ad hoc war crimes tribunal for Yugoslavia. Without his initiative, supported by a number of other NGOs, the tribunal would have never been established. Many human rights NGOs, however, are dedicated to specific issues such as indigenous peoples or India's Dalits. The links between local grassroots groups and the larger international organizations form dense transnational networks. Since 1996 when the OHCHR launched its Web site, NGOs have gained access to both official documents and government reports. As access to official information has become easier, NGOs have become adept at using the technology to communicate with their own constituencies, circulating reports, publicizing abuses, and mobilizing worldwide action networks.

Humanitarian NGOs are concerned traditionally not with rights but with alleviating human suffering, such as by providing food during famines as in Niger or Mozambique; aiding innocent victims of war; and leading relief efforts following natural disasters, such as the 2004 Indian Ocean tsunami and the 2010 earthquake in Haiti. They are distinguished from human rights groups because they often deliberately refrain from advocacy roles. Their neutrality permits them to take a variety of actions that may be unavailable to governments.

The first humanitarian organization to gain recognition in the nineteenth century was the ICRC (and its affiliated Red Crescent Societies in predominantly Muslim states). Working closely with governments during conflicts, the ICRC is known for its neutrality, which has facilitated its work behind the scenes to ensure that prisoners of war receive fair treatment and to assist victims of war by providing medical care, clothing, shelter, and food. Following the 2003 Iraq War, for example, the ICRC inspected facilities where prisoners of war were being held by American authorities, quietly pressured the US government to follow the Geneva Conventions, and, when they were unable to effect changes in prisoner treatment, leaked reports of prisoner abuses to the international press.[28] Other prominent humanitarian NGOs include Oxfam, Save the Children, Doctors Without Borders (Médecins sans Frontières), and CARE. All the major humanitarian relief groups have been active in providing aid for victims of genocide in Darfur and in the ongoing conflict and humanitarian crisis in the Democratic Republic of the Congo, discussed in Chapter 4.

NGOs have become increasingly important in the promotion and enforcement areas. They have been active in providing education on human rights in Central America, Cambodia, Afghanistan, and other postconflict areas. During the 1992–1995 war in Bosnia-Herzegovina, human rights groups were instrumental in generating and sustaining public interest in the unfolding tragedy of ethnic cleansing. AI, for example, issued three reports on widespread human rights abuses between October 1992 and January 1993, and it was among the NGOs that pressed the Security Council to establish the war crimes tribunal for the former Yugoslavia in 1994. An umbrella group of more than a thousand NGOs, the Coalition for the International Criminal Court, played an important role in mobilizing international support in 1997 and 1998 to create the International Criminal Court, urging its ratification and now its usage. Save Darfur has been the most prominent NGO advocating action in Darfur, while the International Rescue Committee has taken on the task of compiling data on the casualties in the DRC since 1996, including victims of rape.

NGOs, therefore, through monitoring and promoting human rights and humanitarian norms, have become major actors within and alongside the UN system in the development of human rights standards. Yet NGOs (and concerned individuals and states) are frequently frustrated when governments fail to act, or when they limit NGO access to official UN meetings to protect nation-state prerogatives and interests.

In all four case studies of UN human rights activity that follow, the UN has provided a forum for getting the issue onto the international agenda and for setting and monitoring standards. In one case, it undertook enforcement. In another, it is now promoting implementation of norms. In each case, NGOs have played key roles, working both within and outside the UN system.

CASE STUDIES OF THE UN SYSTEM IN ACTION

The Anti-Apartheid Campaign

One of the major human rights issues faced by the UN from 1946 to the early 1990s was the apartheid policy of the Republic of South Africa. A political and economic policy supporting the legal "separateness" of the races, apartheid was embodied in a series of South African laws dating from 1948 that enveloped the country's black majority population as well as its coloreds and Asians in increasingly restrictive regulations that violated all human rights standards. To quell domestic opposition, the government used detention, torture, and state-sanctioned murder.

These gross violations of human rights directed against the black majority by the white minority provoked an international campaign against apartheid that was conducted inside and outside the UN by a core group of Third World states and a group of NGOs. The UN General Assembly, the main forum for the campaign, passed its first resolution on the subject in December 1946. Led by India, the assembly approved annual resolutions that rejected South Africa's claims that the Charter's human rights provisions constituted no special obligations for member states and that there was no widely accepted definition of these rights and freedoms.

When South African troops fired on demonstrators in the Sharpeville massacre of 1960, the international community was outraged. Twenty-six newly independent African countries, along with other countries, began in 1962 to call for members to break diplomatic ties with South Africa and impose economic sanctions. This marked an acceptance by a majority of the UN's members that enforcement was necessary. In 1963, a voluntary embargo on military sales to South Africa was adopted by the Security Council. Other assembly resolutions called for sanctions against oil, trade, investment, and International Monetary Fund credits, as well as diplomatic and cultural isolation. The Commission on Human Rights created the first monitoring body, the Ad Hoc Working Group on Southern Africa. When ECOSOC agreed to allow the commission to examine gross violations of human rights in 1967, the practice of apartheid was the focus of investigation.

Beginning in 1974, South Africa was prohibited from taking its seat in the General Assembly; subsequently, the assembly granted observer status to two of the opposition groups—the African National Congress (ANC) and the Pan African Congress. These resolutions passed by large majorities, and pressure mounted for enforcement action by the Security Council. In 1976, the International Convention on the Suppression and Punishment of the Crime of Apartheid went into effect, establishing apartheid as an international crime. In 1977, after a series of particularly egregious actions by the South African government, including the death in detention of the well-known black activist Steve Biko, a mandatory arms embargo was approved by the Security Council under Chapter VII. Pressure for economic sanctions continued, and the General Assembly declared 1982 the International Year of Mobilization for Sanctions Against Apartheid.

The three Western permanent members of the Security Council—the United States, Great Britain, and France—had economic and security interests at stake, however; they persistently opposed assembly resolutions calling for economic sanctions and thereby thwarted further Security Council action. Britain and France were major trading partners of South Africa, and the United States was loathe to apply pressure for a change in regime and thereby risk political instability. These examples illustrate that states often have priorities that conflict with concern for human rights, particularly when there is pressure for enforcement actions.

The international campaign against apartheid took other directions as well, some orchestrated by the General Assembly's Special Committee on Apartheid.[29] For example, there were UN aid programs for victims of apartheid-related abuse through the UN Trust Fund for South Africa. Virtually every international meeting held under UN auspices singled out apartheid for examination. The WHO scrutinized health care for blacks; the ILO probed labor practices. During the 1970s and 1980s, South Africa became a "pariah" state, its sports teams banned from international competition and its cultural activities boycotted, all owing to the egregious violation of the human rights of its own majority population.

The campaign was joined by NGOs such as the World Council of Churches, World Peace Council, International Confederation of Free Trade Unions, and International League for Human Rights; all lobbied governments to approve sanctions and isolate South Africa. Numerous national and subnational NGOs, including church groups, university students, trade unions, and women's and civil rights groups, joined these international NGOs in support of the cause.[30] One tactic was to promote better working conditions for black South Africans by getting American corporations that invested in South Africa to adopt a code of conduct. Another pressured universities, state pension funds, and local governments to refrain from doing business with companies that had investments in South Africa or to divest (sell their stocks in those companies) or both.

The UN and NGOs also provided aid to groups resisting apartheid and became instrumental in publicizing and educating the world about apartheid. Scholarships were given to black South African students, legal aid was provided for those imprisoned for apartheid-related offenses, and relocation was offered for refugees from the regime. This UN support enabled the exiled South African opponents of apartheid to survive decades of severe repression.[31]

In the 1980s, the campaign against apartheid inside and outside the UN grew stronger as apartheid itself became more repressive. Media coverage of violence in South Africa increased public awareness of the problem. High-profile black leaders in South Africa who were not imprisoned, such as Bishop Desmond Tutu, the winner of the 1985 Nobel Peace Prize, actively advocated economic sanctions. In the United States, for example, public pressure and a campaign of civil disobedience by prominent politicians and civil rights activists led both liberal Democrats and conservative Republicans in Congress to approve the Comprehensive Anti-Apartheid Act, including sanctions, over a presidential veto. Britain followed suit in imposing sanctions. This was one instance where grassroots pressure and the strength of moral condemnation mattered.

In 1990, the white-controlled South African regime announced a political opening that led to the dismantling of apartheid and the change to black majority rule. Nelson Mandela, the ANC leader, was freed from prison after twenty-seven years. Open elections were held in 1994, and a black majority government has governed South Africa since then. Apartheid laws have been systematically eliminated, sanctions and the country's diplomatic isolation have ended, and although racism persists in South Africa, the long process of promoting human rights among blacks and whites is under way.

What role did the UN and the international anti-apartheid campaign, including economic sanctions, play in this change? For one, the UN General Assembly and other UN bodies where majority voting was the rule were crucial forums for sustained criticism of South Africa over almost forty years, for isolating the apartheid government diplomatically, and for giving the domestic opposition and exiles visibility, legitimacy, and material aid. The Western permanent members of the Security Council, however, used their veto power to block Third World proposals for comprehensive sanctions, approving only the 1978 arms embargo. The imposition of sanctions by Britain and the United States in the 1980s was a morale boost for the anti-apartheid campaign as well as a means to inflict pain on the South African business community and, through them, on the government. Enlightened white leaders realized that internal opposition could no longer be suppressed and that sanctions were having a damaging effect on the economy.[32] In testimony to the UN's role in delegitimizing and defeating apartheid, Nelson Mandela made one of his earliest public speeches after being freed to the UN General Assembly, thanking members for their support.

In some sense, apartheid might be considered an "easy" case. The discrimination was systematic and egregious, and the campaign against apartheid found early and widespread support for which the UN provided an important forum.

Women's Rights as Human Rights

Women have faced various forms of discrimination in virtually every country and culture. In the 1940s, however, women's rights were viewed as separate and different from human rights, even though Article 2 of the Universal Declaration of Human Rights states that "rights and freedoms set forth in this Declaration" must be given "without distinction as to race, color, sex, or language." Yet it was a long process within the UN system and outside before women's rights came to be seen as human rights.

Initially, it was the political status of women that appeared on the UN agenda because the Western liberal democracies and the socialist states agreed on the importance of granting women political rights. The Commission on the Status of Women had primary responsibility for ensuring women's right to vote, hold office, and enjoy various legal rights. In 1952, ECOSOC addressed the status of women in public and private law and led to the drafting of the Conventions on the Political Rights of Women (1952), Nationality of Married Women (1957), and Consent to Marriage (1962). During the 1960s and 1970s, more attention was given to elevating the status of women as economic actors through the women-in-development initiatives (see Chapter 5). That discussion, however, was never framed in terms of women's rights as human rights.

During the 1980s and 1990s, a major change occurred in the discussion of women's issues, as they were increasingly viewed within the rubric of universal human rights.[33] The shift began with the 1979 Convention on the Elimination of All Forms of Discrimination Against Women (CEDAW), which set the standard for states "to eliminate discrimination against women in the political and public life of the country (Article 7) [and] to modify the social and cultural patterns of conduct of men and women, with a view to achieving the elimination of prejudices and customary and all other practices which are based on the idea of inferiority or the superiority of either of the sexes or on stereotyped roles for men and women (Article 5[a])." CEDAW did not, however, establish initially a system for reviewing complaints of violations of women's rights, although in 2000, the Optional Protocol to CEDAW provided procedures for individual and group complaints.

One hundred eighty-six states have ratified CEDAW, the major legal instrument for women's rights, but those ratifications have often been accompanied by reservations and understandings that provide room for major differences in treaty interpretation. For example, Algeria declares reservations in articles that contradict the Algerian Family Code. Egypt's reservations are in areas in conflict with Muslim sharia law, and Israel expresses reservation on articles that conflict with laws on personal status binding on its various religious communities. Those differences point to cultural relativism—whether human rights are applicable universally or not. The preamble to the 1995 Beijing declaration attempted to put that to rest by affirming: "While the significance of national and regional particularities and various historical, cultural and religious background must be borne in mind, it is the duty of states, regardless of the political, economic and cultural systems, to promote and protect all human rights and fundamental freedoms." But the issue is not dead, and the UN does not have enforcement capabilities on this issue.

The four successive UN-sponsored World Conferences on Women in Mexico City (1975), Copenhagen (1980), Nairobi (1985), and Beijing (1995) raised awareness of women's rights and mobilized action at new levels. In 1975, 6,000 people attended the NGO forum; twenty years later, 300,000 were in attendance. The four conferences greatly expanded women's international NGOs and led to new networks, representing every hue in the ideological rainbow, from secular to religious, radical to conservative, grassroots to elite. They also led to coalitions around issues affecting women, on population, the environment, and development. As the NGOs gained experience with UN procedures, they became more effective in their lobbying efforts, organizing participation in preparatory meetings, developing strategies to push selected issues, gathering information, and monitoring governments' positions. By cross-mobilizing ninety human rights and women's NGOs through the Global Campaign for Women's Human Rights prior to the 1993 Vienna World Conference on Human Rights, the women's groups successfully linked women's rights to human rights.[34]

The new UN Women, discussed in Chapter 5, provides an institutional home for women's activities in economic development and human rights. Michelle Bachelet, its executive director, has long been an advocate for women's rights, empowerment, and gender equality. The mandate for UN Women specifically includes leading, supporting, and coordinating UN work on gender equality as well as the empowerment of women at the global, regional, and country levels.

UN Women has taken up the issue of gender-based violence, an age-old problem largely hidden in the private sphere of the family and communal life. Forced marriages at a young age; physical abuse by spouses, including disfigurement and rape; crippling dowry payments; female genital mutilation; and honor killings all occur within the home and family. A gendered division of labor forces women into sweatshop labor, prostitution, and trafficking in their bodies; in wars, women are raped, tortured, and forced into providing sexual services for troops.

NGO work on the issue dates from 1976, when women organized the International Tribunal on Crimes Against Women. Activists heard testimonials of women who had experienced domestic violence (honor killings, death) or community violence (rape, sexual slavery). The tribunal was ironically a reaction to the 1975 UN Conference on Women that failed to address violence against women. The tribunal provided an impetus for networking, building alliances, and agenda setting and contributed to CEDAW in 1979, even though that treaty did not address violence against women.

Among those working in the UN system, violence against women became recognized as a criminalized activity during the 1980s as a result of intergovernmental meetings of experts from multiple UN agencies, including the Division for the Advancement of Women and the Crime Prevention and the Criminal Justice Division of the UN Department of International Economic and Social Affairs. The first UN survey on violence against women was published in 1989. And in conjunction with the 1993 Vienna Conference on Human Rights, women's NGOs organized another tribunal, with international judges hearing testimony from those abused, putting a human face on domestic violence, torture, political persecution, and denial of economic rights.

The joint efforts of women's and human rights groups produced Article 18 of the Vienna Declaration and Programme of Action, which declared: "The human rights of women and of the girl-child are an inalienable, integral and indivisible part of universal human rights. . . . The human rights of women should form an integral part of the United Nations human rights activities, including the promotion of all human rights instruments relating to women." Violence against women and other abuses in situations of war, peace, and domestic family life, including sexual harassment, were also identified as breaches of both human rights and humanitarian norms. Their elimination was to be pursued through national and international legal means. Later in 1993, the General Assembly approved the Declaration on the Elimination of Violence Against Women and called for states to take steps to combat violence in accordance with provisions of that declaration.[35] Although still soft law, the declaration makes states responsible for providing and enforcing human rights guarantees to women not only in public life but also in private life in the sanctity of the home, a responsibility that many states have so far failed to uphold.

The use of rape as a tool of war is not new, but recognition of it is. The war in Bosnia in the 1990s brought widespread recognition of its systematic use. And a decision by the International Criminal Tribunal for Rwanda concluded that rape, a strategy used against Tutsi women, is a crime of genocide. In 2008, the Security Council unanimously adopted Resolution 1820, declaring rape to be a "tactic of war to humiliate, dominate, instill fear in, disperse and/or forcibly relocate civilian members of a community or ethnic group" and a threat to international security. Sexual violence is a major problem in the ongoing violence in the Democratic Republic of the Congo, which has been named the "rape capital of the world," according to the UN. An estimated 200,000 women have been raped during the past decade; a more detailed study of sexual violence in South and North Kivu provinces finds nearly 40 percent of women report having suffered sexual assault and 23 percent of men.[36] Although the UN peacekeeping force there is one of the largest ever mounted, not only has it been unable to stop sexual violence and protect the innocent, but peacekeepers themselves have also been accused of rape in some well-publicized cases. Pressure has mounted on the UN to increase efforts to stop such violence. In early 2010, the secretary-general responded by appointing a special representative on sexual violence in conflict, with emphasis on the DRC. In September 2010, the Security Council condemned the rape of more than 200 individuals in late summer near a UN base. It admitted that the UN's actions were inadequate, "resulting in unacceptable brutalization of the population." An investigation into UN failures has followed.

Various UN agencies have been mobilized to support programs both to stop the violence and to help the victims. For example, a team from the US Special Forces, with Department of State contractors, is training a new model battalion of Congolese soldiers on human rights and international law and specifically on rape prevention. The inclusion of more women in UN peacekeeping missions is designed to enhance sensitivity to the issue. UNICEF supports a mobile clinic for survivors of sexual violence, and OHCHR, with funding from UN Women, is sponsoring projects to improve women's ability to earn income after being violated. Numerous NGOs offer assorted services. Still, the violence continues, and the UN's failure to protect the population has been a black mark on its peacekeepers' record.

Human Trafficking and Other Slavelike Practices

Violence against women is part of the larger problems of human trafficking and other "slavelike" practices that are conducted against not only women and children, but also men. While institutionalized slavery disappeared at the end of the nineteenth century due to the tireless efforts of the first human rights advocates, the antislavery groups, slavelike practices of forced labor and trafficking in persons continue today. The scope of human trafficking owes much to the rapid pace of globalization following the dissolution of the Soviet Union that opened doors to not only the free flow of ideas, capital, and people but also illicit industries like human trafficking. Many of those trafficked are women and children who are tricked with promises of education, work, and a better life; held against their will once they discover what has happened; work long hours with no breaks; often suffer beatings and other abuse; and are denied contact with their families

It is estimated that between 12 and 27 million people may be "enslaved" in forced labor, and approximately one-quarter of those are trafficked. The difficulty of establishing more firm figures has to do both with varying definitions of what constitutes trafficking and with the often clandestine nature of the problem. It has been framed as both a human rights issue and a transnational crime, with profits in the tens of billions annually. This dual framing of human trafficking has produced two separate lines of action within the UN system.

Human rights framing means setting standards and securing victims' rights to legal and rehabilitative remedies. The UN system has long been actively involved in establishing norms against slavelike practices. The Universal Declaration on Human Rights included the right to be free from slavery or servitude among the articles addressing civil rights. In 1951, the Convention for the Suppression of Traffic in Persons went into effect, prohibiting trafficking in persons for the explicit purpose of prostitution (even with their consent). In 1956, the General Assembly explicitly identified contemporary practices that were considered "slavelike," among them serfdom, forced marriage, child labor, debt bondage, and trafficking in human beings, when it approved the Supplementary Convention on the Abolition of Slavery, Slave Trade, and Institutions and Practices Similar to Slavery. The ILO banned forced labor in a 1957 convention and addressed abuses of migrant workers in a 1975 convention. Other related UN actions include the conventions on women (CEDAW), children, and migrant workers; the Optional Protocols on Children in Armed Conflict and on the Sale of Children, Child Prostitution, and Child Pornography (2002); and the appointment of a special rapporteur appointed to study child trafficking, prostitution, and pornography. (See Table 6.1.)

Framing policy formulation under the rationale and language of criminal justice meant focusing on ensuring aggressive prevention and prosecution of traffickers. Because of this, the General Assembly established the Commission on Crime Prevention and Criminal Justice under ECOSOC in 1992. Under the commission's auspices, a global conference on transnational crime was convened in 1994. This produced a formal action plan against transnational organized crime. Subsequently, ECOSOC directed the secretary-general to solicit the opinions of UN member states on drafting a new convention concerning transnational organized crime. The consensus was that current UN legal instruments were insufficient to address criminal enterprises especially in drug and arms trafficking. Thus, in 1997, the General Assembly authorized the drafting of a new treaty.

Early in the drafting of the Convention Against Transnational Organized Crime, work began on a separate protocol on trafficking in persons. The initiative for this came from Argentina, which was concerned that human rights perspectives were insufficient to address the problem of trafficking in minors.[37] This coincided with other states' growing cognizance of human trafficking, in particular the United States, and a growing sense that vastly expanded migration patterns were obviating national immigration laws.

The drafting process for the protocol on trafficking, which lasted from late 1998 through 2000, was highly contentious and drew active NGO advocacy. The most heated tug-of-war concerned the definition of sex trafficking. One camp, supported prominently by the Coalition Against Trafficking in Women, insisted that prostitution in all its forms was exploitative and should qualify for global criminalization. The opposing view advanced by the Human Rights Caucus posited that noncoerced, consensual migrant sex work should not be prohibited by the protocol. The debate hinged on the definition of sex trafficking and "force" as a required element as well as on whether "consent" should serve as a delineating concept between noncoerced sex work and sex trafficking or whether the coerced consent of victims would allow traffickers to escape prosecution. Both camps sought to influence the delegates directly as well as national governments.[38] The final language maintains a distinction between consensual sex work and sex trafficking, but does not permit the consent of victims to be used as a shield for prosecution if other elements of exploitation are apparent.

The Convention Against Transnational Organized Crime, with the additional protocol for trafficking in persons as well as protocols for migrant smuggling and arms trafficking, was adopted by the General Assembly in 2000 and entered into force in 2003. All three are often referred to as the Palermo Convention and protocols. The trafficking protocol defines trafficking in persons as

the recruitment, transportation, transfer, harbouring or receipt of persons, by means of the threat or use of force or other forms of coercion, of abduction, of fraud, of deception, of the abuse of power or of a position of vulnerability or of the giving or receiving of payments or benefits to achieve the consent of a person having control over another person, for the purpose of exploitation. Exploitation shall include, at a minimum, the exploitation of the prostitution of others or other forms of sexual exploitation, forced labour or services, slavery or practices similar to slavery, servitude or the removal of organs.[39]

As of 2011, 143 states had become party to the trafficking protocol. Because of its link to the transnational crime convention, the Palermo Protocol uses the language of criminal law rather than of human rights. This means that the focus of implementation is not so much monitoring and promotion but law enforcement. The UN Office of Drugs and Crime (UNODC) works to combat trafficking under the convention and both protocols. It assists signatory states in crafting comprehensive policies against human trafficking and provides training resources, primarily for law enforcement officials and lawmakers. Notably excluded from its antitrafficking initiatives are resources and assistance for other "first responders" to human trafficking such as health care professionals, victims' advocates, or social service providers.

The Geneva-based UN human rights organs have continued their antitrafficking work. The HRC has maintained the special rapporteurs for contemporary forms of slavery as well as for trafficking in persons. These rapporteurs are a primary means of monitoring as well as promoting specific human rights by conducting country visits, receiving complaints from individuals, issuing reports to the HRC and General Assembly, and sending letters to governments concerning violations. There is also a special rapporteur on the sale of children, child prostitution, and child pornography as well as a special representative of the secretary-general on children in armed conflict. Among the treaty-based bodies, the Committee on the Rights of the Child in recent reports to the General Assembly, for example, has taken note of the special vulnerabilities of children to human trafficking.

To generate publicity about slavelike practices, the UN General Assembly declared the year 2004 as the International Year to Commemorate the Struggle Against Slavery and Its Abolition and sponsored programs, exhibits, and educational programs. Likewise, the ILO undertook major studies in 2001 and 2005 of forced labor, including human trafficking, calling for a broad effort to eliminate forced labor within ten years.[40] Both reports linked human trafficking with globalization and the ways it promotes forced labor, such as the pressure to cut costs, the surplus of migrant workers, and the deregulation of labor markets.

In 1991, the General Assembly established the UN Voluntary Trust Fund on Contemporary Forms of Slavery to provide financial assistance to individuals who are victims as well as to NGOs dealing with these issues. The aid to individuals is based on needs for security, education, independence, and reintegration and can include housing, legal aid, medical care, food, training, and psychosocial support. In 2010, the Voluntary Fund provided grants to more than three hundred NGOs and communities in eighty countries.

A second source of assistance for all stakeholders dealing with human trafficking, including governments, business, academic, civil society, and the media, is the United Nations Global Initiative to Fight Human Trafficking, better known as UN.GIFT. It was established in 2007 by the ILO, UNHCHR, UNICEF, UNODC, the International Organization for Migration, and the Organization for Security and Cooperation in Europe with funding from the United Arab Emirates, a number of other states, UNIFEM, UNDP, and public donations. UN.GIFT's primary focus is on eradicating trafficking by supporting partnerships for joint action, promoting effective rights-based actions, and capacity building of state and nonstate stakeholders.

One of the things that is striking about efforts to deal with human trafficking is the absence of a single dominant NGO coalition such as formed to deal with violence against women or with slavery itself or to push for the International Criminal Court. The two coalitions active during the drafting of the Palermo Protocol have not formed a single network to coordinate and facilitate antitrafficking efforts. Anti-Slavery International includes human trafficking among its activities and works to raise awareness and lobby countries to ratify conventions and strengthen their antitrafficking efforts. Yet many NGOs continue to prefer to operate independently and often see other NGOs as competitors for funding and attention; obviously, some focus primarily on women, others focus on children, some address women and children, while still others address all victims and forms of trafficking.

Despite all of the human-rights-oriented and crime-oriented activities within the UN system (and by other IGOs) as well as by NGOs and governments, human trafficking remains a highly lucrative form of transnational organized crime. The scope of the problem continues to increase. Lack of public awareness of the problem in countries where trafficking originates (particularly many Southeast Asian and Eastern European countries) as well as in destination countries, including the United States, is an obstacle to antitrafficking efforts. Hence, antitrafficking efforts inside and outside the UN system must continue to raise awareness of the problem. Setting standards, monitoring, promotion, and even enforcement are not enough.

Genocide, Crimes Against Humanity, and War Crimes

During the twentieth century, millions were victims of genocide, ethnic cleansing, other crimes against humanity, and war crimes. The Holocaust is often singled out for the deaths of some 6 million Jews, gypsies, and other "undesirables" under the Nazi German regime, but there were other incidents of what is now called **genocide** before World War II as well as several since. The post–World War II trials of war criminals held in Nuremburg, Germany, and Tokyo, Japan, organized by the victors, made it painfully obvious that there was no international law prohibiting genocide. In fact, prior to 1944, the term *genocide* did not exist. It was coined by a Polish lawyer, Raphael Lemkin, who, along with Chilean and Greek jurists, was largely responsible for drafting the genocide convention as part of the Ad Hoc Committee on Genocide created by ECOSOC. Some countries believed that such a convention was worthless because it could never be enforced. In 1948, however, the General Assembly unanimously adopted the Convention on the Prevention and Punishment of Genocide. The treaty defines the crime of genocide and lists acts that are prohibited. It calls for persons committing genocide to be punished, for states to enact legislation, and for persons charged to be tried either in the state where the crimes were committed or by an international tribunal. (See Box 6.1 for key provisions.)

The Genocide Convention was rapidly signed and ratified and widely recognized as a major advance in international human rights law. Yet it contained ambiguities that could create problems with interpretation and enforcement. For example, it does not specify how many people have to be killed for the incident to be considered genocide, but only addresses the intention on the part of the perpetrators to destroy a group of people "in whole or in part." In contrast to later human rights treaties, the convention created no permanent body to monitor situations or provide early warnings of impending or actual genocide. And for many years, it seemed to have little effect. In Cambodia, Sudan, China, and the former East Pakistan (now Bangladesh), millions of people were killed or forced to flee their homelands as a result of war or deliberate government actions. The international community paid little attention. Still, the norm had been established.

Along with the legal prohibition against genocide came the codification of other **crimes against humanity** and crimes committed during warfare, albeit outside the UN system. These norms are contained in four 1949 Geneva Conventions, two additional protocols concluded in 1977, and related treaties dealing with use of specific weapons. They are designed to protect civilians, prisoners of war, and wounded soldiers, as well as to ban particular methods of war (e.g.,

---

BOX 6.1. The Genocide Convention

Article I . . . genocide, whether committed in time of peace or in time of war, is a crime under international law which they undertake to prevent and punish.

Article II . . . genocide means any of the following acts committed with intent to destroy, in whole or in part, a national, ethnical, racial or religious group, as such:

(a) Killing members of the group;
(b) Causing serious bodily or mental harm to members of the group;
(c) Deliberately inflicting on the group conditions of life calculated to bring about its physical destruction in whole or in part;
(d) Imposing measures intended to prevent births within the group;
(e) Forcibly transferring children of the group to another group.

Article III . . . The following acts shall be punishable:

(a) Genocide;
(b) Conspiracy to commit genocide;
(c) Direct and public incitement to commit genocide;
(d) Attempt to commit genocide;
(e) Complicity in genocide.

Article IV . . . Persons committing genocide or any of the other acts enumerated in article III shall be punished, whether they are constitutionally responsible rulers, public officials or private individuals.

Article V . . . The Contracting Parties undertake to enact . . . the necessary legislation to give effect to the provisions of the present Convention and to provide effective penalties for persons guilty of genocide or any of the other acts enumerated in article III.

---

bombing hospitals) and certain weapons that cause unnecessary suffering (e.g., poisonous gases). Together these form the foundations of **international humanitarian law** and establish the legal basis for **war crimes**. International human rights law—including the Universal Declaration of Human Rights, the Covenant on Political and Civil Rights, and the conventions on torture, genocide, refugees, and children—and the fundamental principle of nondiscrimination between peoples enshrined in Article 1 of the UN Charter establish the basis for crimes against humanity. These are all now incorporated in Article 8 of the International Criminal Court Statute (see Box 6.2).

BOX 6.2. Crimes Against Humanity

- attack against or any effort to exterminate a civilian population
- enslavement
- deportation or forcible transfer of population
- imprisonment or other severe deprivation of physical liberty
- torture
- rape, sexual slavery, forced prostitution, pregnancy, and sterilization
- persecution of any group or collectivity based upon political, racial, national, ethnic, cultural, religious, or gender grounds
- enforced disappearance of persons

The enforcement of norms against genocide, crimes against humanity, and war crimes has proved problematic. Only in the 1990s, with the humanitarian crises in the former Yugoslavia, Rwanda, and Sierra Leone, did the international community begin to pay attention to evidence of ethnic cleansing, genocide, and other crimes and demand action, although too late to prevent atrocities. Only then was there pressure to create mechanisms for prosecuting those accused of crimes against humanity and of war crimes, initially on an ad hoc basis and then through the ICC.

The former Yugoslavia illustrates the dilemmas associated with application of the conventions against genocide, crimes against humanity, and war crimes. During the Yugoslav civil war, the term *ethnic cleansing* was coined to refer to systematic efforts by Croatia and the Bosnian Serbs to remove peoples of another group from their territory, but not necessarily to wipe out the entire group, or part of it, as specified in the Genocide Convention. In Bosnia, Muslim civilians were forced by Serb troops to flee towns for Muslim areas within Bosnia or for neighboring countries. Some were deported to neighboring Macedonia, others placed in concentration camps. Sixty thousand Bosnian women were raped by Serb forces.

The UN Commission on Human Rights appointed envoys to investigate the situation. Initially, in 1992, they reported "massive and grave violations of human rights." Several months later, another report concluded that Muslims were the principal victims and were being threatened with extermination. In 1992, the General Assembly passed a resolution describing Serbia's ethnic cleansing of Bosnia's Muslims as a form of genocide and condemned its actions. In 1993, the International Court of Justice issued a unanimous order to Serbia to follow the Genocide Convention, and the World Conference on Human Rights appealed to the Security Council to take measures to end the genocide in Bosnia. The council created a Commission of Experts, which heard hundreds of hours of taped testimony and sifted through intelligence information, concluding that although all sides were committing war crimes, only the Serbs were conducting a systematic campaign of genocide. It also created the International Criminal Tribunal for the Former Yugoslavia, imposed an arms embargo on all parties, and imposed trade sanctions on Serbia, condemning it for human rights violations.

Was ethnic cleansing in Bosnia equivalent to genocide? If so, who was guilty? The UN Commission of Experts and the Commission on Human Rights both said that Serbia had a policy of systematic genocide. Some states and NGOs, such as Doctors Without Borders, disagreed. Still others maintained that all sides were guilty. Only in 2007, after procedural delays, did the ICJ rule on the merits, concluding that although Serbia failed to prevent the 1995 Srebrenica genocide, the state neither committed genocide nor conspired or was complicit in the act of genocide. The judges pointed to insufficient proof of intentionality to destroy the Bosnians as a whole or in part.[41] In reality, Security Council members lacked the political will to stop the killing in Bosnia. The same was true in 1994 in Rwanda, where the evidence of genocide was much clearer, particularly in retrospect. As evidence mounted of the systematic slaughtering of the minority Tutsis by Hutu extremists in the Rwandan military and police, both the P-5 of the Security Council and the UN Secretariat ignored the evidence and never used the word *genocide*.[42] More recently, despite affirmations of "never again," the response was too little and too late for the 300,000 victims of genocide in the western region of Darfur, Sudan. UN agencies and NGOs provided humanitarian relief beginning in 2003, but not until 2007 was a stronger hybrid UN/AU peacekeeping force of 25,000 approved, let alone mobilized, as discussed in Chapter 4. In this instance, however, the UN Security Council took the unprecedented action of calling on the International Criminal Court to indict Sudan's president, Omar al-Bashir.

Two contemporary cases of alleged genocide and war crimes illustrate the political sensitivity of the issue. Following the end of the Sri Lankan civil war in 2009, a UN panel was charged with investigating allegations of war crimes. Leaked in 2011, the report found that while both the government and the Tamil Tigers had committed war crimes, most civilian casualties in the final days were committed by government troops. This directly contradicted the Sri Lankan government commission's findings.[43] Perhaps even more controversial has been the investigation of the human rights violations during the Gaza war of 2008–2009 between Israel and Hamas. The report of a mission appointed by the UN Human Rights Council, the so-called Goldstone Report, found evidence of potential war crimes and possible crimes against humanity by both Hamas and Israel. Like Sri Lanka, Israel launched its own investigation and found no evidence of deliberate targeting

CARTOON 6.1. "Genocide Enough," by Steve Greenberg. *Reprinted with permission of Cagle Cartoons, Inc. All rights reserved.*

of civilians. Although the Goldstone Report was initially hailed as evidence of Israel's violations and the HRC's own neutrality, in 2011, Goldstone himself retracted his findings, suggesting, "If I had known then what I know now, the Goldstone Report would have been a different document."[44] Other members of the commission have stood by their findings, setting off a storm of controversy, indicative of the sensitivity of states to charges of genocide and war crimes. Further evidence of this sensitivity is seen in Rwanda's rejection of the OHCHR report on genocide in the DRC and its threat to withdraw its peacekeepers from UNAMID.

Although UN members failed to completely stop, let alone prevent, genocide, ethnic cleansing, and crimes against humanity or war crimes, the idea of individual responsibility for such crimes has been revived in the face of the atrocities committed during conflicts in the 1990s. Both ad hoc approaches and new institutions have developed to hold individuals responsible.

Ad Hoc International War Crimes Tribunals. To bring those responsible for crimes during interstate or civil wars to justice, the Security Council under Chapter VII of the Charter established the International Criminal Tribunal for the Former Yugoslavia (ICTY) in 1993, followed in 1994 by the International

Criminal Tribunal for Rwanda (ICTR). In a somewhat different procedure, the UN negotiated an agreement with the government of Sierra Leone in 2002 to establish the Special Court for Sierra Leone. Still another approach was used by the UN to establish the Khmer Rouge Tribunal in agreement with the Cambodian government. Initially, these ad hoc courts lacked established structures and procedures, as well as actual criminals in custody. Yet they recruited prosecutors, investigators, administrators, and judges; devised rules of procedure and evidence; and worked to gain the cooperation of states to carry out their tasks. Deciding whom to indict, arresting those individuals, and trying them in a timely fashion have been ongoing challenges. Let us look briefly at two of the tribunals: the ICTY and the ICTR.

Employing sixteen judges and three separate proceedings, as well as more than 1,200 staff members from around the world, the ICTY developed answers to questions of authority, jurisdiction, evidence, sentencing, and imprisonment that have aided other tribunals. By the end of 2010, 161 individuals had been indicted, and procedures have been concluded for 124 persons. Of those cases, more than 50 percent resulted in sentencing, 10 percent were transferred to local courts, while the other 40 percent were terminated for different reasons. The most well-known defendant, former Serbian president Slobodan Milošević, died in custody in 2006 before the conclusion of his trial. Thirty-eight trials continue, the most famous being those of Radovan Karadžić, the wartime leader of the Bosnian Serbs, and General Ratko Mladić, who was indicted for genocide in the killing of almost 8,000 Bosnian Muslim men and boys in Srebrenica in 1995. These trials are not expected to be completed until 2013 or 2014.

One scholar wrote, "The real success of the ICTY lies in the fact that . . . it is a functioning international criminal court that is providing a forum for victims to accuse those who violated civilized norms of behavior . . . stigmatizing persons . . . and forcing them to relinquish any official power . . . and generating a body of jurisprudence that will undoubtedly continue to build over time."[45] Its judgments have elaborated on the Geneva Conventions, for example, by defining sexual violence, and especially rape, as a war crime; the elements of crimes of genocide and torture; and the application of international humanitarian law to internal armed conflicts.

The Rwandan tribunal has also had problems securing cooperation in arresting suspects and been slow in processing cases. In mid-2011, thirty-eight cases had been completed, nineteen were pending appeal, eight individuals had been acquitted, and seven individuals had been released after completing their sentences. Twenty-one cases were in process. The ICTR's most important contributions to international criminal law are the convictions for using media to incite and coordinate Hutu violence against the Tutsis of Jean Kambanda, the former prime minister of Rwanda, for the crime of genocide—the first such conviction of a head of government—and of four former military officers for conspiracy to commit genocide. Still, because there are more than 120,000 people in custody awaiting trial in Rwanda, it is uncertain how either the ICTR or indigenous Rwandan judicial proceedings will process all the cases.

Both of these ad hoc tribunals were scheduled to conclude their work in 2010. Both, however, have revised the termination dates to 2013 for the ICTY and 2012 for the ICTR.

The International Criminal Court. In 1998, in light of the difficulties posed by the ad hoc nature of the Yugoslav and Rwandan tribunals, and in response to a longstanding movement to create a permanent international criminal court, UN members concluded the Rome Statute for the International Criminal Court. The statute had been drafted by the International Law Commission over several years at the request of the General Assembly. The Coalition for the ICC (a group of more than 1,000 NGOs) played an important role in mobilizing international support for the ICC and continues to promote ratification and implementation. The ICC is officially independent of the UN system, but reports its activities to the UN; it has observer status in the General Assembly and access to UN conference and other services. Under Article 13 of the Rome Statute, the Security Council may refer cases to the ICC, as it has done with two cases as of early 2011—those of Sudan and Libya.

In contrast to the ICJ, the ICC has not only compulsory jurisdiction but also jurisdiction over individuals. Called by one "the most ambitious initiative in the history of modern international law,"[46] the court has jurisdiction over only "serious" war crimes that represent a "policy or plan" rather than just random acts in wartime. They must also have been "systematic or widespread," not single abuses. Four types of crimes are covered: genocide, crimes against humanity, war crimes, and crimes of aggression. The latter were left undefined in the statute, but at the 2010 Review Conference of the Rome Statute, a major step was taken toward adopting a definition, one that would preserve the Security Council's primacy in determining when aggression has taken place. No individuals (save those younger than eighteen) are immune from ICC jurisdiction, including heads of states and military leaders. The ICC functions as a court of last resort and hears cases only when national courts are unwilling or unable to deal with grave atrocities. Prosecution is forbidden for crimes committed before July 1, 2002, when the court came into being, and individuals must be present during trial. Furthermore, the ICC may act only in cases where the state on whose territory the crime was committed, or whose nationals are accused, has ratified the Rome Statute. Anyone—an individual, a government, a group, or the UN Security Council—can bring a case before the ICC. In 2003, the court became operational. At the end of 2010, 139 states had signed the Rome Statute, and 114 states had ratified it. Among those who had not were the United States, China, and India, while Russia had signed but not ratified.

Although the United States has historically supported international accountability for war crimes, there has been strong opposition within the US to the ICC, with President Bush taking the unprecedented action of unsigning the Rome Statute in 2001. One major concern is the possibility that the ICC might prosecute US military personnel, or even the president, without American approval. More generally, the United States asserts that the ICC infringes on its sovereignty and that as a world power it has a unique role to play in international relations. For this reason, the United States would prefer an international court whose powers depend upon approval by the UN Security Council and are thus subject to veto.

To protect itself, the United States negotiated bilateral immunity agreements with more than 100 states that promised not to turn over indicted US nationals, as permitted under Article 98 of the ICC statute. US economic aid to countries not signing such agreements can be suspended. The 2003 American Service-Members Protection Act offers another measure of protection, prohibiting the United States from assisting the ICC in any way and prohibiting military aid to countries who are ICC members but have not signed Article 98 waivers with some key exceptions.

It is significant, however, that the ICC came into being in spite of American objections. Its establishment moved international adjudication and international law far more in the direction of accepting individuals and nonstate entities such as terrorist and criminal groups as subjects of international law, where only states historically have enjoyed such status. Although not an official part of the UN system, the ICC has observer status in the General Assembly and enjoys mechanisms for cooperation with the Security Council and access to UN conference and other services.

In 2011, four cases were pending before the ICC, an investigation of Kenya's 2007 postelection violence had been opened, and a sixth case—that of Libya—had been referred to the court. All involved crimes committed in African countries. With the exception of Darfur and Libya, all involved conflicts and atrocities that had attracted little attention in the Western media. The Congo's case, for example, involves the deaths of more than 4 million people, mostly women and children, since 1998; five individuals have been indicted, and the trial of one Congolese warlord, Col. Thomas Lubanga, is the ICC's first trial, setting important precedents, with more than ninety victims participating as witnesses. The Ugandan case involves the abduction and enslavement of more than 30,000 children by the Lord's Resistance Army; five individuals have been indicted, but at least two of them have since been killed. And while the case was initially referred to the ICC by the Ugandan government, the latter subsequently tried to withdraw it when it appeared to be interfering with efforts to conclude a peace agreement with LRA leader Joseph Kony.

The Darfur situation was the first to be referred by the Security Council to the ICC, an important precedent, especially as the United States first opposed the referral because of its objections to the ICC in general and then later abstained. Six individuals have been indicted, including Omar Hassan al-Bashir, Sudan's president. The first sitting president indicted by the ICC, he is accused of genocide, war crimes, and crimes against humanity for what the court called his "essential role" in the murder, rape, torture, and pillage of civilians. President al-Bashir himself has openly defied the court with the support of the Arab League and African Union and, like several other indictees, was not in custody as of early 2011. The Security Council voted unanimously in February 2011 to refer the crisis in Libya and violent repression by the government of Colonel Muammar Qaddafi against its own people. This action signaled a further shift in the US position on the court.

In addition to the indictments and referrals, the ICC has received almost 9,000 communications from more than 140 countries, the majority from individuals in the United States, Great Britain, Germany, Russia, and France. These referrals and communications are reviewed to see if they meet the statutory threshold; the vast majority are declared outside of the court's jurisdiction.

In sum, the UN has been central to efforts to codify standards relating to genocide, crimes against humanity, and war crimes. It has also been instrumental in more recent efforts to apply those standards in preventing these egregious crimes and to establishing judicial bodies to try those accused of committing them. Yet the ICC's credibility is not ensured: It cannot be a pawn of great-power politics, it needs the cooperation of skeptical African governments, and it needs strong legal cases and adherence to judicial procedures.[47]

EVALUATING THE
UN'S HUMAN RIGHTS RECORD

The four case studies above illustrate the variations in the UN's role with respect to human rights issues. They also show the complex processes by which human rights norms have gained acceptance as well as the challenges of promoting their application and enforcement. The UN's inability to prevent the well-publicized human rights tragedies in Bosnia, Rwanda, and the Sudan has called into question the organization's human rights record, just as did its earlier inability to put a prompt end to apartheid in South Africa. Unquestionably, the UN has failed to address many egregious human rights violations. When it has cataloged abuses, its follow-up activities have too often been weak and ineffectual. The monitoring mechanisms may be too diverse and state dominated to be effective. The funds allocated for these activities are limited. But this harsh indictment does not tell the whole story.

The UN has played a central role in institutionalizing human rights norms in world politics. In 1948, only slavery, genocide, and abuses against aliens were legally proscribed. By 2011, that list had expanded to include extensive protection for individuals as well as women, children, minorities, indigenous peoples, and persons with disabilities. The vast majority of states have ratified the two international covenants and many of the other human rights conventions. It is broadly recognized that human rights are internationally protected and universally applicable, even if enforcement still lags.

The UN itself has moved a long way from the time when mere reporting by states themselves was the only mechanism of monitoring and enforcement. The focus of public monitoring of violations and activities has moved beyond the longtime pariah states of South Africa and Israel. NGOs have played a key role in this process, providing independent monitoring of human rights activities, filing petitions on behalf of victims, publicizing gross violations in a way that the UN cannot, promoting ratification of human rights treaties, and mounting international campaigns against gross violators, including boycotts and sanctions. Moreover, human rights NGOs have been increasingly integrated into the work of the various UN bodies. In this respect, there is a partnership between the UN and NGOs representing civil society.

The UN's activities on human rights have been complemented by the even more extensive development of human rights norms and institutions at the regional level. By far, the most developed is the human rights regime in Europe, where governments are held accountable for actions against their citizens through the European Court of Human Rights. Although the Inter-American human rights regime has witnessed substantive innovations, human rights regimes are weak in Africa and Southeast Asia and nonexistent in the Middle East.

UN and other international efforts to address human rights issues confront challenges relating to our three dilemmas because states traditionally were free to treat their own citizens however they chose. And although liberalism provides a basis for explaining the UN's role and the expansion of international human rights law, it is constructivism that provides the framework for understanding how new norms emerge and become widely accepted.

Dilemma 1: Expanding the Need for Governance Versus the UN's Weakness

With the expansion of democracy and the communication revolution, there is much greater knowledge about violations of human rights in different areas of the world and demands for international action by victims and human rights advocates. Those demands for action face the reality, however, that the UN's monitoring and enforcement mechanisms are weak instruments. The UN has been even less successful in enforcement, precisely because enforcement offends the states that are its constituents. Thus, the UN has been slow to use the "naming and shaming" approach that human rights NGOs frequently employ. The 1990s marked a major shift in this regard, but it is still a relatively small number of violators that get singled out for action, especially by the Security Council. The increasing visibility of the high commissioner and a revived Human Rights Council may bring shame and pressure on errant states.

Dilemma 2: Human Rights at the Nexus of State Sovereignty

Attempts to protect individuals and groups from human rights abuses occurring within the borders of states directly challenge traditional interpretations of state sovereignty and Article 2(7) of the UN Charter that proscribes intervention in matters within the domestic jurisdiction of states. Thus, key to the increased UN attention to human rights is a shift in the understanding of what states are free to do and in the evolving interpretation of what the international community through the UN can and ought to do. Through its role as a forum for bringing human rights into the center of world affairs, the UN has sharpened the sovereignty dilemma.

States still assert the principle of noninterference in internal affairs, especially on human rights issue. China, a strong proponent of the sovereignty argument, for example, expends enormous amounts of diplomatic capital to defend itself and to avert public criticism. Rwanda's attempt to keep reports of its atrocities quiet and Israel's vehement defense of its record in light of the Goldstone Report confirm that state sovereignty is not a dead issue. Likewise, the United States pressured the UN in 2005 to eliminate the position of its human rights investigator in Afghanistan following a report critical of human rights abuse by the US military.

Dilemma 3: The Need for Leadership Versus the Dominance of a Sole Superpower

The establishment of the ICC over the active objections of the United States clearly demonstrated the unwillingness of many states to allow the world's sole superpower to prevent the advance of international criminal law. In fact, historically, no major power has played a leading role in promoting human rights through the UN. The United States has a poor record for signing and ratifying human rights conventions. Instead, leadership has come from the Netherlands, Norway, India, Canada, Costa Rica, and a handful of other states. NGOs such as Amnesty International, Human Rights Watch, and Anti-Slavery International have been prime movers, and grassroots groups of all stripes are important sources of information and advocacy. Thus, human rights are an area where leadership does not depend on traditional sources of power and where the powerless have made a difference.

It is because of the evolution of international human rights norms that new conceptions of security have emerged. These conceptions reject the idea that security applies only to states and embrace the notion that poverty, disease, gross violations of human rights, and environmental degradation threaten the security and well-being of human beings.

Notes

1. Zbigniew Brzezinski, *The Grand Failure: The Birth and Death of Communism in the Twentieth Century* (New York: Charles Scribner's Sons, 1989), 256.

2. Kathryn Sikkink, "Transnational Politics, International Relations Theory, and Human Rights," *PS: Political Science and Politics* 31, no. 3 (1998): 517–521.

3. Franklin D. Roosevelt, *Annual Message to Congress,* January 6, 1941, Congressional Record 44 (1941): 46–47.

4. See Samuel Moyn, *The Last Utopia: Human Rights in History* (Cambridge: Harvard University Press, Belknap Press, 2010).

5. The seven references appear in Articles 1, 13(1), 55, 56, 62, 68, and 76.

6. See Sarah Zaidi and Roger Normand, *The UN and Human Rights Ideas: The Unfinished Revolution* (Bloomington: Indiana University Press, 2006).

7. Mrs. Franklin D. Roosevelt, "General Assembly Adopts Declaration of Human Rights," statement before the General Assembly, December 9, 1948, Department of State Bulletin (December 19, 1948): 751.

8. On the UN and colonialism, see Rupert Emerson, *From Empire to Nation: The Rise to Self-Assertion of Asian and African People* (Cambridge: Harvard University Press, 1960); and Harold K. Jacobson, "The United Nations and Colonialism: A Tentative Appraisal," *International Organization* 16 (Winter 1962): 27–56.

9. James H. Lebovic and Eric Voeten, "The Politics of Shame: The Condemnation of Country Human Rights Practices in the UNHCHR," *International Studies Quarterly* 50, no. 4 (2006): 863.

10. Julie Mertus, *The United Nations and Human Rights: A Guide for a New Era,* 2nd ed. (New York: Routledge, 2009), chap. 2.

11. For details, see the International Court of Justice, *Advisory Opinions on Western Sahara (Spain v. Morocco)* (1975); *Legal Consequences for States of the Continued Presence of South Africa in Namibia* (1971); and the contentious case *Bosnia and Herzegovina v. Yugoslavia* [Serbia and Montenegro] (2007).

12. Louis Henkin, "The Universal Declaration and the U.S. Constitution," *PS: Political Science and Politics* 31, no. 3 (1998): 512.

13. Abdullahi A. An-Na'im, "The Cultural Mediation of Human Rights: The Al-Arqum Case in Malaysia," in *The East Asian Challenge for Human Rights,* ed. Joanne R. Bauer and Daniel A. Bell (Cambridge: Cambridge University Press, 1999), 147. This volume is an excellent set of critical essays on the Asian-values debate.

14. Quoted on the Web site for the UN High Commissioner for Human Rights, www.unhchr.ch.

15. David Weissbrodt, "Do Human Rights Treaties Make Things Worse?" *Foreign Policy* 134 (January–February 2003): 89.

244   *The United Nations in the 21st Century*

16. On this evolution, see Paul Gordon Lauren, *The Evolution of International Human Rights: Visions Seen,* 3rd ed. (Philadelphia: University of Pennsylvania Press, 2011), chaps. 8–9.

17. See Howard Tolley Jr., *The UN Commission on Human Rights* (Boulder: Westview Press, 1987); and Mertus, *The United Nations and Human Rights,* 56–64.

18. For extensive discussion of the treaty bodies, see Mertus, *The United Nations and Human Rights,* chap. 4.

19. Emilie Hafner-Burton and Kiyoteru Tsutsui, "Human Rights in a Globalized World: The Paradox of Empty Promises," *American Journal of Sociology* 110, no. 5 (2005): 706.

20. Emilie Hafner-Burton, "Sticks and Stones: Naming and Shaming the Human Rights Enforcement Problem," *International Organization* 62, no. 4 (2008): 706.

21. Ann Kent, "China and the International Human Rights Regime: A Case Study of Multilateral Monitoring, 1989–1994," *Human Rights Quarterly* 17 (1995): 1–47.

22. "UN: China Torture Still Widespread," www.cbsnews.com/stories/2005/12/02 /world/main1093457.shtm.

23. UN Office of the High Commissioner for Human Rights, *The Democratic Republic of Congo, 1993–2003: Report of the Mapping Exercise* (August 2010), available at www.ohchr.org/Documents/Countries/ZR/DRC_MAPPING_REPORT_FINAL _EN.pdf. Rwanda's reactions are documented in numerous reports in August and October 2010.

24. Joel E. Oestreich, *Power and Principle: Human Rights Programming in International Organizations* (Washington, DC: Georgetown University Press, 2007), 35. See this book for a detailed description of the process.

25. Margaret E. Keck and Kathryn Sikkink, *Activists Beyond Borders: Advocacy Networks in International Politics* (Ithaca: Cornell University Press, 1998), 96.

26. On Amnesty International, see Stephen Hopgood, *Keepers of the Flame: Understanding Amnesty International* (Ithaca: Cornell University Press, 2006); Ann Marie Clark, *Diplomacy of Conscience: Amnesty International and Changing Human Rights Norms* (Princeton: Princeton University Press, 2001); and for Amnesty's own voluminous publications, see www.amnesty.org.

27. James Ron, Howard Ramos, and Kathleen Rodgers, "Transnational Information Politics: NGO Human Rights Reporting, 1986–2000," *International Studies Quarterly* 49, no. 3 (2005): 557–587.

28. David Forsythe, *The Humanitarians: The International Committee of the Red Cross* (Cambridge: Cambridge University Press, 2005).

29. See Audie Klotz, *Norms in International Relations: The Struggle Against Apartheid* (Ithaca: Cornell University Press, 1995).

30. For a comprehensive treatment of the actions of international, national, and local NGOs, see Janice Love, *The U.S. Anti-Apartheid Movement: Local Activism in Global Politics* (New York: Praeger, 1985).

31. Klotz, *Norms in International Relations,* 53.

32. For an analysis of the role sanctions played in the end of apartheid, see ibid., chap. 9.

33. See Charlotte Bunch, "Women's Rights as Human Rights: Toward a Re-Vision of Human Rights," *Human Rights Quarterly* 12, no. 4 (1990): 486–498; and Radhika Coomaraswamy, *Reinventing International Law: Women's Rights as Human Rights in the International Community* (Cambridge: Harvard Law School Human Rights Program, 1997).

34. Donna J. Sullivan, "Women's Human Rights and the 1993 World Conference on Human Rights," *American Journal of International Law* 88 (1994): 152.

35. See Jutta Joachim, *Agenda Setting, the UN, and NGOs: Gender Violence and Reproductive Rights* (Washington, DC: Georgetown University Press, 2007).

36. Reported in Kirsten Johnson et al., "Association of Sexual Violence and Human Rights Violations with Physical and Mental Health in Territories of the Eastern Democratic Republic of the Congo," *Journal of the American Medical Association* 304, no. 5 (2010): 553–562.

37. Anne Gallagher, "Human Rights and the New UN Protocols on Trafficking and Migrant Smuggling: A Preliminary Analysis," *Human Rights Quarterly* 23, no. 4 (2001): 982.

38. Philip Shenon, "Feminist Coalition Protests U.S. Stance on Sex Trafficking Treaty," *New York Times,* January 13, 2000.

39. *Protocol to Prevent, Suppress, and Punish Trafficking in Persons, Especially Women and Children,* to the Convention on Transnational Organized Crime, often referred to as the Palermo Protocol.

40. International Labour Organisation, *A Global Alliance Against Forced Labour: Report of the Director-General* (Geneva: International Labour Office, 2005), available at www.ilo.org/public/english/standards/relm/ilc/ilc93/pdf/rep-i-b.pdf.

41. International Court of Justice, Case concerning application of *Convention on the Prevention and Punishment of the Crime of Genocide* (Bosnia and Herzegovina v. Serbia and Montenegro) (2007).

42. There are many good sources on the failure of international responses to genocide; among them, see Samantha Power, *"A Problem from Hell": America and the Age of Genocide* (New York: Basic Books, 2002); and Michael Barnett, *Eyewitness to a Genocide: The United Nations and Rwanda* (Ithaca: Cornell University Press, 2002).

43. Lydia Polgreen, "Report by U.N. Panel Says Sri Lanka Attacked Civilians Near End of War on Rebels," *New York Times,* April 19, 2011, A9.

44. Richard Goldstone, "Reconsidering the Goldstone Report on Israel and War Crimes," *Washington Post,* April 1, 2011.

45. Sean D. Murphy, "Progress and Jurisprudence of the International Criminal Tribunal for the Former Yugoslavia," *American Journal of International Law* 93, no. 1 (1999): 96–97.

46. Marlise Simons, "World Court for Crimes of War Opens in The Hague," *New York Times,* March 12, 2003.

47. "Dim Prospects: The ICC and Africa," *Economist* (February 19, 2011): 66.

7

Human Security:
The Environment and Health

The concept of security must change—from an exclusive
stress on national security to a much greater stress on people's
security, from security through armaments to security through
human development, from territorial security to food,
employment, and environmental security.
                              —1993 *Human Development Report*

Traditionally, international peace and security has meant states' security and
the defense of states' territorial integrity from external threats or attack. Yet out
of the people-oriented concept of sustainable human development, articulated
in the late 1980s and early 1990s, and the evolution of international human
rights norms has come the broader concept of human security. "Making human beings secure," it is argued, "means more than protecting them from
armed violence and alleviating their suffering."[1] This conceptualization has
major implications not only for how the UN and its member states think about
security but also for how the UN and other multilateral institutions are organized and conduct their work, for a human-security-oriented approach cuts
across traditional divisions between peace and security issues and economic
and social issues. Some states, such as Canada, have adopted it as a foundation
of their foreign policies.

AN EXPANDED
VIEW OF SECURITY

Although some scholars argue that the concept of human security lacks precision and is too expansive,[2] it has been increasingly accepted within the UN system as a useful way to conceptualize a variety of threats that affect states, vulnerable groups such as women and children, and individuals—threats that go beyond physical violence. In 2000, for example, the Millennium Declaration set the goal of attaining "freedom from fear" and "freedom from want" for all people. In 2004, the High-level Panel on Threats, Challenges, and Change incorporated many ideas relating to human security in its report. Among the threats it identified were poverty, infectious diseases, and environmental degradation, in addition to such traditional threats as interstate conflict, civil war, genocide, nuclear weapons, terrorism, and transnational organized crime. This evolution in thinking about security "has recognized the security needs of individuals and the responsibilities of states and organizations in attending to those needs."[3] An important part of that evolution involves the roles of nonstate actors—NGOs, civil society, private corporations, scientists, foundations, and IGOs—in empowering individuals and communities to act on their own behalf. "Correspondingly," as two members of the Commission on Human Security noted, "human security requires strong and stable states."[4]

Viewed in this way, human security has already been addressed in the previous three chapters through the examination of threats to peace and security, including humanitarian crises and the R2P norm, nuclear nonproliferation, terrorism, and the Security Council's initiatives on women in conflict, child soldiers, and civilians at risk; through the UN's efforts to eradicate poverty, reduce economic inequalities, and promote human and sustainable development; and through the UN's role in promoting greater respect for human rights. In this chapter, the focus is on the need for protecting the environment and human health. Neither of these issues is new on the UN's agenda; indeed, health is one of the oldest areas of functional cooperation. What has changed is recognition that failure to address either environmental degradation or major threats to health has a fundamental impact on human security. They can also have "a direct impact on peace and stability within and between states."[5] In short, issues once perceived as "merely environmental" or "merely social" have far-reaching security implications when people rather than states become the primary concern. In a few cases, fragile, weak states are challenged by multiple threats to human security. In this chapter, we examine one such state, Haiti, to see how the UN has responded to the multiple crises affecting its people and to the difficulties of building a stronger, more stable state.

PROTECTION OF THE ENVIRONMENT

The desire to protect the environment dates from the nineteenth century when commissions were established between neighboring states to coordinate cross-border environmental issues (such as the United States and Canada on the Great Lakes and interstate river commissions in Europe). NGOs also formed to protect specific species (for example, the Society for the Protection of Birds in 1898) or to promote general environmental awareness (the Sierra Club in 1892). In the twenty-first century, the threat posed by major environmental degradation is much greater. As one scholar noted, "Climate change, land degradation and de-sertification, the largest wave of species extinctions since the dinosaurs, and multifarious pollutants are real and growing sources of insecurity."[6] International cooperation in pursuit of environmental security had also grown, especially with the proliferation of environmental treaties. At the forefront have been NGOs, in-dustries, scientists, the UN, and other IGOs. Much of this activity has taken place since the early 1970s, with the UN playing a major role in promoting new think-ing about the economic, social, and environmental aspects of resource manage-ment, the global commons, and the links between environment and development.

Although some states and a few NGOs recognized the need for environmental protection at the time, neither the League of Nations Covenant nor the UN Char-ter contained specific provisions to that effect. This is not surprising because envi-ronmental issues did not emerge on most states' agendas until the late 1960s. Inspired by books such as Rachel Carson's *Silent Spring* and Garrett Hardin's essay "Tragedy of the Commons," and photographs of the earth taken by Apollo 2 as-tronauts in 1969, an entirely new image of the planet as a single ecosystem began to emerge.[7] Concerns about the consequences of economic growth on the earth's environment and on human health grew. The UN, responding to this growing en-vironmental consciousness, played a key part in the emergence of an international environmental agenda. The UN's role included the development of a global poli-cymaking framework as a result of UN-sponsored global conferences, the articula-tion of new norms, and the drafting of numerous environmental conventions. NGOs, industries, and major scientific and professional groups have all had im-portant inputs along with developed and developing states. From the beginning, divisions between the developed and developing world have marked the politics of environmental issues.

In response to scientists' growing concerns about the biosphere, the UN Edu-cational, Scientific, and Cultural Organization sponsored the first international environmental conference in 1968. In that same year, Sweden offered to host a larger UN conference. The 1972 UN Conference on the Human Environment (UNCHE), or Stockholm Conference, was the first UN-sponsored conference on a major issue of global concern. At this time, there was little recognition that environmental degradation might become so severe that it would lead to conflict between states and among groups for precious resources, let alone threaten human security.

The Genesis of an Idea: The Stockholm Conference

The Stockholm Conference put environmental issues on the UN and global agendas, as well as on many national governments' agendas. It initiated a process that has led to the piecemeal construction of international environmental institutions, expansion of the global environmental agenda, increasing acceptance by states of international environmental standards and monitoring regimes, and extensive involvement of both NGOs and scientific and technical groups in policymaking efforts. Putting environmental issues on the UN's agenda was an innovation as important to development as peacekeeping was to the UN's role in maintaining international peace and security.

During the preparatory meetings for the 1972 conference, UNCHE Secretary-General Maurice Strong provided the leadership for trying to bridge the divergent interests of North and South. The developed countries saw environmental issues as stemming from the population explosion in the less developed countries, hence greater pressures for natural resource utilization and greater strains on the environment. States must be willing to pay the costs for a safe and healthy environment. In contrast, the developing countries blamed environmental problems on the overutilization of natural resources and the pollution caused by the consumption excesses of the developed countries. They feared that environmental regulation could hamper economic growth and divert resources from economic development. Many developing countries were reluctant even to attend the Stockholm Conference; indeed, they had to be persuaded that environmental problems were neither a concern simply of developed, industrialized countries nor a plot to keep developing countries underdeveloped. It was incumbent on Strong and others to forge conceptual links between development and the environment.

The Stockholm Declaration suggested such a conceptual link: the principle that it is states' obligation to protect the environment and their responsibility not to cause damage to the environment of other states or areas beyond their national jurisdiction. Delegates also endorsed the principle that environmental policies should enhance developing countries' development potential and not hamper the attainment of better living conditions for all. Environmental concerns are not to be used to justify discriminatory trade practices or as a way to restrict access to domestic markets. Finally, the conference called for the creation of a new UN body to coordinate environmental activities and promote intergovernmental cooperation. That body—the UN Environment Programme (UNEP)—is discussed below.

The Stockholm Conference also inaugurated the important practice of a parallel forum of NGO representatives, run simultaneously with the official conference. This has proved critical for generating new ideas and involving a key set of actors. The almost two hundred groups that participated in the NGO forum at Stockholm set important precedents for similar forums at various UN-sponsored global conferences.

Solidification of an Idea: Sustainable Development

The ideas generated at Stockholm on integrating the environment and development continued to be challenged during the next two decades. A series of other UN-sponsored global conferences dealt with specific issues such as food, population, desertification, water, human settlements, and climate (see Box 2.2). The tension between the developing countries that sought economic growth and developed states that were increasingly questioning the costs and the unintended side effects of economic growth led the UN General Assembly in 1983 to establish the Brundtland Commission, discussed in Chapter 5, whose report *Our Common Future* introduced the concept of sustainable development by making the link between economic development and the necessity of balancing environmental concerns. It underscored that developing countries could not follow the path of the industrialized countries in exploiting resources in view of the degradation of global life support systems.

The Brundtland Commission's approach was adopted in 1987 by the UN General Assembly, UNEP, and later by the World Bank, NGOs, and many national development agencies; it became the rallying cry of the environmental movement, including activists, state officials, and leading scientists. The commission acknowledged that poverty is a critical source of environmental degradation; it called on people to think about critical links among agriculture, trade, transportation, energy, and the environment, and it called attention to the long-term view. In 1989, the General Assembly decided to convene a second global conference on the environment twenty years after Stockholm.

The Rio Conference and Sustainability. The 1992 UN Conference on the Environment and Development (UNCED)—or Earth Summit—in Rio de Janeiro and its extensive preparatory process were major outgrowths of the debate over sustainable development and the necessity of balancing economic growth with preserving the environment. The Rio Conference and its preparatory process were influenced, like Stockholm before it, by a series of important scientific findings during the 1980s, including the discovery of the ozone hole over Antarctica; the growing evidence of global warming, or climate change; and the accumulating data on loss of biodiversity and depletion of fisheries. Rio was further influenced by three agreements dealing with ozone depletion: the 1985 Vienna Convention for Protection of the Ozone Layer, the 1987 Montreal Protocol on Substances That Deplete the Ozone Layer, and the 1990 London amended protocol phasing out ozone-depleting chemicals. The largest developing countries, most notably China, India, Brazil, and Indonesia, were successful in bargaining with the industrialized countries for unprecedented guarantees of technology and resource transfers and for additional financing—a major victory for the developing world.

These developments shaped the Rio Conference agenda and were crucial steps in the continuing struggle to get the developed and developing world working together to address environmental issues without lessening the shared commitment to promoting economic growth and greater well-being for rich and poor.

The 1992 Rio Earth Summit was the largest of the UN-sponsored global conferences not only in the number of participants but also in the scope of the agenda. As with other conferences, a series of preparatory meetings were used to articulate positions, hammer out basic issues, and negotiate the text for all conference documents. NGOs played significant roles in the preparatory process as well as in the conference. Although the environmental movement continued to be dominated by northern NGOs, by the 1980s it had spread beyond. UNCED provided even further impetus through opportunities for networking among the unprecedented number of participating NGOs. The 1,400 accredited environmental organizations included not only traditional, large, well-financed northern NGOs, such as the World Wide Fund for Nature and the International Union for the Conservation of Nature but also many new groups pursuing grassroots activities in developing countries that typically were poorly financed and had few previous transnational linkages.

In retrospect, what did the Rio Earth Summit accomplish? First, it is credited with integrating environmental and development policies worldwide by demonstrating the interconnections between various human activities such as industry, agriculture, and consumption patterns and the environment. They included the Rio Declaration of Twenty-seven Principles, Agenda 21, the UN Convention on Biological Diversity, and the UN Framework Convention on Climate Change. Broader issues of global economic reform were incorporated into Agenda 21, Chapters 2, 3, 4, and 12. Each program area (debt, structural adjustment, trade and commodities, poverty, and multinational corporations) needs to include not only cost evaluations but also human resource development and capacity building. While the principle of sovereignty over natural resources was reaffirmed, states also accepted that deforestation, the degradation of water supplies, atmospheric pollution, and desertification were threats to global security and that states were responsible for exercising control over environmentally damaging activities within their boundaries. Second, the linkage between development and the environment was made not only in the UN but also in the trade and development agenda of the WTO and the gradual "greening" of World

Bank programs. This suggests a growing consensus around the concept of sustainable development both in the UN system and beyond.

A third outcome of Rio was the acceptance of direct NGO participation in dealing with environmental issues. The goal of sustainable development depends not only on governments, businesses, and IGOs but also on ordinary people whose interests NGOs often purport to represent. Although the member states excluded NGOs from negotiating the final documents, NGOs' persistence paid off. Section II (Chapter 4) of Agenda 21 recognized the unique capabilities of NGOs and recommended that they participate at all levels, from decision-making to implementation. What began as a parallel informal process of participation within the UN system evolved into a more formal role. Indeed, Rio marked a high point for NGOs and the international environmental movement. For the small grassroots organizations from the developing world, participation in Rio and in the UN system was viewed as a significant breakthrough, making the UN more representative of the "peoples of the world."

Finally, just as Stockholm led to the establishment of UNEP, Rio led to the creation of the Commission on Sustainable Development (CSD) in 1993 as the body to encourage and monitor the implementation of Agenda 21. It also led to the restructuring of the Global Environmental Facility (GEF), leading one observer to conclude, "Institutionalization of sustainable Third World development within the UN system may be the most important consequence of Rio for the less industrialized world."[8]

Beyond Rio: The Challenges of Implementing Sustainable Development.
Moving from promises and commitments to implementing sustainable development as articulated in the Rio documents has proved difficult. Other international environmental conventions were signed, including the UN Convention to Combat Desertification and the UN Fish Stocks Agreement. A plethora of conferences also followed: the 1994 International Conference on Population and Development in Cairo, the 1995 Social Summit in Copenhagen, the 1995 Fourth Women's Conference in Beijing, and the 1996 Habitat II Conference in Istanbul. Each reinforced the discourse of sustainable development. The Millennium Declaration and the Millennium Development Goals adopted in September 2001 represented yet another effort to bring together outcomes from these various conferences and to integrate environmental concerns with other threats to human security (see Box 5.1). In particular, MDG 7 calls for ensuring environmental sustainability. The stated targets are to integrate principles of sustainable development into country policies and programs and reverse the loss of environmental resources.

Rio Plus 10 convened in Johannesburg, South Africa, in 2002. Yet compared to previous meetings, the outcome was disappointing. Among the regional groups, only the European Union had held adequate preparatory meetings. Although the gathering was large (10,000 delegates and almost 1,000 NGOs), NGOs could not fully participate. The summit's Plan of Implementation included some targets, like access to clean water and proper sanitation consistent with the MDGs. But on other issues like restoration of fisheries, reversing biodiversity loss, the better use of chemicals, and more use of renewable energy, no specific target or plan was set. These long-term goals were to be achieved through partnerships between governments, citizen groups, and business (called action coalitions), many of which had already been forged before Johannesburg.

Part of the explanation for the disappointing results was that by the time the Johannesburg Summit convened in 2002, there was increasing disillusionment with the notion of sustainable development. The term was perceived as a "buzz-word largely devoid of content," and some officials, especially in the developing world, had begun to argue that "sustainable" refers to continuity of economic growth without even acknowledging the term's environmental dimension.[9] The timing is especially ironic because, just as disillusionment set in during the early years of the new millennium, there was growing recognition that environmental degradation can cause conflicts between states. In the Middle East, the degradation of water resources has exacerbated conflict between Israel and Jordan, as well as between Turkey and Syria; in Asia, water conflicts linked to degradation have led to conflicts between India and Bangladesh and states around the Caspian and Aral Seas. A widely read book, *Collapse*, argues that environmental degradation and the ensuing struggle for scarce resources led not only to the collapse of states and empires in the past but also to state failure in Rwanda and Haiti.[10] And as the Indian Ocean tsunami (2004), Hurricane Katrina in the United States (2005), and the earthquakes in Kashmir (2005), Haiti and Chile (2010), and Japan (2011) illustrate, humans living in environmentally fragile zones are vulnerable to natural disasters, some of which may be linked to global climate change.

With the ongoing debates on climate change and the economic downturn caused by the global financial crisis beginning in 2008, it is no wonder there is pessimism about whether Rio Plus 20 in 2012 will yield any more positive results. The UN's Commission on Sustainable Development has invited contributions by all the stakeholders and has submitted a detailed road map leading to the 2012 meetings. Focusing on two issues—the green economy in the context of sustainable development and poverty eradication and a reexamination of the institutional framework—the goal is to produce more tangible outcomes at Rio Plus 20. Although questions remain on whether such global conferences are still useful, issue-specific institutions are attacking the environmental agenda in a piecemeal fashion.

The Institutional Framework for Environmental Protection

The creation of international environmental institutions, including new organizations and a large number of environmental treaties, has been a permanent legacy of UN-sponsored activities since the early 1970s. These have set standards and contributed to the evolution of key ideas. The organizations coordinate initiatives; encourage and support treaty negotiations; monitor state compliance; aid member states, NGOs, and other IGOs in the promotion of environmental standards; and, occasionally, enforce environmental norms. One scholar put it this way: "The clearest evidence for the ecological turn in world politics is the astonishing array of recent treaties on a host of environmental problems, including marine pollution, acid rain, stratospheric ozone depletion, loss of biodiversity, and the export of toxic waste to developing countries."[11] (See Table 7.1.) While some of the conferences discussed above have been more productive than others, they have led, not only to new organizations and treaties, but also to General Assembly resolutions, intergovernmental negotiating committees, meetings and conferences of treaty parties, and decisionmaking by consensus.

United Nations Environment Programme. The United Nations Environment Programme was the chief product of Stockholm and was established by the General Assembly in 1972. With Maurice Strong as its first executive director, UNEP became the champion of the emerging environmental agenda, and, by establishing its headquarters in Nairobi, Kenya, it became the first UN agency based in a developing country. With a relatively small professional staff and a small budget that relies heavily on states' voluntary contributions, its mandate is to promote international cooperation in the field of the environment, serve as an "early warning system" to alert the international community to environmental dangers, provide guidance for the direction of environmental programs in the UN system, and review implementation of these programs. UNEP's Governing Council sets general policy and reports to the General Assembly through ECOSOC. Its fifty-eight members are elected by the UN General Assembly for four-year terms. Its secretariat is organized around its various programs, such as early warning and environmental assessment, environmental policy implementation, and supporting existing environmental conventions. As one scholar notes, "The UNEP secretariat is the hub of global environmental information." Its strongest source of influence is its expertise on the state of the environment and on international environmental law.[12]

UNEP has four major responsibilities.[13] First, UNEP plays a key role in negotiating international environmental agreements and in providing the secretariat and oversight for more than a dozen treaty bodies. In a number of instances, it

TABLE 7.1. UN Environmental Agreements

Year	Convention
1971	Convention on Wetlands of International Importance Especially as Waterfowl Habitat
1972	Convention for the Protection of the World Cultural and Natural Heritage
1973	Convention to Regulate International Trade in Endangered Species of Wild Fauna and Flora (CITES)
1979	Convention on the Conservation of Migratory Species of Wild Animals
1982	UN Convention on the Law of the Sea
1985	Vienna Convention for the Protection of the Ozone Layer
1987	Montreal Protocol on Substances That Deplete the Ozone Layer
1987	Convention on Long-Range Transboundary Air Pollution Concerning the Control of Emissions of Nitrogen Oxides or Their Transboundary Fluxes
1989	Convention on the Control of Transboundary Movements of Hazardous Wastes and Their Disposal
1991	Protocol on Environmental Protection to the Antarctic Treaty
1992	Convention on Biological Diversity
1992	UN Framework Convention on Climate Change
1994	Convention to Combat Desertification in Those Countries Experiencing Serious Drought and/or Desertification, Particularly in Africa
1997	Kyoto Protocol to Convention on Climate Change
1998	Convention on the Prior Informed Consent Procedure for Certain Hazardous Chemicals and Pesticides in International Trade
2000	UN Fish Stocks Agreement
2001	Stockholm Convention on Persistent Organic Pollutants

has been a catalyst for negotiations. For example, in the mid-1980s, UNEP executive director Mustafa Tolba provided leadership for the negotiation of the Montreal Protocol on Substances That Deplete the Ozone Layer and the 1990 London Amendment that further tightened states' agreement to phase out ozone-depleting chemicals. In the process leading to the successful negotiations on ozone, Tolba mobilized an international constituency and initiated consultations with key governments, private interest groups, and international organizations. He argued for flexibility, applied pressure, and floated his own proposals as a stimulus to participants. He organized the negotiating process and procedures expeditiously, subdividing the issues into smaller problems.[14] Senior UNEP officials have played similar leadership roles in negotiations that led to the Mediterranean Action Plan, the 1992 UN Convention on Biological Diversity, the 1989 Basel Convention on Hazardous Waste Substances and Their Disposal, and the 2001 Stockholm Convention on Persistent Organic Pollutants. UNEP provides secretariat support for all of these.

Second, UNEP is charged with monitoring the international environment, drawing on a variety of sources. For actual research, it commissions outside experts. Together with the World Meteorological Organization, it monitors atmospheric quality and, in 1988, initiated the Intergovernmental Panel on Climate Change. UNEP shares ocean-quality monitoring with the International Oceanographic Council and together with the FAO and WHO, it conducts studies of freshwater quality. The monitoring and assessments enable UNEP to play an agenda-setting role on particular issues. For example, it has framed discourse on chemical pollutants and hazardous wastes and catalyzed action on desertification and marine pollution.[15]

Third, UNEP launched the Regional Seas Programme in 1974 to address degradation of oceans and coastal areas and develop comprehensive actions to manage them. The program has built on UNEP's initial success with the Mediterranean Action Plan and now protects thirteen regional seas, with more than 140 states participating. Although the program is often seen as one of UNEP's major successes, the plans for various seas have faced a number of difficult problems, including contentious political relationships among participating states.

Fourth, UNEP manages the multistakeholder project entitled the Dams and Development Project that builds on the work of the World Commission on Dams. The project is designed to improve decisionmaking, planning, and operation of dams so that it is done in an environmentally sustainable fashion.

Although UNEP is often given credit for its role in the ozone "solution," it is not an implementing agency as such except in its role of building states' capacity in environmental law. As a result, it collaborates with a number of other UN agencies. In this respect, it is handicapped by its limited leverage over the UN specialized agencies and national governments, as well as by its location in Nairobi far removed from other UN centers, its limited budget, the multiplicity of issues and institutions under its purview, and its inability to coordinate these. UNEP is not a funding agency, but it disburses small amounts from a number of funds including the Environment Fund and trust funds linked to particular environmental issues such as organic pollutants.

UNEP, like many UN agencies and programs, has long been a venue for North-South confrontation over the need to square environmental concerns with development priorities. Developed countries and UNEP need the cooperation of developing countries to address environmental problems and strengthen international environmental governance. Yet the developed countries fear that UNEP is too heavily influenced by LDC interests and have been reluctant to support a strong, more independent UNEP bureaucracy.

Commission on Sustainable Development. The Commission on Sustainable Development was created following the Rio Conference to encourage and monitor implementation of Agenda 21, review reports from states, and coordinate sustainable development activities within the UN system, overlapping in part with UNEP. Since it first convened in 1993, an important task for the CSD has been strengthening the participation of major societal groups, including NGOs, indigenous peoples, local governments, workers, businesses, women, and the young in decisionmaking. Located in New York and reporting to ECOSOC, the commission, with its fifty-three members elected by ECOSOC for three-year terms, is the venue for discussing issues related to sustainable development. Every two years, the CSD focuses on a particular theme or cluster of issues. For 2012–2013, for example, the theme is forests, biodiversity, biotechnology, tourism, and mountains. Over time, the themes are supposed to cover the major elements of Agenda 21. As part of its monitoring role, the CSD is supposed to review national reports and information from other UN programs on actions relating to Agenda 21 recommendations. The record on both counts, however, has been poor. The CSD is also charged with preparations for the follow-ups to Rio—the Rio Plus 5 special session of the General Assembly, the 2002 Johannesburg Summit (Rio Plus 10), and the Rio Plus 20 conference in 2012. One analyst notes, "It is difficult to determine what the influence of this institution has been. It is not charged with creating any new obligations for states and has no legal authority to compel states to act. Its primary impact is in the generation of information, the creation of norms, and the development of capacity." She adds, however, that we should not entirely dismiss the CSD since it has played a valuable role in bringing nonstate actors into discussions and increasing their access within the UN.[16] Rather than UNEP or the CSD, it is the World Bank and other economic institutions that have been able to provide more significant financial resources for environmental activities.

Global Environmental Facility. In 1991, the Global Environmental Facility was created at the suggestion of France and Germany to provide funds to address global environmental issues, initially biodiversity, climate change, ozone depletion, and international waters, and to fund environmental projects in low- and middle-income countries. Although the World Bank is the dominant partner in administering the facility, organizing the application process, and implementing projects using facility funds, two other UN agencies participate in implementation. UNEP provides scientific oversight and helps in selecting priorities, and UNDP coordinates with other bilateral donors. NGOs are involved in the planning and execution of projects. As a result, the GEF has emerged as a useful complement to other sources of financial assistance for environmental projects in less developed countries. It has enabled the World Bank to call itself a "green" institution and has augmented the amount of funding for environmental activities.

GEF funds are designed to induce the developing countries to take environmental actions, with the fund covering the cost differential between a project initiated with environmental objectives and an alternative project undertaken without attention to global environmental concerns. GEF began with $1 billion in pledges; each periodic replenishment has increased in size, but not without difficult negotiations. Perhaps most important, however, the GEF funds help leverage other funding for projects so that by late 2010, it had disbursed some $9.2 billion itself, supplemented by $40 billion in cofinancing. In addition, through a series of small grants ($50,000–$250,000), the GEF subsidizes grassroots groups, thereby building on its commitment to NGO participation.

GEF's priorities include financing the commitments under the UN Convention on Biological Diversity, with more than 50 percent of its funding aimed at biodiversity-related projects. It also provides funding for projects related to the UN Framework Convention on Climate Change and the Kyoto Protocol, with small grants for energy efficiency, renewable energy, emissions inventories, and adaptation projects. GEF grants also support projects on land degradation, protection of international waters, and persistent organic pollutants. Most ozone-related funding is handled through the Montreal Protocol Multilateral Fund, not the GEF.

In the mid-1990s, the GEF was restructured to better accommodate various interests. The GEF Council is composed of thirty-two states, with sixteen from developing countries, fourteen from developed countries, and two from the former Soviet bloc. It meets twice a year to approve work programs and projects. Decisions require double majorities of the funder and developing member states. Every three years, the GEF, assembly composed of all member countries and implementing agencies and the conventions that use the GEF, reviews general policies and approves any changes to the GEF agreement. Since the restructuring, funds have been replenished and programmatic initiatives have become more cohesive. NGOs enjoy an open invitation to participate, a unique privilege not often found in other international institutions. To many countries in the developing world, GEF, because of its association with the World Bank, overrepresents the interests of the industrialized states, while failing to address more localized problems, such as soil erosion and urban air pollution, in the developing world.

Although these environmental institutions within the UN system have their flaws, their creation and functioning over the past forty years represent one of the UN's main accomplishments in this issue area. In addition, the goals for environmental sustainability have been elucidated in a variety of UN resolutions as well as in the substantial number of environmental treaties. Multilateral and bilateral financial resources have been marshaled, though not nearly enough to meet the demands. Global successes have included reducing the threat to the ozone layer caused by chlorofluorocarbons, cleaning up international waters, developing standards to decrease the prevalence and malevolent effects of persistent organic pollutants, and creating fruitful partnerships with state and local institutions to mitigate soil erosion and plant emissions.

Case Study: Lessons Learned from Ozone and Climate Change Initiatives

Looming large on the international agenda as a threat to human security is global climate change. What lessons can be drawn from the above successes, especially in dealing with the ozone problem, which may be relevant for climate change?[17] The general approaches to both issues have been similar—several General Assembly resolutions, conclusion of a framework convention followed by a protocol, creation of various institutional structures, meetings and conferences of the parties, and consensus as the decisionmaking mode. Yet there was rapid progress in addressing the problem of ozone in the mid-1980s and repeated refinements of the legal commitments through subsequent agreements since then. In contrast, there have been more than twenty years of diplomacy surrounding climate change to date, each round of which has been protracted, yielding relatively few hard commitments and marked by confrontations between developed and developing countries.

Five lessons stand out. First, the nature of the environmental problem itself must be acknowledged. Ozone depletion was thrust onto the international agenda in 1975 when two American scientists submitted a report attributing the depletion of the ozone layer to use of chlorofluorocarbons (CFCs). The correlation between use of CFCs and ozone depletion was contested for several years among scientists, but in a little less than a decade following publication of new data confirming a widening ozone hole over Antarctica, most states and scientific experts acknowledged the problem. In contrast, the acknowledgment of global climate change, or greenhouse warming, has proved more contested. After almost twenty years of debates over the scientific data, the UN's Intergovernmental Panel on Climate Change (IPCC)—an independent network of scientists formed in 1988 at the urging of bureaucrats in the World Meteorological Organization and UNEP—released its fourth assessment in 2007 that the evidence of global warming is "unequivocal" and that human activity is very likely (more than 90 percent likely) to be responsible. Most greenhouse gas emissions come from automobile emissions and from the use of fossil fuels for power generation in the industrialized northern countries and, increasingly, from China, India, and other emerging economies. The IPCC's findings substantiated a 2006 report from the US National Academy of Sciences. Just as those findings were gaining widespread acceptance, reports surfaced in 2009 and 2010 questioning the veracity of the IPCC data and the implications drawn. Although those reports have been largely discredited, there remains a very public and politically charged debate over whether there is human-induced global climate change taking place. Without consensus on the nature and magnitude of the problem, fashioning a solution has proved difficult. Furthermore, climate change is a multifaceted problem—far more complex and with more far-reaching implications, and potential winners and losers, than is the case with ozone depletion.

The second lesson is that key states need to support action. The United States and European states were not only the major producers of CFCs but also the major consumers, although usage in the new industrializing economies of India, China, Brazil, and Mexico was rising at about 10 percent annually. US, Canadian, and Norwegian leadership was critical to success in negotiating the Montreal Protocol and subsequent amendments. The support of those countries rested on a mobilized public and on supportive NGOs. The US government was particularly active, and the two important American-based multinational corporations that produced CFCs, Dow Chemical and DuPont, found suitable substitutes for most uses at an acceptable price and, hence, did not oppose phasing them out.

Key European states have provided leadership on climate change, while the United States has been either absent or obstructionist. The issue was first addressed in the 1992 UN Framework Convention on Climate Change, but the convention contained no legally binding obligation to reduce carbon dioxide emissions. In 1997, it was supplemented by the Kyoto Protocol, which aimed to stabilize the concentration of greenhouse gases and required developed countries to reduce their overall greenhouse gas emissions by at least 5 percent below 1990 levels by 2010. Europe has been a leader in pushing for Kyoto and post-Kyoto reductions. EU members who produce between 16 percent and 22 percent of global greenhouse gas emissions agreed to cut, on average, 8 percent from 1990 emission levels, and they proposed significant reductions by 2020 in a post-Kyoto agreement. The United States, however, raised major objections to both the Kyoto Protocol and the 1992 framework convention and has refused to support any international agreement calling for specific mandated cutbacks in emissions. It believes that the costs of compliance would be too high and that the

US economy would be adversely affected. The United States has objected to the fact that countries like China and India are excluded from Kyoto's emission limits, a concern that has grown since China surpassed the United States as the largest carbon emitter in 2009. Nevertheless, the Kyoto Protocol came into force in early 2005 with 156 parties, accounting for 55 percent of greenhouse gas emissions. Absent US participation and in the face of flagging European commitment, the goals have not been attained.

Just as the Kyoto agreement came into force, a series of meetings, with the US participating, began on negotiations for its successor since the targets set by the protocol end in 2012.[18] Each has focused on a particular issue or set of issues. In Bali in 2007, for example, there was agreement that China and India should be included in a follow-on agreement. In 2008 meetings, it was agreed that states should be given credit for saving forests and expanding a fund to help poorer countries adapt to climate change. The Copenhagen conference in 2009, although reported as a failure by the press, resulted in 140 parties (80 percent of global emissions) agreeing to provide both technology and financing ($30 billion annually and up to $100 billion by 2020) to decrease emissions and mitigate the effects of climate change. The 2010 Cancun conference, the sixteenth meeting of parties, built on pledges for mitigation for the developing countries. Still, the series of meetings have shown that the ozone example where major powers agreed to take significant measures relatively quickly is unworkable for the climate change issue. Climate change diplomacy under the UN, in fact, has a twenty-year reputation for being dysfunctional, with procedural issues often taking precedence over substantive ones, with a problem of framing and poor management, and a pattern of last-minute—if any—breakthroughs.[19] The negotiations over Kyoto's successor show "where the U.N. process has the most potential to be useful and avoids other areas where the U.N. process is a dead end. The outcome does not change the fact that most of the important work of cutting emissions will be driven outside the U.N. process," as discussed below.[20] And suffice it to say, if there were consensus among key states on the need for and the type of action to take, there would have been progress long since.

The third lesson to be drawn from looking at the two cases is that multilateral institutions are needed to monitor provisions and settle controversies. For ozone, such institutions developed slowly. In approving the 1985 Vienna Framework Convention, states promised to cooperate on research and data acquisition. The 1987 Montreal Protocol, the 1990 London Amendment, and three subsequent amendments further strengthened states' commitment to phase out ozone-depleting chemicals. The industrialized countries agreed to pay for the incremental costs of compliance for developing countries, creating the Multilateral Fund for the Implementation of the Montreal Protocol. The GEF has provided financial assistance to Central and Eastern European countries. The Implementation

Committee handles cases of noncompliance. In addition, there is a procedure for states to ask UNEP's Ozone Secretariat (after consultation with a technical committee) for relief should specific industries be adversely affected by the chemical restrictions.

In contrast, with the eight-year lag between conclusion of the Kyoto Protocol and its entry into force, very little institutional structure was created to aid in implementation. There is a Compliance Committee with both facilitative and enforcement tasks. Parties found to be noncompliant are not entitled to use the flexible mechanisms to offset emission standards. The GEF finances projects for increasing energy efficiency and energy conservation and for promoting renewable energy sources, as discussed above. Under the Kyoto Protocol, the Clean Development Mechanism provides funds to be used by developed states and private companies to meet domestic emission targets by financing projects in developing countries. Overseen by the special UN secretariat created under the convention, projects are assigned one carbon emission credit for every ton of greenhouse gas saved. These credits may be sold on the international carbon exchanges, ten of which are managed by the World Bank. More than half of these projects have been in either India or China. Under the Nairobi Framework (2006), a program under UNEP, UNDP, and the World Bank has been developed to build national capacity in African states to develop projects to reduce their emissions and enhance sinks through reforestation. In 2010, the first bilateral arrangement between Norway and Indonesia was forged under the REDD process (reducing emissions from deforestation and degradation process), a collaborative project of UNEP, the FAO, and UNDP. In 2011, the World Bank signed an agreement with mayors from forty of the world's largest cities to fund climate change–reduction projects. Unlike the ozone case where affordable substitutes were found in relatively short order, climate change demands long-term major changes in use of fossil fuels and major funding for mitigation of effects already experienced.

The fourth lesson is that international environmental agreements need flexibility—a way to change standards when new scientific information becomes available—without renegotiating the entire treaty. The Montreal Protocol is a flexible instrument that can and has been made more restrictive as the scientific evidence warranted through a series of amendments; its provisions could also be relaxed should the ozone problem become less severe. The Kyoto Protocol provides flexible mechanisms for states to meet emission requirements, including emission trading permits, investment credits for the joint implementation of projects, and credits for forested land, each of which have been affirmed. The core disagreement, however, comes from the overarching "principle of common but differentiated responsibilities." Should all states take responsibility? Do some states have more responsibility than others? Do developing states have time to catch up in terms of economic development? Answers to these questions depend, in part, on one's assessment of the urgency of the climate change problem.

Fifth, there is evidence showing that improvement in the ozone layer has occurred as a result of states' compliance with the protocol and its amendments, although the final verdict on whether the change is permanent is still out. The Kyoto Protocol has not reduced the emissions of greenhouse gases, even though some countries have met their targets. Given current global dependence on oil and gas as major sources of energy to sustain global economic growth, the issue of climate change is clearly too complex to be addressed in a single treaty regime. That is why we are unlikely to see a narrowly focused legal approach like the ozone treaty with climate change. In other words, at least part of the problem is trying to get a comprehensive agreement rather than taking a piecemeal approach. As Keohane and Victor conclude, "Both political reality and the need for flexibility and diversity suggest that it is preferable to work for a loosely linked but effective regime complex for climate change."[21]

One of the challenges in addressing environmental threats to human security is the longtime lag before major effects may be felt. Thus, for example, changes made now may take a generation or more to show their effects. Inevitably, this tends to decrease the sense of urgency in addressing the sources of degradation since policymakers tend to focus primarily on short-term rather than long-term issues. In contrast, with infectious diseases and health threats, short-term actions can have immediate effects.

HEALTH AND HUMAN SECURITY

Public health and disease are hardly new issues, but globalization has had a dramatic effect on the transmission, incidence, and vulnerability of individuals and communities to disease through migration, air transport, trade, and troop movements. Intensified human mobility poses major problems for containing outbreaks of cholera, influenza, HIV/AIDS, tuberculosis, West Nile virus, severe acute respiratory syndrome (or SARS), avian (bird) influenza, H1N1 virus (a form of swine flu), and other diseases that can be carried in a matter of hours from one part of the globe to another long before symptoms may appear. Globalization has thus exacerbated the urgency and the scope of the threats that infectious diseases can pose to human security. The issue is not only vulnerability to large-scale loss of life, however; it is also one of disease impeding development and weakening societies, as the WHO-appointed Commission on Macroeconomics and Health has argued.[22]

Rudimentary international rules to prevent the spread of epidemics, including procedures for instituting quarantines, date back hundreds of years, and institutionalized collaboration can be traced to 1851. With the HIV/AIDS epidemic and recent outbreaks of SARS and avian flu, there has been a substantial strengthening of global health governance. The linkage of health and human security was made most directly by the UN Security Council in its first-ever special session devoted to the challenge of HIV/AIDS, in January 2000. Three of the MDGs deal with health; MDG 6 specifically targets HIV/AIDS, malaria, and other diseases.

Developing International Responses to Health Issues

Between 1851 and 1903, a series of eleven international conferences developed procedures to prevent the spread of contagious and infectious diseases. In 1907, the Office International d'Hygiène Publique (OIHP) was created with a mandate to disseminate information on communicable diseases such as cholera, plague, and yellow fever. More than a decade later, at the request of the League of Nations Council, the International Health Conference met to prepare for a permanent International Health Organization, but the OIHP did not become part of this new health organization. Following the UN's creation, in 1948, the World Health Organization came into being. In membership and budget, WHO is one of the largest UN specialized agencies, a sign of the universality of health concerns. With its strong regional offices located on every continent, it is also one of the more decentralized functional organizations. The WHO secretariat, located in Geneva, is highly technical, the director-general, other secretariat officials, and many delegates being medical doctors. The medical and allied health communities form a strong epistemic community based on their technical expertise and training.

The main decisionmaking body is the World Health Assembly (WHA) composed of three delegates from each member state, including delegates from the scientific, professional, and nongovernmental communities. Each country, however, has only one vote, unlike the ILO, where representatives of each functional group have a separate vote. The executive board is a smaller group of thirty members elected by the WHA. By "a gentlemen's agreement," at least three of the Security Council members are supposed to be represented.

WHO Initiatives. WHO's activities include three major areas.[23] The first area, building on the work of predecessor organizations, is providing security against the spread of communicable diseases. In 1951, WHO passed the International Health Regulations (IHR), requiring states to report outbreaks of four communicable diseases (yellow fever, cholera, plague, and smallpox) and take appropriate measures without interrupting international commerce. Those regulations covered only a few diseases, they were not legally binding, and reports were accepted only from states. During the 1980s and 1990s, new communicable diseases emerged that were not covered under the IHR, including Ebola, West Nile virus, HIV/AIDS, and avian flu. Newly revised IHR took effect in 2007 to deal with the consequences of globalization and the accelerated movement of people through migration, air transport, trade, and troop movements. As a result, WHO is better equipped to address public health emergencies, and member states are required to notify the WHO command center within twenty-four hours of any emerging global health threat. WHO can also now utilize non-governmental sources like the Internet and the press to publicize potential problems, even over state objections.

These changes occurred as a result of the problems encountered during the SARS outbreak in 2002–2003 when China initially suppressed information on the outbreak, was slow to permit WHO officials to visit potentially affected areas, and failed to undertake preventive measures for several months. Although the epidemic killed fewer than 1,000 individuals, the potential for a global pandemic was widely recognized, and the economic repercussions on the most affected countries—China, Vietnam, Singapore, and Canada—were significant. WHO took unprecedented measures, serving as a conduit for information, working with public health officials, helping to establish national monitoring systems, and providing technical assistance.

Those tasks were institutionalized, and WHO was ready to act with its new Strategic Operations Center for the Global Outbreak Alert and Response Network when avian flu broke out in 2005–2006 and the H1N1 virus in 2009. There is a medical strike force, a "fire brigade," that has the capacity on six hours' notice to send experts to distribute antiviral drugs in an area affected by an outbreak. Longer term, the aim is to train nationals in developing countries to identify outbreaks, provide essential technology for surveillance, and encourage states to develop national plans. Regional offices of WHO, national health institutes, and developed states are all involved in this urgent initiative.[24]

The second area of WHO activity is eradication programs for certain diseases and working with state health authorities to improve health infrastructure. The malaria- and polio eradication campaigns are examples. Those have followed the widely acclaimed and successful eradication of smallpox and yaws as well as WHO's contributions to the successful treatment of river blindness. With the support of Rotary International, the Bill and Melinda Gates Foundation, and other groups, the goal of polio eradication was close to realization in 2006; then resistance to vaccination in Nigeria led to outbreaks that subsequently spread in neighboring countries and in South Asia. The World Bank is providing major funding for the global effort to recontain the disease. After years of stagnation, the campaign against malaria is now showing steady improvement, thanks in part to an increase in funding for control and provision of insecticide-treated bed nets that have been effective in protecting the young from the scourge of malaria.

The third area of WHO activity includes interaction with the pharmaceutical industry. Developing countries have been concerned about the quality of imported drugs, and they have sought technical assistance in monitoring quality control. WHO approved guidelines for drug-manufacturing quality control in 1970, covering such issues as labeling, self-inspection, and reporting adverse reactions. As discussed below, WHO also dealt with the pharmaceutical industry on the issue of pricing AIDS drugs in poor countries. In several cases, WHO has entered into the contentious issue of regulation of MNCs, no more so than the World Health Assembly's adoption in 1981 of the Code of Marketing for Breast-Milk Substitutes. This called for states to adopt regulations banning marketing and advertising of infant formula that discouraged breast-feeding, while acknowledging a "legitimate market" for breast-milk substitutes. In the late 1990s, the accessibility and affordability of drugs in developing countries remained on WHO's agenda. How to get equitable access to vaccines and pharmaceuticals to meet pandemic threats is of continuing urgency.

In recent years, WHO's campaign against tobacco illustrates the continuing dilemmas in health governance and a newer, fourth, area of focus—lifestyle-related health issues. When the issue first appeared in the World Health Assembly, the large tobacco companies mounted stiff opposition, as did some key states. Yet in 2003, member states approved the Framework Convention on Tobacco Control that bans advertising of tobacco products, requires health warnings on packages, and mandates broader liability for manufacturers. The convention took effect in 2005 and has been ratified by 172 state parties as of 2010 (but not the United States). But progress on implementation has been slow: Smoking rates continue to rise in developing countries, and the marketing restrictions have not been implemented. There appears to be a loss of momentum on this controversial issue. In contrast, HIV/AIDS has occupied a top spot on the international agenda for almost twenty-five years, posing a significant challenge to human security.

Case Study: The Challenge of AIDS

One of the greatest challenges for international cooperation and human security is the HIV/AIDS epidemic. Not just a health or humanitarian problem, it threatens economic development, security, and social stability in the world's poorest regions. There is no cure. The disease is highly mutable, and some mutations are resistant to drugs. It disproportionately affects those in the most productive years, between fifteen and forty-five years, including military personnel. Indeed, soldiers serving in peacekeeping forces in Africa have helped spread the disease. As the International Crisis Group notes, "Where it reaches epidemic proportions, HIV/AIDS can be so pervasive that it destroys the very fibre of what constitutes a nation: individuals, families and communities; economic and political institutions; military and police forces. It is likely then to have broader security consequences."[25]

International responses to the AIDS epidemic have mirrored evolving awareness of the multifaceted nature of the problem. Initially, in 1986, the World Health Organization took the lead. The earliest WHO actions, for example, were to stimulate the creation of national AIDS programs. That was based on the idea that governments' willingness to acknowledge HIV/AIDS as a major problem and their commitment to enlarging public health budgets would be vital steps needed to address the problem. Yet both measures were controversial because some states refused to acknowledge the problem, and others did not have the resources to devote to it.

Other UN agencies gradually became involved when it became evident that the effects of AIDS reached beyond health. In 1996, the UN Joint Programme on HIV/AIDS (UNAIDS) was created by UNICEF, UNDP, the UN Fund for Population Activities, UNESCO, WHO, and the World Bank was to be the lead agency for global action, with the UN Drug Control Programme, WFP, and the ILO subsequently joining. UNAIDS illustrates the importance of network approaches to governance problems through partnerships among UN agencies, national governments, corporations, religious organizations, grassroots groups, and NGOs. It tracks the epidemic, monitors responses, distributes strategic information, mobilizes resources, and reaches out to diverse groups. In addition, the UN has convened global AIDS conferences every two years to raise awareness and mobilize responses. Both the UN General Assembly and the UN Security Council have held special sessions to address the issue, with the council identifying the AIDS pandemic as a threat to global security in 2000, the first time a health issue was elevated to such status.

The UN-led partnership has proved unsatisfactory, however. The lack of local ownership of programs, inadequate institutional accountability measures, politicization of some programs, and the need for a steady stream of financial resources resulted in the creation of the Global Fund to Fight AIDS, Tuberculosis, and Malaria. It is an independent institution that includes all stakeholders and provides for multisectoral participation at all stages of the process, from funding to implementation.[26] Funding decisions are made by the board, which includes representatives of donor countries, NGOs, foundations, those living with the diseases, and private companies, plus four nonvoting advisory seats, occupied by WHO, UNAIDS, the World Bank, and a Swiss member. As of 2011, Global Fund has allocated $22 billion for three programs: supplying 3 million people with antiretroviral treatments, 7.7 million tuberculosis treatments, and insecticide-treated nets for 163 million people. Despite some problems, it gets high marks for its independence and professionalism.

The Global Alliance for Vaccines and Immunization (GAVI), which supports AIDS vaccines, receives funding from the Bill and Melinda Gates Children's Vaccine Program, the Rockefeller Foundation, and the International Federation of Pharmaceutical Manufacturers Associations, as well as UNICEF, WHO, and the World Bank. As antiretroviral multidrug "cocktails" became increasingly effective in the late 1990s, their expense raised economic and ethical questions that the UN proved ill-equipped to handle. The high cost made their use in poorer countries in Africa and Asia problematic, and the budgets of the UN and related specialized agencies were inadequate to subsidize long-term treatments. The major Western pharmaceutical companies were reluctant to cooperate, citing the need to protect intellectual property rights against cheaper generic substitutes manufactured in Brazil and India. Faced with an outpouring of pressure from NGOs, IGOs, and affected developing countries, organized in part in the transnational Treatment Action Campaign, the major pharmaceutical companies were forced to alter pricing strategies in poor countries and stop their efforts to thwart the sale of generics.

The UN's recognition that the AIDS epidemic and other health issues directly link to human security is illustrated by their inclusion in the Millennium Development Goals. Goal 6 calls for combating HIV/AIDS, malaria, and other diseases, with the major target of halting and reversing the spread of HIV/AIDS by 2015. Goal 4 calls for the reduction of child mortality, and Goal 5 addresses the need for the improvement of maternal health. Child and maternal mortality have both dropped significantly; so have the rates of new HIV infection in many parts of the world. Still, the goals are unlikely to be met unless actors and resources outside of the UN are brought together.

WHO remains important for identifying health problems, suggesting solutions, and coordinating negotiations, but it is no longer the central institution in HIV/AIDS specifically or in global health more generally. Other IGOs such as the World Bank and regional organizations are key actors, bilateral donors and foundations like the Gates Foundation provide financial resources, and program implementation is dependent on not only the technical resources of MNCs but also states and other actors in public-private partnerships.[27] Just as with climate change, contemporary health issues cannot be addressed through a single institution.

Good health and a sustainable environment are just two of the necessary ingredients for human security. Physical security, economic well-being, and respect for human rights are also needed for individuals to thrive. In the international state system, it is the state's responsibility to provide that security. Yet one of the phenomena of the post–Cold War era has been that of failing states—states unable to control their own borders—to meet even the basic needs of their citizens. Although Somalia is often singled out as an example of such states, in recent years it is Haiti that has come to demonstrate the scope of the human insecurity that can accompany a weak and failing state, particularly when it suffers from a large-scale natural disaster. We turn, then, to a discussion of how the UN system has responded to the multiple human security threats in Haiti.

STATEBUILDING FOR HUMAN SECURITY: THE CASE OF HAITI

On January 12, 2010, a 7.0-magnitude earthquake devastated Port-au-Prince and nearby areas of Haiti, killing more than 220,000 people, injuring at least that many, leaving close to 1 million people homeless, and leveling or heavily damaging many government buildings as well as private homes of rich and poor alike. One-third of Haiti's civil servants died, along with hundreds of its police. The UN Stabilization Mission in Haiti (MINUSTAH) lost 102 peacekeepers, including the special representative of the secretary-general, his principal deputy, and the UN police commissioner. These were the largest casualties for the UN in a single incident. Haiti's national police were in disarray. As a result of the earthquake, one-half of the prisoners, many of whom had been jailed for gang-related violence, had escaped from prison, and weapons were stolen.

In short, the natural disaster severely affected the small island country, long identified as a failing state. Less than two years before, in 2008, Haiti had also been heavily hit by three major hurricanes. Decades of political instability, crime, violence, drug trafficking, illiteracy, high infant mortality, AIDS, deforestation, overpopulation, and widespread poverty made Haiti the poorest country in the Americas, even before the earthquake struck. It ranks 146 out of 169 countries worldwide on the Human Development Index. Throughout much of its two-hundred-year history, Haiti's governments have failed to provide basic services for its citizens, generate economic development, or deal effectively with violence and disorder.

Thus, Haiti's precarious situation did not just occur on January 12, 2010. The UN has a long history of development projects in Haiti. There were fourteen major World Bank projects in Haiti at the time of the earthquake, including projects for infrastructure, community development, education, economic governance, and, ironically enough, disaster management. The grants and interest-free credits came from the International Development Association—the World Bank's arm for lending to the poorest countries; many projects were implemented by NGOs. UNEP had designated Haiti as a focus country of its environmental programs since extreme poverty has led people to cut down trees for firewood, leaving less than 2 percent of Haiti's territory covered by forests, resulting in both soil erosion and devastating floods and mud slides during the an-

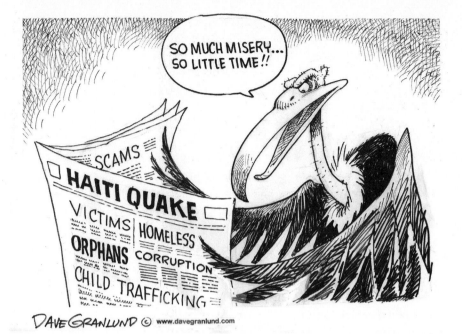

nual hurricane and storm seasons. Already in 2008, for example, environmental degradation was identified as one of the key challenges facing Haiti, according to the UN Development Assistance Framework. The Haiti Regeneration Initiative aimed to restore the country's ecosystems.

NGOs, too, have a long history of involvement in Haiti, often choosing to work outside of government channels even as long ago as the early 1970s because of high levels of corruption. By 1984, the number of NGOs operating in Haiti was estimated at between 200 and 300, and a decade later, the number had increased to 800. By 2010, although there was no confirmed count, there were an estimated 10,000 NGOs working in Haiti, with about 500 of them registered with the government.[28] Such well-known NGOs as Catholic Relief Services, CARE, and Habitat for Humanity were among those with years of experience. Over time, NGOs have been "used as substitutes by international institutions and donor countries to implement programs that were once administered by the state," weakening further the already troubled state apparatus.[29] This has led Haiti to be described as a "republic of NGOs" since so much aid has come through NGOs rather than through the Haitian government.[30]

Haiti's major bilateral donors—the United States and Canada—have also long been involved in all sectors, from education to health care and infrastructure, increasingly using NGOs as well to implement the programs. Although there have been some programs aimed at improving public administration, thereby increasing state capacity, most of the funding is outside of government channels, and NGOs report directly to the donors.

In the early 1990s, there were high hopes for changes in Haiti's long cycle of dictatorship, misrule, and poverty when Jean-Bertrand Aristide won the 1990 presidential election that was overseen by the UN, the OAS, and US observers. He had campaigned with an agenda for social justice. When he was overthrown in a 1991 military coup, it was one of the turning points in the Americas and for the UN in advancing the right of democracy. The coup led to UN- and OAS-approved comprehensive sanctions on Haiti that caused its economy to shrink about 30 percent between 1991 and 1994 and, along with looting of the state treasury by the military regime, deepened the misery of the people. In 1994, the Security Council authorized a multinational force to expel the military regime and restore Aristide as the legitimate president, initiating seven years of international peacekeeping, peacebuilding, and human rights–monitoring initiatives. Despite the expenditure of more than $2 billion, these UN-led efforts failed to achieve credible results in terms of an independent police force, governmental reforms, or economic improvement.[31] In fact, political turmoil deepened, the poverty rate grew, crime and violence increased along with corruption, and the police and judicial system remained ineffective.

In 2004, following the outbreak of armed conflict, the Security Council authorized a US-led interim force followed by a new UN Stabilization Mission in Haiti to help stabilize the interim government, protect civilians, reform the Haitian national police, disarm and demobilize armed groups, undertake police and judicial reform, and monitor human rights.[32] By 2008, there was sufficient progress in dealing with crime, gang activities, and rebuilding the police that the UN began planning for an eventual drawdown. Then the three hurricanes struck, hindering progress; food prices rose; the global financial crises hit; and there was a political stalemate in Haiti. Still, with $350 million pledged for Haiti's recovery and development, Secretary-General Ban Ki-moon appointed former US president Bill Clinton in May 2009 as his special envoy for Haiti to provide a focal point for improving both human security and state capacity. The following January, the earthquake struck, totally transforming the situation in Haiti.

The extent of Haiti's human security crisis and devastation called for extraordinary responses. Immediately, the US military deployed more than 20,000 troops to Haiti—its largest humanitarian response to a natural disaster ever. Their task was to provide critical logistical support and emergency supplies.

Working with teams from forty-three countries, they reopened the Port-au-Prince airport in twenty-four hours and the seaport ten days later. MINUSTAH's logistics base in Port-au-Prince was spared much damage and became the operations center for US, UN, and other actors participating in emergency relief efforts. With an infusion of more police and military personnel authorized by the Security Council, MINUSTAH mobilized to increase neighborhood patrols and control key locations such as warehouses to prevent looting and worked with the Haitian National Police in the overcrowded camps for some 1.5 million displaced persons where gender-based violence became a particular problem and a UN priority. To address it, MINUSTAH provided additional training for troops in how to prevent and respond to such violence and deployed a unit of female officers.

Humanitarian aid agencies immediately mobilized people and material. Within a few days, the World Food Programme was feeding more than 600,000 people with MINUSTAH's help; UNICEF was distributing health kits, water, and food, trying to meet the needs of unaccompanied children. WHO coordinated the health sector, working with its regional affiliate, the Pan American Health Organization, to vaccinate against potential diseases, while the UNHCR organized camp housing for displaced persons, providing tarps, tents, blankets, and mosquito nets. The UN Population Fund equipped maternity wards and provided reproductive health services in the camps. The UN Office for the Coordination of Humanitarian Affairs, along with MINUSTAH, managed relief teams composed of representatives from various agencies. And along with the UN-related programs and organization, there were teams from the United States with its unparalleled logistical capacity as well as Canada, Japan, other countries, and countless NGOs providing emergency assistance. Although many of the latter suffered losses that undermined their own capacity to act, they continued to provide services.

At the first UN-convened donor conference in March 2010, donor governments pledged $5.3 billion over the following two years and more than $10 billion for the following ten years. This demonstrated the deep resonance the earthquake's devastation called forth, despite Haiti's long history of failed efforts by outsiders to remedy its endemic weakness and poverty.

The international financial institutions have also been mobilized. Following the earthquake, the Inter-American Development Bank canceled Haiti's $479 million debt; now that debt relief has added up to $1.21 billion through the Heavily Indebted Poor Countries Initiative and the Multilateral Debt Relief Initiative. The World Bank announced grants of $100 million to Haiti the day after the earthquake struck.

The recovery efforts now involve UNDP. Its cash-for-work and labor-intensive initiatives have been extensive, building on programs long in place. In partnership with the WFP and others, UNDP employs Haitians to clear debris, clean water channels, and collect garbage in return for food and cash payments, an effort to inject cash into the economy. In addition, UNDP is continuing in its traditional role of providing technical assistance to Haitian government agencies severely impacted by the earthquake, including providing operational support for the November 2010 and March 2011 elections, constructing space and providing office equipment for the Ministry of Justice, and enhancing training for legal offices as part of a longer term project for enhancing government capacity. UNDP has convened meetings of donors at UN headquarters to support the Interim Haiti Recovery Commission. Pledges of $10.2 billion in aid for reconstruction have been made, but by March 20011, only $1.28 billion paid out. Since much of that aid money goes to pay salaries and for foreign workers, one aid worker warned, aid alone is unlikely to "fix Haiti."[33]

Through subsequent donor conferences, an economic development agenda has begun to take shape. Namely, the idea is to create "growth poles" beyond the capital of Port-au-Prince, focusing on agriculture, manufacturing, and tourism, with "development corridors" linked to the growth poles.[34] That plan depends on not only donor funding and MNC investment but also enhanced government capacity.

Yet Haiti experienced still another crisis that diverted attention from long-term recovery beginning in October 2010 when there was an outbreak of cholera that killed more than 4,000 persons, sickening an estimated 253,000 persons and counting. The epidemic created an immediate public health crisis and threat to Haiti's human security. WHO and health-related NGOs took quick action to improve the water supply and sanitation system, the source of the epidemic, but infrastructural programs are a long-term commitment. With evidence that the cholera strain came from South Asia, possibly from Nepalese troops in MINUSTAH, the UN's reputation was tarnished and the future of the UN mission placed in doubt after outbreaks of violence against peacekeepers.

The questions for Haiti's future human security not only concern the ability of the UN and other outsiders to help build a stronger government but also the ability of Haiti's own leaders, such as Michel Martelly, the political outsider who was elected president in March 2011, to tackle the widespread corruption and the host of other problems that have long plagued Haiti. Will he be able to utilize the outpouring of the international community assistance to address the needs of both Haiti's government and its ordinary people who have suffered so much? Will he be able to develop partnerships with the UN agencies, international donors, and NGOs to build a stronger, more stable, and more responsive Haitian government? Likewise, will UN agencies, international donors, and NGOs learn the lessons of the past when their attention to Haiti has often been episodic and their efforts fragmented and incoherent? Addressing the multifaceted threats to human security in a place like Haiti is a long-term task and one that requires both better Haitian leadership and outside assistance.

DILEMMAS IN HUMAN SECURITY

Environmental degradation, pandemics, and natural disasters are only three of many human security issues. As illustrated by the case of Haiti, extreme poverty, physical insecurity, environmental and health challenges, as well as weak states are among other threats to human security. The disparities that a country such as Haiti represents have critical ramifications, as a UN panel warned several months before the September 11, 2001, attacks: "In the global village, someone else's poverty very soon becomes one's own problem: of lack of markets for one's products, illegal immigration, pollution, contagious disease, insecurity, fanaticism, terrorism."[35] Because they represent new needs for governance that cut across traditional ways of defining issues, challenge state sovereignty, and require leadership, human security issues pose major dilemmas for the United Nations system.

Dilemma 1: Needs for Governance Versus the UN's Weakness

Human security issues are now widely accepted as a permanent part of the UN's agenda, though framing environmental degradation and health as human security issues has occurred only since the mid-1990s. Institutionalization, however, has tended to be ad hoc and piecemeal, often with little thought to how coordination was to occur. There is a perennial shortage of funds to tackle the governance challenges posed by human security issues. Should there be greater centralization of these international activities under UN authority, or is a more decentralized approach more effective?

The debate over environmental governance exemplifies this dilemma. On one side are those who argue for the greater centralization of environmental institutions through a world or global environmental organization. They note that often there are multiple institutions within a given issue area, addressing different aspects of a problem or different types of solutions. The result is overlapping mandates, too many meetings, and competition for scarce resources. They see a single global organization also as a remedy for UNEP's weak mandate, insufficient powers, and inadequate resources.[36] On the other side are those who suggest that restructuring or creating a new architecture will divert attention from the major institutional and policy issues, including confusion over the norm of sustainable development and the challenge of integrating nonstate actors and civil society into the governance process. In all likelihood, the only suitable approach to international environmental issues is a multilevel one with a wide variety of partnerships.[37] On the issue of global warming, clearly the latter approach is ascendant.

The UN and various specialized agencies play valuable roles in dealing with human security issues, but their weaknesses as institutions mean they cannot accomplish the tasks alone. Whether in the issues of the environment or health or the multiple human security issues illustrated by Haiti, decentralized approaches and partnerships among global, regional, national, and local entities, both public and private, with or without the UN, are the modus operandi.

Dilemma 2: Sovereignty Versus Challenges to Sovereignty

Human security issues are boundary-spanning issues because epidemics and pollution do not stop at states' borders; neither do the effects of state weakness and failure. What prompted US concern about Haiti in the 1990s, for example, was the flood of Haitian refugees finding their way to US shores. As a result, these issues and responses to them challenge state sovereignty. That challenge is just as fundamental as it is to human rights issues and to humanitarian intervention. States, quite predictably, continue to be wary of such challenges, just as they have resisted interference in their domestic affairs on other issues. Although the hard shell of sovereignty has been breached, the tension still remains, and the shell is not yet broken. The SARS epidemic illustrates the necessity of gathering all possible information on infectious disease despite the reluctance of governments to admit there is a problem or cooperate with WHO to provide data. Ozone depletion and climate change illustrate the potential for cooperation when there is shared recognition of a problem and a willingness to deal with it, including providing assistance to developing countries in making necessary adjustments. These cases also illustrate the variety of factors, including a powerful state that can block action. And in a few cases where state sovereignty and capacity is weak, as in Haiti, UN agencies, international donors, and NGOs may usurp the role of the state rather than strengthen state capacity, leading to further weakness and the necessity for statebuilding efforts if the threats to human security are to be addressed.

Dilemma 3: The Need for Leadership

For action to occur, all issues require leaders who seize an issue, publicize it, mobilize constituencies, forge potential solutions, and work for implementation. On human security issues, this may come from among the handful of states, including Japan and Canada, that have made human security an integral part of their foreign policy or from a group of states such as those that have ratified the Kyoto Protocol and demonstrated their determination to forge ahead in its implementation even without the participation of the United States. Leadership can come from the UN secretary-general, the executive-director of UNEP, the director-general of WHO, an ambassador such as Richard Holbrooke who played a key role in convening the first Security Council session on the threat of HIV/AIDS, or even prominent individuals such as former president Bill Clinton, who has played a key role in Haiti.

Given the wide recognition of threats to human security now, no one state or one international organization (even the UN) is apt to be in the lead on all issues. Nonstate actors of various kinds are important partners in addressing these issues. Commitments of governmental funding are important, but private foundations such as the Bill and Melinda Gates Foundation have shown how much can be done with private initiative.

The challenges posed by human security issues reinforce what we have seen with respect to peace and security issues, economic development, and human rights, namely, that reform of the UN system is imperative. When has the UN been successful? When has it failed? What can we learn from those experiences? It is to that topic we now turn.

Notes

1. Thomas G. Weiss, David P. Forsythe, and Roger A. Coate, *The United Nations and Changing World Politics,* 4th ed. (Boulder: Westview Press, 2004), 278.

2. See, for example, Roland Paris, "Human Security: Paradigm Shift or Hot Air?" *International Security* 26, no. 2 (2001): 87–102.

3. Richard Jolly, Louis Emmerij, and Thomas G. Weiss, *The Power of UN Ideas: Lessons from the First 60 Years* (New York: United Nations Intellectual History Project, 2005), 34.

4. Sadako Ogata and Johan Cels, "Human Security: Protecting and Empowering the People," *Global Governance* 9, no. 3 (2003): 275. Sadako Ogata was cochair of the Commission on Human Security and former UN high commissioner for refugees. Johan Cels was the commission's project coordinator for conflict.

5. Edward Newman, "Human Security and Constructivism," *International Studies Perspectives* 2, no. 3 (2001): 241. For a somewhat different approach to the link between environmental degradation and state security, see Thomas Homer-Dixon, *Environment, Scarcity, and Violence,* 2nd ed. (Princeton: Princeton University Press, 1999). Also see Michael T. Klare, *The New Landscape of Global Conflict* (New York: Metropolitan/Owl Book, 2001).

6. Karen T. Litfin, "Constructing Environmental Security and Ecological Interdependence," *Global Governance* 5, no. 3 (1999): 364.

7. See Rachel Carson, *Silent Spring* (Boston: Houghton Mifflin, 1962); and Garrett Hardin, "The Tragedy of the Commons," *Science* 162 (December 13, 1968): 1243–1248.

8. Craig N. Murphy, "The United Nations Capacity to Promote Sustainable Development: The Lessons of a Year That 'Eludes All Facile Judgment,'" in *The State of the United Nations: 1992,* ed. Albert Legault, Craig N. Murphy, and W. B. Ofuatey-Kodjoe,

ACUNS Reports and Papers no. 3 (Academic Council on the United Nations System, 1993), 60.

9. Daniel C. Esty, "A Term's Limits," *Foreign Policy* 126 (September–October 2001): 74.

10. Jarod Diamond, *Collapse: How Societies Choose to Fail or Collapse* (New York: Penguin, 2005).

11. Litfin, "Constructing Environmental Security and Ecological Interdependence," 367.

12. Steffen Bauer, "The Secretariat of the United Nations Environment Programme: Tangled Up in Blue," in *Managers of Global Change: The Influence of International Environmental Bureaucracies,* ed. Frank Biermann and Bernd Siebenhüner (Cambridge: MIT Press, 2009), 185.

13. Elizabeth R. DeSombre, *Global Environmental Institutions* (London: Routledge, 2006), 14–20.

14. Richard Elliot Benedick, *Ozone Diplomacy: New Directions in Safeguarding the Planet,* enlarged ed. (Cambridge: Harvard University Press, 1998).

15. See Bauer, "The Secretariat of the United Nations Environment Programme."

16. DeSombre, *Global Environmental Institutions,* 34.

17. See Michele M. Betsill, "Global Climate Change Policy: Making Progress or Spinning Wheels?" in *The Global Environment: Institutions, Law, and Policy,* ed. Regina S. Axelrod, David Leonard Downie, and Norman J. Vig, 2nd ed. (Washington, DC: CQ Press, 2005), 103–124.

18. See Stephen Peake, "Turbulence in the Climate Regime," *Current History* (November 2010): 349–354.

19. See Lorraine Elliott, "Climate Diplomacy: Two Steps Forward, One Step Back," in *The Oxford Handbook of Modern Diplomacy,* ed. Andrew Cooper, Jorge Heine, and Ramesh Thakur (New York: Oxford University Press, forthcoming), for discussion of the climate change diplomacy.

20. Michael A. Levi, quoted in John M. Broder, "Climate Talks End with Modest Deal on Emissions," *New York Times,* December 11, 2010.

21. Robert O. Keohane and David G. Victor, "The Regime Complex for Climate Change," *Perspectives on Politics* 9, no. 1 (2011): 20.

22. World Health Organization, *Macroeconomics and Health: Investing in Health for Economic Development, Report of the Commission on Macroeconomics and Health* (Geneva: World Health Organization, 2001), available at www.who.int/macrohealth /documents/en. For an extended treatment on health and security, see Andrew T. Price-Smith, *Contagion and Chaos: Disease, Ecology, and National Security in the Era of Globalization* (Cambridge: MIT Press, 2009).

23. See Mark W. Zacher and Tania J. Keefe, *The Politics of Global Health Governance: United by Contagion* (New York: Palgrave Macmillan, 2008).

24. David Brown, "Preparing for the Worst," *Washington Post National Weekly Edition,* December 5–11, 2005.

25. International Crisis Group, "HIV/AIDS as a Security Issue" (2001), www.intl -crisis-group.org.

26. Barrett Wallace Brown, "Multisectoralism, Participation, and Stakeholder Effectiveness: Increasing the Role of Non-State Actors in the Global Fund to Fight AIDS, Tuberculosis, and Malaria," *Global Governance* 15, no. 2 (2009): 169–178.

27. See David P. Fidler, "The Challenges of Global Health Governance," Working Paper, Council on Foreign Relations, International Institutions and Global Governance Program (May 2010).

28. Data from various sources compiled in François Pierre-Louis, "Earthquakes, Nongovernmental Organizations, and Governance in Haiti," *Journal of Black Studies* 42, no. 2 (2011): 189.

29. Ibid., 191.

30. See United States Institute of Peace, "Haiti: A Republic of NGOs?" *Peacebrief* 23 (April 26, 2010).

31. Marlye Gélin-Adams and David Malone, "Haiti: A Case of Endemic Weakness," in *State Failure and State Weakness in a Time of Terror,* ed. Robert I. Rotberg (Washington, DC: Brookings Institution, 2003), 297–298.

32. See Carlos Chagas Vianna Braga, "MINUSTAH and the Security Environment in Haiti: Brazil and South American Cooperation in the Field," *International Peacekeeping* 17, no. 5 (2010): 711–722.

33. "Rebuilding Haiti: The Long, Hard Haul," *Economist* (March 19, 2011): 46–47.

34. See Robert Maguire, "Rebuild Haiti, Not Just Its Capital," *Current History* (February 2011): 81–82.

35. United Nations General Assembly, *Report of the High-level Panel on Financing for Development Appointed by the United Nations Secretary-General,* Fifth-fifth Session, Agenda item 101, June 26, 2001, A/55/1000, 3, www.un.org/esa/ffd/a55–1000.pdf.

36. Frank Biermann, "The Case for a World Environment Organization," *Environment* 42, no. 9 (2000): 22–31. See also Frank Biermann and Steffen Bauer, eds., *A World Environment Organization* (Aldershot, UK: Ashgate, 2005).

37. See Adil Najam, "The Case Against a New International Environmental Organization," *Global Governance* 9, no. 3 (2003): 367–384.

8

Is There a Future for the United Nations?

The United Nations today leads what seems at times like a double life. Pundits criticize it for not solving all the world's ills, yet people around the world are asking it to do more, in more places, than ever before.

—Secretary-General Ban Ki-moon,
Sidney Morning Herald, December 31, 2010

Secretary-General Ban Ki-moon's words echo a refrain often heard from supporters of the UN: "If the UN did not exist, a similar institution would have to be created." In this final chapter, we explore some of the ways in which the UN has made a difference over more than sixty-five years and identify areas where it has failed. We examine factors that have shaped its successes and failures and the question of whether, in fact, the UN can be reformed to play a more vigorous role in global governance.

DOES THE UN MAKE A DIFFERENCE?

You might imagine in a book on the UN that the automatic, unequivocal answer to this question would be "of course." If you were to pick up literature from the UN's Department of Public Information, you would find it filled with a list of UN achievements over the years, including the positioning of peacekeepers along fragile borders in the Middle East and Cyprus, energizing the voices of the newly independent colonies on behalf of self-determination and economic development, pushing an international human rights agenda for marginalized peoples, and improving global health through the WHO's eradication of small-pox and UNAIDS partnerships. Some books that dwell on the UN's achieve-ments also note its shortcomings, much as we have. Still others are critiques of the UN or even polemics that emphasize that the institution is overtly politi-cized, criticizing states like Israel and not others or responding to threats to the peace emanating from smaller states while neglecting those posed by the P-5. These critics point to the UN's failures, its inability to halt genocides, to stop weapons proliferation, and to close the gap between the rich and the poor. For some American pundits, the only logical response is for the United States to pull out and withdraw its support.

Before we answer the question of how much of a difference the UN actually makes, we must return to the notion that there is not just one UN, but three UNs, each of which plays and has played a role in shaping what the UN does. As three experts put it, there is "the UN of governments, the UN of staff mem-bers, and the UN of closely associated NGOs, experts, and consultants."[1] It is the third UN that has been most neglected by scholars, diplomats, and govern-ments because of the longstanding state-centric focus of international relations. All three have influenced what the UN has and has not been able to do over the years. Yet it is admittedly difficult to differentiate these three UNs in the area of one of the UN's major accomplishments, the development of new ideas.

Developing New Ideas

Thanks to the United Nations Intellectual History Project (UNIHP), which over a decade (1999 to 2009) produced fifteen books and seventy-nine in-depth oral history interviews that trace and document the history of key ideas and concepts about security and economic and social development within the UN system, we have important insights into those areas where the UN has had a major impact. The final volume, *UN Ideas That Changed the World*, brings to-gether the wealth of insights that emerged from the project. The authors con-clude that ideas are among the most significant contributions the UN has made to the world and to human progress. And all three UNs have played various roles "collectively . . . sometimes in isolation and sometimes together or in par-allel" in generating ideas, providing a forum for debate, giving ideas legitimacy, promoting adoption of ideas for policy, implementing or testing ideas and poli-cies at the country level, generating resources for implementing, monitoring progress, and sometimes burying ideas.[2]

In the area of peace and security, the UN has advanced an idea that has proven of tactical importance to the UN's own role as well as proven flexible over time to encompass a variety of types of tasks. *Peacekeeping*, the idea that the military personnel, police, and civilians from states acting on behalf of the international community, wearing the UN's blue berets, could insert themselves into conflict situations represents an institutional innovation that was not explicit in the UN Charter. Peacekeepers can separate, disarm, and demobilize combatants; police cease-fires; and, in limited circumstances, even use more coercive measures under Chapter VII mandates to preserve international peace and security. They can protect aid workers, monitor human rights violations, undertake security sector reform, repatriate refugees, and provide interim civil administration. The idea has been implemented on every continent, using small to large contingents, some with pronounced effect and others deemed as mixed successes or even failures. Peacekeeping has become an integral part of the UN's approaches to addressing threats to peace and security, along with mediation, preventive diplomacy, and enforcement.

The UN has also been instrumental in expanding the very concept of security from state security to *human security*. Humans, too, need to be secure in their own person, from violence, economic deprivation, poverty, infectious diseases, human rights violations by states, and environmental degradation. While it is governments' responsibility to provide for security within the state, some states may need assistance in controlling cross-border arms, human, and drug trafficking as well as funding for economic development, monitoring disease, and adaptations to reverse or protect against environmental threats. In implementing the idea of human security, then, the UN can help states protect individuals and carry out their responsibilities of sovereignty.

Following from this, the UN has legitimized the new norm of states' *responsibility to protect* their own citizens, particularly from war crimes or crimes against humanity. This particular idea is and will likely remain contested because of its potential for abuse—for providing a justification for outside intervention. Yet the concept introduces a new interpretation of both state sovereignty and the obligations of the international community.

In the area of economic development, the UN has benefited from the creativity of innovative economists who have at one time or another been employed by the UN or served as consultants and who have contributed to key UN ideas. *Sustainability*, as enunciated in the Brundtland Report, clearly showed that economic development cannot occur without consideration of the future, resources cannot be exploited without assurance that there are not detrimental side effects, and resource uses need to be managed with an eye to future generations. As a result, the UN and other development institutions began to weigh development needs with environmental imperatives.

Just as security has been redefined as human security, development, too, has been reconceived as *human development*. This idea represents a sea change in thinking from traditional economic theory that measured development in terms of growth in a state's GNP over time and in comparison to that of other states. UNDP and some of the specialized agencies began to think of development in terms of how it affected people: their health, educational level, income and overall well-being, and the differential effects of gender. Thinking about human development led to the MDGs and the concerted action to attain human development goals.

Universalizing *human rights for all* represents a key normative idea where all three UNs share credit. NGOs, in particular, were instrumental in getting provisions relating to human rights into the UN Charter, and they continue to play critical roles in the promotion and monitoring of human rights. As one noted scholar has said, "Among the most improbable developments of the previous hundred years or so is the spectacular rise of human rights to a position of prominence in world politics. This rise cuts across the grain of both the structure of world order and the 'realist' outlook of most political leaders acting on behalf of sovereign states."[3]

And in human rights, as well as in peace and security and development, new categories of individuals as well as groups have been recognized as not enjoying equal protection. The UN has added to its agenda in all these issues the notion that not only white men merit protection but all vulnerable people do, whatever their race, ethnicity, age, physical condition, place of residence, or gender. Of these groups, the UN system has devoted the most attention to enhancing the status and role of women. The UN did not initiate efforts to improve the status of women—key states and NGOs played that role—and the League of Nations provided the first international forum for promoting women's rights. But as the founding director of UNIFEM has said, "The global women's movement would be lost or at least much weaker without the UN."[4] Indeed, the four world women's conferences played a major role in the creation of the global women's movement. And countless UN resolutions "have forced their [*sic*] governments to be more accountable . . . showing that this is the way that governments should behave, or corporations should behave, or men should behave."[5] Another major achievement on the long road for gender equality was the creation of UN Women in 2010.

Developing ideas is, therefore, an important way in which the UN has made a difference, but ideas alone are inadequate. Furthermore, some ideas took hold, while others did not. The UN itself sometimes implemented ideas, sometimes buried them. What, then, are other ways in which the UN has made a difference?

Filling Knowledge Gaps, Gathering Data

In the early years, the UN played a key role in helping states gather basic data and measure outcomes. That data collection largely reflected the perspective and methods of liberal economists and dominant states. But as new ideas emerged, the data collected had to change. Just as critical as monitoring deaths and refugee flows from interstate wars is knowing death rates and displacements during civil wars. Did economic development projects really benefit everyone, as liberal economists anticipated? We did not know the answer until data were collected comparing women and men on various development indicators. We now have a variety of indicators and data that help us to provide numbers to the ideas, but also help us to set goals, another key UN contribution.

Setting, Promoting, and Monitoring Goals

The UN is often criticized as a forum for empty rhetoric and hot air, for resolutions and declarations that make no difference. One of the surprising conclusions from the UNIHP is the importance of goal setting; indeed, setting targets for economic and social development is seen as a "singular UN achievement."[6] Some fifty economic and social goals in all, beginning with the First Development Decade in 1960 and including the most recent set—the MDGs for poverty reduction—have been set, promoted, and monitored. The long list of human rights treaties negotiated under UN auspices established the normative foundation for global human rights and, hence, a set of goals of rights for all. The UN has established international machinery for their promotion through the OHCHR, as well as mechanisms for monitoring states' human rights records and the implementation of the treaties. In the areas of arms control and counterterrorism, the UN has also set goals and provided assistance for both state and international monitoring. In short, "Goals have also served over the years as a focus for mobilizing interests, especially the interests of NGOs, and for generating pressures for action."[7]

Agenda Setting: The UN's Value as a Forum

The value of the UN as a general forum, and particularly the General Assembly as a voice of the "peoples of the world," means that member states have used it to raise and act on new issues, thereby setting agendas for the UN itself, for other IGOs, for NGOs, and for states themselves. No one doubts the forum's value over time for promoting self-determination and decolonization in the 1950s and 1960s, calling attention to apartheid and pressuring South Africa to change over more than forty years, negotiating the comprehensive law of the sea over nine years in the 1970s, recognizing the unique position of small island states in the global climate debate, or putting on the agenda the rights of the disabled, migrant workers, and indigenous peoples. In view of the stalemate in Israeli-Palestinian peace negotiations, the Palestinians and their supporters proposed to ask the General Assembly in 2011 to recognize the state of Palestine and to admit it as a full member of the UN. To be sure, in the eyes of some, the forum has been abused, as when it was used to repeatedly link Zionism with racism in General

Assembly resolutions over many years. Still, the value of having a place where issues can be raised, resolutions can be put forward, and consensus can be built or votes taken is to serve both an agenda-setting function and a steam-releasing function for the international community.

Partnerships

Given its state-centric structures and rather limited resources, the UN's various organs, programs, and agencies must now work with a variety of partners to accomplish their objectives. Thus, partnerships are an important modus operandi. UN specialized agencies and programs not only work in tandem, as illustrated by the creation of UNAIDS, but also work with the burgeoning number of NGOs in responding to humanitarian disasters, administering economic development projects, and contributing to peacebuilding and statebuilding missions. Increasingly, they work with the private sector as well in improving labor and environmental policies (Global Compact) and in tackling specific health threats (Global Fund). Partnerships are essential for augmenting financial resources and marshaling expertise, in providing broader participation from donors, and for improving "buy in" and, hence, legitimacy for recipient states and individuals.

Yet as much as the UN has demonstrated how it has made a difference, history has also made evident what the UN cannot do.

LESSONS ABOUT
WHAT THE UN CANNOT DO

At its core, the UN remains a product of the international state system, an IGO whose member states retain sovereignty and whose policy outcomes must reflect state agreement. As Ruggie reminds us, "International organizations remain anchored in the state system. . . . Their [international organization] role in actual enforcement remains tightly constrained by states."[8] Indeed, it is in the area of enforcement in which the UN remains constrained.

Enforcement

Referring to the UN, Weiss and Thakur acknowledge that "no ways exist to enforce decisions and no mechanisms exist to compel states to comply with decisions."[9] Although that may sound extreme, the fact is most UN bodies can only make recommendations. Hence, as the same authors explain, "One of the main tactics used in the face of these constraints has been to embarrass those who do not comply. This tactic is used when UN secretariats or NGOs generate and publicize information and data about noncompliance."[10] In the human rights area, this tactic has been successful *if* it is accompanied by strong domestic measures for compliance, particularly in the form of NGO pressure. On other issues, however, publicly naming and shaming states for noncompliance may not yield the desired results.

The UN Security Council, under Chapter VII, clearly can authorize sanctions and direct, coercive military action if the P-5 concur (or do not exercise their vetoes). Although sanctions have been extensively used since the Cold War's end, military enforcement action is still rare, despite the greater use of Chapter VII authority in mandates for peace operations. Even if there is consensus on some type of enforcement, it may be for a relatively brief period of time, and member states may not back up that commitment with sufficient resources to ensure success. With sanctions, the possibility of cheating is always present, and the longer they are in place, the greater the possibility of leakage. For military enforcement, a clear lesson of the early post–Cold War years is that the UN must rely on major powers, a coalition of the willing, or NATO with its alliance capabilities for joint action developed over many years. States are unwilling to provide the UN with the types of military resources necessary for major coercive action; they are also very often reluctant to see the UN intervene in some situations—sometimes because of their own national interests, be they economic or political, as one would predict from a realist view of what is possible in IGOs.

Managing Large Long-Term Projects

Whether it is sanctioning, peacebuilding, statebuilding, or economic development, UN undertakings often demand long-term commitments. The IAEA's role in the nuclear nonproliferation regime illustrates this well. Inspections must be done at periodic intervals indefinitely, with particular vigilance in those instances where states such as Iran or North Korea are suspected of developing nuclear weapon programs. Complex multidimensional peace operations with large numbers of personnel and varied responsibilities—keeping the peace, organizing elections, rebuilding the police, creating a new judicial system, stimulating economic development, and even serving as an interim government—require a long-term commitment. It was for this reason that the PBC was created—to provide the institutional means to support such postconflict peacebuilding endeavors.

Economic development—human development—is an even longer term undertaking that the UN was really never designed to address. As shown in Chapter 5, both the UN and even the World Bank (the institution designed for reconstruction and development) changed approaches over time, making it more difficult to evaluate whether they had any positive effect. The fact is that no one knows precisely how to achieve development—what combination of factors and steps will yield positive results in each unique setting—and the UN's record of moving in fits and starts seems to parallel that of other actors.

Coordinating the Activities of a Variety of Agencies

As numerous UN staff and NGOs have remarked, "Everyone is for coordination, but nobody wants to be coordinated."[11] This has been a chronic problem, as seen in ECOSOC's coordination or lack of coordination of the multiple overlapping economic and social programs and agencies. It can also be seen in the problems of uncoordinated responses to complex humanitarian crises or to late and feeble responses to HIV/AIDS. Weiss refers to the "spaghetti junction" of the UN organizational chart (see Figure 2.1) and suggests that it creates either "productive clashes over institutional turf and competition for resources, or paralysis. Both are less-than-optimal outcomes resulting from the structure of decentralized silos instead of more integrated, mutually reinforcing, and collaborative partnerships among the various moving parts of the United Nations."[12]

Yet if the UN cannot coordinate itself, how can it participate effectively in broader partnerships involving regional organizations, NGOs, or the private sector that are requisite for addressing the challenges of the twenty-first century? Will it be able to form those partnerships so necessary to help secure Haiti's future? With these lessons of what the UN cannot do, is it possible to judge success and failure?

FACTORS IN UN SUCCESS AND FAILURE

How can we judge success and failure of the UN (or of any institution)? What criteria can be employed? What measures can be used? Did the UN meet the objectives of the founders as reflected in the Charter? Has the UN met the demands of 2012, with new issues and challenges? What frame of reference should we use—an individual program or a particular period of time? And for whom has the UN been a success or a failure—for dominant states, small states, or certain groups or individuals? For an institution with many moving parts, can we really measure success or failure as a whole, or must we evaluate particular parts? Although it is important to be explicit about our evaluation criteria, we can set forth some generalizations about the probability of success and failure.

First, if the UN's actions reflect consensus among member states and have financial backing from key donor states or private foundations, then it has a greater likelihood of success. Second, if the relevant UN program or agency takes responsibility and seizes the initiative for that action, then there is a greater probability of success. Third, endorsement and support of professionals, outside experts, scholars, NGOs—that is, the third UN—will increase the probability even more. Yet given the size of the UN's diverse membership of sovereign member states, getting these conditions "right" is rare.

The UN's actions are more likely to lead to failure when it tries to tackle an issue that, by institutional design, the founders did not intend. That includes having a strong role in international economic relations. If major powers oppose UN action, it will likely fail. Barring Security Council reform, P-5 power is assured. Barring finding independent sources of funding, economically strong states will wield the power of the purse, leading to greater assurance that their policies will be followed. If member states turn to new institutions and programs that bypass the UN, this will marginalize the UN and undermine its legitimacy as the primary global institution. States may do this either because they do not approve of UN actions or because they anticipate UN weak performance. Or other global institutions will replace the UN because the demands of the twenty-first century may really outrun the capacity of the UN in any form.

CAN THE UN BE REFORMED?

Because the UN has rarely lived up to the full expectations of all member governments, its own staff, and its supporters as well as critics, the topic of reform has been what Mark Malloch Brown, former deputy secretary-general under Kofi Annan and former administrator of UNDP, calls "an occupational obsession."[13] This has been particularly true with regard to Security Council reform and the perception for many years that the council's makeup reflects a world long gone. As we discussed, however, in Chapter 2, Security Council reform is only a small part of the puzzle, and although there has been no change in its makeup, there have been other changes in the Security Council's operation and many types of changes in the Secretariat and other parts of the first and second UNs. There have been a host of reforms in peacekeeping since the early 1990s as well as in human rights institutions, as noted in earlier chapters.

To make more substantial reforms, Brown asserts, there is no alternative "to a real commitment by member states to a better UN. . . . Real reforms will require major concessions from powerful and weak countries alike. The intergovernmental gridlock between the big contributors and the rest of the membership concerning governance and voting is the core dysfunction. To overcome it, both sides would have to rise above their own current sense of entrenched rights and privileges and find a grand bargain to allow a new, more realistic governance model for the UN."[14]

What will it take to break the deadlock and change the political equation for a major overhaul of the UN? Will it take some type of international crisis? In Brown's view, it will take something of the sort: "When politicians reach for a solution for climate change or a war and cannot find it, this absence will build the case for a better UN."[15] That's what it took for the League of Nations—the outbreak of World War II—to make the creation of the League's replacement, a stronger League, if you will, possible. Brown adds, "Until the sense of crisis at the UN is strong enough to make governments let go of their own agendas, there cannot be the kind of cathartic recommitment and renewal of the UN proper that is required."[16] So what might such a crisis look like? An terrorist attack more horrific than the 9/11 attacks? Some environmental catastrophe? A global recession or depression greater than the financial meltdown in 2008? The outbreak of war in the Middle East involving Iran, Israel, others, and perhaps even nuclear weapons or a war in Northeast Asia involving North and South Korea, Japan, the United States, and China?

To undertake major reform of the UN will require member states—both powerful and weak—to be willing to make major concessions. They will need to create a new system of representation in the Security Council and other bodies that not only accommodates today's emerging powers but is also flexible enough to adjust to future power shifts. They will have to overcome their reluctance to bring modern management principles and procedures into the UN Secretariat and empower the secretary-general to exercise more authority. They will need to devise a means for the third UN—civil society, NGOs, the private sector—to gain more formal means of involvement in the work of the organization. Or, one might ask, will they scrap the UN itself and create an entirely new institution for global governance?

LINKING THE UN TO GLOBAL GOVERNANCE

The fact is that the UN must reform to meet the demands for governance, meet the challenges of diminished sovereignty, and find states and coalitions able and willing to lead. Unless those dilemmas are addressed, the UN will become increasingly irrelevant. Global governance—rather, pieces of global governance to manage a wide variety of international issues and problems—is already now a reality with many different actors, including the UN, having authority, resources, and processes in place. Yet none of these other actors, be they regional security organizations, the G-20, NGOs, MNCs, even powerful states, can begin to replace the UN in its entirety. The real question for the UN is whether it will be a central or a marginal player in global governance in the twenty-first century.

Notes

1. Richard Jolly, Louis Emmerij, and Thomas G. Weiss, *UN Ideas That Changed the World* (Bloomington: Indiana University Press, 2009), 32–33.

2. Ibid., 34–35.

3. Quoted in Thomas G. Weiss, "The John W. Holmes Lecture: Reinvigorating the International Civil Service," *Global Governance* 16, no. 1 (2010): 52.

4. Jolly, Emmerij, and Weiss, *UN Ideas That Changed the World,* 73.

5. Ibid., 75.

6. Ibid., 43.

7. Ibid., 44.

8. John Gerard Ruggie, foreword to *Global Governance and the UN: An Unfinished Journey,* by Thomas G. Weiss and Ramesh Thakur (Bloomington: Indiana University Press, 2010), xvii.

9. Weiss and Thakur, *Global Governance and the UN,* 21.

10. Ibid.

11. Quoted in Thomas G. Weiss, *What's Wrong with the United Nations and How to Fix It* (Malden, MA: Polity Press, 2009), 81.

12. Ibid., 14.

13. Mark Malloch Brown, "The John W. Holmes Lecture: Can the UN Be Reformed?" *Global Governance* 14, no. 1 (2008): 1.

14. Ibid., 6.

15. Ibid., 7.

16. Ibid., 11.

Appendix

Charter of the United Nations (Selected Selections)

The Charter of the United Nations was signed on 26 June 1945, in San Francisco, at the conclusion of the UN Conference on International Organization, and it came into force on 24 October 1945. The Statute of the International Court of Justice is an integral part of the Charter.

Amendments to Articles 23, 27, and 61 were adopted by the General Assembly on 17 December 1963 and came into force on 31 August 1965. A further amendment to Article 61 was adopted by the General Assembly on 20 December 1971 and came into force on 24 September 1973. An amendment to Article 109, adopted by the General Assembly on 20 December 1965, came into force on 12 June 1968.

PREAMBLE TO THE CHARTER OF THE UNITED NATIONS

WE THE PEOPLES OF THE UNITED NATIONS DETERMINED

to save succeeding generations from the scourge of war, which twice in our lifetime has brought untold sorrow to mankind, and

to reaffirm faith in fundamental human rights, in the dignity and worth of the human person, in the equal rights of men and women and of nations large and small, and

to establish conditions under which justice and respect for the obligations arising from treaties and other sources of international law can be maintained, and

to promote social progress and better standards of life in larger freedom,

AND FOR THESE ENDS

to practice tolerance and live together in peace with one another as good neighbours, and

to unite our strength to maintain international peace and security, and

to ensure, by the acceptance of principles and the institution of methods, that armed force shall not be used, save in the common interest, and

to employ international machinery for the promotion of the economic and social advancement of all peoples,

HAVE RESOLVED TO COMBINE OUR EFFORTS TO ACCOMPLISH THESE AIMS.

Accordingly, our respective Governments, through representatives assembled in the city of San Francisco, who have exhibited their full powers found to be in good and due form, have agreed to the present Charter of the United Nations and do hereby establish an international organization to be known as the United Nations.

CHAPTER I

Purposes and Principles

Article 1

The Purposes of the United Nations are:

1. To maintain international peace and security, and to that end: to take effective collective measures for the prevention and removal of threats to the peace, and for the suppression of acts of aggression or other breaches of the peace, and to bring about by peaceful means, and in conformity with the principles of justice and international law, adjustment or settlement of international disputes or situations which might lead to a breach of the peace;

2. To develop friendly relations among nations based on respect for the principle of equal rights and self-determination of peoples, and to take other appropriate measures to strengthen universal peace;

3. To achieve international co-operation in solving international problems of an economic, social, cultural, or humanitarian character, and in promoting and encouraging respect for human rights and for fundamental freedoms for all without distinction as to race, sex, language, or religion; and

4. To be a centre for harmonizing the actions of nations in the attainment of these common ends.

Article 2

The Organization and its Members, in pursuit of the Purposes stated in Article 1, shall act in accordance with the following Principles.

1. The Organization is based on the principle of the sovereign equality of all its Members.

2. All Members, in order to ensure to all of them the rights and benefits resulting from membership, shall fulfill in good faith the obligations assumed by them in accordance with the present Charter.

3. All Members shall settle their international disputes by peaceful means in such a manner that international peace and security, and justice, are not endangered.

4. All Members shall refrain in their international relations from the threat or use of force against the territorial integrity or political independence of any state, or in any other manner inconsistent with the Purposes of the United Nations.

5. All Members shall give the United Nations every assistance in any action it takes in accordance with the present Charter, and shall refrain from giving assistance to any state against which the United Nations is taking preventive or enforcement action.

6. The Organization shall ensure that states which are not Members of the United Nations act in accordance with these Principles so far as may be necessary for the maintenance of international peace and security.

7. Nothing contained in the present Charter shall authorize the United Nations to intervene in matters which are essentially within the domestic jurisdiction of any state or shall require the Members to submit such matters to settlement under the present Charter; but this principle shall not prejudice the application of enforcement measures under Chapter VII.

CHAPTER II

Membership

Article 3

The original Members of the United Nations shall be the states which, having participated in the United Nations Conference on International Organization at San Francisco, or having previously signed the Declaration by United Nations of 1 January 1942, sign the present Charter and ratify it in accordance with Article 110.

Article 4

1. Membership in the United Nations is open to all other peace-loving states which accept the obligations contained in the pres-

ent Charter and, in the judgment of the Organization, are able and willing to carry out these obligations.

2. The admission of any such state to membership in the United Nations will be effected by a decision of the General Assembly upon the recommendation of the Security Council.

Article 5

A Member of the United Nations against which preventive or enforcement action has been taken by the Security Council may be suspended from the exercise of the rights and privileges of membership by the General Assembly upon the recommendation of the Security Council. The exercise of these rights and privileges may be restored by the Security Council.

Article 6

A Member of the United Nations which has persistently violated the Principles contained in the present Charter may be expelled from the Organization by the General Assembly upon the recommendation of the Security Council.

CHAPTER III

Organs
Article 7

1. There are established as the principal organs of the United Nations: a General Assembly, a Security Council, an Economic and Social Council, a Trusteeship Council, an International Court of Justice, and a Secretariat.

2. Such subsidiary organs as may be found necessary may be established in accordance with the present Charter.

Article 8

The United Nations shall place no restrictions on the eligibility of men and women to participate in any capacity and under conditions of equality in its principal and subsidiary organs.

CHAPTER IV

The General Assembly
Composition
Article 9

1. The General Assembly shall consist of all the Members of the United Nations.

2. Each Member shall have not more than five representatives in the General Assembly.

Functions and Powers
Article 10

The General Assembly may discuss any questions or any matters within the scope of the present Charter or relating to the powers and functions of any organs provided for in the present Charter, and, except as provided in Article 12, may make recommendations to the Members of the United Nations or to the Security Council or to both on any such questions or matters.

Article 11

1. The General Assembly may consider the general principles of co-operation in the maintenance of international peace and security, including the principles governing disarmament and the regulation of armaments, and may make recommendations with regard to such principles to the Members or to the Security Council or to both.

2. The General Assembly may discuss any questions relating to the maintenance of international peace and security brought before it by any Member of the United Nations, or by the Security Council, or by a state which is not a Member of the United Nations in accordance with Article 35, paragraph 2, and, except as provided in Article 12, may make recommendations with regard to any such questions to the state or states concerned or to

the Security Council or to both. Any such question on which action is necessary shall be referred to the Security Council by the General Assembly either before or after discussion.

3. The General Assembly may call the attention of the Security Council to situations which are likely to endanger international peace and security.

4. The powers of the General Assembly set forth in this Article shall not limit the general scope of Article 10.

Article 12

1. While the Security Council is exercising in respect of any dispute or situation the functions assigned to it in the present Charter, the General Assembly shall not make any recommendation with regard to that dispute or situation unless the Security Council so requests.

2. The Secretary-General, with the consent of the Security Council, shall notify the General Assembly at each session of any matters relative to the maintenance of international peace and security which are being dealt with by the Security Council and shall similarly notify the General Assembly, or the Members of the United Nations if the General Assembly is not in session, immediately the Security Council ceases to deal with such matters.

Article 13

1. The General Assembly shall initiate studies and make recommendations for the purpose of:

A. promoting international cooperation in the political field and encouraging the progressive development of international law and its codification;

B. promoting international cooperation in the economic, social, cultural, educational, and health fields, and assisting in the realization of human rights and fundamental freedoms for all without distinction as to race, sex, language, or religion.

2. The further responsibilities, functions, and powers of the General Assembly with respect to matters mentioned in paragraph 1(b) above are set forth in Chapters IX and X.

Article 14

Subject to the provisions of Article 12, the General Assembly may recommend measures for the peaceful adjustment of any situation, regardless of origin, which it deems likely to impair the general welfare or friendly relations among nations, including situations resulting from a violation of the provisions of the present Charter setting forth the Purposes and Principles of the United Nations.

Article 15

1. The General Assembly shall receive and consider annual and special reports from the Security Council; these reports shall include an account of the measures that the Security Council has decided upon or taken to maintain international peace and security.

2. The General Assembly shall receive and consider reports from the other organs of the United Nations.

Article 16

The General Assembly shall perform such functions with respect to the international trusteeship system as are assigned to it under Chapters XII and XIII, including the approval of the trusteeship agreements for areas not designated as strategic.

Article 17

1. The General Assembly shall consider and approve the budget of the Organization.

2. The expenses of the Organization shall be borne by the Members as apportioned by the General Assembly.

3. The General Assembly shall consider and approve any financial and budgetary arrangements with specialized agencies referred to in Article 57 and shall examine the administrative budgets of such specialized

agencies with a view to making recommendations to the agencies concerned.

Voting
Article 18

1. Each member of the General Assembly shall have one vote.

2. Decisions of the General Assembly on important questions shall be made by a two-thirds majority of the members present and voting. These questions shall include: recommendations with respect to the maintenance of international peace and security, the election of the non-permanent members of the Security Council, the election of the members of the Economic and Social Council, the election of members of the Trusteeship Council in accordance with paragraph 1(c) of Article 86, the admission of new Members to the United Nations, the suspension of the rights and privileges of membership, the expulsion of Members, questions relating to the operation of the trusteeship system, and budgetary questions.

3. Decisions on other questions, including the determination of additional categories of questions to be decided by a two-thirds majority, shall be made by a majority of the members present and voting.

Article 19

A Member of the United Nations which is in arrears in the payment of its financial contributions to the Organization shall have no vote in the General Assembly if the amount of its arrears equals or exceeds the amount of the contributions due from it for the preceding two full years. The General Assembly may, nevertheless, permit such a Member to vote if it is satisfied that the failure to pay is due to conditions beyond the control of the Member.

Procedure
Article 20

The General Assembly shall meet in regular annual sessions and in such special sessions as occasion may require. Special sessions shall be convoked by the Secretary-General at the request of the Security Council or of a majority of the Members of the United Nations.

Article 21

The General Assembly shall adopt its own rules of procedure. It shall elect its President for each session.

Article 22

The General Assembly may establish such subsidiary organs as it deems necessary for the performance of its functions.

CHAPTER V
The Security Council
Composition
Article 23

1. The Security Council shall consist of fifteen Members of the United Nations. The Republic of China, France, the Union of Soviet Socialist Republics, the United Kingdom of Great Britain and Northern Ireland, and the United States of America shall be permanent members of the Security Council. The General Assembly shall elect ten other Members of the United Nations to be non-permanent members of the Security Council, due regard being specially paid, in the first instance to the contribution of Members of the United Nations to the maintenance of international peace and security and to the other purposes of the Organization, and also to equitable geographical distribution.

2. The nonpermanent members of the Security Council shall be elected for a term of two years. In the first election of the non-permanent members after the increase of the membership of the Security Council from eleven to fifteen, two of the four additional members shall be chosen for a term of one year. A retiring member shall not be eligible for immediate reelection.

3. Each member of the Security Council shall have one representative.

Functions and Powers
Article 24

1. In order to ensure prompt and effective action by the United Nations, its Members confer on the Security Council primary responsibility for the maintenance of international peace and security, and agree that in carrying out its duties under this responsibility the Security Council acts on their behalf.

2. In discharging these duties the Security Council shall act in accordance with the Purposes and Principles of the United Nations. The specific powers granted to the Security Council for the discharge of these duties are laid down in Chapters VI, VII, VIII, and XII.

3. The Security Council shall submit annual and, when necessary, special reports to the General Assembly for its consideration.

Article 25

The Members of the United Nations agree to accept and carry out the decisions of the Security Council in accordance with the present Charter.

Article 26

In order to promote the establishment and maintenance of international peace and security with the least diversion for armaments of the world's human and economic resources, the Security Council shall be responsible for formulating, with the assistance of the Military Staff Committee referred to in Article 47, plans to be submitted to the Members of the United Nations for the establishment of a system for the regulation of armaments.

Voting
Article 27

1. Each member of the Security Council shall have one vote.

2. Decisions of the Security Council on procedural matters shall be made by an affirmative vote of nine members.

3. Decisions of the Security Council on all other matters shall be made by an affirmative vote of nine members including the concurring votes of the permanent members; provided that, in decisions under Chapter VI, and under paragraph 3 of Article 52, a party to a dispute shall abstain from voting.

Procedure
Article 28

1. The Security Council shall be so organized as to be able to function continuously. Each member of the Security Council shall for this purpose be represented at all times at the seat of the Organization.

2. The Security Council shall hold periodic meetings at which each of its members may, if it so desires, be represented by a member of the government or by some other specially designated representative.

3. The Security Council may hold meetings at such places other than the seat of the Organization as in its judgment will best facilitate its work.

Article 29

The Security Council may establish such subsidiary organs as it deems necessary for the performance of its functions.

Article 30

The Security Council shall adopt its own rules of procedure, including the method of selecting its President.

Article 31

Any Member of the United Nations which is not a member of the Security Council may participate, without vote, in the discussion of any question brought before the Security Council whenever the latter considers that the interests of that Member are specially affected.

Article 32

Any Member of the United Nations which is not a member of the Security Council or any state which is not a Member of the United Nations, if it is a party to a dispute under consideration by the Security Council, shall be invited to participate, without vote, in the discussion relating to the dispute. The Security Council shall lay down such conditions as it deems just for the participation of a state which is not a Member of the United Nations.

CHAPTER VI

Pacific Settlement of Disputes

Article 33

1. The parties to any dispute, the continuance of which is likely to endanger the maintenance of international peace and security, shall, first of all, seek a solution by negotiation, enquiry, mediation, conciliation, arbitration, judicial settlement, resort to regional agencies or arrangements, or other peaceful means of their own choice.

2. The Security Council shall, when it deems necessary, call upon the parties to settle their dispute by such means.

Article 34

The Security Council may investigate any dispute, or any situation which might lead to international friction or give rise to a dispute, in order to determine whether the continuance of the dispute or situation is likely to endanger the maintenance of international peace and security.

Article 35

1. Any Member of the United Nations may bring any dispute, or any situation of the nature referred to in Article 34, to the attention of the Security Council or of the General Assembly.

2. A state which is not a Member of the United Nations may bring to the attention of the Security Council or of the General Assembly any dispute to which it is a party if it accepts in advance, for the purposes of the dispute, the obligations of pacific settlement provided in the present Charter.

3. The proceedings of the General Assembly in respect of matters brought to its attention under this Article will be subject to the provisions of Articles 11 and 12.

Article 36

1. The Security Council may, at any stage of a dispute of the nature referred to in Article 33 or of a situation of like nature, recommend appropriate procedures or methods of adjustment.

2 The Security Council should take into consideration any procedures for the settlement of the dispute which have already been adopted by the parties.

3. In making recommendations under this Article the Security Council should also take into consideration that legal disputes should as a general rule be referred by the parties to the International Court of Justice in accordance with the provisions of the Statute of the Court.

Article 37

1. Should the parties to a dispute of the nature referred to in Article 33 fail to settle it by the means indicated in that Article, they shall refer it to the Security Council.

2. If the Security Council deems that the continuance of the dispute is in fact likely to endanger the maintenance of international peace and security, it shall decide whether to take action under Article 36 or to recommend such terms of settlement as it may consider appropriate.

Article 38

Without prejudice to the provisions of Articles 33 to 37, the Security Council may, if all the parties to any dispute so request, make recommendations to the parties with a view to a pacific settlement of the dispute.

CHAPTER VII

Action with Respect to Threats to the Peace, Breaches of the Peace, and Acts of Aggression

Article 39

The Security Council shall determine the existence of any threat to the peace, breach of the peace, or act of aggression and shall make recommendations, or decide what measures shall be taken in accordance with Articles 41 and 42, to maintain or restore international peace and security.

Article 40

In order to prevent an aggravation of the situation, the Security Council may, before making the recommendations or deciding upon the measures provided for in Article 39, call upon the parties concerned to comply with such provisional measures as it deems necessary or desirable. Such provisional measures shall be without prejudice to the rights, claims, or position of the parties concerned. The Security Council shall duly take account of failure to comply with such provisional measures.

Article 41

The Security Council may decide what measures not involving the use of armed force are to be employed to give effect to its decisions, and it may call upon the Members of the United Nations to apply such measures. These may include complete or partial interruption of economic relations and of rail, sea, air, postal, telegraphic, radio, and other means of communication, and the severance of diplomatic relations.

Article 42

Should the Security Council consider that measures provided for in Article 41 would be inadequate or have proved to be inadequate, it may take such action by air, sea, or land forces as may be necessary to maintain or restore international peace and security. Such action may include demonstrations, blockade, and other operations by air, sea, or land forces of Members of the United Nations.

Article 43

1. All Members of the United Nations, in order to contribute to the maintenance of international peace and security, undertake to make available to the Security Council, on its call and in accordance with a special agreement or agreements, armed forces, assistance, and facilities, including rights of passage, necessary for the purpose of maintaining international peace and security.

2. Such agreement or agreements shall govern the numbers and types of forces, their degree of readiness and general location, and the nature of the facilities and assistance to be provided.

3. The agreement or agreements shall be negotiated as soon as possible on the initiative of the Security Council. They shall be concluded between the Security Council and Members or between the Security Council and groups of Members and shall be subject to ratification by the signatory states in accordance with their respective constitutional processes.

Article 44

When the Security Council has decided to use force it shall, before calling upon a Member not represented on it to provide armed forces in fulfilment of the obligations assumed under Article 43, invite that Member, if the Member so desires, to participate in the decisions of the Security Council concerning the employment of contingents of that Member's armed forces.

Article 45

In order to enable the United Nations to take urgent military measures, Members shall hold immediately available national air-force contingents for combined international enforcement action. The strength and degree of readiness of these contingents and plans for their combined action shall be determined within the limits laid down in the special agreement or agreements referred to in Article 43, by the Security Council with the assistance of the Military Staff Committee.

Article 46

Plans for the application of armed force shall be made by the Security Council with the assistance of the Military Staff Committee.

Article 47

1. There shall be established a Military Staff Committee to advise and assist the Security Council on all questions relating to the Security Council's military requirements for the maintenance of international peace and security, the employment and command of forces placed at its disposal, the regulation of armaments, and possible disarmament.

2. The Military Staff Committee shall consist of the Chiefs of Staff of the permanent members of the Security Council or their representatives. Any Member of the United Nations not permanently represented on the Committee shall be invited by the Committee to be associated with it when the efficient discharge of the Committee's responsibilities requires the participation of that Member in its work.

3. The Military Staff Committee shall be responsible under the Security Council for the strategic direction of any armed forces placed at the disposal of the Security Council. Questions relating to the command of such forces shall be worked out subsequently.

4. The Military Staff Committee, with the authorization of the Security Council and after consultation with appropriate regional agencies, may establish regional sub-committees.

Article 48

1. The action required to carry out the decisions of the Security Council for the maintenance of international peace and security shall be taken by all the Members of the United Nations or by some of them, as the Security Council may determine.

2. Such decisions shall be carried out by the Members of the United Nations directly and through their action in the appropriate international agencies of which they are members.

Article 49

The Members of the United Nations shall join in affording mutual assistance in carrying out the measures decided upon by the Security Council.

Article 50

If preventive or enforcement measures against any state are taken by the Security Council, any other state, whether a Member of the United Nations or not, which finds itself confronted with special economic problems arising from the carrying out of those measures shall have the right to consult the Security Council with regard to a solution of those problems.

Article 51

Nothing in the present Charter shall impair the inherent right of individual or collective self-defence if an armed attack occurs against a Member of the United Nations, until the Security Council has taken measures necessary to maintain international peace and security. Measures taken by Members in the exercise of this right of self-defence shall be immediately reported to the Security Council and shall not in any way affect the authority and responsibility of the Security Council under the present Charter to take at any time such action as it deems necessary in order to maintain or restore international peace and security.

Chapter VIII
Regional Arrangements
Article 52

1. Nothing in the present Charter precludes the existence of regional arrangements or agencies for dealing with such matters relating to the maintenance of international peace and security as are appropriate for regional action provided that such arrangements or agencies and their activities are consistent with the Purposes and Principles of the United Nations.

2. The Members of the United Nations entering into such arrangements or constituting such agencies shall make every effort to achieve pacific settlement of local disputes through such regional arrangements or by such regional agencies before referring them to the Security Council.

3. The Security Council shall encourage the development of pacific settlement of local disputes through such regional arrangements or by such regional agencies either on the initiative of the states concerned or by reference from the Security Council.

4. This Article in no way impairs the application of Articles 34 and 35.

Article 53

1. The Security Council shall, where appropriate, utilize such regional arrangements or agencies for enforcement action under its authority. But no enforcement action shall be taken under regional arrangements or by regional agencies without the authorization of the Security Council, with the exception of measures against any enemy state, as defined in paragraph 2 of this Article, provided for pursuant to Article 107 or in regional arrangements directed against renewal of aggressive policy on the part of any such state, until such time as the Organization may, on request of the Governments concerned, be charged with the responsibility for preventing further aggression by such a state.

2. The term "enemy state" as used in paragraph 1 of this Article applies to any state which during the Second World War has been an enemy of any signatory of the present Charter.

Article 54

The Security Council shall at all times be kept fully informed of activities undertaken or in contemplation under regional arrangements or by regional agencies for the maintenance of international peace and security.

Chapter IX
International Economic and Social Cooperation
Article 55

With a view to the creation of conditions of stability and well-being which are necessary for peaceful and friendly relations among nations based on respect for the principle of equal rights and self-determination of peoples, the United Nations shall promote:

   A. higher standards of living, full employment, and conditions of economic and social progress and development;

   B. solutions of international economic, social, health, and related problems; and international cultural and educational cooperation; and

   C. universal respect for, and observance of, human rights and fundamental freedoms for all without distinction as to race, sex, language, or religion.

Article 56

All Members pledge themselves to take joint and separate action in cooperation with the Organization for the achievement of the purposes set forth in Article 55.

Article 57

1. The various specialized agencies, established by intergovernmental agreement

and having wide international responsibilities, as defined in their basic instruments, in economic, social, cultural, educational, health, and related fields, shall be brought into relationship with the United Nations in accordance with the provisions of Article 63.

2. Such agencies thus brought into relationship with the United Nations are hereinafter referred to as "specialized agencies."

Article 58

The Organization shall make recommendations for the co-ordination of the policies and activities of the specialized agencies.

Article 59

The Organization shall, where appropriate, initiate negotiations among the states concerned for the creation of any new specialized agencies required for the accomplishment of the purposes set forth in Article 55.

Article 60

Responsibility for the discharge of the functions of the Organization set forth in this Chapter shall be vested in the General Assembly and, under the authority of the General Assembly, in the Economic and Social Council, which shall have for this purpose the powers set forth in Chapter X.

CHAPTER X

The Economic and Social Council
Composition
Article 61

1. The Economic and Social Council shall consist of fifty-four Members of the United Nations elected by the General Assembly.

2. Subject to the provisions of paragraph 3, eighteen members of the Economic and Social Council shall be elected each year for a term of three years. A retiring member shall be eligible for immediate reelection.

3. At the first election after the increase in the membership of the Economic and Social Council from twenty-seven to fifty-four members, in addition to the members elected in place of the nine members whose term of office expires at the end of that year, twenty-seven additional members shall be elected. Of these twenty-seven additional members, the term of office of nine members so elected shall expire at the end of one year, and of nine other members at the end of two years, in accordance with arrangements made by the General Assembly.

4. Each member of the Economic and Social Council shall have one representative.

Functions and Powers
Article 62

1. The Economic and Social Council may make or initiate studies and reports with respect to international economic, social, cultural, educational, health, and related matters and may make recommendations with respect to any such matters to the General Assembly, to the Members of the United Nations, and to the specialized agencies concerned.

2. It may make recommendations for the purpose of promoting respect for, and observance of, human rights and fundamental freedoms for all.

3. It may prepare draft conventions for submission to the General Assembly, with respect to matters falling within its competence.

4. It may call, in accordance with the rules prescribed by the United Nations, international conferences on matters falling within its competence.

Article 63

1. The Economic and Social Council may enter into agreements with any of the agencies referred to in Article 57, defining the terms on which the agency concerned shall be brought into relationship with the United Nations. Such agreements shall be subject to approval by the General Assembly.

2. It may co-ordinate the activities of the specialized agencies through consultation with and recommendations to such agencies and through recommendations to the General Assembly and to the Members of the United Nations.

Article 64

1. The Economic and Social Council may take appropriate steps to obtain regular reports from the specialized agencies. It may make arrangements with the Members of the United Nations and with the specialized agencies to obtain reports on the steps taken to give effect to its own recommendations and to recommendations on matters falling within its competence made by the General Assembly.

2. It may communicate its observations on these reports to the General Assembly.

Article 65

The Economic and Social Council may furnish information to the Security Council and shall assist the Security Council upon its request.

Article 66

1. The Economic and Social Council shall perform such functions as fall within its competence in connection with the carrying out of the recommendations of the General Assembly.

2. It may, with the approval of the General Assembly, perform services at the request of Members of the United Nations and at the request of specialized agencies.

3. It shall perform such other functions as are specified elsewhere in the present Charter or as may be assigned to it by the General Assembly.

Voting
Article 67

1. Each member of the Economic and Social Council shall have one vote.

2. Decisions of the Economic and Social Council shall be made by a majority of the members present and voting.

Procedure
Article 68

The Economic and Social Council shall set up commissions in economic and social fields and for the promotion of human rights, and such other commissions as may be required for the performance of its functions.

Article 69

The Economic and Social Council shall invite any Member of the United Nations to participate, without vote, in its deliberations on any matter of particular concern to that Member.

Article 70

The Economic and Social Council may make arrangements for representatives of the specialized agencies to participate, without vote, in its deliberations and in those of the commissions established by it, and for its representatives to participate in the deliberations of the specialized agencies.

Article 71

The Economic and Social Council may make suitable arrangements for consultation with non-governmental organizations which are concerned with matters within its competence. Such arrangements may be made with international organizations and, where appropriate, with national organizations after consultation with the Member of the United Nations concerned.

Article 72

1. The Economic and Social Council shall adopt its own rules of procedure, including the method of selecting its President.

2. The Economic and Social Council shall meet as required in accordance with its

rules, which shall include provision for the convening of meetings on the request of a majority of its members.

CHAPTER XI

Declaration Regarding Non-Self-Governing Territories

Article 73

Members of the United Nations which have or assume responsibilities for the administration of territories whose peoples have not yet attained a full measure of self-government recognize the principle that the interests of the inhabitants of these territories are paramount, and accept as a sacred trust the obligation to promote to the utmost, within the system of international peace and security established by the present Charter, the well-being of the inhabitants of these territories, and, to this end:

A. to ensure, with due respect for the culture of the peoples concerned, their political, economic, social, and educational advancement, their just treatment, and their protection against abuses;

B. to develop self-government, to take due account of the political aspirations of the peoples, and to assist them in the progressive development of their free political institutions, according to the particular circumstances of each territory and its peoples and their varying stages of advancement;

C. to further international peace and security;

D. to promote constructive measures of development, to encourage research, and to co-operate with one another and, when and where appropriate, with specialized international bodies with a view to the practical achievement of the social, economic, and scientific purposes set forth in this Article; and

E. to transmit regularly to the Secretary-General for information purposes, subject to such limitation as security and constitutional considerations may require, statistical and other information of a technical nature relating to economic, social, and educational conditions in the territories for which they are respectively responsible other than those territories to which Chapters XII and XIII apply.

Article 74

Members of the United Nations also agree that their policy in respect of the territories to which this Chapter applies, no less than in respect of their metropolitan areas, must be based on the general principle of good-neighbourliness, due account being taken of the interests and well-being of the rest of the world, in social, economic, and commercial matters.

CHAPTER XIV

The International Court of Justice

Article 92

The International Court of Justice shall be the principal judicial organ of the United Nations. It shall function in accordance with the annexed Statute, which is based upon the Statute of the Permanent Court of International Justice and forms an integral part of the present Charter.

Article 93

1. All Members of the United Nations are ipso facto parties to the Statute of the International Court of Justice.

2. A state which is not a Member of the United Nations may become a party to the Statute of the International Court of Justice on conditions to be determined in each case by the General Assembly upon the recommendation of the Security Council.

Article 94

1. Each Member of the United Nations undertakes to comply with the decision of

the International Court of Justice in any case to which it is a party.

2. If any party to a case fails to perform the obligations incumbent upon it under a judgment rendered by the Court, the other party may have recourse to the Security Council, which may, if it deems necessary, make recommendations or decide upon measures to be taken to give effect to the judgment.

Article 95

Nothing in the present Charter shall prevent Members of the United Nations from entrusting the solution of their differences to other tribunals by virtue of agreements already in existence or which may be concluded in the future.

Article 96

1. The General Assembly or the Security Council may request the International Court of Justice to give an advisory opinion on any legal question.

2. Other organs of the United Nations and specialized agencies, which may at any time be so authorized by the General Assembly, may also request advisory opinions of the Court on legal questions arising within the scope of their activities.

CHAPTER XV

The Secretariat

Article 97

The Secretariat shall comprise a Secretary-General and such staff as the Organization may require. The Secretary-General shall be appointed by the General Assembly upon the recommendation of the Security Council. He shall be the chief administrative officer of the Organization.

Article 98

The Secretary-General shall act in that capacity in all meetings of the General Assembly, of the Security Council, of the Economic and Social Council, and of the Trusteeship Council, and shall perform such other functions as are entrusted to him by these organs. The Secretary-General shall make an annual report to the General Assembly on the work of the Organization.

Article 99

The Secretary-General may bring to the attention of the Security Council any matter which in his opinion may threaten the maintenance of international peace and security.

Article 100

1. In the performance of their duties the Secretary-General and the staff shall not seek or receive instructions from any government or from any other authority external to the Organization. They shall refrain from any action which might reflect on their position as international officials responsible only to the Organization.

2. Each Member of the United Nations undertakes to respect the exclusively international character of the responsibilities of the Secretary-General and the staff and not to seek to influence them in the discharge of their responsibilities.

Article 101

1. The staff shall be appointed by the Secretary-General under regulations established by the General Assembly.

2. Appropriate staffs shall be permanently assigned to the Economic and Social Council, the Trusteeship Council, and, as required, to other organs of the United Nations. These staffs shall form a part of the Secretariat.

3. The paramount consideration in the employment of the staff and in the determination of the conditions of service shall be the necessity of securing the highest standards of efficiency, competence, and integrity. Due regard shall be paid to the importance of

recruiting the staff on as wide a geographical basis as possible.

CHAPTER XVIII

Amendments

Article 108

Amendments to the present Charter shall come into force for all Members of the United Nations when they have been adopted by a vote of two-thirds of the members of the General Assembly and ratified in accordance with their respective constitutional processes by two-thirds of the Members of the United Nations, including all the permanent members of the Security Council.

Article 109

1. A General Conference of the Members of the United Nations for the purpose of reviewing the present Charter may be held at a date and place to be fixed by a two-thirds vote of the members of the General Assembly and by a vote of any nine members of the Security Council. Each Member of the United Nations shall have one vote in the conference.

2. Any alteration of the present Charter recommended by a two-thirds vote of the conference shall take effect when ratified in accordance with their respective constitutional processes by two-thirds of the Members of the United Nations including all the permanent members of the Security Council.

3. If such a conference has not been held before the tenth annual session of the General Assembly following the coming into force of the present Charter, the proposal to call such a conference shall be placed on the agenda of that session of the General Assembly, and the conference shall be held if so decided by a majority vote of the members of the General Assembly and by a vote of any seven members of the Security Council.

Suggested Sources for Additional Research

General Sources on International Organizations and the United Nations

Books

Barnett, Michael, and Martha Finnemore. *Rules for the World: International Organizations in Global Politics*. Ithaca: Cornell University Press, 2004.

Claude, Inis L., Jr. *Swords into Plowshares: The Problems and Progress of International Organization*. 4th ed. New York: Random House, 1984.

Commission on Global Governance. *Our Global Neighborhood: Report of the Commission on Global Governance*. Oxford: Oxford University Press, 1995.

Emmerij, Louis, Richard Jolly, and Thomas G. Weiss. *Ahead of the Curve? UN Ideas and Global Challenges*. Bloomington: Indiana University Press, 2001.

Fasulo, Linda. *An Insider's Guide to the UN*. 2nd ed. New Haven: Yale University Press, 2009.

Heinbecker, Paul, and Patricia Goff, eds. *Irrelevant or Indispensable? The United Nations in the 21st Century*. Waterloo, Canada: Wilfred Laurier Press, 2005.

Karns, Margaret P., and Karen A. Mingst. *International Organizations: The Politics and Processes of Global Governance*. 2nd ed. Boulder: Lynne Rienner, 2010.

Mazower, Mark. *No Enchanted Palace: The End of Empire and the Ideological Origins of the United Nations*. Princeton: Princeton University Press, 2009.

Muldoon, James P., Jr., JoAnn Fagot Aviel, Richard Reitano, and Earl Sullivan, eds. *The New Dynamics of Multilateralism: Diplomacy, International Organizations, and Global Governance*. Boulder: Westview Press, 2011.

Reinalda, Bob, and Bertjan Verbeek, eds. *Decision Making Within International Organizations*. London: Routledge, 2004.

Schlesinger, Stephen C. *Act of Creation: The Founding of the United Nations*. Boulder: Westview Press, 2003.

Smith, Courtney B. *Politics and Process at the United Nations: The Global Dance*. Boulder: Lynne Rienner, 2006.

Taylor, Paul, and A. J. R. Groom, eds. *The United Nations at the Millennium*. New York: Continuum, 2007.

Weiss, Thomas G. *What's Wrong with the United Nations and How to Fix It*. Malden, MA: Polity Press, 2009.

Weiss, Thomas G., and Sam Daws, eds. *The Oxford Handbook on the United Nations*. New York: Oxford University Press, 2007.

Weiss, Thomas G., David P. Forsythe, Roger A. Coate, and Kelly-Kate Pease. *The United Nations and Changing World Politics*. 6th ed. Boulder: Westview Press, 2010.

Weiss, Thomas G., and Ramesh Thakur. *Global Governance and the UN: An Unfinished Journey*. Bloomington: Indiana University Press, 2010.

Journals

Three excellent journals on international organizations, global governance, and the United Nations are *Global Governance*, the *Review of International Organizations*, and *International Organization*. The *UN Chronicle* is also an excellent resource on many UN-related topics and activities.

Official UN Web Sites

International Court of Justice: www.icj-cij.org
UN home page: www.un.org
UN Reform: www.un.org/reform
UN system of organizations: www.unsystem.org

Academic and Policy-Related Web Sites

Academic Council on the United Nations System: www.acuns.org
American Society of International Law: www.asil.org
Belfer Center for Science and International Affairs: belfercenter.ksg.harvard.edu
Carnegie Endowment for International Peace: www.carnegieendowment.org
Council on Foreign Relations Global Governance Monitor: www.cfr.org/global-governance
    /global-governance-monitor/p18985
Global Policy Forum: www.globalpolicy.org
UN Association of the USA: www.TheInterdependent.com
UN Foundation/UN Wire: www.unfoundation.org/unwire
UN Intellectual History Project: www.unhistory.org
United Nations Association of the United States: www.unausa.org
United States Institute of Peace: www.usip.org

The Organs of the United Nations

Books

Bailey, Sydney D., and Sam Daws. *The Procedure of the UN Security Council*. 3rd ed. New York: Oxford University Press, 1999.

Bosco, David L. *Five to Rule Them All: The UN Security Council and the Making of the Modern World*. Oxford: Oxford University Press, 2009.

Chesterman, Simon, ed. *Secretary or General? The UN Secretary-General in World Politics*. Cambridge: Cambridge University Press, 2007.

Cronin, Bruce, and Ian Hurd, eds. *The UN Security Council and the Politics of International Authority*. New York: Routledge, 2008.

Gordenker, Leon. *The UN Secretary-General and Secretariat*. 2nd ed. London: Routledge, 2010.

Hurd, Ian. *After Anarchy: Legitimacy and Power in the United Nations Security Council*. Princeton: Princeton University Press, 2007.

Kille, Kent. *From Manager to Visionary: The Secretary-General of the United Nations*. New York: Palgrave, 2006.

———, ed. *The UN Secretary-General and Moral Authority: Ethics and Religion in International Leadership*. Washington, DC: Georgetown University Press, 2007.

Malone, David, ed. *The UN Security Council: From the Cold War to the 21st Century*. Boulder: Lynne Rienner, 2004.

Marin-Bosch, Miguel. *Votes in the UN General Assembly*. The Hague: Kluwer Law International, 1998.

Newman, Edward. *The UN Secretary-General from the Cold War to the New Era: A Global Peace and Security Mandate?* New York: St. Martin's Press, 1998.

Peterson, M. J. *The UN General Assembly*. London: Routledge, 2006.

Schechter, Michael G. *United Nations Global Conferences*. London: Routledge, 2005.

Thompson, Alexander. *Channels of Power: The UN Security Council and U.S. Statecraft in Iraq*. Ithaca: Cornell University Press, 2009.

United Nations Association of the USA, eds. *Global Agenda: Issues Before the United Nations*. New York: UNA-USA (published annually).

Actors in the United Nations System: States and Nonstate Actors

Books

Alger, Chadwick F., Gene M. Lyons, and John E. Trent, eds. *The United Nations and the Politics of Member States*. Tokyo: United Nations University Press, 1995.

Drifte, Reinhard. *Japan's Quest for a Permanent Security Council Seat: A Matter of Pride or Justice?* New York: St. Martin's Press, 2000.

Friedman, Elizabeth, Kathryn Hochstetter, and Ann Marie Clark. *Democracy, Sovereignty, and Global Civil Society*. Albany: State University of New York Press, 2005.

Joachim, Jutta, and Birgit Locher, eds. *Transnational Activism in the UN and the EU: A Comparative Study*. London: Routledge, 2009.

Karns, Margaret P., and Karen A. Mingst, eds. *The United States and Multilateral Institutions: Patterns of Changing Instrumentality and Influence*. Boston: Unwin Hyman, 1990.

Keck, Margaret E., and Kathryn Sikkink. *Activists Beyond Borders: Advocacy Networks in International Politics*. Ithaca: Cornell University Press, 1998.

Krause, Keith, and W. Andy Knight, eds. *State, Society, and the UN System: Changing Perspectives on Multilateralism*. Tokyo: United Nations University Press, 1995.

Luck, Edward C. *Mixed Messages: American Politics and International Organization, 1919–1999*. Washington, DC: Brookings Institution Press, 1999.

McKeon, Nora. *The United Nations and Civil Society: Legitimating Global Governance— Whose Voice?* London: Zed Books, 2009.

Paolini, Albert J., eds. *Between Sovereignty and Global Governance: The United Nations, the State, and Civil Society*. Basingstoke, UK: Palgrave, 2003.

Patrick, Stewart. *The Best-Laid Plans: The Origins of American Multilateralism and the Dawn of the Cold War*. Lanham, MD: Rowman and Littlefield, 2009.

Patrick, Stewart, and Shepard Forman, eds. *Multilateralism and U.S. Foreign Policy: Ambivalent Engagement*. Boulder: Lynne Rienner, 2002.

Scholte, Jan Aart, ed. *Building Global Democracy? Civil Society and Accountable Global Governance*. Cambridge: Cambridge University Press, 2011.

Traub, James. *The Best Intentions: Kofi Annan and the UN in the Era of American World Power*. New York: Farrar, Straus, and Giroux, 2006.

Weiss, Thomas G., and Leon Gordenker, eds. *NGOs, the UN, and Global Governance*. Boulder: Lynne Rienner, 1996.

Whitfield, Teresa. *Friends Indeed? The United Nations, Groups of Friends, and Resolution of Conflict*. Washington, DC: United States Institute of Peace Press, 2007.

Willetts, Peter. *Non-Governmental Organizations in World Politics*. New York: Routledge, 2011.

Peace and Security

Books

Abiew, Frances Kofi. *The Evolution of the Doctrine and Practice of Humanitarian Intervention*. The Hague: Kluwer Law International, 1999.

Adebajo, Adekeye. *UN Peacekeeping in Africa: From the Suez Crisis to the Sudan Conflicts*. Boulder: Lynne Rienner, 2011.

Aoi, Chiyuki, Cedric de Coning, and Ramesh Thakur, eds. *Unintended Consequences of Peacekeeping Operations*. Tokyo: United Nations University Press, 2007.

Autesserre, Séverine. *The Trouble with the Congo: Local Violence and the Failure of International Peacebuilding*. Cambridge: Cambridge University Press, 2010.

Barnett, Michael, and Thomas G. Weiss. *Humanitarianism Contested: Where Angels Fear to Tread*. New York: Routledge, 2011.

Berdal, Mats. *Building Peace After War*. London: International Institute for Strategic Studies, 2009.

Berdal, Mats, and Spyros Economides, eds. *United Nations Interventionism, 1991–2004*. Cambridge: Cambridge University Press, 2007.

Boulden, Jane, and Thomas G. Weiss, eds. *Terrorism and the UN: Before and After September 11*. Bloomington: Indiana University Press, 2004.

Call, Charles T., with Vanessa Wyeth, eds. *Building States to Build Peace*. Boulder: Lynne Rienner, 2008.

Chesterman, Simon. *Just War or Just Peace? Humanitarian Intervention and International Law*. New York: Oxford University Press, 2001.

———. *You, the People: The United Nations, Transitional Administration, and State-Building*. New York: Oxford University Press, 2004.

Cortright, David, and George A. Lopez. *Sanctions and the Search for Security*. Boulder: Lynne Rienner, 2002.

Diehl, Paul F. *Peace Operations: War and Conflict in the Modern World*. Malden, MA: Polity Press, 2008.

Diehl, Paul F., and Daniel Druckman. *Evaluating Peace Operations*. Boulder: Lynne Rienner, 2010.

Dobbins, James, et al. *The UN's Role in Nation-Building: From the Congo to Iraq*. Santa Monica, CA: Rand, 2005.

Doyle, Michael W., and Nicholas Sambanis. *Making War and Building Peace: United Nations Peace Operations*. Princeton: Princeton University Press, 2006.

Fortna, Virginia Page. *Does Peacekeeping Work? Shaping Belligerents' Choices After Civil War*. Princeton: Princeton University Press, 2008.

———. *Peace Time: Cease-Fire Agreements and the Durability of Peace*. Princeton: Princeton University Press, 2004.

Howard, Lise Morjé. *UN Peacekeeping in Civil Wars*. New York: Cambridge University Press, 2008.

Hudson, Natalie Florea. *Gender, Human Security, and the UN: Security Language as a Political Framework*. London: Routledge, 2009.

Jentleson, Bruce W. *Opportunities Missed, Opportunities Seized: Preventive Diplomacy in the Post–Cold War World*. Lanham, MD: Rowman and Littlefield, 1999.

Kuehnast, Kathleen, Chantal de Jonge Oudraat, and Helga Hernes, eds. *Women and War: Power and Protection in the 21st Century*. Washington, DC: United States Institute of Peace Press, 2011.

Malone, David M. *The International Struggle over Iraq: Politics in the UN Security Council, 1980–2005*. New York: Oxford University Press, 2006.

Mamdani, Mahmood. *Saviors and Survivors: Darfur, Politics, and the War on Terror*. New York: Random House, 2009.

Mayall, James, ed. *The New Interventionism, 1991–1993: United Nations Experience in Cambodia, Former Yugoslavia, and Somalia*. New York: Cambridge University Press, 1996.

Paris, Roland. *At War's End: Building Peace After Civil Conflict*. New York: Cambridge University Press, 2004.

Paris, Roland, and Timothy D. Sisk, eds. *The Dilemmas of Statebuilding: Confronting the Contradictions of Postwar Peace Operations*. New York: Routledge, 2009.

Price, Richard M., and Mark W. Zacher, eds. *The United Nations and Global Security*. New York: Palgrave Macmillan, 2004.

Pugh, Michael, and Waheguru Pal Singh Sidhu. *The United Nations and Regional Security: Europe and Beyond*. Boulder: Lynne Rienner, 2003.

Ramcharan, Bertrand G. *Preventive Diplomacy at the UN*. Bloomington: Indiana University Press, 2008.

Ratner, Steven R. *The New UN Peacekeeping: Building Peace in Lands of Conflict After the Cold War*. New York: St. Martin's Press, 1996.

Robinson, Geoffrey. *"If You Leave Us Here, We Will Die": How Genocide Was Stopped in East Timor*. Princeton: Princeton University Press, 2009.

Romaniuk, Peter. *Multilateral Counter-Terrorism*. New York: Routledge, 2010.

Sorenson, David S., and Pia Christina Wood, eds. *The Politics of Peacekeeping in the Post–Cold War Era*. London: Frank Cass, 2005.

Stedman, Stephen John, Donald Rothchild, and Elizabeth M. Cousens. *Ending Civil Wars: The Implementation of Peace Agreements*. Boulder: Lynne Rienner, 2002.

Thakur, Ramesh. *The United Nations, Peace, and Security*. New York: Cambridge University Press, 2006.

Thakur, Ramesh, and Albrecht Schnabel, eds. *United Nations Peacekeeping Operations: Ad Hoc Missions, Permanent Engagement*. Tokyo: United Nations University Press, 2001.

United Nations. *The Blue Helmets: A Review of United Nations Peace-Keeping*. 3rd ed. New York: UNDPI, 1996.

Weiss, Thomas G., ed. *Beyond UN Subcontracting: Task-Sharing with Regional Security Arrangements and Service-Providing NGOs*. New York: St. Martin's Press, 1998.

———. *Humanitarian Intervention: War and Conflict in the Modern World*. Malden, MA: Polity Press, 2007.

Weiss, Thomas G., and Cindy Collins. *Humanitarian Challenges and Intervention: World Politics and the Dilemmas of Help*. 2nd ed. Boulder: Westview Press, 2000.

Zanotti, Laura. *Governing Disorder: UN Peace Operations, International Security, and Democratization in the Post–Cold War Era*. Philadelphia: Pennsylvania State University Press, 2011.

Journals and Specialized Publications

Two excellent sources on peacekeeping are the journal *International Peacekeeping*, published by Frank Cass and Company, London, and the *Annual Review of Global Peace Operations*, a Project of the Center on International Cooperation at New York University, published by Lynne Rienner Publishers. On the responsibility to protect, see the journal *Global Responsibility to Protect*, published by Martinus Nijhoff Publishers and available online.

Peace and Security-Related Web Sites

International Atomic Energy Agency: www.iaea.org
International Campaign to Ban Landmines: www.icbl.org
International Commission on Intervention and State Sovereignty: www.dfait-maeci.gc.ca
  /iciss-ciise
International Crisis Group: www.crisisgroup.org
International Relations and Security Network: www.isn.ethz.ch
Stockholm International Peace Research Institute: www.sipri.org
UN Counter-Terrorism Committee: www.un.org/en/sc/ctc
UN Department of Peacekeeping Operations: www.un.org/en/peacekeeping
UN Office of Disarmament Affairs: www.un.org/disarmament
UN Peacebuilding Commission: www.un.org/peace/peacebuilding

Economic Development and Sustainability

Books

Berthelot, Yves, ed. *Unity and Diversity in Development Ideas: Perspectives from the UN Regional Commissions.* Bloomington: Indiana University Press, 2004.

Boas, Morten, and Desmond McNeill, eds. *Global Institutions and Development: Framing the World?* London: Routledge, 2004.

Clapp, Jennifer, and Rorden Wilkinson, eds. *Global Governance, Poverty, and Inequality.* New York: Routledge, 2010.

Goldman, Michael. *Imperial Nature: The World Bank and Struggles for Social Justice in the Age of Globalization.* New Haven: Yale University Press, 2005.

Grunberg, Isabelle, and Sarbuland Khan, eds. *Globalization: The United Nations Development Dialogue, Finance, Trade, Poverty, Peacebuilding.* Tokyo: United Nations University Press, 2000.

Hoekman, Bernard M., and Petros C. Mavroidis. *The World Trade Organization: Law, Economics, and Politics.* New York: Routledge, 2007.

Hulme, David. *Global Poverty: How Global Governance Is Failing the Poor.* New York: Routledge, 2010.

Jain, Devaki. *Women, Development, and the UN: A Sixty-Year Quest for Equality and Justice.* Bloomington: Indiana University Press, 2005.

Jolly, Richard, Louis Emmerij, Dharam Ghai, and Frederic Lapeyre. *UN Contributions to Development Thinking and Practice.* Bloomington: Indiana University Press, 2004.

Kapur, Devesh, John P. Lewis, and Richard Webb, eds. *The World Bank: Its First Half Century.* Vol. 1, *History.* Vol. 2, *Perspectives.* Washington, DC: Brookings Institution Press, 1997.

Marshall, Katherine. *The World Bank: From Reconstruction to Development to Equity.* New York: Routledge, 2008.

Murphy, Craig N. *The United Nations Development Programme: A Better Way?* Cambridge: Cambridge University Press, 2006.

O'Brien, Robert, Anne Marie Goetz, Jan Aart Scholte, and Marc Williams. *Contesting Global Governance: Multilateral Economic Institutions and Global Social Movements.* New York: Cambridge University Press, 2000.

Peet, Richard. *Unholy Trinity: The IMF, World Bank, and WTO.* 2nd ed. New York: Zed Books, 2009.

Sagafi-nejad, Tagi, with John Dunning. *The UN and Transnationals: From Code to Compact.* Bloomington: Indiana University Press, 2006.

Shaw, John. *Global Food and Agricultural Institutions.* New York: Routledge, 2009.

Stiglitz, Joseph E. *Globalization and Its Discontents.* New York: W. W. Norton, 2002.

Stone, Randall W. *Controlling Institutions: International Organizations and the Global Economy.* New York: Cambridge University Press, 2011.

Tabb, William K. *Economic Governance in the Age of Globalization.* New York: Columbia University Press, 2004.

Taylor, Ian. *UN Conference on Trade and Development.* New York: Routledge, 2007.

Ul Haq, Mahbub, et al., eds. *The UN and the Bretton Woods Institutions.* New York: St. Martin's Press, 1995.

Vreeland, James Raymond. *The International Monetary Fund: Politics of Conditional Lending.* New York: Routledge, 2007.

Ward, Michael. *Quantifying the World: UN Contributions to Statistics.* Bloomington: Indiana University Press, 2004.

Weaver, Catherine. *Hypocrisy Trap: The World Bank and the Poverty of Reform.* Princeton: Princeton University Press, 2008.

Weiss, Thomas G., Tatiana Carayannis, Louis Emmerij, and Richard Jolly. *UN Voices: The Struggle for Development and Social Justice.* Bloomington: Indiana University Press, 2005.

Economic Development–Related Web Sites

Center for Global Development: www.cgdev.org

Commission on Sustainable Development: www.un.org/esa/sustdev/csd/review.htm

Food and Agriculture Organization: www.fao.org

Group of 20: www.g20.org

Group of 77: www.g77.org

Human Development Reports: www.hdr.undp.org

Institute of Development Studies: www.ids.ac.uk

Inter-American Development Bank: www.iadb.org

International Development Association: www.worldbank.org/ida

International Labour Organization: www.ilo.org

International Monetary Fund: www.imf.org

UN Conference on Trade and Development: www.unctad.org

UN Development Programme: www.undp.org

UN Global Compact: www.unglobalcompact.org

UN Millennium Development Goals: www.un.org/millenniumgoals

World Bank: www.worldbank.org

World Food Programme: www.wfp.org

World Trade Organization: www.wto.org

Human Rights

Books

Barnett, Michael. *Eyewitness to Genocide: The United Nations and Rwanda.* Ithaca: Cornell University Press, 2002.

Devaki, Jain. *Women, Development, and the UN: A Sixty-Year Quest for Equality and Justice.* Bloomington: Indiana University Press, 2005.

Donnelly, Jack. *Universal Human Rights in Theory and Practice.* 2nd ed. Ithaca: Cornell University Press, 2003.

Forsythe, David, ed. *The Encyclopedia of Human Rights.* 5 vols. New York: Cambridge University Press, 2009.

———. *The Humanitarians: The International Committee of the Red Cross.* New York: Cambridge University Press, 2005.

———. *Human Rights in International Relations.* 3rd ed. New York: Cambridge University Press, 2012.

Gallagher, Anne T. *The International Law of Human Trafficking.* Cambridge: Cambridge University Press, 2010.

Hafner-Burton, Emilie M. *Forced to Be Good: Why Trade Agreements Boost Human Rights.* Ithaca: Cornell University Press, 2009.

Hopgood, Stephen. *Keepers of the Flame: Understanding Amnesty International.* Ithaca: Cornell University Press, 2006.

Joachim, Jutta. *Agenda Setting, the UN, and NGOs: Gender Violence and Reproductive Rights.* Washington, DC: Georgetown University Press, 2007.

Khagram, Sanjeev, James V. Riker, and Kathryn Sikkink, eds. *Restructuring World Politics: Transnational Social Movements, Networks, and Norms.* Minneapolis: University of Minnesota Press, 2002.

Lauren, Paul Gordon. *The Evolution of International Human Rights: Visions Seen.* 3rd ed. Philadelphia: University of Pennsylvania Press, 2011.

Lischer, Sarah Kenyon. *Dangerous Sanctuaries: Refugee Camps, Civil War, and the Dilemmas of Humanitarian Aid.* Ithaca: Cornell University Press, 2005.

Mertus, Julie A. *The United Nations and Human Rights: A Guide for a New Era.* 2nd ed. New York: Routledge, 2009.

Meyer, Mary K., and Elisabeth Prugl, eds. *Gender Politics in Global Governance.* Lanham, MD: Rowman and Littlefield, 1999.

Neuffer, Elizabeth. *The Key to My Neighbor's House: Seeking Justice in Bosnia and Rwanda.* New York: Picador, 2001.

Oestreich, Joel E. *Power and Principle: Human Rights Programming in International Organizations.* Washington, DC: Georgetown University Press, 2007.

Peterson, V. Spike, and Anne Sisson Runyan. *Global Gender Issues in the New Millennium.* 3rd ed. Boulder: Westview Press, 2010.

Ramcharan, Bertrand G. *Contemporary Human Rights Ideas.* New York: Routledge, 2008.

———. *The UN Human Rights Council.* New York: Routledge, 2011.

Romano, Cesare P. R., ed. *The Sword and the Scales: The United Nations and International Courts and Tribunals.* New York: Cambridge University Press, 2009.

Schiff, Benjamin N. *Building the International Criminal Court.* Cambridge: Cambridge University Press, 2008.

Shelley, Louise. *Human Trafficking: A Global Perspective.* New York: Cambridge University Press, 2010.

Simmons, Beth A. *Mobilizing for Human Rights: International Law in Domestic Politics.* New York: Cambridge University Press, 2009.

Skinner, E. Benjamin. *A Crime So Monstrous: Face-to-Face with Modern-Day Slavery.* New York: Free Press, 2008.

United Nations. *The United Nations and Apartheid, 1948–1994.* Blue Book vol. 1. New York: United Nations, 1995.

————. *The United Nations and Human Rights, 1945–1995*. Blue Book vol. 7. New York: United Nations, 1996.

————. *The United Nations and the Advancement of Women, 1945–1996*. Blue Book vol. 6. New York: United Nations, 1997.

Zaidi, Sarah, and Roger Normand. *The UN and Human Rights Ideas: The Unfinished Revolution*. Bloomington: Indiana University Press, 2006.

Human Rights–Related Web Sites

Amnesty International: www.amnesty.org
Anti-Slavery International: www.antislavery.org
Coalition for the International Criminal Court: www.iccnow.org
Human Rights Watch: www.hrw.org
International Commission of Jurists: www.icj.org
International Committee of the Red Cross: www.icrc.org
International Criminal Court: www.icc-cpi.int/Menus/ICC/
International Criminal Tribunal for Rwanda: www.unictr.org
International Criminal Tribunal for the Former Yugoslavia: www.icty.org/
International Organization for Migration: www.iom.int
UN Children's Fund: www.unicef.org
UN High Commissioner for Human Rights: www.unhchr.ch
UN High Commissioner for Refugees: www.unhcr.org
University of Minnesota Human Rights Library: www.umn.edu/humanrts
UN Office for the Coordination of Humanitarian Affairs: ochaonline.un.org
UN Office of Drugs and Crime: www.unodc.org
UN Women: www.unwomen.org

Human Security

Books

Benedict, Richard Elliot. *Ozone Diplomacy: New Directions in Safeguarding the Planet*. Enlarged ed. Cambridge: Harvard University Press, 1998.

Conca, Ken, and Geoffrey D. Dabelko, eds. *Green Planet Blues: Four Decades of Global Environmental Politics*. 4th ed. Boulder: Westview Press, 2010.

Delmas, Magali, and Oran R. Young, eds. *Governing the Environment: Interdisciplinary Perspectives*. New York: Cambridge University Press, 2008.

DeSombre, Elizabeth R. *Global Environmental Institutions*. New York: Routledge, 2006.

Elliott, Lorraine. *The Global Politics of the Environment*. London: Macmillan, 1998.

Garrett, Laurie. *The Coming Plague*. New York: Farrar, Straus, and Giroux, 1994.

Heine, Jorge, and Andrew Thompson, eds. *Fixing Haiti: MINUSTAH and Beyond*. Tokyo: United Nations University Press, 2010.

Hoffmann, Matthew J. *Climate Governance at the Crossroads: Experimenting with a Global Response after Kyoto*. New York: Oxford University Press, 2011.

Homer-Dixon, Thomas. *Environment, Scarcity, and Violence*. 2nd ed. Princeton: Princeton University Press, 1999.

Lee, Kelley. *The World Health Organization*. New York: Routledge, 2009.

Lisk, Franklyn. *Global Institutions and the HIV/AIDS Epidemic: Responding to an International Crisis*. New York: Routledge, 2010.

MacFarlane, S. Neil, and Yuen Foong Khong. *Human Security and the UN: A Critical History*. Bloomington: Indiana University Press, 2006.

Mitchell, Ronald B. *International Politics and the Environment*. Thousand Oaks, CA: Sage, 2010.

Newell, Peter. *Governing Climate Change*. New York: Routledge, 2010.

Price-Smith, Andrew T. *Contagion and Chaos: Disease, Ecology, and National Security in the Era of Globalization*. Cambridge: MIT Press, 2009.

Rich, Bruce. *Mortgaging the Earth: The World Bank, Environmental Impoverishment, and the Crisis of Development*. Boston: Beacon Press, 1994.

Simmons, P. J., and Chantal de Jonge Oudraat, eds. *Managing Global Issues: Lessons Learned*. Washington, DC: Carnegie Endowment for International Peace, 2001.

Tolba, Mostafa K., with Iwona Rummel-Bulska. *Global Environmental Diplomacy: Negotiating Environmental Agreements with the World, 1973–1992*. Cambridge: MIT Press, 1998.

Victor, David. *Global Warming Gridlock: Creating More Effective Strategies for Protecting the Planet*. Cambridge: Cambridge University Press, 2011.

World Commission on Environment and Development. *Our Common Future*. Brundtland Commission report. Oxford: Oxford University Press, 1987.

Young, Oran R. *Institutional Dynamics: Emergent Patterns of Change in International Environmental Governance*. Cambridge: MIT Press, 2010.

———. *International Governance: Protecting the Environment in a Stateless Society*. Ithaca: Cornell University Press, 1994.

Human Security–Related Web Sites

Climate Action Network: www.climatenetwork.org

Database of International Environmental Agreements: iea.uoregon.edu/page.php?file=home.htm&query=static

Global Environment Facility: www.gefweb.org

Global Fund to Fight AIDS, Malaria and Tuberculosis: www.theglobalfund.org

Human Security Bulletin: www.humansecurity.info

Human Security Report Project: www.hsrgroup.org

Intergovernmental Panel on Climate Change: www.ipcc.ch

Interim Haiti Recovery Commission: www.cirh.ht

International Rescue Committee: www.rescue.org/

Relief Net: www.reliefweb.net

UNAIDS: www.unaids.org

UN Climate Change Gateway: www.un.org/climatechange

UN Division for Sustainable Development: www.un.org/esa/sustdev

UN Environment Programme: www.unep.org

UN Framework Commission on Climate Change: unfccc.int/2860.php

US Centers for Disease Control and Prevention: www.cdc.gov

World Health Organization: www.who.org

Glossary

Advisory opinion   An opinion issued by the International Court of Justice based on a request by an international organization for advice on a general question of international law.

Apartheid   An Afrikaans term meaning "separateness"; the policy in South Africa from the 1950s to 1992 of official discrimination touching all aspects of public and private life, designed to keep the different races separate.

Arms control and disarmament   Efforts to induce states to limit, reduce, or eliminate specific types of weapons and armaments.

Arrearages   Unpaid assessed contributions to an international organization.

Balance of payments   The flow of money into and out of a country from trade, tourism, foreign aid, sale of services, profits, and so on.

Basic human needs   Proposals in the development community to shift from emphasizing economic growth to progress in meeting the population's basic needs, including better health care, education, and water supplies.

Bretton Woods institutions   The international economic institutions—the World Bank and the International Monetary Fund—created in 1944 to promote global monetary stability and economic growth. Also includes the trade procedures established under the General Agreement on Tariffs and Trade (GATT), now the World Trade Organization (WTO).

BRICS   Brazil, Russia, India, China, and South Africa. An informal group of emerging economic powers.

Coalition of the willing   An ad hoc group of states that volunteer to carry out a peace-enforcement or humanitarian mission with or without Security Council authorization.

Collective legitimation   The garnering of votes at the UN in support of a particular state's policy or a new international norm.

Collective security   The concept behind the League of Nations and the United Nations, namely, that aggression by one state is aggression against all and should be defeated collectively.

Concert of Europe, or Concert system   The nineteenth-century practice of multilateral meetings of leaders of major European powers to settle problems.

Constructivism   An approach to the study of international relations that examines how shared beliefs, rules, norms, organizations, and cultural practices shape state and individual behavior.

Crimes against humanity   International crimes that include murder, enslavement, forcible transfer of populations, ethnic cleansing, and torture.

Democratization   The process whereby states become increasingly democratic; that is, citizens vote for representatives who rule on their behalf, and the political system is marked by the rule of law.

Dependency theory   Derived from Marxism, an explanation of poverty and underdevelopment in less developed countries based on their historical dependence on and domination by rich countries.

Economic liberalism   The theory that the free interplay of market forces leads to a more efficient allocation of resources, to the benefit of the majority.

Enforcement actions   The use of direct actions—economic sanctions, withdrawal of aid, or military force—by the UN to ensure compliance with Security Council directives.

Exceptionalism   Belief held in the United States that because of its tradition of democracy and adherence to human rights norms that it has a unique role to play in international relations and is not subject to the same restraints as others.

First-generation human rights, or negative rights   The civil or political rights of citizens that prevent governmental authority from interfering with private individuals in civil society.

Functionalism   The belief that cooperation in solving social and economic issues can be separated from politics but will ultimately contribute to peace. UN specialized agencies are functionalist organizations.

Genocide   The systematic killing or harming of a group of people based on racial, religious, or ethnic characteristics, with the intention of destroying the group.

Global Compact   Voluntary principles that multinational corporations agree to accept and work toward in cooperation with the UN and NGOs.

Global governance   The rules, norms, activities, and organizations designed to address the international problems that states alone cannot solve.

Globalization   The idea that economies, social relations, and cultures are rapidly being linked by international market processes, international institutions, and NGOs in such a way that state sovereignty and distinctiveness are undermined; the internationalization of the capitalist economy in which states, markets, and civil society are restructured to facilitate the flow of capital.

Group of 7 (G-7)   The major economic powers, which meet annually to address world economic problems.

Group of 20 (G-20)   Group of emerging powers, including India, Brazil, and South Africa, who play important roles in international trade and finance.

Group of 77 (G-77)   A coalition of LDCs that pressed for reforms in economic relations between developing and developed countries; also referred to as "the South." Now includes 132 countries.

Human development   The concept that economic growth alone does not ensure improvement in human standards of living, measured by such indicators as average life expectancy, infant mortality, adult literacy, and per capita nutritional level.

Humanitarian intervention   UN or individual states' actions to alleviate human suffering during violent conflicts without necessarily obtaining the consent of the host country.

Human security   The idea that security includes not only the security of the state and territory but also security of individuals from civil and economic turmoil and health and environmental threats.

Interdependence   The sensitivity and vulnerability of states to each other's actions resulting from increased interactions generated by trade, monetary flows, telecommunications, and shared interests.

International Bill of Rights   A term for the three primary human rights documents: the Universal Declaration of Human Rights, the Covenant on International Civil and Political Rights, and the Covenant on Economic, Social, and Cultural Rights.

International humanitarian law   International laws holding states and individuals accountable for actions during war, specifically including protection of and assistance to military and civilian victims of war.

International intergovernmental organizations (IGOs)   International agencies or bodies set up and controlled by member states to deal with areas of common interest.

Liberalism   A theoretical perspective, based on the goodness of the individual and the value of political and legal institutions, holding that there are multiple actors in international politics and that the state has many different, sometimes conflicting, interests.

Millennium Development Goals (MDGs)   Goals agreed to by UN member states in 2000 to improve the economic and social conditions of people; includes specific targets and a procedure for tracking progress toward attainment of the goals.

Multilateralism   The conduct of international activities by three or more states in accordance with shared general principles, often through international or multilateral institutions.

Multinational corporations (MNCs)   Private enterprises with production facilities, sales, or activity in more than one country; also called transnational corporations.

New International Economic Order (NIEO)   A list of demands by the G-77 to reform economic relations between the North and the South, that is, between the developed countries and the less developed countries.

Nonaligned Movement (NAM)   Group of developing countries held together by principles of anticolonialism, opposition to racism, and neutrality toward the Cold War.

Noncompulsory jurisdiction   When states are not obligated to bring disputes to a body such as the International Court of Justice for settlement.

Nongovernmental organizations (NGOs)   Private associations of individuals or groups that engage in political activity, often across national borders.

Nonintervention   The principle that obliges states and international organizations not to interfere in matters within the domestic jurisdiction of other sovereign states.

Peacebuilding   Postconflict activities to strengthen and preserve peace settlements, such as development aid, civilian administration, and election and human rights monitoring.

Peaceful settlement   Various techniques by which disputes are settled, including adjudication, arbitration, mediation, conciliation, and good offices.

Peacekeeping   Use of multilateral forces to achieve different objectives: traditionally, observation of cease-fire lines and cease-fires and separation of forces; multidimensional complex operations may employ both military and civilian personnel and involve use of force to deliver humanitarian aid and promote law and order.

Politicization   The linkage of different issues for political purposes, as in the introduction of a clearly political topic to an organization dealing with health problems.

Poverty alleviation   Programs designed to improve food supply, nutrition, health, housing, and the standard of living for the poorest people, particularly in remote areas of developing countries and in minority groups whose poverty is not reduced by general economic growth and development.

Preventive diplomacy   The practice of engaging in diplomatic actions to prevent the outbreak of conflict; the monitoring of hot spots before conflict erupts.

Privatization   Belief held by economic liberals that economies function more efficiently if there is private ownership of industries and services.

Realist theory, or realism   A theory of world politics that emphasizes states' interest in accumulating power to ensure security in an anarchic world.

Regime   The rules, norms, and decisionmaking procedures developed by states and international organizations to address common concerns and to organize common activities relating to specific issue areas or problems, such as human rights, trade, or nuclear proliferation.

Responsibility to protect (R2P)   Emerging norm in response to massive human rights abuses that the international community has the responsibility to help individuals suffering at the hands of their own state or other states.

Second-generation human rights, or positive rights   The social and economic rights that states are obligated to provide for their citizenry; may include the right to an education, the right to decent housing, and the right to medical care.

Self-determination   The principle according to which nationalities and colonial peoples have the right to determine who will rule them; thought to minimize war for territorial expansion.

Sovereignty   The authority of the state, based on recognition by other states and non-state actors, to govern matters within its own borders that affect its people, economy, security, and form of government.

Specialized agencies   UN-related organizations established by separate agreements to deal with specific issues, such as health, working conditions, weather, air and sea transport, and education.

Statebuilding   Activities taken by international actors to create, reform, or strengthen the governmental institutions of a state and their relationships to society.

Structural adjustment programs   IMF policies and recommendations to guide countries out of payment deficits and economic crises through changes in domestic economic policies and practices.

Sustainable development   An approach that tries to reconcile current economic growth and environmental protection with future needs and resource supplies.

Technical assistance   The provision of human skills and resources necessary for economic development, including education, training, and expert advice.

Terms of trade The ratio of the price of imports to the price of exports. When import prices are greater than the value of exports, a state experiences adverse or declining terms of trade.

Third-generation human rights   The collective rights of groups, such as the rights of children or indigenous people; includes the right to democracy and to development.

Third UN   External experts, consultants, citizens, and NGOs who work with UN agencies and the Secretariat.

Trade preferences   The granting of special trade arrangements, usually giving trade advantages to less developed countries.

United Nations system   Includes not only the UN based in New York but also the specialized agencies and other autonomous organizations headquartered in different parts of the world.

Uniting for Peace Resolution   The resolution that enables the General Assembly to assume responsibility for peace and security issues if the Security Council is deadlocked.

Veto   A negative vote cast in the UN Security Council by one of the permanent members that effectively defeats a decision.

Voting blocs   Groups of states voting together in the UN General Assembly or in other international bodies.

War crimes   Illegal activities committed during war, including deliberately targeting civilians, abusing prisoners of war, and committing crimes such as torture and rape.

Weighted voting systems   Systems in which states have unequal votes, based on financial contributions, population, or geographic representation. Used in the Bretton Woods institutions.

Index